THE
CONSERVATIVES

THE
CONSERVATIVES

A History from their Origins to 1965

by

Norman Gash
Donald Southgate
David Dilks
and
John Ramsden

edited with an introduction and epilogue
by
The Rt Hon. LORD BUTLER
KG, PC, CH

London
GEORGE ALLEN & UNWIN LTD
Boston   Sydney

Printed in Great Britain
in 11 on 12 pt Baskerville by
William Clowes and Sons, Limited
London, Beccles and Colchester

CONTENTS

INTRODUCTION
by The Rt Hon. Lord Butler, KG, PC, CH

It has for long been my ambition to be responsible for publishing a book about Conservatism as it has existed and flourished for the last century and three-quarters. I have been exceptionally fortunate in securing four distinguished historians to divide up the period from the last days of the younger Pitt to the assumption of power by Edward Heath. Professor Norman Gash is particularly well qualified to take the story as far as the immense contribution of his hero, Sir Robert Peel. Dr Donald Southgate has wanted to write on Disraeli, while the book he edited on Conservative leadership shows his ability to describe the contributions of Salisbury and Balfour. Professor Dilks carries on after Bonar Law with Baldwin and Chamberlain, and Dr Ramsden concludes with a study of Churchill, Eden, Macmillan and up to 1965. I have had the responsibility of editing the book and ensuring that it has both continuity and completeness.

I have been anxious that the work should not be overlong, that it should be easy to handle and read, and that it should in relatively short compass indicate the themes and achievements of the greatest and longest surviving party in the State, and also serve as a guideline for the future activities, prospects and philosophy of Conservatism. A study of the past will be all the more worthwhile, because things are not easy at the present time and because in my view it is imperative to revivify Conservatism. Where there has been inspiration this can be carried forward; where there have been mistakes these can be avoided. As Geoffrey Butler, the Senior Burgess for Cambridge University, wrote in his book *The Tory Tradition**, 'the Tory tradition

* Sir Geoffrey Butler, *The Tory Tradition*; John Murray, 1914.

is the Tory hope'. In his quest he went back as far as Bolingbroke.

We do not propose to go as far back as that or to the origins
of the Tory Party in the early seventeenth century or earlier.
The reasons for this are twofold; first, that the Tory Party
suffered a virtual extinction between the period before the
supremacy of Robert Walpole and its revival in the early
writings of George Canning, and second, that Sir Keith Feiling
has already written an early *History of the Tory Party 1640–
1714**. It would be impossible to add anything useful to this
attractive and picturesque study of the Cavaliers, of the
Revolution of 1688, of Clarendon and Danby and Harley.
Feiling writes, 'the Tory débâcle in 1714 was essentially brought
about by their association with the Pretender's cause'. The
author describes the party '. . . which boasted Falkland and
George Herbert among its prophets, Strafford and Laud in its
roll of martyrs; the party which in robust youth figured as the
cavalier, and walked after death with the Jacobites; which
counts Hooker, Bacon and Swift in its spiritual lineage and was
led successively by Clarendon, Danby, Harley and Bolingbroke;
that party which after living for three-quarters of a century
crowded with heroism, passion and suffering, disappeared with
the last Stuart and vanished as though it had never been'.

Feiling, in his *The Second Tory Party*†, attempts to trace its
history mostly underground during the eighteenth century. He
notices signs of rebirth in 1794 when Burke deserted Fox.
Feiling's second volume is not so captivating as the first, largely
because his quarry is so elusive and partly because, to requote
his own words, the first Tory Party had 'vanished as though it
had never been'. In any case Feiling was writing before Sir
Lewis Namier revolutionised our way of looking at eighteenth-
century politics by demonstrating the essential non-party basis
of parliamentary activity in the period between the fall of
Walpole and the rise of the younger Pitt. We thus take up the
theme at the beginning of the nineteenth century and pursue
it with increasing interest into modern times.

If the 'Tory tradition is the Tory hope' we must gain some

---

* Keith Feiling, *A History of the Tory Party, 1640–1714*; The Clarendon Press,
Oxford, 1924.
† Keith Feiling, *The Second Tory Party, 1714–1832*; Macmillan 1938.

idea of what this tradition is before we study the following pages. Geoffrey Butler wonders

'. . . whether there does not exist today a life-giving, a revivifying marrow, to the Tory doctrine, which it is well to understand before that doctrine is rejected. This fundamental force of strength exists indeed and takes on, I think, three aspects. It may be considered first of all as an abiding criticism and rejection of the utilitarian canon, at any rate as that canon is usually interpreted. In other words, as a perpetual warning, that the state no less than the individual does well to fear lest it do evil in order that good may come. It may be considered secondly as a distrust of sectional control whatever the merits may be, however righteous the demands of the section which is in question. This distrust will find embodiment in the old belief in the safeguard provided by historic institutions, and it will base that belief on an insistence that historic evolution is capable of providing checks, the necessity of which any given generation may be unable to realise; and the fairness of which any one interest (however great) may unduly depreciate. Lastly, it may take the form of emphasising the importance of national duties, every bit as much as, indeed probably more than, the importance of emphasising national well-being.'

I do not apologise for quoting this passage, written in 1914, because it is I think very apt to the circumstances of today when we are hoping so keenly for a Conservative revival. Of course, a revival in the 1970s could not be based solely on the general principles stated. The structure of the State and of politics have changed radically in the interval.

Butler's book goes back over sixty years. The period which we cover has been one of colossal, cumulative and in several ways catastrophic change, brought about primarily by technology and affecting every aspect of human existence. Though the pace is not slackening, it has been unprecedented in previous history, so that in all material things a greater gulf separates us from Sir Robert Peel than separated him from Julius Caesar. If, therefore, we look to discover why the same party (quite recognisably the same) has existed throughout, and still does, and will go on, one finds the clue in a defensive response to these ineluctable changes which is part not merely of politics but of human nature.

The range of defensive response has always varied widely in degree of sophistication – all the way from the dunderhead stand-patters thundering '*on ne passe pas*' while dying in penultimate ditches, to the supple and subtle intellectuals who, each in his or her own very different way, have said: 'alas, feudalism and monasticism and lordship and kingship and vicinage and other features of the organic society cannot conceivably survive the impact of the almighty machine, but the *values* of that older society can and must somehow be made to survive, and that is what politics should really be about'. All the best minds and pens of the period have thought or said that, some not at all regarding themselves as Conservatives any more than Pitt ever regarded himself as a Tory, and of course just a few practising politicians, Benjamin Disraeli obviously, but also Stanley Baldwin and Sir Robert Peel.

I quite see that as a practitioner of the art of the possible I am comfortable in the important world of political immediacy and of the eager machinery of parliamentary measures; but we must not forget that our ancestors stood for values which we practising politicians must never forget in an age of Marxism and terrorism and violence.

Of all writers I shall say most of Burke. From the earliest times the party not only profited by Burke's wisdom but has stoutly defended his dictum, 'a man should not be deprived of his legitimate expectations'. We have a bitter fight before us today to defend these rights and exemplify their duties. In many homes the wealth tax and the capital transfer tax will destroy for ever the enjoyment of traditional inheritance and will refute the doctrine of Burke that we live not only for our generation but for those who have gone before and those who come after. All sections of society have their legitimate expectations, some to avoid redundancy and to obtain or keep their jobs, others to enjoy their homes and have freedom to spend their earnings.

We thus turn from literary and human values to economics. Before the first great war there was an apparent lack of emphasis on 'national well-being'. It was not usual for a Prime Minister or even a leading statesman to be trained in or immersed in economics. It is interesting that Pitt, Liverpool and Peel, not to mention Huskisson, were particularly knowledge-able in this field. True there was Goschen, whom Lord Randolph Churchill 'forgot', but if Lord Salisbury had had as much gift for economics as he had for foreign policy, and if, as Robert Rhodes James has said, the Tory Party had not been for so long shut up in the 'Hotel Cecil', there might have been more striking progress towards the third of Disraeli's principles of 1872, namely to 'elevate the condition of the people'. Advance towards social progress and fiscal reform was really reserved for the Asquith Government and a yawning gap was left into which Keir Hardie and the first socialists stepped, gradually creating the size and strength of the present Labour movement. Stanley Baldwin, after the Coalition, did much to accustom this Labour movement to power and to heal class divisions and to bring about a social revolution or change in a peaceful man-ner. He set monarchy on a firm path and, by his policy towards India, started the dismantling of that Empire of which Disraeli had been so proud.

Disraeli's other two principles – to maintain the institutions of the country and to uphold the Empire – have, particularly in relation to the second of these, changed with time. The almost hectic rush between 1947 and 1963 to grant self-government to the Empire has altered Britain's imperial face and caused us to turn towards a future in Europe. As for our institutions, it is our intention to defend them, as I have indicated, against what Nigel Birch* describes as an oligarchy. Warnings against the misuse of power of the State and of sectional control should be the creed of Conservatism today and tomorrow. Disraeli warned us that the repositories of power succeed one another. The King defeats the Barons, Parliament reduces the supremacy of the King, and now the authority of Parliament itself is questioned. Men of all parties realise this danger, but it particu-larly behoves the modern Tory Party to defend parliamentary democracy. As Plato observed in the city states of his day, monarchy gave way to aristocracy, aristocracy to democracy and that led in his experience to dictatorship. No dictatorship of the right or left has ever suited Britain.

Having cited Disraeli I must turn to Peel. Birch quotes me

* Nigel Birch, *The Conservative Party*; Collins, 1949. Britain in Pictures series.

as being a follower of Peel and this is true. I am, therefore, all the more glad to welcome Professor Gash's study in this volume. When Winston Churchill made me chairman of the committee which produced the Industrial Charter in 1947, I and my colleagues studied the *Tamworth Manifesto*. It is true that the contents of the two documents are dissimilar, but each had a similar effect in attracting voters to Conservatism. Our contribution, flanked by the Workers Charter, attempted to give capitalism a human look. In our approach to economics we were inspired by Keynes's *General Theory*. We have missed the opportunity of a new look by Maynard Keynes today. One lasting feature of Conservatism throughout the century has been its tendency to swing against the abuse of the day, thus we opposed '*laissez-faire*', that is the extreme licence of free enterprise in the nineteenth century, and have stood out against nationalisation, that is the extreme of state control in the twentieth century. It is when we have sought the middle ground that we have been successful. Professor Gash wisely quotes, later in this volume, passages from Burke which show the impossibility of government being able efficiently and wisely to regulate the many and complex activities of society. There is nothing in Conservatism which is against using the power of the State for beneficial purposes; that power should be opposed when it brings abuse and evil waste in its train. 'Modern Conservatism inherits the principles of Toryism which are favourable to the activity and the authority of the state', wrote Lord Hugh Cecil in 1912*.

Cecil is one of two modern contributors to Conservative philosophy, both in slim volumes of small compass. His is *Conservatism*, published in 1912; the other is *The Case for Conservatism*, which I asked Quintin Hogg, now Lord Hailsham, to write in 1947†. These two inspiring books deal with fundamentals, namely the connection between our political faith and the Christian religion, and our belief in the duties and obligations which prosperity entails. While in its early stages Toryism was very closely allied with the Established Church, today, quite rightly, no party has a monopoly of religion.

---

* Lord Hugh Cecil, *Conservatism*; Williams & Norgate, 1912.
† Quintin Hogg (Lord Hailsham), *The Case for Conservatism*; Penguin Books, 1947.

A vital expression of Burke's, much used by Baldwin, is 'ordered liberty'. At the start of our study in this book we note that modern Conservatism started in opposition to something, namely the radical change of the French Revolution. Canning published the *Anti-Jacobin*, and anti-Jacobinism was a great component of our thought in the early nineteenth century. With Burke we were horrified by the excesses of the revolutionaries. Ever since the time of Pitt and Liverpool, Conservatism has been firm on the subject of preserving order, because liberty without order begets violence and licence. Peel was an advocate of order, but he also practised reform at the Home Office. I think that he was wrong to oppose the Reform Act of 1832, but it was he who, at a later date, accepted the consequences and helped to build our modern creed.

Part of 'ordered liberty' is to protect the Rule of Law and the Supremacy of Parliament. We strongly support the bicameral system, and if practicable a reform of the House of Lords.

For political and economic reasons we have been ardently keen to work with and in Europe to extend international co-operation and to care for the needs of poorer nations. As is described in Kenneth Rose's book, *The Later Cecils**, Lord Robert as a Conservative did more than any other man to found the League of Nations, from which sprang the United Nations. In these days of great-power politics, 'the one nation one vote' principle of the United Nations has tended to obscure reality. Nevertheless, in the Middle East, whether in Cyprus or Sinai, there is place for an international force, and the United Nations anyway forms an invaluable forum.

Where the foreign policy of the great nations hangs behind is in help and succour to the world's poor. Overseas aid is often costly and quite often unrewarding. Nevertheless, a frightening number of millions live below the poverty and starvation level.

'The best immediate hope of international co-operation lies in concentrating upon the satisfaction of simple human needs for food, clothes and shelter without making these the excuse for ideological discrimination. For although Conservatives put the political freedoms and the moral rights and dignities first, the satisfaction of real need by acts of generosity and by work of

* Kenneth Rose, *The Later Cecils*; Weidenfeld & Nicolson, 1975.

co-operation setting up a mutual dependence, is the best road from one man's heart to another's.'*

As Hearnshaw says in his *Conservatism in England*†, progress and continuity are complementary political conceptions. If we tear up our roots as the Tribune Group would wish, the tree will die.

The chapters in this book illustrate how, whenever we have adapted ourselves to change, we and the nation have prospered. Professor Gash describes the ordered and sober mind of Peel. Dr Southgate treats the youth of Disraeli and his novels with eloquence. As Disraeli gets older, Dr Southgate gives us in the Crystal Palace speech a summary of Conservative doctrine which is accepted to this day. He has also followed Lord Salisbury from his youth, as Lord Robert Cecil with his many articles and speeches, each of them more strikingly diehard in the old sense than the last. The same author ably covers the hiatus created after A. J. Balfour's resignation.

Professor Dilks writes on Baldwin and Chamberlain. Despite his lethargic later years, Baldwin was probably the most important Conservative leader in modern times and his long series of public speeches reveals a great literary sense and adds much to the philosophy of Conservatism. Professor Dilks, who is writing a separate book on Chamberlain, reminds us of Chamberlain's contribution as Minister of Health and Chancellor of the Exchequer.

Dr Ramsden has not found it easy to discuss Churchill as a Conservative leader. In his book, *The Road to 1945*‡, Mr Addison describes the decline of Conservatism in 1943-5. This was precisely the period when Churchill was occupied – and how much – with the war. Yet we must not underestimate his contribution to the story of our party. He set up the Reconstruction Committee representing the two parties of the Coalition under the impartial chairmanship of Lord Woolton. It prepared the launching of the Beveridge scheme and the Welfare State. During this period the 1944 Education Act was born. I was proud of the Conservatives' part in these achievements, the

* Quintin Hogg (Lord Hailsham), op. cit.
† F. J. C. Hearnshaw, *Conservatism in England*; Macmillan, 1933.
‡ Paul Addison, *The Road to 1945*; Jonathan Cape, 1975.

implementation of which followed during the initial phase of the Labour Government of 1945.

All this and much else is described in this volume. The instance which I have just quoted indicates that Conservatives have been responsible for pushing many of the reforms of the modern State. The following chapters also show that Conservatives have often had to wait a long time for their chance to come again. It has done so before and will do so again. Our party is not only the oldest in the State but it always responds to the national instincts of the people.

Part One

From the Origins to Sir Robert Peel

by

Norman Gash

*Professor of History
at the University of St Andrews*

CHAPTER 1

The Origins

I

Though Conservatism first became a discernible basis of domestic policy during the administration of Lord Liverpool between 1815 and 1827 and was only formally embodied in an explicit political party under Sir Robert Peel after 1832, its origins are clearly traceable to the age of the French Revolution which began in 1789. It was born of reaction: part of the defensive mechanism which British society devised to counter first the ideas and then the armed threat of the revolutionary French state. Its prophet was Edmund Burke, its political hero William Pitt the Younger. It was true that the two men differed sharply in the nature and timing of their reaction to the events in France. The emotional vehemence which shaped and sometimes distorted Burke's powers of political judgement made him a passionate, almost premature intellectual enemy of revolutionary France. The place of Pitt in the pantheon of Conservative statesmen owes more to the accident of history than is commonly allowed. But the world of Burke and Pitt remains as the great uplands from which the headwaters of Conservatism descended to the plains of Victorian party politics below.

The reaction in Britain to the French Revolution was, however, conditioned not only by the actual happenings in France but by the kind of society in Britain which observed and interpreted those happenings. The character of British eighteenth-century politics was as important as the nature of the revolutionary process in France. Burke and Pitt were products not only of their age but of their country, and their reaction to the French Revolution can only be understood in terms of their pre-1789 background. It was because of this background that, though both men called themselves Whig,[1] both in their different ways were founders of the Conservative tradition.

It is a mark of the tenacity of British political habits that the terms Whig and Tory, coined in the second half of the seventeenth century, were still in use a century later. Those terms, however, did not provide a useful basis for understanding how politicians differed from each other or organised themselves for the pursuit of political power. They were part of the vocabulary rather than the grammar of politics. No 'Tory Party' existed; and though there were 'Whig' parties, there was no 'Whig Party'. The contemporary division of politicians into Court, Opposition, and Independents was a more realistic analysis of parliamentary life in the reign of George III than the party nomenclature devised in the reign of Charles II. Nevertheless, the old names survived to indicate types, temperaments, traditions and connections. To Dr Johnson a Tory was a man who had an instinctive reverence for what was established, a respect for government and the Crown, a loyalty towards the Church of England, a prejudice in favour of the landed interest. A Whig, on the other hand, was a creature predisposed to innovation, jealous of the executive power (the Devil, after all, was the first Whig), distrustful of ecclesiastical authority, favourable to trade and finance, and a champion (when he thought it expedient) of the popular interest. These were stereotypes, useful for understanding contemporary modes of thought but of little value in deciding how individual Whigs and Tories (if in fact a politician chose to designate himself as either) would act in a specific set of circumstances. An observer of the political scene might be forgiven if he concluded that a Tory out of office behaved like a Whig and a Whig in office like a Tory.

The tendency of ministers to resemble their predecessors in office rather than themselves in Opposition is a phenomenon not confined to the eighteenth century. From the closing years of George II's reign, however, there was increasing talk of the extinction of party. Paradoxically there was also a perceptible recovery in the political reputability of Toryism. The two developments were not unconnected. The failure of the Forty-Five Rebellion, the accession in 1760 of a young prince who was British, patriotic and religious, enabled Jacobitism to be rele-

gated to the lumber-room of history where it was subsequently
retrieved by Sir Walter Scott. To be a Tory was vastly more
respectable in 1770 than it had been in 1740. Nevertheless, the
long period of Whig ascendancy had left an indelible mark on
political society. Nearly all those who looked to the Court for
social advancement, or to government for office and a career,
enrolled in the traditional if shapeless mass of Whigs. Vagueness
and confusion of nomenclature were therefore inevitable. The
elder Pitt, a Whig who disclaimed party connection, was
supported by Tories. The North ministry from 1770 to 1782, because it was the King's ministry defending royal and parliamentary supremacy against colonial sedition, was stigmatised as
Tory though North himself had entered political life as a Whig.
Conversely, the body of Tory back benchers, who respected the
Crown but disliked the Court, who wanted sound government
but distrusted professional politicians, found themselves increasingly courted not as 'Tories' but as the 'independent
country gentlemen'.

Behind this loose terminology and fluid political structure
was a fundamentally static view of politics and the constitution.
Though there was criticism of excessive political patronage, of
electoral abuses, of House of Commons pretentiousness and
executive officiousness, the system was in general accepted. The
object of political activity was office rather than policy. The
concept of the State itself was of an established, not an evolving
institution. The Glorious Revolution of 1688 and the less
glorious but eminently satisfactory Hanoverian Succession had
enshrined the notion of a perfected British Constitution which
might require amendment in detail but not alteration in principle. In the stereotyped image of the post-Newtonian scientific
age, it was viewed as a complicated machine incorporating
various checks and balances which by their reciprocal action
produced a steady equilibrium of forces. In this delicate adjustment of the constitution lay the secret of that combination
of liberty and order which won the admiration of continental
observers like Montesquieu and de Lolme and was the proud
boast of patriotic Englishmen. Government was regarded as a
matter of mechanics. All that was needed were honest and efficient engineers to ensure that the machine ran smoothly. Even
Dr Johnson, for all his anti-Whig prejudices, virtually accepted

this mechanistic view of the constitution when he admitted to Boswell in a moment of intellectual candour that 'a wise Tory and a wise Whig, I believe, will agree. Their principles are the same, though their modes of thinking are different. A high Tory makes government unintelligible . . . a violent Whig makes it impracticable.'²

That observation was made in 1781. Eight years later came the start of the French Revolution which was to shatter for ever the Augustan calm of which Johnson was the last great intellectual representative.

II

Burke's *Reflections on the Revolution in France* was published in November 1790, after the fall of the Bastille and the promulgation of the new constitution but before the destruction of the monarchy, the outbreak of war, and the Terror. Its significance was that it initiated a fundamental debate on the French Revolution at a time when British opinion was largely divided between two views, equally natural and equally short-sighted: enthusiasm at the rapid dawn of liberty in what had been the greatest of continental despotisms, and circumspect satisfaction at the disablement for a long period of Britain's greatest European rival. It elicited a number of replies, notably from Mackintosh and Paine; and Burke's tendency to extremism of language and argument (already noted in the Regency debates of 1788–9) was a further hindrance to immediate acceptance of his views by the respectable and propertied classes even though they bought edition after edition of his book in the first twelve months. The *Annual Register* for 1791 could still talk with a certain condescension of 'the well-known irritability of Mr Burke upon the subject of the French politics', and the young intellectual Huskisson was probably not the only future Pittite who (in February 1791) declared himself shocked by Burke's 'strange romantic doctrines'.

But when the imprisonment of the French King in 1791 was followed in 1792 by the declaration of war against the emperor, the expulsion of priests, the flight of the *émigrés*, the establishment of a republic, the victory of Valmy and the decree of fraternisation with all subject nations, all that Burke had written seemed to be vindicated. Towards the end of the parliamentary session of 1792 there was a flood of loyal addresses and Lord Grenville, the Foreign Secretary, opined to his brother in November that the body of landed gentlemen were 'thoroughly frightened'. Liberal sympathies among the well-to-do withered quickly; there were calls for loyalist associations to counter the activities of radical societies; and by the end of the year it was apparent that the Government had realised both the possibility of war abroad and the need to keep firm control of dissident elements at home. When hostilities started in February 1793 it was, for some Englishmen at least, not merely a war of self-defence but a war of principle.

Burke's reputation, therefore, was not only favoured by a change in public opinion, but fortified as a prophet whose words had come true. Yet this alone does not account for the unique position in British political writings occupied by the *Reflections*. Burke was no blind reactionary; had he been, his polemics would have disappeared with the generation for whom they were written. His previous career as a Rockingham supporter, his hatred of cruelty, his views on the American colonies, on Irish Catholicism, on slavery, were proof of the essentially liberal strain in his political outlook. Though he reacted strongly and unfairly against demagogic radicalism at home and either misunderstood or was blind to certain aspects of the French Revolution, he was essentially a constructive thinker. The importance of the *Reflections* was that for the first time it provided an explicit and penetrating philosophy of conservatism, marked by observations of enduring value for the study of politics and expressed in a superb literary style. It has remained a treasure-house of precept and quotation for Conservative writers and politicians ever since. His work outlived his age because it was based not simply on the historical circumstances of his time but on a profound insight into the nature of man in society.

Nevertheless, what is less often noticed is that the date of publication of the *Reflections* was important not only for the nature of their reception by the public, but even more fundamentally for the kind of book which Burke was obliged to write.

Had he waited another two years, he could have contented himself with a mere attack on the visible dangers and excesses of the French Revolution. Argument would have been unnecessary; the facts would have spoken for themselves. But to win conviction for his views in the relatively calm period before the Terror, Burke had to demonstrate that the apparently innocent liberal and intellectual principles on which the early revolutionary movement in France was based were in fact false principles of political action, that they would be exploited by corrupt and dangerous men, and that the inevitable outcome would be weakness and anarchy, followed by tyranny and military despotism. Similarly, because his chief object was to combat the spread of those doctrines in Britain, he had to demonstrate that, any superficial appearance to the contrary, there was no real idenfity between the principles of the French Revolution of 1789–90 and those of the English Revolution of 1688 and the political system which had resulted from it. To achieve these two ends, he had of necessity to embark on historical and political analyses which in their range and subtlety were in a different class to the legalistic, mechanistic descriptions of the constitution on which the educated men of his generation had been brought up. The very isolation of his position during 1790 required a new and fundamental approach to the problems of political society. The 'prematureness', so to speak, of his *Reflections* was not an accidental feature but an integral reason for the form in which he cast them. To convince his own reluctant and unprepared contemporaries in 1790 he had to lay bare the roots of the issues which he believed confronted them. What in an academic philosopher might have been the fruits of a lifetime's meditation, with Burke came from a rapid concentration of nervous energy to distil the lessons which his long political career had taught him for the purpose of warning his fellow-countrymen against dangers of which they seemed unconscious. It was this which made what has since become a classic of political thought the most influential political pamphlet of its time.

Fundamentally Burke's philosophy rested on three principles: history, society and continuity. Like all real Conservatives his ideas were conditioned by a certain view of humanity. Because he was conscious of the frailty, ignorance and evil in human nature, he believed that it needed the discipline of ordered society to liberate the best elements in mankind and restrain the worst. Society in this sense could only be an historical product, a thing of slow, natural growth: an organic entity, with unity and character, with a place for patriotism, a place for morals and religion. It was a framework for conduct, a defence against the excesses of individuals and the caprice of tyrants. For Burke unrestrained individualism and political tyranny derived from the same source: arbitrary behaviour. He rejected therefore both libertarianism and despotism. Liberty for him was the product of social order and social discipline; liberty and restraint were inseparable. A large measure of freedom was necessary for the full expansion of the human spirit, but it was a freedom that arose naturally from well-ordered society. No governmental or doctrinal prescription could satisfactorily mark the boundaries of human activity or the progress of civilisation. 'The nature of man is intricate; the objects of society are of the greatest possible complexity; and therefore no simple disposition or direction of power can be suitable either to man's nature, or to the quality of his affairs.'

Change was part of political life, as of all organisms; time itself was the greatest innovator. 'A state without the means of some change is without the means of its conservation.' But the continuity of the social fabric must be respected. Change should come in small gradations; by way of evolution not revolution; by adaptation not destruction: 'A disposition to preserve, and an ability to improve, taken together, would be my standard of a statesman.'

For the doctrinaire reformer who acted as though human nature and existing society could be disregarded in the pursuit of abstract justice, he had nothing but scorn. 'I cannot conceive how any man can have brought himself to that pitch of presumption, to consider his country as nothing but *carte blanche*, upon which he may scribble whatever he pleases.' Continuity, therefore, the inheritance from the past both individual and collective, was the stabilising attribute of society. 'The idea of inheritance furnishes a sure principle of conservation, and a sure principle of transmission; without at all excluding a principle of improvement.' It was not surprising that in the deliberate overthrow of the old order in France he saw the seeds of rapine and anarchy, and in the enunciation of abstract rights by political intellectuals the foreshadowing of bloodshed and tyranny. 'In the groves of *their* academy,' he wrote in one of his most haunting phrases, 'at the end of every vista, you see nothing but the gallows.'

The nature of Burke's philosophy is clear. He reintroduced human nature into political philosophy; he replaced a static by an evolutionary view of society; he substituted an organic view of the state for the older mechanical concept of the constitution. If much of what he taught was implicit in the outlook of the governing class of his day, he made it explicit. Out of reaction against the French Revolution – 'that shocking Conspiracy', as one contemporary described it, 'against Religion, order and government' – was born a luminous and profound statement of the fundamental conservative attitude. Yet that achievement should not obscure the fact that Burke was writing for his own generation and with a purpose. It was not enough that the greater part of educated Englishmen in his day became his pupils. It was not enough that they should be, in his own words, 'alarmed into reflection'. He wished to alarm them into action as well. His *Reflections* forced a national debate on the fundamentals of political society, just as his *Appeal from the New to the Old Whigs* in 1791 forced a decision on the future of the opposition Whigs. A feature of his writing, which became more prominent as time went on, was his insistence on the connection of the war against Jacobin principles abroad with the contest against democratic movements at home. Radical politics in late-eighteenth century Britain did not start with the French Revolution; their roots went back to the agitation of Wilkes and the War of American Independence. The first part of the *Reflections* was taken up with an attack on a recent sermon delivered by the dissenting minister and political pamphleteer Dr Richard Price on the principles of the English Revolution of 1688; and in his *Letters on a Regicide Peace* in 1796, the last writings to come from his pen before his death the following year, Burke reiterated that 'it is with an *armed doctrine* that we are at war . . . It is a colossus which bestrides our channel. It has one foot on a foreign shore, the other upon the British soil.'

His bitter complaint against the Government was that it treated the war as a separate issue, English sedition as a purely domestic concern. For Burke they were part of a whole. Of the independent, educated British public (which he reckoned at less than half a million) who constituted the political nation, he estimated that a fifth were Jacobin. 'They desire a change; and they will have it if they can', if necessary with the assistance of the French. Their assiduity and activity made up for their lack of numbers, while the sound and loyal majority were weakened by their own shortsightedness and by the temporising of their political leaders. He admitted that the parties of 'the old whigs' and the 'ancient tories' had become 'nearly extinct by the growth of new ones, which have their roots in the present circumstances of the times'. The real dividing line in politics by the end of the century, he argued, was between those who stood for 'the conservation in England of the ancient order of things' and the other party 'which demands great changes here, and is so pleased to see them everywhere else, which party I call Jacobin'.[3] Prophetically forecasting that the war against France would prove long and exhausting, he believed that the national will to sustain that war would never be adequate until the British public was made to realise that the safety of their own constitution was dependent on the outcome of the conflict abroad.

In this analysis of 1796 there was realism as well as exaggeration. The mass of the upper and middle classes had accepted Burke's teaching and the outbreak of war in 1793 saw an immediate rallying to the Government of peers and politicians previously in Opposition. The incorporation in the ministry of the Portland Whigs in 1794 was only a formal symbol of the disintegration of the powerful Rockingham opposition which up to 1793 could claim to be the embodiment of the old historic Whig Party. The Foxite rump of some fifty members which remained in Opposition was isolated and discredited, out of touch with respectable opinion and only saved from parliamentary annihilation by its substantial possession of pocket boroughs. By the time Canning and other young Government wits ran their famous but short-lived weekly *The Anti-Jacobin* during the 1797–8 session to ridicule the liberal, humanitarian, cosmopolitan attitudes once fashionable on both sides of the Channel, the battle as far as the propertied and governing classes were concerned had already been won.

The real danger in conservative eyes was the extra-parliamentary radicalism of the reform and corresponding societies, and the clear signs of democratic stirrings in the new industrial areas. The English 'Jacobinism' against which Burkean Conservatism aligned itself was not violence and terrorism but doctrinaire democracy. It was a movement which denounced existing governments in the name of an abstract principle; which denied legitimacy to what was established because it was not based on democratic consent. 'A Jacobin', wrote that indefatigable pamphleteer John Bowles, who disseminated a popular form of Burkean Conservatism at the start of the new century, 'is one who maintains, as his first and fundamental principle, that every individual in society has a right to concur in the choice of representatives; and that representatives, so chosen, can *alone* constitute a *legal* Government.'[4] The definition, if not the epithet, was equally clearly accepted by the other side. When a radical society in industrial Yorkshire could defy Parliament in the name of popular sovereignty and a leading Whig peer propose a toast to 'Our sovereign – the Majesty of the People', Burke's analysis of the cleavage in British society did not seem widely misplaced. The great spokesman of the radical movement himself defined the issue in similarly stark terms. 'The present war', wrote Tom Paine in his *Dissertation on First Principles of Government* (1795), 'is a conflict between the representative system, founded on the rights of the people, and the hereditary system, founded in usurpation.' Paine and Burke agreed on the nature of the struggle; the issue for Burke was whether it was also a definition accepted by Pitt.

Of all the leading men in politics Pitt seemed best situated to profit from the Burkean reaction. He had come to power in 1783 as the King's choice to save the Crown from the dictation of the Fox–North coalition. The General Election of 1784 had consolidated his position as champion of constitutional monarchy and loyal feeling against the sordid intrigues of oligarchic politicians. In the golden, prosperous years which followed he had established a record of moderate, enlightened and efficient administration in almost every branch of government. He enjoyed the respect and confidence of the King, the support of the country gentlemen, and the warm regard of the commercial world. On the eve of the French Revolution his handling of the

Regency crisis, brought about by George III's first prolonged mental illness, had confirmed his reputation as the great constitutional minister defending the monarchy against the unprincipled ambitions of the Foxite Whigs. His integrity of character, his cool sagacious temperament, his devastating debating skill and unequalled administrative talent enabled him to dominate politics singlehanded as no minister had done since Walpole or was to do after him until Peel.

Yet Pitt was always more of an administrator than a politician. His outlook was practical and flexible; his stock-in-trade of political principles slender. At the outset of his career he had called himself an independent Whig, and the adjective was more significant than the noun. Though sensitive on personal matters, on public issues his mind always seemed to work at a lower temperature than those of his colleagues or adversaries. Calm, reserved, unmarried, his intimates were few. His personal parliamentary following was small and he made little attempt to build a party of his own. Like his father, the great Chatham, he was content to rest his claims on his public reputation and a proud consciousness of his own talents. Between Pitt and Burke there could scarcely have been a greater contrast; and Pitt was left unmoved by the warmth and eloquence which Burke poured into his political writings. In 1795, when Lord Auckland's pamphlet on the desirability of peace with France brought him a stately letter of remonstrance from Burke, Auckland passed it on to Pitt. The Prime Minister replied in a brief, cool postscript: 'I return Burke's letter, which is like other rhapsodies from the same pen, in which there is much to admire, and nothing to agree with.'[5]

In entering the war in 1793 Pitt's motive was self-defence; his object security. He had no ideological ends in view; he was financially and militarily unprepared for prolonged European hostilities, and once engaged revealed an over-optimistic trust in the vigour of his continental allies and the financial weakness of the new French state. The short war he had expected turned into a long one; and when rising prices, bad harvests and popular discontents were added to the lack of military success abroad, he was ready in 1795 and 1797 to make peace. Though three successive sets of negotiations broke down on the exorbitance of French demands, Pitt in 1800 was more convinced

than ever that the financial embarrassments of the Government
and the growing war-weariness of the country made peace a
national necessity. While in the end it was left to Addington in
1801 to negotiate the treaty of Amiens which secured a breath-
ing-space of eighteen months in the twenty-two-year struggle
against France, Pitt in retirement was party to the arrangements
and defended them in Parliament.

His peace policy in the 1790s, which even envisaged leaving
Belgium in French hands and Holland as a French dependency,
was the more remarkable since he had to press it against the
views of some of his chief collaborators. Lord Grenville, his
Foreign Secretary, was closer to Burke and his patron Earl
Fitzwilliam than to Pitt in his conviction that the war was
a conflict of rival systems in which the existence of one or the
other was at stake. But it was proof of Pitt's statesmanship and
skill that he never forfeited his position as the embodiment of
all those conservative forces in British society which rallied to
the defence of the Crown, the Constitution and the Church in
the last decade of the eighteenth century. Though the Fitzwilliam circle railed at his hypocrisy, his political flexibility
enabled him to conciliate the undoubted war-weariness in the
country while continuing to strike the right note of patriotic
resistance. He abandoned his earlier advocacy of parliamentary
reform, he passed the repressive measures, such as the Acts
against seditious meetings and treasonable practices, which his
supporters demanded. For all his practical contempt at Burke's
emotional attitude, he was astute enough to use Burke's arguments when exhorting the House of Commons to fresh national
endeavours. All through the war he employed language in
debate hardly distinguishable from, sometimes a direct echo
of, Burke's phraseology. 'The moment will never come,' he
announced in 1794, 'when I shall not think any alternative
preferable to that of making peace with France, upon the system
of its present rulers.' In 1797 he described French hostilities as
directed 'against the very essence of your liberty, against the
foundation of your independence, against the citadel of your
happiness, against your constitution itself'. 'We are at war',
he said in 1799, 'against armed opinions', and as late as 1803,
in his speech on the renewal of hostilities, he referred to 'the
liquid fire of Jacobinical principles desolating the world.'

Despite the repeated failure of his coalition policies, Pitt's patience, his determination, his courage and skill, above all the supreme quality of national leadership which he displayed to the country, made him the only acceptable head of government while the war continued. Not only was he without an equal as war-leader, there was not even a rival. Addington's ministry which made the peace survived the resumption of hostilities by only one year – not so much because of its intrinsic defects but because of the general conviction, even among its own members, that any wartime administration that was not under Pitt was a patent absurdity. By that time Pitt had become a symbol; and as a symbol he was perhaps more potent after 1801 than as a politician. As long as he lived, all others suffered by contrast; and after his death in 1806 he was almost deified. Outside the small circle of the Foxite Whigs, politicians of all shades and descriptions who could claim some connection with him contested for the honour of his name. 'Upon every measure,' wrote the liberal Whig Romilly bitterly of the opposition to the Talents ministry in 1806, 'they talk of the opinions and the plans of Mr Pitt, or, in their language, the great statesman whose death the nation finds every day more reason to deplore.'[6] To the mass of his countrymen he was, in the words of Canning's famous song, 'the Pilot that weathered the Storm'. To the fervent Tories of the post-Waterloo era he remained, as one clerical pamphleteer expressed it in 1820, 'the Immortal William Pitt' who 'had, in England, bound the Jacobinism of France' and had he lived, would ultimately have extinguished the Radicalism in which it was reincarnated.[7]

Yet, by another of those paradoxes which run through Pitt's career, the dead statesman himself had largely been responsible for the almost insuperable difficulties which seemed to confront any attempt after 1801 to recreate the 'party of Mr Pitt'. Though his personal following had been small, what was at stake was the possession of Pitt's name and the loyalty of that silent majority in the Commons and in the country who had supported what Pitt seemed to them to embody between 1793 and 1800. The 'party of Mr Pitt' had a symbolic significance. Yet Pitt's actions as a politician in the last five years of his life had gone far to disintegrate the Coalition over which he presided. His policy of following Irish Union in 1800 with a measure of final Catholic Emancipation had alienated the King, split the Cabinet and brought about his own resignation. Though he returned to office in 1804 his second administration was only a shadow of the first and his death in 1806 completed the process of disintegration. For the remainder of the war, parliamentary politics seemed to revert to the old pattern of rival personal groups – Pittites, Addingtonians, Grenvillites, Foxites, the Canning – Wellesley coterie, and others – not one strong enough to provide a basis for an administration and few able to work comfortably together.

From 1804 to 1812 almost every combination of these groups was attempted, to the growing disillusionment of the public which began to see in the kaleidoscope of Westminster politics little more than a greedy and corrupt scramble for office. Scandals at home and defeats abroad added to the public cynicism and provided fresh disagreements among politicians. Not for a generation had government seemed so weak and opposition so strong as in the first dozen years of the new century. After Pitt's long rule from 1783 to 1801 a succession of six prime ministers in less than twelve years seemed to destroy all unity and to put the highest prize of politics within the grasp of any politician who considered himself endowed with the requisite qualifications. Yet the disintegration of party was never so complete as appeared on the surface. The deaths of two Prime Ministers in office while a third (Portland) was a dying man, like the King's madness, were accidental strokes of fate. The rapid succession of chief ministers concealed a large degree of continuity in their Cabinets. The one exception was the Talents ministry of 1806–7. But of the remaining administrations Hawkesbury (the future Lord Liverpool), Castlereagh, Eldon and Westmoreland served as Cabinet members in all five; Sidmouth, Chatham, Portland, Camden and Mulgrave in four. In this nucleus of senior ministers there was after 1803 fundamental agreement on the elements of a Pittite policy: vigorous prosecution of the war, discouragement of radical reform movements at home, abandonment of the Catholic question for the time being, and respect for the wishes and constitutional authority of the King.

For such a policy there was considerable support in the political world at large. What most people wanted was a government that would apply itself with courage and integrity to the business of winning the war abroad while avoiding contentious policies at home. The strength of unfashionable ministers like Sidmouth and Perceval was that they represented solid, homespun Tory qualities which the country gentlemen in the House of Commons, and a good deal of influential public opinion outside, thought were more important than flashy genius or aristocratic pretentiousness. Yet any administration, if it hoped to last, had to possess a measure of unity and more than a modicum of talent. In a loose House of Commons, where an organised Opposition of over two hundred could make the life of any administration unendurable, it was particularly important to have prestige and a show of parliamentary ability. It was here that the lack of sustained leadership and the internecine quarrels of the Pittites had their most damaging effects. Perceval, who became Prime Minister in 1809, was not indifferent to the Pittite legacy. At a dinner in 1810 to celebrate the anniversary of Pitt's birthday, he told his audience that, inspired by Pitt's example, the Cabinet would carry on the struggle against 'democrats and levellers' and maintain the campaign in the Peninsula against all the defeatist talk of the Whigs. Yet he admitted privately that 'we are no longer the sole representatives of Mr Pitt' and that 'the magic of that name is in a great degree dissolved'. Liverpool, who succeeded to Perceval's position, Cabinet and problems in 1812, looked on matters in much the same light. The real danger, he observed when finally confirmed in office, was not so much from the official Opposition but from the parties of Wellesley and Canning, who would claim that 'they have as much right to be considered as the successors of Mr Pitt's party as ourselves, and whose object will consequently be to detach as many of our friends as possible.'[8]

Only gradually was the old corps of Pitt's followers reunited. Castlereagh and Sidmouth were brought back to the fold by Perceval. The brilliant but over-ambitious Canning, having refused the Foreign Office in 1812, finally wrote off his losses and rejoined the Government as head of the India Board in 1816. The post-war social disorders brought Lord Grenville firmly over to the side of the executive, and though he never took office again, the faded Grenville connection, including

Wellesley, made their formal and long-expected junction with
the ministers in 1822. 'Mr Pitt's party' in a ghost-like form was
perpetuated in Liverpool's post-war administration and as long
as that ministry lasted a conscious Pittite tradition remained.
Liverpool, a disciple of Adam Smith and an admirer of Edmund
Burke, reserved his greatest reverence for the man whose friend
and follower he had been in his younger days. In the House of
Lords he once described Burke and Pitt, in a carefully balanced
phrase, as the one 'perhaps the greatest philosopher, the other
certainly the greatest practical statesman, that ever existed'.
Castlereagh, as late as 1822, could attempt to rally support by
invoking the name of Pitt, 'that illustrious individual, consecrated as his name must ever be, no less by the important truths
which he established, than by the splendid acts which he
achieved' and by appealing to 'the Commons of England who
supported that great statesman through the long, dark and
dreary career of our contest with revolutionary France'.[9]

No party, however, can subsist on the memory of its great
men. Liverpool's Cabinet had to live on the merits of their own
policies and a persuasion of their own efficiency and integrity.
The needs of the war and the victories of Wellington enabled
them to survive the first testing years. But once the war was
over, Parliament was able to demonstrate that it was more
independent of the executive than it had been for a century.
Between adherents of the ministry and the regular Opposition
was a mass of independent MPs whose support, though indispensable for legislation, was fluctuating and often incalculable. If there was party in politics, there was hardly a party
system. The Opposition Whigs could be described as a party
within limits, but there was no counteracting Tory Party.
Though contemporary opponents and later critics called Lord
Liverpool's administration Tory, it was an epithet rarely used
by its own members. In their eyes they were simply the King's
ministers, carrying on the government of the country, and when
they spoke of their own 'party', it was in the vaguest of terms.
'United as I am with the party now in the Government,' wrote
Goulburn when he took the Irish Secretaryship in 1821; and
when Wellington entered the Cabinet in 1818 he referred in
the same anonymous manner to 'the party of which the present
Government are the head.' Party in this sense was little more

than a group of men in office and their adherents, on personal or public grounds, in Parliament. Though the Foxite Whigs had persisted in calling Pitt's administration 'Tory' because it was a creation of the King, the Pittites had never accepted that description. Only gradually was the name 'Whig' successfully monopolised by the Opposition; only by default did the Pittite party passively acquiesce in the label 'Tory' in the years after Waterloo. But by the reign of George IV such distinctions lacked much significance other than historical.

CHAPTER 2

Lord Liverpool and the Foundation of Conservative Policy

The politics of the period from 1815 to 1827 were marked by two paradoxes. One was the evolution of a conservative policy without the parallel evolution of a conservative party. The other was the phenomenon of a long administration in terms of years which was not a strong administration in terms of parliamentary organisation. The two paradoxes explain each other. The fact that substantially the same set of men continued in office under the same Prime Minister for fifteen years at a time of great social and economic difficulty not only permitted but virtually demanded the eventual formulation of some settled line of policy. The contemporary structure of politics, on the other hand, which was in essence the old eighteenth-century system in its final weak but purified stage, effectively denied the possibility of controlling the legislature either through patronage or through party. It was natural in those circumstances that the emergence of a recognisable conservative policy should historically precede and not result from the emergence of a recognisable conservative party. This inversion of the logical sequence does much to explain the apparent time-lag between the thinking of the party leadership and that of the party back benchers in the 1840s.

What enabled the ministry to survive for another twelve years after Waterloo was the political skill of Lord Liverpool, the collective talents of his colleagues, and their ability to adjust themselves to the problems of post-war society. Even at its weakest, Lord Liverpool's administration was more impressive than any of Pitt's Cabinets. While their intrinsic parliamentary capabilities enabled them in the long run to impress their authority on the House of Commons, they also developed under the grinding pressure of events statesmanlike qualities of a kind that could hardly have been predicted in 1812. It was not, however, an unnatural development. Though by training and circumstances Liverpool and his colleagues were firm defenders of the existing order, most of them were at the same time anxious to stand well with the 'respectable' as distinct from the popular or radical elements in the country. Given their social and political backgrounds, they could hardly have wished otherwise. Very few of them belonged to the old aristocracy. Most of them, and nearly all their leading figures, were drawn from middle-class families. Of the four peers who formed the more ornamental section of the Cabinet – Westmorland, Bathurst, Harrowby and Melville – only the first two had any claims to length of lineage. Harrowby's grandfather was a successful political barrister who became Lord Chief Justice in George III's reign; Melville was the son of Pitt's ally, the rough-tongued Scots advocate Henry Dundas. Of the rest, Liverpool's father was a commoner who had made his career and earned his earldom by unflagging political service to George III; Vansittart was the son of an East India nabob from a London merchant family; Sidmouth's father was a fashionable doctor; Eldon's a coal-factor at Newcastle-on-Tyne. Huskisson came from the Staffordshire small gentry class. Peel's grandfather was a Lancashire yeoman and his father a cotton millionaire. Canning's father was the disinherited elder son of a small Irish landowner whose widow had to take to the stage to earn a living. Though any collective description has its exceptions, it would be nearer the truth to regard Liverpool's Cabinet as a set of industrious middle-class administrators with a high, almost evangelical, sense of duty rather than as a group of careless, hardbitten aristocrats. As a group they formed a recognisable type of Conservative. It was natural for them to think

well of a political system which had given them a career, office
and power. At the same time, lacking the easy assurance of
broad acres and long genealogy, they were in varying degrees
responsive to opinion in the country and as professional politicians could not be indifferent to their own public reputation.

Nevertheless the Government was never able to command a
majority in Parliament, least of all in the Commons. It could
persuade, cajole, and occasionally threaten. But essentially it
had to work its measures through Parliament, relying on its
prestige, the necessities of the public service, and superior
argument. The limits of its powers were decided by the independent MPs, whose numbers, as time went on, seemed to
grow rather than diminish. 'The striking *feature* – to use a
Castlereaghism – of the day,' wrote C. W. Wynn after the 1818
election, 'is the unwillingness of most of the new members to be
considered as belonging to Government, to receive notes or
answer whip.'[1] The one saving grace in the situation from the
ministers' point of view was that at no time between 1815 and
1827 did the majority of MPs wish to drive out the existing
ministers and let in the Whigs; and when pushed to the wall
Liverpool was prepared to let it be known that defeat on a
particular issue would entail resignation. This, however, was a
weapon which could only be sparingly used if its force was not
to be blunted by repetition. Between thwarting ministerial
policy and forcing ministers to resign was a wide field which the
independent members of the Commons did not hesitate to
exploit. Though often ignorant, self-willed and misguided, they
were not entirely capricious or irresponsible. But many of them
had large constituencies which they had to consider; others
were sensitive to public opinion especially when it coincided
with their own social and economic interests; all of them valued
their reputation. They expected Government to make a case
for its proposals; and if necessary to defer to the opinion of the
legislature when strongly held and widely supported.

Two early events illustrated the power of Parliament and the
weakness of the executive. The first was the passing of the Corn
Law of 1815, prohibiting the entry of foreign corn until the
domestic price reached 80s a quarter; the second was the defeat
in 1816 of the Government's proposal to prolong the property-
tax, as Pitt's wartime income tax was generally known. Liver-

pool had reluctantly yielded to public and parliamentary pressure for a Corn Law inquiry in 1814, partly because of the importance of easing the transition of the inflated agricultural industry to peace conditions, partly to reconcile the country gentry to his postwar financial measures. But though nominally a government bill, the actual terms were drafted by an all-party committee which rejected the Prime Minister's own recommendation for a sliding scale. The loss of the income tax was an even more decisive rebuff. It had not been expected and it left the ministry with only twelve millions of ordinary revenue to meet an estimated expenditure of thirty millions. More subtly, the abolition of the income tax transferred a substantial financial burden from the rich and placed it on the mass of the population through the medium of indirect taxation. Liverpool himself was not deceived. No other tax, he observed in 1815, 'could be so equal or so just'; and seven years later he reminded the peers that 'it was by no means in conformity to the opinions and wishes of H.M. Government that the revenue was so hastily and materially curtailed.'[2]

As it was, the two events together crippled the Government for years. The Corn Law, the first prohibitory measure of its kind in British history, though perhaps less significant in its operation than believed at the time, was a double handicap. On the one side it held out to the agriculturists the illusory promise of a security which in practice was never, and could never be, realised, with the consequent alienation and exasperation of farmers and many country gentry. At the same time it saddled the ministry with the odium of having passed a piece of blatant class legislation. It provoked popular riots at the time and remained for the next thirty years one of the stock radical grievances against the aristocratic system. The loss of the income tax, despite the Cabinet's proposal to halve the wartime rate, wrecked their financial plans and forced them back on a ruinous policy of borrowing and deficit budgeting for another five years. A large part of the history of the Liverpool administration could be written in terms of the Cabinet's prolonged and painful efforts to recover from these two false steps.

Even without the financial strait-jacket in which the Cabinet was encased after 1816, the difficulties confronting them were unprecedented in their nature and severity. The aftermath of the most expensive and prolonged war the country had ever fought was only one element in the situation. The rest derived from the great economic and social changes that had been going on in British society since the last quarter of the eighteenth century. Wartime inflation, post-war slump, industrialisation, a rapidly growing population, and equally rapid urbanisation, created a set of problems for which the country was singularly ill-adapted either by its outlook or institutions to find a solution. If conservative policy was not a direct product of the Industrial Revolution, at least it was a product of a situation in which the harsher aspects of early industrialisation aggravated the evils which the twenty-two-year struggle against revolutionary France brought in its train. The difficulties and discontents of the years after Waterloo clearly demanded some response from Government; the only issue was what kind of response.

War rarely leaves societies where it finds them, and the Britain of 1815 had changed considerably since 1783. Public opinion was more educated, more articulate, more critical. There was a wide diffusion of radical opinion which extended from a few MPs and leading figures in the metropolis like Hunt, Cobbett, Cartwright and Burdett to shopkeepers, Dissenters, London craftsmen and Methodist-educated weavers in Yorkshire and Lancashire. All in varying degrees agreed with Cobbett's analysis as defined in Bamford's famous aphorism: the true cause of their sufferings was misgovernment; its proper corrective parliamentary reform. In the wilder fringes of the radical movement the continued use of the slogans and emblems of the French Revolution – tricolour flags, cockades, Phrygian caps, trees of liberty – kept alive the emotional fears of Jacobinism. Romilly in 1807 had pessimistically remarked that 'the influence which the French Revolution has had over this nation has been in every way unfavourable to them. Among the higher orders it has produced a horror of every kind of innovation; among the lower, a desire to try the boldest political experiments, and a distrust and contempt of all moderate reforms.'[3] It was a comment that seemed even more applicable ten years later.

As the columns of newspapers and a spate of pamphlets witnessed, the well-to-do themselves were deeply concerned at the state of the country. Agriculture, the largest single industry, suffered like the rest from the post-war depression; and when farmers complained, the country gentry were quick to demand remedies. At the time of the General Election of 1818 Huskisson reported to the Prime Minister that the radical press had affected even the yeomanry. 'They despise the Whigs; but they are no longer what they were ten years ago in their attachment to the old Tory interests and principles which are prevalent in the Nobility & Gentry.'[4] Lower down the social scale the libertarian habits of British society made it easy for the discontents of the poor to find outlet in disorder and destruction. Political power had always been in the hands of a few; and for the mass of the population government was an arcane institution capable of being influenced, if at all, by protest and criticism from outside the closed political oligarchy rather than from within. But a feature of the post-war years was that the gap between government and the country seemed to be widening every year. Peel, settling down in England after six years as Chief Secretary in Ireland, was particularly struck by this unwelcome and dangerous development.

'Do not you think [he asked his friend Croker in March 1820] that the tone of England . . . is more liberal, to use an odious but intelligible phrase, than the policy of the Government ? Do not you think that there is a feeling, becoming daily more general and more confirmed . . . in favour of some undefined change in the mode of governing the country ?'[5]

A curious situation, he thought, had grown up in which public opinion, with more influence than it had ever enjoyed before, was never more dissatisfied with the share it possessed.

Peel was writing in the wake of Peterloo and the Six Acts which had added more items to the depressing catalogue of alternate bouts of disorder and repression after 1814 – Luddit-ism, the East Anglian riots, the march of the Blanketeers, the Pentrich rising, the Huddersfield rising, the Spa Fields riots, the Cato Street Conspiracy, and their inevitable consequences in the shape of Special Commissions, secret committees of inquiry, suspension of Habeas Corpus, and Seditious Meetings Acts. In purely parliamentary terms (but only in those) riot and disorder were among the least of the ministerial problems. Government was never stronger in the legislature than when there were plots and disturbances in the country. The efforts of the Opposition Whigs to exploit such situations, like their anti-war policy before 1815, invariably recoiled on their own heads and convinced the respectable of their unfitness for office. The House of Commons was always ready to rally round the Government in time of social unrest and the repressive legislation passed was backed by the governing class as a whole. Ministers were acting in response to a genuine alarm and on the evidence before them could scarcely have done less than they did. They were often urged to do more in language more extreme than they themselves would have used.

Yet events like Peterloo could only increase the widespread feeling that the country was in a state of crisis. The crisis indeed seemed worse than in the 1790s since it was not a matter of a specific danger to British society from without, but a more pervasive atmosphere of violence and disunion within. Tories, Whigs and Radicals alike could feel with justice that these were symptoms of an unhappy and divided nation, even though they disagreed both on causes and remedies. Ministers could reiterate the arguments of the political economists to which most educated men subscribed: that the laws of economics were inexorable and legislative intervention likely to do more harm than good. But if the educated public were ready to accept this doctrine in the abstract, they also felt strongly if illogically that something was missing in practice. Discontent and distress in society, even if not the fault of the Government, materially weakened its prestige and damaged its influence. To be seen to do nothing was to invite unpopularity and worse. Ministers were not indifferent to the problems of the economy and the hardships of the poor; nor indeed to the general dissatisfaction of the public with the conduct of government. Their difficulty was to know what, if anything, they could do about it. Direct concession to political agitation, which meant in effect making changes in the actual fabric of the constitution, was out of the question. In the immediate post-Waterloo period there was no inclination for that in either Parliament or the Cabinet. As Romilly had observed, the effect of the revolutionary struggle had been to harden the resistance of the governing classes to

any organic change. The only exception was Catholic Emancipation, the issue left unresolved by Pitt. On this the House of
Commons was evenly divided. But the Cabinet's agreement in
1812 to remain neutral on the question precluded any ministerial initiative; and the House of Lords, with Liverpool's
personal example to fortify them, offered an insuperable
barrier to independent action in the Commons.

Yet there was an alternative road of advance for a ministry
that wished to be both progressive and conservative. The
eighteenth-century school of practical reformers, of whom
Adam Smith was the great British representative, had concerned themselves not with doctrinaire plans for ideal constitutions or attacks on established institutions but with an
examination of the methods whereby enlightened legislators
could improve the lot of society as a whole. The object of this
new political science was not to take power from the governing
classes but to teach them how to promote the happiness of the
mass of people in their charge. That in the continental states
they had to educate the despotic princes and in Britain a
middle-class Cabinet was only an accident of history and
geography. For Lord Liverpool, a student of political economy,
the increasingly urgent duty of the British Government was to
tackle the administrative problems which had dogged it since
1815 – finance, trade, and the state of the country.

Although by 1818 the wartime tax burden of about £70
millions had been cut by £18 millions, the pressure by Parliament and the public for retrenchment had not slackened. The
more the Government made concessions, the greater the public
appetite for economy seemed to grow. In 1817 and 1818 the
ministry was forced into a desperate defensive to preserve the
mere skeleton of the necessary machinery of the State. The
peace-time establishments for the armed forces agreed in 1816
were again reduced; the civil establishment drastically pruned;
a 10 per cent reduction made in official salaries; and the Civil
List cut still further. These, however, were little more than
face-saving expedients. The plain fact was that beyond certain
limits there was little the Government could do to reduce taxation. Of the total expenditure of £69 millions for the financial
year ending January 1818, for example, no less than £54
millions were absorbed by servicing the National Debt, interest

on exchequer bills, and the legacy of the great war represented
by the 'deadweight' of £5 millions for service pensions and
half-pay. With a revenue of only £56 millions Vansittart had
in effect a disposable surplus of only £2 millions with which to
meet expenditure on normal government services of £15 millions. It was a preposterous situation and in 1819 the ministers
at last made up their mind to stand and fight. 'If we cannot
carry what has been proposed,' the Prime Minister wrote to
Lord Eldon in May 1819, 'it is far, far better for the country
that we should cease to be the Government.'[6]

The outcome of the new mood of resolution was a determined
effort to regain the initiative in a number of fields of executive
policy. The year 1819 is the crucial date in the history of the
Liverpool administration, not for the irrelevant episode of
Peterloo, but for the beginning of a new constructive attitude
to national problems. The first imperative task was to bring
the country and the Government back to a system of sound
conservative finance. The post-war depression and the drastic
reduction of State expenditure had already acted as a powerful
deflationary weapon. From a low point of 30 per cent devaluation in 1813 the pound had recovered to a level of only 4 per
cent devaluation in 1819. As a final deflationary step the
ministers took the plunge of returning to a metallic-based currency. Despite the qualms of the Bank of England, the 1819
Currency Committee, chaired by Peel but containing all the
leading House of Commons ministers, resulted in legislation
the same year to return to the gold standard by graduated
stages between 1820 and 1823. In the wider field of government
finance the new era was heralded by Vansittart's budget of
1819 which imposed £3 millions of new taxes and stripped
£12 millions from the Sinking Fund. The object of this 'new
system of Finance', as it was described in a government
pamphlet, was to meet current expenditure by actual revenue;
maintain, for the support of public credit rather than for any
intrinsic value, the Sinking Fund at £5 millions; and gradually
to reduce the capital debt by conversion of stock to a lower rate
of interest.

The success of this policy depended largely on rendering
more productive the standard source of revenue, customs and
excise, which constituted about two-thirds of the total taxation.

To Lord Liverpool, bred in the school of Adam Smith, as Pitt and Grenville had been before him, the problem of stimulating the sluggish post-war economy was susceptible to only one solution: the dismantling of part of the high tariff barrier which surrounded British trade and industry, and a progressive reduction in the mass of commercial restrictions. His great Free-Trade speech of May 1820 was the first time that a British Prime Minister so firmly and unequivocally stated his conviction of the great advantages offered by unrestricted freedom of trade. Of that, he told the House of Lords, 'I can entertain no doubt'. Though the existing British system was historically one of high protection, and many believed that it owed its greatness to that system, 'others, of whom I am one, believe that we have risen *in spite* of that system.'[7]

The reports of the committees of both Houses on foreign trade appointed in 1820 laid down the strategy of the new commercial policy. When presenting the report of the Commons Committee Wallace, the Vice-President of the Board of Trade, laid down the precept on which future policy should rest: that all restrictions on trade were justifiable only on grounds of political expediency and, where no political expediency was evident, should be abolished. In the course of the next half-dozen years the first great instalment of the nineteenth-century Tariff Reform and Free-Trade policy was carried out in accordance with this principle. The methods employed were the reduction of a high tariff system to a low one; the simplification and easing of the Navigation Acts and other shipping regulations; and the opening of colonial trade to foreign countries on a reciprocal basis. The prime object was to promote commerce by extending Britain's world market and to stimulate domestic production and consumption. The pace of reform was inevitably conditioned by the financial situation but with returning prosperity Robinson's budgets of 1824 and 1825 – the first true 'Free Trade' budgets of the century – showed surpluses which enabled large tariff reductions to be made. Even the Corn Law of 1815 came under review; and though the 1822 Act was too cautious to effect its purpose, from 1826 Liverpool and Huskisson were preparing a radical new bill on the principle of adjusting protection to the new monetary levels and introducing a sliding scale of duties to minimise the disruptive effect of foreign imports. As early as April 1823 the Prime Minister could talk with satisfaction of British commerce and manufactures 'advancing to a degree of prosperity which they never before enjoyed'; and two years later, with the confidence born of 'the unprecedented, unparalleled prosperity of every part of the country', he re-enunciated the general principle of Free Trade as the great foundation of economic success and 'the need to move further down the road which government initiative had opened up.[8]

Though continued parliamentary pressure made it expedient to yield occasional concessions to economy and tax-reduction, Liverpool's eyes were fixed on the expansion of trade and industry rather than on parsimony and retrenchment as the means of lifting the country out of the post-war depression. He had vigorously denied in 1822 that the economic difficulties of the country were due to high taxation. By 1824, in fact, the four millions of direct taxation imposed on the country was less in proportion to total revenue than in any other state in Europe. As he wrote privately to Canning the same year, 'if we *could* do, what we *ought* to do (do not be alarmed, I am not going to propose it) we should make an augmentation in our direct taxes of at least two millions, and, as a compensation, take off indirect taxes to the amount of four or five millions'.[9] Tax the rich, encourage the economy, ease the burden on the mass of the people by reducing the cost of raw materials and articles of consumption: this in brief was Liverpool's concept of true national policy. To the charge that the Government was unduly favouring the commercial interest, his answer was brief and emphatic. It was complete folly, he told the peers in 1820, to think that 'the great interests of the country, the agricultural, the manufacturing and the commercial interests, can ever justly be set at variance . . . What is for the benefit of the one, must be beneficial to the rest . . . any attempt exclusively to favour the one, must be prejudicial to all.'[10]

The new 'liberal' policies of the Liverpool ministry in the 1820s had little direct connection with the reshuffle of Cabinet posts which took place between 1821 and 1823. To speak of the replacement of 'reactionary Tories' by 'liberal Tories' in these years is to misunderstand both the temper of the Cabinet and the political circumstances of the time. Some of the changes arose from immediate necessities; others were part of the normal process of renewal in an administration that had already lasted ten years. The purpose of the main group of new appointments at the end of 1821 was not so much to initiate a change of direction as to reorganise the ministerial team for policies already set in motion. The motives were exclusively political: to rehabilitate the administration after the disastrous episode of the Queen's trial in 1820, to deny the King the possibility of an alternative ministry, and to reinforce Castlereagh in the House of Commons.

Though Canning's ostentatious detachment from despotic monarchies abroad and shrewd cultivation of public opinion at home subsequently consolidated his reputation for liberalism, it would be a distortion to ascribe the new policies of the ministry solely or even mainly to his influence. Had he, as so nearly happened, spent the last five years of his career as Governor-General of India, his absence would have been unnoticeable. It was only the delay to the Government's programme caused by the parliamentary difficulties of 1820–1 that invested the succeeding ministerial changes with any policy significance. It was a matter of appearance rather than reality. If Vansittart had remained at the Exchequer instead of Robinson, or Wallace, the energetic Vice-President, become President of the Board of Trade, instead of Huskisson, it is unlikely that the commercial and financial policies of the mid-1820s would have been different or less successful. Canning's isolationist attitude in foreign affairs had been foreshadowed in Castlereagh's state-paper of 1820; and the first of Peel's criminal reforms had been prepared under Sidmouth. Yet appearances were important. After 1822 the ministry looked stronger and the impression gained ground that it was prepared to do more than had seemed either possible or desirable in the years immediately after Waterloo.

What was of even greater significance was that the new policies owed almost everything to the initiative of the Cabinet and very little to public pressure. Though Peel's legal reforms, for example, could not be disconnected from the sustained campaign led in previous years by Romilly and Mackintosh, his emphasis on the interdependence of criminal reform and a more efficient police was a view that found little echo among the Whig legal reformers, though, as an issue of law and order, it was central to Peel's thinking. It took the Home Secretary six years to convert the House of Commons to the need for a unified and disciplined Metropolitan Police. The situation was much the same in the more central field of commercial legislation. Though Free Trade as an abstract economic ideal commanded wide acceptance among the educated public, few individual industries or great mercantile interests wished to expose themselves voluntarily to the winds of competition; and most were able to bring forward plausible arguments why they should be excepted from the general rule. The famous petition of the London merchants in 1820, prepared by the economist Tooke, met with lukewarm response until it was taken up by the influential banker Henry Thornton and actively encouraged by the Prime Minister. There is no reason to doubt the truth of Tooke's subsequent comment that the ministers were 'more sincere and resolute Free Traders than the Merchants of London'. The petitions provided useful background for executive action but it was the favourable reception in the Commons that enabled the Cabinet to press forward with the appointment of committees to examine the whole question of foreign trade.

While the country gentry were ready to support the Government in matters of currency and commercial reform, however, it was a different matter when it came to Corn Laws and the grievances of farmers. The agricultural depression of 1819–23 (the result mainly of abnormally good harvests) produced campaigns for greater protection, tax relief, and retrenchment, which ran directly counter to Government policy. The agricultural committees appointed in 1821 and 1822 deflected part of the attack; and independent action in the Commons to reduce taxation still further was defeated on two occasions by the threat of Government resignation. But though most MPs outside the official Opposition were beginning to realise by 1822 that retrenchment had reached its limit, a new danger emerged with the conversion of many of the country gentlemen to the view that their economic troubles stemmed from the 1819 policy of deflation and the return to gold, and could be solved by an inflationary policy of paper money and unrestricted credit. What faced the Government in these years in fact was something approaching an organised agricultural revolt in the House of Commons more formidable than any threat from the Whigs.

Though the 'Boodle Cabinet', as this group was known (from the club of that name), kept themselves and their followers separate from the official Opposition, their existence was a serious danger to Government policy. 'The country gentlemen,' wrote Wellington acidly in March 1822, 'treat the Government exceedingly ill . . . What I complain of is their acting in concert, and as a party independent of, and without consultation with, the Government, which they profess to support, but really oppose.'[11]

While ready to make tactical concessions, however, Liverpool was no more disposed to allow the powerful agricultural interest to shape his policy than the vested interest of manufacturers and merchants. The real cause of farming distress he ascribed to the inflation, over-investment and over-production of the war years and the failure to adjust to peace conditions. 'What the agriculturalist really wants is a market,' he said in an outspoken speech in the House of Lords in February 1822. 'But it is not in the power of Parliament immediately to give the farmer a market adequate to his wants.' For that time and the slow recovery of the national economy were necessary. Manufacture, trade and agriculture, he reiterated, were interdependent and none could be treated in isolation or as a special case. 'It is the duty of Government and of Parliament to hold the balance between all the great interests of the country, *as even as possible* . . . The agricultural is not the *only* interest in Great Britain. It is not even the *most numerous*.' Though farmers complained of low prices, he could not blind himself to the fact that low prices for food benefited the great and growing mass of the people. It would be a material benefit, he asserted roundly, to the other classes of the community if they could buy meat at 4d a pound instead of 8d, and other necessities of life equally cheaply. An alteration in the Corn Laws would do little good; the only real hope for farmers lay in more efficient methods and increased consumption.[12]

The agriculturists were not to hear such forceful language from a prime minister again until Peel abolished the Corn Laws in 1846. But implicit in this speech was Liverpool's whole economic outlook. In essence it was not so much an economic as a social policy. The Government was ready to reform provided that the fabric of the constitution remained intact. They wished to show themselves responsive to public needs, not in the sense of reacting deferentially to particular pressures but in recognising national problems, finding the right solutions, and taking the initiative in putting those solutions into effect. The promotion of national prosperity, and equally important a clear demonstration that ministers were watching over the interests of all classes, was the best answer to radical attacks on the governing structure of the country. To close the gap between State and society, to allay social discontent and agitation, to avoid organic change by administrative reform, to vindicate aristocratic rule by following national and not class policies: this was the broad pattern into which were woven the various strands of the new Government policies after 1819.

It was a strategy that in the short term was remarkably successful. In the mid-twenties the Whig Opposition found themselves outflanked by Liverpool's reforming Government in a bid for support from central moderate opinion in the country. There was truth rather than flattery in Bathurst's remark to Liverpool in May 1825 that he stood 'at the height of your power, at the head of the most popular administration which this country has for some time had'. Another member of the Cabinet, exactly a year earlier, passed another judgement which in a different way was also an epitaph on Liverpool's work. Defending himself to the Prime Minister against royal criticism for attending the radical Lord Mayor Waithman's Banquet, Canning observed that he had spent nearly thirty years of his life in fighting the battle against Jacobinism. 'But I think that battle is now fought. I think we have gained the victory.'[13]

Yet these comments represented only part of the truth. Popularity could wane; Jacobinism, at least in the watered-down sense of a demand for parliamentary reform, could revive. In setting his face so rigidly against organic reform, Liverpool had left traps for his successors and opportunities for his opponents. His real achievement after 1815 was to guide the country through the difficult transition from war to peace, from the discontents of the age of Peterloo to the prosperity of the mid-twenties, and in the process to evolve a conservative policy that went far beyond anything Pitt had done, in circumstances which Pitt could scarcely have envisaged. It was Liverpool and not Pitt who created the tradition and formulated the principles which were behind the work of Peel's great ministry of 1841–6 when a Conservative Party, explicit and organised, regained power after the Whig interlude of 1830–41. What remained to be seen was whether that policy, framed by a set of able administrators in a looser, unreformed political world, could be sustained in the sharper party conflicts of the post-reform era.

CHAPTER 3

The Emergence of the Conservative Party

I

It is arguable that the collapse of the political defences of the old order between 1827 and 1830 was a necessary condition for the emergence of a conscious conservative movement in the country at large. In making British society more content, Liverpool had made an organised defence of its institutions less urgent. Canning's classic expositions of the virtues of the unreformed parliamentary constitution, framed largely on Burke's arguments, won widespread acceptance in the 1820s because that constitution was demonstrably providing sensible and efficient government. With the country prosperous and the voice of Radicalism stilled, there seemed little cause for alarm among the traditional defenders of the State. Nobody could guess in 1826 how short the Indian summer of the old regime would prove.

The end in fact came with startling rapidity. In ten months a succession of unpredictable events transformed the face of British politics: Liverpool's stroke, Canning's accession and the consequent resignation of half the Cabinet, Canning's death after four months of power, the collapse of the Canningite–Whig Coalition, and finally the appointment as Prime Minister of Wellington, the man of whom Liverpool had written in 1822 that nothing would be more inexpedient for his own sake and his public usefulness than 'to put him permanently into any political office'.[1] Even this was only the beginning. The temperamental clash between Huskisson and the Duke destroyed Peel's policy of re-uniting the old Liverpool party. The endemic weakness of the Wellington ministry made inevitable the judicious surrenders to Dissenting and Irish Catholic agitation embodied in the repeal of the Test and Corporations Acts and Catholic Emancipation. The resultant alienation of High Tory sentiment and the continued failure to conciliate the Canningites left Wellington an ever-narrowing basis of political support which finally vanished from under him when he made his defiant declaration of faith in the old constitution in November 1830. His defeat brought the Whigs to power for the first time in quarter of a century, pledged to a substantial measure of parliamentary reform.

The character of the bill brought forward in March 1831, more sweeping than nearly every politician outside the Cabinet thought either possible or desirable, owed everything to Grey's determination to find a complete and final solution to the problem. But though he obtained the instant and enthusiastic support of the country as a whole, he had profoundly miscalculated the temper of the aristocratic legislature through which his measure had to pass. Before his bill won through to the statute book in 1832, he had been forced to dissolve the 1830 House of Commons, coerce the House of Lords and bring unprecedented political pressure to bear on the King. For eighteen months there was a running national debate, punctuated by outbursts of popular demonstrations, disorder, bloodshed and riot. It was the methods as much as the contents of the Reform Bill that shocked the Opposition. Over principles, details and tactics, they were deeply divided; but they were at one in thinking that the Whig Cabinet, by arbitrarily imposing its will on all three branches of the legislature in the name of the people, had provoked the greatest constitutional crisis in British history since the Revolution of 1688.

All these things had a profound effect on the conservative classes in British society. Within four years the three great organic measures which Liverpool had consistently opposed were put on the statute book: the repeal of the Test and Corporations Acts, Catholic Emancipation, and Parliamentary Reform. The ironic circumstances that the first two had come at the hands of a Wellington ministry merely added to the bitterness of defeat and to the disunion of the Tories. The revolutionary trilogy of great constitutional reforms awoke fears deeper than any experienced since the days of Pitt and the French wars. In both Church and State the way seemed open to the enemies of the classic eighteenth-century constitution. With the Opposition reduced to some 150 members by the first election under the new system, the inaugural meeting of the reformed Parliament in January 1833 appeared to herald an era of fundamental change. It was a common view among men of all parties that with the Reform Act the Tories were out for a generation at least and that the political battle of the future would be between the central body of Whigs and the extreme Radicals. There was little confidence among the Opposition that the ministers would be able to offer much resistance to their new and dangerous allies. At the end of the session Wellington and Rosslyn, the Opposition chief whip in the House of Lords, were agreed that 'there will be no blow-up, no bloodshed' but that 'all our ancient institutions will be destroyed by due course of law'.[2]

The rapid spread of the term 'Conservative' between 1830 and 1832 marked the widespread reaction to these epoch-making events. Originally a word borrowed, like 'liberal', from continental politics, the adjective 'conservative' had been used in its French form for several years. '*Principes conservateurs*' appears in the *Wellington Despatches* for 1819 and Wellington himself spoke in 1827 of the '*parti conservateur*' in Britain. But it was a phrase employed by an anonymous writer in the *Quarterly Review*[3] in January 1830 – 'we are now, as we always have been, decidedly and conscientiously attached to what is called the Tory, and which might with more propriety be called the Conservative Party' – that seems to have popularised the use of the word as a convenient designation for those who stood for the conservation of the great institutions of the state. Despite the occasional appearance of the alternative form 'conservator', the term spread with remarkable rapidity. By the end of the following year it was in common use by the public, the press and the politicians themselves. Two circumstances, perhaps, were responsible for this sudden adoption of a new political label. In the first place the Reform crisis evoked a need for some generic title less negative than 'anti-reformer' to describe the opponents of radical reform. In addition, it was a wider and more respectable appellation than the word 'Tory'. Not only had there been a widespread feeling during George IV's reign that Whigs and Tories were simply aristocratic factions that were increasingly meaningless and outmoded but a flavour of reaction still clung to the second of these ancient party names. 'I may be a Tory, I may be an illiberal,' Peel had said ironically in the House of Commons after his resignation in 1827; but the implication was that he regarded himself as neither. Indeed, the point of his argument was that neither Canning nor the Whigs held a monopoly of reforming policy; and that opposition to Catholic Emancipation did not necessarily imply an obscurantist attitude on other national issues.

The term Conservative was thus a product of the Reform crisis and from the start signified something different from Tory. The general use of the phrase 'Conservative Party' by 1832 did not, however, imply that an organised political party was already in being. Before such a party could come into existence, it was necessary for a large section of the public to have a sense of common interest on which such a party could be based. What happened in 1830 and 1831 was a successful search for a political identity among those who were opposed to radical reform. In establishing that identity they looked back to their historical origins rather than forward to an unknown future. At a Constitutional Meeting at Edinburgh in November 1831, for example, protesting against the Reform Bill and the threat to the independence of the House of Lords, there were innumerable references to the 'Conservative Party' as well as to 'Conservative principles'; but what was referred to was a public rather than a parliamentary manifestation. The preface to the printed report of the proceedings stated unequivocally that

'the question which now divides the country, is no question of party politics: it is the deeper and wider question, whether the institutions of the country are to stand or fall. The conservative portion of the state unites in its ranks men of all parties and of all political opinions . . . That great and numerous body are influenced by no petty hostility to a particular party or a particular ministry. It is against measures, not men, that their opposition is directed.'

The chief orator at the meeting, the famous Professor John Wilson, made clear his definition of what he called 'the great Conservative Party in the state' when he recalled the loyalty and patriotism which that party had displayed when rallying round the 'Good old king' George III at the time of the French Revolution. References by other speakers to Pitt, Burke, and Canning merely underlined the nature of the historical tradition to which they felt heirs. To such men the word 'Conservative' merely made explicit what had long been present as a force in British society.[4]

It was precisely to allow time for this force to develop that Peel had wished the contest over the Reform Bill to be fought to the last. But he was equally anxious that 'Conservative' should not merely be 'Tory' writ large. As early as May 1831 he had written to Croker that

'there are two parties amongst those who call themselves Conservatives – one which views the state of the country with great alarm; which sees a relaxation of all authority, an impatience of all that restraint which is indispensable to the existence, not of this or that, but of all Government; which is ready to support monarchy, property and public faith whenever attacked. There is another party, and that by far the more numerous, which has the most presumptuous confidence in its own fitness for administering public affairs . . . and which . . . prefers chaos to the maintenance of the present Government. Now to this latter section I do not, and will not, belong. I will not play the game which, played by the Ultra-Tories against us, is the main cause of the present evils.'

That game – and he listed some of its recent manifestations: an inflationary money policy, attacks on the new metropolitan police, readiness to ally with O'Connell or the Radicals, a factious desire to criticise the Government at all costs – was one he had experienced as minister of the Crown in the 1820s. He was not prepared to join in it now simply to evict the Whigs. A Conservative Party for Peel, and for others like him, was even in Opposition a party of government. 'There is nothing half so dangerous,' he added, 'as the man who pretends to be a Conservative, but is ready to be anything, provided only he can create confusion.'[5]

Conservatism, as far as Peel was concerned, was an attitude towards politics rather than a new tactic in party warfare: an attitude that saw in law, order, and stable rule the first principle of government; the conservation and steady improvement of the institutions of the state the necessary corollary of that principle. The practical weakness of ultra-Tories like Knatchbull and Vyvyan was that they had no policies commensurate with the real problems of the time, and insufficient talent to form a government even if the Whigs were driven to resign. The ejection of Lord Grey's administration would simply lead to parliamentary anarchy and the strengthening of the forces of disorder in the country. The proper task for Conservatives therefore was to stiffen the will and ability of the Whigs to resist their radical allies. The weakness of the Opposition after the general election of 1832 made this role even more appropriate.

'As there is no use in defeating, [he wrote to Goulburn in January 1833] no use in excluding a Government, unless you can replace it by one formed on principles more consonant to your own – our policy ought to be rather to conciliate the goodwill of the sober-minded and well-disposed portion of the community, and thus lay the foundation of future strength, than to urge an opposition on mere party grounds and for any purpose of mere temporary triumph.'[6]

Unlike Wellington, Peel's attitude at the start of the first session of the reformed Parliament was one not of pessimism but of patience. His main objective was to strengthen the links between the parliamentary Opposition and the new conservative feeling in the country; and in the process create a true Conservative party.

His immediate policy was therefore one of deliberate moderation. He was not the party's leader: no one was. Although peers and politicians were talking freely of Conservative principles, the Conservative cause, and the Conservative party, the fact remained that the Opposition had no acknowledged head, no identifiable policy, and – despite the foundation of the Carlton Club in 1832 – little in the way of organisation. Peel was the most prominent politician on the Opposition benches in the Commons but he abstained from, even discouraged, attempts to hold party meetings and issue whips. There was enough agreement on certain topics, he believed, to form a bond of union as the session developed; and where there was disagreement, he preferred to be free to take his own line. What he was not prepared to do was to buy the leadership by making concessions to ultra-Tories, agriculturalists, and inflationists.

Instead of attempting to reconcile the irreconcilable, Peel preferred to erect a standard of his own. His first important speech in the reformed Parliament was made in the debate on the Address: a protracted and disorderly affair which seemed to confirm the worst fears of the new legislature. He could hardly have chosen a more significant occasion for his statement of the course he proposed to follow. He declared his support for the Government's Irish Coercion Bill (which had caused most of the uproar among the Irish and Radicals), not because he had confidence in the Government but because their measure was in the public interest. In the new political conditions in which they found themselves the maintenance of law, order and the rights of property was more important than the harassment of the King's ministers. As for the future, he said boldly that he accepted the Reform Act as a final settlement of a great controversy; and that, taking the constitution as it existed, he would make a stand only on essential issues. He had never been an enemy of gradual and temperate reform; and he was in favour of reforming any institution that required reform. But 'he was for doing it gradually, dispassionately, and deliberately, in order that reform might be lasting.'

It was an impressive speech, both in matter and manner, and its effect was unmistakable. As Greville observed, he had 'contrived to transfer to himself personally much of the weight and authority which he had previously held as the organ and head of a great and powerful party'. This establishment of his personal ascendancy in the opening weeks of the reformed Parliament was crucial both for Peel's career and for the evolution of a Conservative Party. In effect he had served notice that

if he was to head a party again, these were the terms on which
he would do it. At the same time, by asserting his authority
as the greatest parliamentarian of the day, he made it certain
that if the thinned and divided ranks of the Opposition were
ever to become a united party, it would be under his leadership.

The events of the first two sessions of the reformed Parliament
did nothing to relieve the fears of the conservative classes of
society. The secession from the Government of Stanley, Graham,
Richmond and Ripon in May 1834, followed within six weeks
by the resignation of Lord Grey, the apparent influence of
Radicals, Dissenters and O'Connell on Cabinet policy, the
attacks on the Irish Church and on the House of Lords, reinforced the view that the old moderate Whig Party had been
destroyed by the Reform Act and that Whiggery would soon be
as obsolete as Toryism. The real question after 1832 was how
the new system would work and what direction the Whigs
would take under pressure from their Irish and Radical allies.
On this men who had been reformers in 1831 might well have
differing views. Already there was a perceptible drift away from
the Reform ministry of 1833–4 among those who had supported
them in earlier years. Peel made it his business to accelerate
that process.

Initially the best way to achieve this was to strengthen his
position in the country by the sense and moderation of his
actions in Parliament. These were qualities, however, which
were more likely to appeal to the public at large than to the
more bellicose members of the Opposition. In both Houses
Peel and Wellington had to counter the activities and encounter
the criticisms of the ultra-Tories; and there were limits to the
influence of either man. There was still no united Opposition
and still no leader. Greville, in February 1834, could still write
admiringly of Peel's enviable position, 'unshackled by party
connections and prejudices'. Peel himself was in no hurry to
move from that position. He told Aberdeen a couple of months
later that he preferred his existing situation, enjoying great
influence in the Commons independent of party, to any he could
possess as member of a ministry. It was an attitude with which
for once Wellington unexpectedly agreed. Nobody could suppose, he told Lady Salisbury, that if he and Peel consulted their

convenience, they would wish to take over the Government in the present circumstances of the country.[7]

II

By the end of the 1834 session all the elements for a Conservative Party clearly existed, but they had not yet been brought together. The *deus ex machina* was the slightly improbable figure of William IV who for that reason alone deserves a niche in the gallery of Conservative history. His action in dismissing the Melbourne Government in November 1834 had three momentous consequences. It gave Peel as Prime Minister the authority he needed to become party leader; it enabled him, as leader and head of government, to issue in the *Tamworth Manifesto* the first general exposition of Conservative principles; and it precipitated the General Election of 1835 which transformed a small divided Opposition into a substantial, united parliamentary party. If the growth of Conservatism was the product of many years, the birth of the Conservative Party can be assigned with unusual precision to the months of November–December 1834 when Peel was summoned back from his Italian holiday 'to put himself,' as the King expressed it '. . . at the head of the administration of the country.' Only then did the Opposition become a recognisable political party in the sense of having an acknowledged leader, an adequate organisation, and a coherent political philosophy.

The publication of the *Tamworth Manifesto*, in form an address to Peel's constituents, in fact an appeal to the nation, was by the conventions of the time a remarkable and unprecedented action justified only by the exceptional circumstances under which the 1834 administration came into existence. With less than 200 supporters at best it was clearly impossible for the new ministry to face the old House of Commons. An immediate general election was necessary; and in that case a statement of the attitude of the new and untried Government seemed highly advisable. For Peel there was another strong reason for establishing at the outset the character of his Government. The accident of his absence in Italy had put Wellington in charge of the executive as temporary chief minister for some three weeks. For many sections of the public, however, the recollection of the Duke's disastrous administration four years earlier and his unforgettable declaration against Reform in 1830, had turned him into a symbol of reaction, made more sinister by the fact that he was a professional soldier. In refusing Peel's invitation to join the Cabinet Stanley gave as one of his chief reasons the stamp which Wellington's name had already put on the new ministry. For that reason alone it was vital – as interested politicians were quick to point out – to give some official re-assurance to electors of moderate views who were hesitating between their fears of Radicalism and their dislike of Wellingtonian Toryism. The *Manifesto* was essentially an electioneering document, the first of its kind in British political history. It created, as Greville noted, a 'prodigious sensation', and in succeeding weeks innumerable Conservative candidates made its content the basis of their speeches from the election hustings.

The document itself was a mixture of general principles and specific policy statements. At the outset Peel emphasised that he was making a plea to 'that great and intelligent class of society . . . which is far less interested in the contentions of party, than in the maintenance of order and the cause of good government.' He referred to his own record as a reforming minister, repeated his statement that he accepted the Reform Act as a final settlement of a great constitutional question, and promised to govern in the spirit of the Reform Act if by that was meant, not indiscriminate overturning of all traditional rights and authority in a search for instant remedies for every alleged abuse, but 'a careful review of institutions, both civil and ecclesiastical' and the 'correction of proved abuses and the redress of real grievances.' In dealing with current matters he went as far as he could to conciliate the Dissenters; he de-clared himself ready to reform Church finances and to initiate a general inquiry into the organisation of the Establishment; and he promised to support the inquiry into municipal corporations started under his Whig predecessors. His basic attitude was clear: he would defend the essentials of the constitution in Church and State, but outside those essentials he would go to all reasonable lengths to meet the legitimate grievances of all classes and interests.

It was an attitude of conciliation; it was also an attitude of realism. The matters he touched on were the great practical issues raised by the first two years of the Reform ministry and no government which did not appear to be taking them seriously could hope to obtain the confidence of public opinion or of the majority of the electorate. What was more important was that Peel was offering a constructive alternative to Whig-radicalism on the one side, and negative Toryism on the other. It was a policy that admitted change, but change by moderate and evolutionary methods rather than by destruction and confiscation. He offered Reform, but Reform that would save the constitution, not subvert it.

In 1835 the work could not be carried very far. The general election failed to provide a majority for the Government. It could scarcely have been expected to do so since only three-fifths of the total seats were contested by Conservatives, often with improvised machinery and makeshift candidates. Peel placed his ultimate hope in being able to attract a sufficient number of independent, moderate MPs over to his side when the new Parliament met. In this he was disappointed. The stimulus to party unity and discipline administered by the events of November was not confined to one side. The shock of eviction brought Whigs, Radicals and Irish nationalists together, and their Lichfield House compact in February 1835 marks almost as clearly as the *Tamworth Manifesto* for their opponents the beginning of the Victorian Liberal Party. It followed that all Peel's proposed legislation was defeated and the only part of his reforming programme translated into action was the Ecclesiastical Commission set up by royal prerogative. This nevertheless was of prime importance both for what it accomplished and as an illustration of Peel's reforming technique. By setting up a standing body of bishops and senior Cabinet ministers he made it almost impossible for the Whigs to undo his work. By imposing on the Church leaders the responsibility not only for inquiring into abuses but for framing legislative remedies, he ensured that the mass of the clergy would accept and Parliament would not oppose the series of reforms which the Commission produced over the next few years. In forcing the Establishment to reform itself Peel saved the Church of England both from itself and from its enemies.

The significance of the Hundred Days ministry was, however, not in its specific achievements, which were negligible, but in its indirect consequences, which were considerable. Peel himself, in his first essay as Prime Minister, raised his reputation not only with his followers but with the public and even his opponents. The parliamentary party, heartened by the accession of another hundred MPs and a glimpse however brief of office and power, exhibited a discipline which, if patchy, was at least an immeasurable improvement on anything seen before. When early in the session the self-appointed leader of the agriculturalists, Lord Chandos, made an independent move to abolish the malt tax, an issue on which Peel had come to the rescue of the Whigs in 1833, a well-attended party meeting saw leading county MPs declare their readiness to abandon their pledges to constituents rather than risk the defeat of a Conservative ministry. After Peel's resignation a formal address of confidence and gratitude was presented to him by his followers; and this was followed by a shoal of similar addresses from cities and universities, magistrates, clergy, freeholders, merchants, lawyers, and manufacturers, all over the country. In the constituencies, now more than ever seen to be the indispensable basis of political power, the General Election of 1835 gave a powerful impetus to the organisation of Conservative voting strength. As F. R. Bonham, the party's chief electoral expert, observed to Peel later the same year, 'then we had to find candidates, organisers and friends in almost every place. *Now that work is done* and a tenth part of the exertions then applied would at least preserve if not increase our present strength.'[8]

The work thus set on foot did not cease when the election was over. A feature of the years between 1835 and 1837 was the rapid and almost spontaneous spread of constituency Conservative Associations throughout the country. Electioneering clubs had long been a feature of English borough politics; and the Reform Bill excitement in 1831–2 had given rise to innumerable political unions and associations. Though these latter were mostly on the popular side, their opponents did not disdain to copy their methods. The Act itself had led to the formation in many constituencies of local registration societies designed to support the interests of particular parties or candidates at the annual registration courts. At least one Conservative Associa-

tion, moreover, was in existence before 1834. Soon after the
1832 election Lord Londonderry formed the Durham County
Conservative Association complete with a registration committee, dinners for party workers, and general publicity, which
he boasted was the first of its kind in the country.[9]

It was the period from November 1834 to April 1835, however, while Peel was in office, that witnessed the first spontaneous mobilisation of Conservative feeling in the provinces. The
South Lancashire Conservative Association dated from November 1834. In December was founded the Birmingham Conservative Union under the presidency of Lord Dartmouth when
a Conservative candidate was put up to oppose the Radicals.
In March 1835 the Westminster Conservative Association was
started with an annual subscription of one guinea and an array
of committees and sub-committees to promote the election of a
Conservative candidate. April 1835, which saw the foundation
among others of Conservative Associations in Staffordshire,
Denbighshire and Hampshire, was the most fruitful month of
all. Charles Wynn in Denbighshire, who was old-fashioned
enough to deprecate the introduction of party political organisation into provincial society, admitted nevertheless in April
1835 that 'I see our friends promoting them all over the country
and there is frequently utility in acquiescing in what one cannot
prevent. The circumstances of the present time also in some
degree justify it.'[10] The same month *The Times*, which had
warmly supported the new ministry, printed on its leader-page
an extract from the *Liverpool Standard* exhorting its readers to
become members of their local Conservative Associations.

'It is with no small degree of pleasure [added the *Standard*] we
perceive that these valuable and important institutions are
spreading far and wide, taking for their model the principle on
which the South Lancashire Conservative Association has been
established.'[11]

During the next few years the movement extended into all
parts of the country. As early as 1837 a pamphlet entitled
'*Thoughts on the State and Prospects of Conservatism by R.S.S.*'[12]
declared that 'at this moment there is scarcely a county in
England which cannot boast of its Conservative association of

gentry.' The new organisations were not, however, confined to the country aristocracy and their social dependents. They were to be found in industrial towns like Coventry, Halifax, Preston and Warrington as well as in more old-fashioned boroughs such as Thirsk, Lewes, Ripon, Winchester, Cambridge, Canterbury and Reading. In the sprawling metropolitan area associations were founded in the separate constituencies, as for example Lambeth and Tower Hamlets, and even in small outlying suburbs like Hackney and Croydon. Exact statistics are lacking and obviously the incidence varied greatly. In quiet rural Lincolnshire a Conservative Association was started in 1836 in the southern division but a similar society in the northern division did not come until the second Reform Act. In politically-minded Buckinghamshire, on the other hand, no less than four Conservative Associations were founded between 1836 and 1837: in North and South Bucks and in the two boroughs of Aylesbury and Buckingham. It is evident, however, that well before the general election of 1841 the party possessed a wide if loose array of local organisations throughout England. Less headway seems to have been made in Wales and Scotland though even in these more distant parts of the kingdom there were successful imitations of the English models.[13]

A parallel if more localised development was the simultaneous growth of Conservative Operative and Tradesmen's Societies, to which *The Times* was giving publicity and support in the autumn of 1836. These institutions, designed as ancillaries to the main Conservative Associations, were most prominent in Lancashire, the West Riding and the Midlands. The Leeds Operative Society, claimed as the first of its kind, was founded in March 1835 to give support to Conservatism, the Peel administration and the new Conservative member, Sir John Beckett. Another started in Liverpool furnished the occasion for the encouraging notice in *The Times* in October 1836. Operative Societies were not confined to Lancashire and the Midlands; nor did they only emerge in 1835. In some towns they were clearly continuations of earlier societies; and even in their new form must often have retained something of the convivial character of the old pre-Reform benevolent and entertainment clubs catering for the poorer classes of electors. Nevertheless, they represented a significant widening of the party's social base and had a direct if limited electoral value. The author of the 1837 pamphlet was optimistic enough to suggest that while country registration could be supervised by the local Conservative Association, the work of registering supporters and striking off opponents in the boroughs should be undertaken by the Tradesmen's and Operative Societies.

Amateurish and occasionally wasteful as some of the Conservative Associations proved in their early days the cumulative effect must have been considerable. They brought in regular subscriptions, appointed permanent secretaries and treasurers, attended to the business of registration, employed solicitors, often made themselves responsible for seeking out and recommending candidates, and almost always held periodic dinners where MPs, candidates, local landowners and civic dignitaries could meet, speechify and generally demonstrate the party's strength. Provincial activity was not subordinated at one stroke to central control but at least it was given a measure of political organisation which served as a link between the two. Divisions on a party basis already existed in the provinces, sometimes to a marked degree; but the emergence of local party associations had the natural effect of hardening these divisions and making them more exclusive. The old county feeling that sent a man up to Westminster to represent his neighbours and his neighbourhood rather than a party did not immediately disappear; but a feature of provincial politics in the 1830s was the increasing importance of national issues, even if the intensity with which they were taken up depended on the social and economic interests of the particular constituency. The growth of Conservative Associations was at once a proof of these developments and an important strengthening of the parliamentary party. It was a justified tribute that Peel paid when, at his election dinner at Tamworth in July 1841, he spoke of the thousands of 'unobtrusive individuals' up and down the country who had worked harder for the party than candidates themselves in an earlier era had been accustomed to do.

The intensification of party activity in the provinces was matched by improvements and innovations in the machinery of the parliamentary party. The chief whips Peel appointed after 1834 – Sir George Clerk, Sir Thomas Fremantle and Sir John Young – were a marked improvement on the vulgar and indiscreet Billy Holmes who had served in that capacity in the unreformed House of Commons. In the almost forgotten figure of Lord Granville Somerset, Peel's chief of staff, and in the Oxonian ex-MP F. R. Bonham, the party's electoral expert, the Conservatives had officials of higher social standing and better quality than 'Bear' Ellice, and the two radical attorneys, Parkes and Coppock, who performed similar duties for the Liberals in the 1830s and 1840s. Long before the crucial election of 1841 the management of the Conservative parliamentary party was clearly superior to that of its opponents.

Peel himself after 1835 was perfecting his own style of leadership. Small gatherings of ex-ministers and party managers were held, usually at Drayton, a few weeks before the start of session to discuss policy and tactics. During the session there were periodic conferences with leading men and prominent debaters in the Commons, or with Wellington and a few influential members of the House of Lords, on particular issues. Occasionally, though less often, since Peel was not partial to them, a full meeting of the parliamentary party took place at the Carlton, or at Peel's town house in Whitehall Gardens, or at one of the great London mansions of the Conservative peers, to explain decisions and ensure common action. Partly because of this growing practice of discussion and consultation the management of the House of Commons Conservatives provided few serious problems between 1835 and 1841. The high-water mark of Peel's popularity with his party was perhaps the great Conservative banquet in May 1838 when 315 friends and supporters, all but two of them members of the House of Commons, dined him in the Merchant Taylors' Hall under the chairmanship of Lord Chandos.

Though Peel is often accused of being a poor manager of men, his leadership of the Conservative Party in these years of Opposition showed considerable skill and flexibility. His problems arose less from his immediate followers in the Commons than from the need to foster the alliance with Stanley and Graham, the two great Whig seceders of 1834, from the intemperate tendencies of the Tory peers, and from an occasional stiffness and misunderstanding between himself and the Duke. All these were of minor importance, however, compared with the growing power and confidence of the Opposition at the start of Victoria's reign. Further gains in the General Election of 1837 put the Conservatives in a position of parliamentary strength from which the leader of the Opposition was to a large extent able to dictate the limits of Government effectiveness. By accepting some of the Whig legislation, blocking other bills, and emending the rest, the powerful Conservative minority in the Commons and the large Conservative majority in the House of Lords, ensured that Melbourne's ministry could only carry out those reforms which were acceptable to his opponents. At his election celebrations at Tamworth in 1837 Peel was able to point to the continued progress of Conservative recovery and warn his audience to prepare at any time for another general election. Some of their opponents, he added in a reference to O'Connell's watchword for Repealers in 1833, said 'agitate, agitate, agitate'. 'The advice I give to the conservatives is this – "register, register, register".'

But though Peel's parliamentary skill was essential for the consolidation of Conservative strength, this was only part of his work as leader. In the wider society outside Westminster he continued the task started in the *Tamworth Manifesto* of extending the party's social foundations. Organisation without ideas was not enough. Though the standard theme of the defence of the constitution, of the monarchy, of the Church and of the House of Lords furnished the bulk of his, as of other Conservative speeches in this period, the significant feature was that he deliberately and repeatedly addressed himself not to the aristocracy and gentry, but to the great professional, mercantile and manufacturing classes. What was important was not merely what he said, but to whom he said it. His scope was limited, since it was still unconventional, almost indeed unconstitutional, for politicians, especially Privy Councillors, to make great public speeches except in Parliament or in their own constituencies. But the rare opportunities that came his way he took with an alacrity that showed the value he attached to securing a wider publicity for his views. Within a week of the publication of the *Tamworth Manifesto* he was making a speech on the same theme to the merchants and bankers of the City of London. At the conclusion of his 1835 ministry he delivered at another City dinner the most significant political speech he had ever given outside parliament. At Glasgow, where he was elected Rector of the University in 1837, he gave his main address not to the students but to a great civic audience of over three thousand at a special subscription banquet organised in his honour.

To all these audiences he emphasised the same themes. Those who wished to defend the Constitution and the Church were urged to join in the work of the Conservative Party in their own neighbourhoods. The Crown and the House of Lords, he reminded them, could no longer be relied on as barriers to radical encroachments: the essential battle was for the control of the House of Commons. Those who had supported the Reform Act as a means of securing efficient and enlightened government, but had no wish to see it transformed into 'a platform from which a new battery is to be directed against the institutions of the country', were told that their proper place now was with the Conservative Party. He did not desire, any more than they did, that the machine of government should stand still. Like them he wanted to see it 'animating industry, encouraging production, rewarding toil, correcting what is irregular, purifying what is stagnant or corrupt.' But it could only operate well if its foundations were secure and its operations free from perpetual meddling and disturbance. Public order and economic prosperity both depended on that fundamental condition; and these were the real interests of the middle-classes and of the electorate in general. He refuted the charge that the Conservative Party was exclusively aristocratic. There was, or should be, he said, no barrier between it and the new classes enfranchised by the Reform Act. 'We deny that we are separated by any line of interest, or any other line of demarcation, from the middling classes.' To prove his point he was not afraid to advertise his own social origins.

'What was the grand charge against myself – that the King had sent for the son of a cotton-spinner to Rome, in order to make him Prime Minister of England? Did I feel that by any means a reflection on me? . . . No; but does it not make me, and ought it not to make you, gentlemen, do all you can to reserve to other sons of other cotton-spinners the same opportunities, by the same system of laws under which this country has so long flourished, of arriving by the same honourable means at the like destination?'[14]

Reported prominently in the national press and, like many of his more important parliamentary speeches, reprinted in cheap form by the party organisation for wholesale distribution in the constituencies, these speeches reached a vast audience all over the country. The publicity he obtained in this way for Conservative ideas surpassed anything that was achieved for the Whigs by Melbourne or Russell.

As the decade of the 1830s came to an end, Peel had in fact shown himself the most successful Opposition leader that had so far emerged in British political history. From the disaster of the 1832 election, the lowest point to which either of the two main parties sank in the nineteenth century, he had brought the Conservative Party in little more than half a dozen years to the brink of power. The temporary resignation of the Melbourne Cabinet in 1839 and the fiasco of the Bedchamber episode, though it added to the impatience and frustration of the Conservative back benchers, merely condemned the Whig ministry to two more years of barren rule.

It would of course be an exaggeration to attribute the Conservative recovery to Peel alone. Some reaction was bound to have taken place after 1832. The reassertion of normal electoral influences after the abnormal excitement of the 1831–2 crisis, the disappointments which followed the unrealistic expectations raised by the Reform Act, the fears for the Church, for property, for the Corn Laws, English dislike of O'Connell, Protestant dislike of Catholicism, the weakness and equivocation of Melbourne's leadership after the resignation of the tired and disillusioned Lord Grey in 1834: all these things would have reduced in due course the great Reform majority of 1833. The unusual incidence of four general elections in the first nine years of the reformed era helped to translate the reaction more rapidly into electoral terms than could possibly have been anticipated. Nevertheless, what was decisive was that these fears, feelings and interests had been embodied in an organised political party under the greatest parliamentarian of his time; and in the 1841 General Election that party won a clear majority of nearly eighty seats. The magnitude of this achievement, in the narrow and defective electoral structure left by the Reform Act of 1832, is easy to overlook. The year 1841 was the first time in British history that an Opposition, previously in a minority

in the House of Commons, defeated the Government of the day
and took office as the result of a victory at the polls. It was the
only occasion between the first and second Reform Acts that this
happened. It was the only general election in those thirty-six
years which the Conservatives won. To achieve this remarkable
feat national leadership of a kind transcending party was indispensable. It was that which Peel supplied.

III

There was no repetition of the *Tamworth Manifesto* in 1841;
there was no need for one. The party stood squarely on its
proved electoral strength, its superior organisation and morale,
and on the reputation of its leader. *The Times*, that confident
voice of the educated middle-classes, in commenting on the
result of the election spoke of

'a party being installed in power expressly by the voice of a
great people – not for any pledges or promises which they have
given, not for the sake of any particular measure or series of
measures which they have advocated, but solely because the
nation places confidence in their capacity and disinterestedness,
and recognises in them a tone of principle which it feels to be
necessary for wise and good government.'[15]

Yet a party must stand for something. What did Conservatism
in 1841 represent?

It was in the first place a party of law and order, of strong
executive government, the essential basis of any civilised
society. 'He had no other views,' Peel told the House of Commons in 1833, 'than to preserve law, order, property and
morality.' The firm line he took from the start on this issue went
far to ensure that the first indisciplined sessions of the reformed
Parliament did not make the position of the executive completely untenable. For Wellington, with his eternal query, 'How
is the king's government to be carried on?', it was the central
issue in public life. Not the least of the attractions of Peel and
Wellington was that they stood for strong government in a

society which between 1815 and 1848 experienced greater
social disorder than England had known since the seventeenth
century.

It was next a defensive policy. Its spokesmen never failed to
emphasise that primary characteristic. 'If you ask me what I
mean by Conservative principles,' Peel said in his Merchant
Taylors' Hall speech, 'I shall, as we have been so often taunted
with the use of vague generalities, in conclusion briefly state
the meaning I attach to them.' His list contained few surprises:
maintenance of the prerogatives of the Crown, of the constitutional powers of King, Lords and Commons, of the Established
Church in England and Ireland, and the protection of its property against confiscation. With that list no Conservative would
have quarrelled. It summed up the interests which the party
wished to preserve and the issues on which the party had come
together. 'In the main it is undoubted that the Whig Governments fell, and the Conservative Party was formed,' wrote
Stanley objectively after the Corn Law disruption, 'upon questions affecting the maintenance of the Established Church and
the integrity of the institutions of the country, the House of
Lords included.'[16]

Though it could be argued that all or most of these principles
were also professed by the Whigs, the difference was not hard to
find. The Conservatives believed these interests to be threatened
by the radical movement and had no trust in the ability of the
Whigs to resist that threat. Nobody could be sure in 1834 or
even 1836 how 'squeezable', in the contemporary phrase, the
Whigs would prove in the face of radical demands for the
ballot, shorter Parliaments, reform of the House of Lords, and
the disendowment or even disestablishment of the Church of
England. To dismiss these issues as unimportant because in
the event nothing came of them is unhistorical. The threat to
the House of Lords, for example, seemed very real at the time.
For Conservatives the importance of defending the powers of
the upper house after 1832 consisted not merely in the principle
of opposing all further constitutional reforms but in maintaining
the only barrier they possessed against further radical legislation. The consequent Radical demand for curtailment of the
powers of the Lords became one of the crucial issues of the mid-
thirties; the management of the House of Lords to avoid a

constitutional crisis one of the chief preoccupations of Wellington and Peel.

Questions of religion, and the Irish question from which religion could never long be disentangled, were even more important. The prominent place they occupied in the *Tamworth Manifesto* was a sufficient mark of their primacy in post-reform politics. While on the Poor Law the parties were agreed and on English municipal reform could compromise, the matter of the appropriation of Church property for non-religious purposes was the real dividing-line between Liberals and Conservatives. 'Appropriation' brought down Peel's ministry in 1835 and was at the root of the protracted party struggles over Irish Church, municipal, Poor Law, and tithe reform between 1835 and 1839. In a wider British context Church reform raised the whole legal and historical position of the Establishment, involving Church rates, tithe, admittance to universities, dissenting grievances, and the place of the bishops in the House of Lords; and a search for the solution of these problems was embittered by the fact that the Establishment was subject to the secular authority of a Parliament which was no longer by law a Protestant, let alone an Anglican assembly.

In contrast therefore to the Whigs, who were increasingly forced to rely for a majority on the support of Dissenters, Radicals and O'Connell's Irishmen, the Conservative Party was a Church and State party. It was the party of the clergy of the Establishment, the squirearchy, the majority of peers, and of many of the business and professional classes. 'You are supported,' Peel told his followers at the Merchant Taylors' Hall banquet, 'by the clergy, the magistracy, the yeomanry, and the gentry of the country, as well as by a great proportion of the trading community.' Yet if the Conservatives had only been a Church and State Party, it is doubtful whether they would have attained power so quickly, or possibly at any time, between the first and second Reform Acts. Society was changing too rapidly, the consciousness of the need for reform too widespread, the anti-aristocratic feeling too strong, the middle-class borough electoral interest too powerful, for a party to succeed that was no more than the old Tory Party under a different name. It was the fresh element supplied by Tamworth reformism that shifted the balance and created an increasing conviction in the public mind that under Peel the Conservative Party would be sensitive to the needs of the time and promote real reform without endangering the essential fabric of the State.

It is difficult now to recapture the original impact of Tamworth Conservatism, partly because so much of it has become a commonplace of Conservative thought, partly because it is forgotten how novel and creative it appeared to contemporaries. It not only provided a security to which men of property, education and moderate views could turn, it offered a challenge to which the youthful and idealistic could respond. Peel in fact achieved that rare feat among Conservative leaders of appealing to the rising generation. A young fellow of All Souls, T. D. Acland, writing to his friend Gladstone at the time of the *Tamworth Manifesto*, while confessing his innate Toryism, declared that were this to be interpreted as a defence of abuses, 'I should be bound to protest on the grounds that the only true conservative principle is destructive of real abuses.' In reply the 25-year-old Gladstone spoke of the need for men like Acland to enter Parliament who were 'sound in their politics (as the phrase is commonly understood) yet brought something more than such politics to the task of rescuing, rectifying and securing the institutions of the country.'[17] They were not unrepresentative of their age and class. The radical *Westminster Review*, for example, when commenting in 1837 on the steady drift of Whigs over to Conservatism, noted that not only were many old Reformers now Conservatives, but even more significantly the younger generation of traditional Whig families at public schools and in the universities were also transferring their allegiance. The belief that Peel was the best statesman to guide the necessary changes in national life was the greatest moral advantage the Conservatives had over their opponents in 1841.

Conservatism had therefore from the start a dual nature. It was the dualism not of the superficial jibe in *Coningsby*, 'Tory men and Whig measures', but of the two sides of a single coin. It was based on the axiom that the best way to defend what was most valuable in the state was to ensure that those elements never became isolated from the mainstream of national development. This, the Burke formula of preservation and improvement, for Peel represented the greater part of his life's work: 'that practical problem', as he expressed it to his Home

Secretary Graham in 1842, 'which in some case or other requires daily solution – to harmonise as far as possible the satisfaction of new wants and necessities with the framework of time-honoured institutions and the social usages and feelings which are closely interwoven with them.'[18] It was to Burke's teaching on this central point of Conservative philosophy that he appealed in his last great speech in the Corn Law debates of 1846. When reiterating his conviction that in Britain, with its 'ancient constitution, ancient habits and mixed form of government', it was of 'the utmost importance that a territorial aristocracy should be maintained', he reminded the House of Commons of Burke's doctrine that the aristocracy of England had retained its influence because it had identified itself with the people and had never pertinaciously insisted on retaining a privilege when the time had come to surrender it. His appeal failed with his party in 1846 but its failure should not be allowed to obscure the fact that it was this constructive attitude which had given moral strength to the Conservative cause in the 1830s.

Yet politics is not only a matter of ideals and ideas but of interests and men. In electoral terms the Conservative revival was proportionately greatest in the English county constituencies and found in them its great bastion of political strength. Partly this was because the clergy and gentry were, in the conditions of the 1830s, the natural opponents of Radicalism. But this constitutional and religious opposition was in a social context a rural opposition and could not therefore be separated from the economic interests of agriculture and the land. It was true that for the most part rural society was closely knit and that farmers and freeholders were generally ready to accept the leadership of the gentry and great landowners. But it would be a misconception to regard them simply as the electoral infantry of their social superiors. They had opinions and interests of their own, narrower but tenaciously held; and few county MPs could afford to disregard their views. The 'deference' of English rural society worked in more directions than one.

Since 1815 farmers had been a growing force in politics. Raised to affluence by the Napoleonic War they reacted sharply to the threatened decline in their economic status after 1815. Agricultural societies and the developing provincial press con-

tributed to their sense of importance. They helped to agitate
for the new Corn Law in 1815 and against the income tax in
1816. In Webb Hall's Protectionist movement of 1819–20
involving some twenty counties over the southern half of England they experienced their first attempt at national organisation. In the 1820s they had been courted by the Whigs and
harangued by Cobbett on behalf of such diverse remedies for
agricultural distress as paper currency, government retrenchment, and parliamentary reform. Many of them had supported
the Reform Bill in 1831 and as a class had gained by the Chandos clause enfranchising the £50 tenant farmers, proposed by a
Tory back bencher and reluctantly conceded by the Whig
Cabinet. After 1832 the constant radical agitation against the
Corn Laws and the Whig connection with the urban electorate
and Free-Trade economists raised deep suspicions in men who for
the most part were inveterate Protectionists. Great issues of
Church and State touched them less than the price of wheat or
the tax on malt; and over tithe their attitude to the clergy was
sometimes less than dutiful. Yet in the big rural constituencies
their vote was crucial and their interests paramount. Farmers,
moreover, were not an isolated class. Country bankers, lawyers,
millers, corn-merchants reinforced the 'agricultural interest'
and there were always a number of individual back bench
MPs to give an active lead in the constituencies and form the
nucleus of an independent 'country party' in the House of
Commons.

Not many Conservative MPs set out so blatantly as Lord
Chandos did in Buckinghamshire to woo the farmers' vote; but
as early as the 1832 election, in such agricultural counties as
Essex, Lincolnshire and Berkshire, questions of Free Trade and
agricultural protection were already central topics. 'Depend
upon it', said one Tory squire in North Lincolnshire when
nominating a candidate in opposition to the dominant Whig
interest, 'the very first question that will be agitated in the
reformed parliament will be the repeal of the corn laws.'[19] It
proved to be an unfounded assertion, partly because the new
Corn Law of 1828 had gone some way to satisfy Free-Traders,
partly because after 1832 good harvests and low prices deprived
the repeal movement of any urgency. Nevertheless, low prices
fed the farmers' dissatisfaction and the steady growth of local

agricultural associations in the 1830s provided them with a forum for their grievances. Societies founded by well-meaning gentry to promote agricultural reform and the adoption of scientific methods showed a disconcerting tendency to become agitation centres for Protectionist farmers. Not all the gentry relished this undermining of their traditional authority. 'I am not quite satisfied of the utility of these sorts of meetings,' old General Dyott recorded in his diary on the occasion of the founding of a local farmers club in 1843, 'they induce the farmers to feelings above their caste in society and perhaps don't amuse them as practical agriculturalists.'[20]

Despite the private reservations of both gentry and politicians, the circumstances of the 1830s inevitably brought the Conservative Party and the farmers together. The Agricultural and Conservative Club founded in Essex in 1833 to promote the election of Conservative candidates and the cause of agriculture was an unusual advertisement for the alliance; but in most of the rural counties by the mid-thirties the Conservative Party was regarded not only as the party of the Church and State but as the party of the landed and agricultural interest. For the moment, with the Conservatives in Opposition, it was a reasonably harmonious alliance which reaped a rich electoral profit. It was true that among the MPs the 'fanatick Agriculturalists', as Granville Somerset styled them in 1835, were a perpetual source of concern to the party managers and whips. Nevertheless, in the House of Commons after 1835 the malt tax question, which was a periodic irritant to both front benches, was kept under control and the larger issue of the Corn Laws was still quiescent. Though the Cabinet's decision in 1839 to make the repeal of the Corn Laws an open question was a concession to the growing pressure within the Liberal Party, it was also a clear indication of the unwillingness of the Whigs to adopt it as party policy. The annual attempts by the radical MP Charles Villiers after 1837 to have the Corn Laws re-examined, and the foundation of the Manchester Anti-Corn Law League in 1838, were as yet only straws in the wind. Indeed the Corn Laws only emerged as a political issue between the parties in 1841, following the inclusion in the budget of proposals for a low fixed duty on corn. Even then it was not strictly speaking a question of Free Trade *versus* Protection since all that the Whigs proposed was a different method of Protection. But the farming community interpreted it as a step towards repeal; and the conviction that had grown up in the 1830s that the Conservatives were the party of the agricultural interest seemed to be confirmed by this latest manifestation of Whig economic liberalism.

The party which Peel led to victory in 1841 was therefore not only composite in its social support but composite in its conception of fundamental values. What was indisputable, however, was that the largest single economic interest it represented was the land. The electoral basis of the party's strength reflected this simple fact. Already the classic pattern had emerged. The Conservative Party was in the first place the party of England. By 1837 it had attained a clear majority of all the English seats which only Scotland and Ireland turned into a minority in the House of Commons as a whole. But even in 1841, at the peak of its electoral fortunes, it only took 41 per cent of the Irish and Scottish seats. Secondly, it was the party of the counties and small boroughs as opposed to the industrial areas and large towns. In 1841, of the 159 English and Welsh county seats, all but 23 were taken by the Conservatives. A feature of the 1841 election in fact was the net gain of 29 county seats, representing a turnover of nearly 60 in the division, which supplied the bulk of Peel's working majority of 80. Even so, this central strength would not have sufficed had it not been for the substantial margin of seats secured in the boroughs. It was here that the attraction of Tamworth Conservatism and the appeal of a great leader had perhaps their decisive effect. In 1841 the Conservatives gained more than they lost in the borough constituencies; they held 45 per cent of the urban seats; and even in the larger towns with electorates of over 1,000, notoriously unreceptive to Conservatism, they had succeeded in returning 44 members. It was the first general election since 1832 in which the Conservatives won seats in central London, two in the City and one at Westminster. Without these inroads into areas of traditional Liberal feeling, the Conservative majority which put Peel into office could not have been achieved. Urban Conservatism was an indispensable adjunct to rural strength; and the emphasis Peel put on the Conservative successes in the towns, when speaking at his victory dinner at Tamworth in

1841, showed his desire to present the party as something more than a mere product of landed interest and influence.

The problem of the Conservative Party in 1841 was how a party so constituted and barely six years old would react to the next phase of development which would come with the transition from Opposition to office. It had been built up primarily to resist further changes in Church and State; but the mere fact that it was now in office demonstrated that this resistance had been successful. On the other hand Peelite Conservatism was nothing if not constructive; and a belief in the superior governing abilities of Peel and his colleagues was one of the great intangible factors in the general election. The tasks were certainly waiting for him; but they were not those of the 1830s. Before the Whigs left office the old constitutional issues of Church and State were already being displaced by the new problems caused by the economic depression that set in after 1836: budgetary deficits, unemployment, social unrest, and fresh political agitations such as Chartism and the Anti-Corn Law League. These were problems which the Whigs, with their historic tradition of civil and political liberty, their exhausted programme of constitutional reform, and their dismal record of financial ineptitude, were ill-qualified to meet. For Peel on the other hand, it put Conservative policy on a new footing. It was no longer a question of opposing, however moderately and selectively, the policies of his opponents but of demonstrating in office that the aristocratic system could deal successfully with national problems. He had given no indication of how he would proceed when he came to power: the result partly of his natural caution, partly of the political conventions of the time. He took office as uncommitted as any minister could possibly be in such circumstances. But what he had done was to make it clear to opponents and supporters alike that he would govern according to his own concept of national interest.

'If I exercise power, [he said on the eve of accession to office] it shall be upon my conception – perhaps imperfect, perhaps mistaken – but my sincere conception of public duty. That power I will not hold, unless I can hold it consistently with the maintenance of my own opinions; and that power I will relinquish the moment I am satisfied that I am not supported in the maintenance of them by the confidence of this House and of the people of this country.'[21]

He was answering the accusation made by some of his opponents in the debate that in taking office he would have to become the instrument of opinions and feelings which he himself repudiated. Nevertheless, at the end of a decade which had seen the foundation and rise to power of the Conservative Party, there was something significant, and perhaps ominous, in that emphatic declaration.

CHAPTER 4

The Great Disruption

I

When the work of Peel's great ministry of 1841–6 is viewed as
a whole, two features stand out. In Britain he set himself the
task of allaying social unrest and political agitation by restoring
financial stability, promoting national prosperity and reducing
the cost of living. In Ireland he tried to neutralise O'Connell's
dangerous movement for the Repeal of the Union by conciliating the Catholic middle-classes and initiating the first
constructive inquiry into the economic position of the peasan-
try. Both policies were essentially conservative in that their
object was to reconcile the mass of people in both islands to the
existing political and constitutional system. Both aroused deep
disquiet in the Conservative Party. To many of his followers the
first seemed to weaken the party's main economic interest, the
second its traditional alliance with the Established Church. The
division was between two schools of thought, both claiming to
be Conservative, over the nature of Conservative principles, the
definition of Conservative interests, and the most intelligent
way to apply those principles and safeguard those interests. It
was a quarrel not over ends but over means; it was a quarrel
that went on intermittently for most of Peel's ministry. The
disruption of 1846 was not a sudden, unpredictable event but
the culmination of a long period of intensifying strain.

Indeed few political events of its kind were forecast so long
in advance as the revolt of a large section of Peel's party

against their leader. Politicians are under a natural temptation
to predict unpleasant things for their opponents; and it is un-
wise to attach much significance to Cassandrine warnings in
which a certain party gratification may be detected. On the
other hand a hostile eye is sometimes a searching one. It is at
least worth remarking that as early as 1840, when it was clear
that Peel's accession to power was only a matter of time, the
Whigs were confidently forecasting that the unity of the Conservative Party would break under the strain of office. An article
in the *Edinburgh Review* in April, for example, asserted not only
that the divisions among the Conservatives would appear as
soon as Peel began to govern but that they would probably
bring down on him the fate of Canning in 1827. 'His ostracism
may be distant but to us it appears certain.' Macaulay in the
no-confidence debate of January 1840 had taken the same line.
'What then,' he enquired, 'must be the fate of a government
formed by the Rt Hon. Baronet? Suppose that the event of this
debate should make him Prime Minister? Should I be wrong if
I were to prophesy that three years hence he will be more hated
and vilified by the Tory party than the present advisers of the
Crown have been?' Macaulay was arguing from the history of
the 1820s; and both he and the *Edinburgh Review* underestimated
the differences between the Conservative Party of 1840 and the
Tories of Lord Liverpool's day.[1] Nevertheless the historical
analogy was an uncomfortable one since the political situation
in the 1840s was in many respects closer to that of the 1820s
than that of the previous decade.

The problems confronting Peel when he took office in 1841
bore, in fact, a remarkable likeness, though on a larger scale,
to those of 1817: governmental deficits, stagnation in trade and
industry, high prices, huge unemployment, widespread distress,
political agitation and social disaffection. It was a sign of the
permanent ills afflicting British society that the tag of 'Corn,
Currency and Catholics' that had been affixed to the great
issues of Liverpool's administration could equally well be
applied to Peel's ministry twenty years later. If rephrased as
'Finance, Free Trade and Ireland', the parallel is almost exact.
As far as revenue and tariffs were concerned, the situation was
almost untouched since 1828. The Whigs had sheered away
from the difficulties of financial reform and had contented

themselves by responding to the constant pressure for economy with piecemeal reductions in direct taxation. Their consequent increased dependence on indirect taxation made them even more vulnerable to trade depressions and from 1837 onward there were mounting budgetary deficits. The Free-Trade proposals of 1841 were little more than a desperate expedient to extricate themselves from their permanent financial predicament. Had they survived the general election, they would undoubtedly have fallen even deeper into insolvency since they were unwilling or afraid to introduce the one financial safeguard that would have protected their fiscal experiments – a tax on incomes.

In 1830 Peel, Goulburn and Herries had vainly urged on Wellington's Cabinet a restoration of this invaluable but exceptionally unpopular wartime tax as the only sure means of solving the chronic shortage of revenue from which every government had suffered since Waterloo. Its re-introduction in 1842, one of the most courageous as well as most momentous acts of any nineteenth-century administration, at one stroke created the basis for financial stability that had eluded the Whigs and made possible the first large instalment of tariff reductions since the days of Huskisson and Robinson. In 1844 the Bank Charter Act complemented the work of the Currency Committee of 1819 and stabilised the banking system by stiffening the connection between note issue and gold reserves. A second, even more sweeping tariff reform budget in 1845 completed, except for the repeal of the Corn Laws in 1846, Peel's main economic and social policies. For solidity and durability they had few equals in modern British history. On the foundations thus laid down the financial and commercial system of Britain rested until 1914.

By the Conservative Party at the time, however, this great programme was received often with doubt, sometimes with dismay. The bulk of the opposition came from the agricultural wing of the party and the divergency of opinion was evident from the start. As a preliminary to his 1842 budgetary arrangements Peel passed a new Corn Law which lowered by as much as half the protective scale provided by the Act of 1828. Though he had criticised the Whig proposal for a fixed duty and at his Tamworth election in 1841 had reaffirmed the need for agricultural protection, he had been at pains not to commit himself to the maintenance of the 1828 Act. Nevertheless, though it was generally expected that he would modify the existing law, he took care to consult the views of moderate agriculturalists; and the bill he presented to his Cabinet provided a larger degree of protection than he privately thought was necessary to ensure the farmers a fair price. But, as he told the restive young Gladstone, he had to consider what was politically feasible as well as what was economically desirable. It was fully realised by the Cabinet that any tampering with the Corn Laws would arouse uneasiness in the party and Peel went to some trouble to prepare Conservative MPs for the new measure. Though the bill caused the resignation of the former Lord Chandos (now Duke of Buckingham), a meeting of the parliamentary party on the eve of the main debate made it plain that while many would have preferred a higher tariff, the great body of Conservative MPs were ready to support the measure. A Conservative back-bench amendment for a higher scale of duties was comfortably warded off and the judicious mixture of compromise and management employed by the Government enabled the first serious party difficulty to be surmounted without undue strain.

Though their representatives in Parliament proved amenable, however, the farmers in many constituencies were disposed to be more critical. Perhaps as a consequence, Protectionist feeling in the party hardened as the session progressed. Peel's subsequent budget proposals for lowering the import duty on a wide range of agricultural products from potatoes to live cattle aroused a ferment in some parts of the country. The Lincolnshire members had to desert their parliamentary duties and go back to their constituencies to face an angry meeting of farmers. 'They do not care for the income tax,' wrote R. A. Christopher, MP for the northern division, to the Conservative Chief Whip, 'nor are they very rebellious about wheat but on barley, oats and cattle they are, I think, with reason, dissatisfied.'[2] Pressure from the agricultural MPs failed to move the Prime Minister. As a result in May 1842 an amendment was moved by W. Miles, Conservative member for Somerset, which would have had the effect of raising the duty on live cattle. It was defeated by 267 votes, but in the majority were 172 Liberals and in the minority 85 Conservatives. It was the first significant defection by the country party and though no doubt some cast a vote to please their constituents in the knowledge that it would have no effect on Government policy, the size of the defection was a portent.

Less than twelve months therefore after the great electoral victory of 1841 the party was already showing cracks. The question was not simply one of oats or fat cattle. The whole principle of Peel's 1842 budget rested on the economic desirability of greater freedom of trade. George Palmer, Conservative member for Essex, voiced the deeper anxieties of the Protectionists when he said that if the Government were going to adopt Free Trade as their principle, it would only be a matter of time before the Corn Laws were repealed. The pessimistic Knatchbull, put into the Cabinet as a sop to the country party, recorded as early as April 1842 that the Government had lost the goodwill of the greater part of the agriculturalists; and Lockhart, editor of the Tory *Quarterly Review*, wrote to Croker in June about the 'sulky disaffection' among the Conservative back benchers. Peel, however, was not disposed to take a defensive, let alone an apologetic, attitude. In the budget debates he had invoked the tradition of Pitt and Huskisson, and had emphasised that the object of his tariff changes was to reduce the cost of living for the country as a whole. The 'extravagantly high' cost of meat, he argued, was evidence that the British population was outstripping its food resources. Provided farmers received adequate protection, his main concern was to safeguard the mass of the population against exorbitant rises in the price of food in time of shortages.

The unrest and violence the same summer merely hardened his determination. In 1842 the economic depression that had started six years earlier reached its climax. There was massive and prolonged unemployment especially in the textile areas of England and Scotland; official poor relief and private charity were collapsing under the strain; and both Chartists and Anti-Corn Law Leaguers were trying to bring pressure on the Government by fomenting the bitter social discontents. In August there was widespread rioting and destruction with some loss of life in the Midlands, the industrial districts of Yorkshire and Lancashire, on Tyneside, and in parts of Wales and Scotland. For the second time in Peel's life (the first was in 1831) English country houses and the dwellings of the rich were put in a state of defence against possible attack by riotous mobs.

It was the worst year of distress and disorder that Britain experienced in the nineteenth century: and against this background the continuing grumbling of the agriculturalists at good harvests and low prices seemed to Peel indefensibly selfish and short-sighted. To Croker, seeking material for the defence of the Government's policy that appeared in the September *Quarterly*, he wrote sharply that the difficulty would be to prove that they had gone far enough in tariff reductions. Unless there was some improvement soon, they would be on the brink of a social crisis. To Arbuthnot, who warned him of the discontents of the ultra-Tories, he retorted that such men should look to something more important than the price of pigs or wheat. 'My firm belief is that you could not have during the coming winter the high prices of the last four years and at the same time tranquillity and security for property.' The real friend of the discontented Tories, he observed dryly, was the man who endeavoured to avert the consequences which would inevitably follow if they had their way.[3]

Peel's economic policy, like that of Liverpool, was at heart a social policy. The case for the income tax was less its efficiency than its social justice. Whatever their financial difficulties, he told the House of Commons, they must take care not to adopt any measure that would 'bear on the comforts of the labouring classes.' On another occasion he said bluntly that 'it is for the interest of property that property should bear the burden.' Tariff Reform carried this principle one step further. Conservatism in his view would fail, and rightly fail, if it could not come to terms with the problems of an expanding, industrial urban society. The only way open for Government to overcome the human suffering and social dangers in British society was to increase the purchasing power of the masses. Other social reforms pressed on the ministers by individual reformers – changes in the Poor Law, textile factory regulation, assisted emigration, education, and church extension – were little more than palliatives. The only general remedy for the 'Condition of England Question', as Carlyle had called it in 1840, was steady employment and cheap food. 'We must make this country a cheap society for living,' he told Croker in August, 'and thus

induce parties to remain and settle here, enable them to con-
sume more, by having more to spend.' From that conviction he
never receded.

His preoccupation with these central matters dominated the
first two years of his ministry. It was not until 1843 that he
was able to turn to Ireland and not until 1844 that the Cabinet
was converted to his fundamental proposals. O'Connell's vast
agitation for repeal of the Union was brought to a halt in the
autumn of 1843 with the banning of the Clontarf meeting and
the subsequent prosecution of the Irish nationalist leaders. But
this was only the start of a new deal for Ireland. 'Mere force,
however necessary the application of it,' the Prime Minister
observed to his Home Secretary, 'will do nothing as a permanent remedy for the social evils of that country.' The Devon
Commission, drawn from both parties and including one
Roman Catholic, started its inquiry into the relations of landlord and tenant early in 1844. But by its nature no immediate
results could be forthcoming and in the event the end of the
ministry in 1846 left its report as no more than a blue-print for
later Victorian legislators. But a series of trenchant memoranda
in the spring of 1844 made clear to the Cabinet Peel's view that
law and order in Ireland depended on winning the co-operation
of the Catholic middle-classes and that every concession short
of abandoning the Church of Ireland and the Union should be
made to secure that co-operation. His proposals were varied;
but essentially they were designed to be a practical demonstration that the Government was ready to promote the political,
cultural and religious equality of Irish Roman Catholics as a
necessary complement to the legal equality they had won in
1829. Without this, he thought, Catholic Emancipation would
merely operate to strengthen the divisions between the two
countries. Ireland would remain a permanent source of disaffection: a standing problem in time of peace, a national
danger in time of war.

Of the more important measures presented to Parliament in
1844–5, both the Charitable Trusts Bill, facilitating private
endowment of Catholic clergy, and plans for an Irish national
university, received a friendly reception in the House of Commons. It was the third measure, the Maynooth Bill of 1845,
which roused real sectarian passion in Britain. The Catholic

seminary of Maynooth had been started with financial assistance from Pitt's Government in 1795 to fill the gap caused by the suppression at the hands of the revolutionaries of the traditional training colleges of the Irish priesthood in France and the Low Countries. The support was exiguous and in the opinion of many observers the subsequent generation of young Irish priests, bred up in the narrow and impoverished environment of Maynooth College, had served as a formidable reinforcement for O'Connell's nationalist and anti-British agitation. Peel's proposal was for an immediate allocation of £30,000 for new buildings and a greatly enlarged annual grant. Though technically the bill raised no new principle, the scale of the proposed financial provisions clearly represented a new policy. It raised two issues in particular: first the principle of State endowment for religious purposes; the other the expediency of strengthening the Roman Catholic Church in Ireland. Both were calculated to stir up Anglican and Dissenting feeling which was already ultra-sensitive on the Catholic question as a result of the contemporary Tractarian movement in the Church of England which to many seemed Popery disguised.

The bill brought about the resignation of Gladstone and when introduced in the Commons in the spring of 1845 was energetically opposed by many High Anglicans. Outside Parliament a fierce campaign against the bill was launched by evangelical Protestants, Dissenters and the great (and usually Conservative-minded) Methodist organisation. Inside the House of Commons attacks developed from two quarters: from the strong group of Conservative Anglicans and from Radicals who shared the general Dissenting anti-establishment objections to all forms of State assistance to religion. The vote on the second reading in April 1845 revealed a complete cross-party division, with liberal Conservatives, Whigs and Irish opposed by Anglican Conservatives and doctrinaire Radicals. The Conservative Party itself was split in half. On the second reading it divided 159 to 147 in favour of the bill; on the third reading 148 to 149 against.

What was equally damaging to party unity was that as the long debate dragged on, it tended to become less a discussion of fundamental Irish policy than an inquest on the Prime Minister himself. It was a natural reaction both among his opponents and in his own party. Of all Peel's actions, Maynooth came closest to a repudiation of the Church and State principles on which the party had been built up in the 1830s. Inevitably it recalled the 'betrayal' over Catholic Emancipation in 1829 and all the old suspicions of Peel's integrity which that measure had created were revived. Caught in the centre of the storm of controversy Peel defiantly upheld the doctrine of ministerial responsibility which was at the heart of his political philosophy. The Government, any government, he said, must have the right, without too much regard for personal consistency or party loyalty, to do what it thought right in any given set of circumstances. Proud as he was of his party's confidence, he could never admit that he owed any personal obligation to those who had placed him in office. 'I claim for myself the right to give to my sovereign, at any time, that advice which I believe the interests of the country require.'[4]

Maynooth, like Catholic Emancipation, went through with comfortable majorities; but, like the earlier measure, the split among the Government's usual supporters was disastrous. It was this episode, more than anything else, that finally destroyed the morale of the party and broke the last emotional tie between Peel and many of his followers. Both Graham and Aberdeen thought that the political consequences would be similar to those of Emancipation and that it was only a matter of time before the shattered party broke up. 'The bill will pass,' wrote Graham heavily in April, 'but our party is destroyed . . . The old High Tories will not see that they can only govern on Peel principles in a Reformed Parliament and if they reject the only man who has the wisdom and capacity to lead them thro' the difficulties of the Age in which we live, they must be content to see power transferred to their political opponents.'[5] Though the position of the Prime Minister was undermined, however, for the moment he was unassailable. There was no issue on which he could be defeated and the Conservatives had no man who could replace him. 'Everybody expects that he means to go on,' observed Greville dryly in August 1845, 'and in the end to knock the Corn Laws on the head, and endow the Roman Catholic Church, but nobody knows how or when he will do these things.'

II

As the Maynooth debate showed, the growing divergence
between Cabinet policy and the views of many Conservative
back benchers involved the whole question of the proper
relationship between party loyalty, individual conviction, and
ministerial responsibility. In one form or another it was a
recurrent and almost insoluble problem. In 1843, for example,
Stanley's bill to admit Canadian corn at a nominal duty provoked a large number of protest meetings in agricultural districts and some Conservative MPs publicly pledged themselves
to oppose the measure. The Cabinet were well aware of the
danger and before the bill was introduced a special party meeting was held in Downing Street to hear explanations by Peel
and Stanley. Hampered rather than assisted by the diversionary
tactics of some of the Whigs, the threatened revolt petered out
in a series of desultory and easily defeated amendments. In
1844, however, the problem of party discipline became more
acute. In that year the Government was twice defeated on a
major bill as a result of the opposition of a section of its normal
supporters. Each time it had to exert its full executive influence
to compel the House of Commons to reverse the decision.

The first defeat, on Ashley's amendment to reduce the maximum hours of work for women and children in textile mills,
owed something to genuine humanitarian feeling among the
younger Conservatives, but a good deal also to the class
resentment of the country gentry against the Manchester mill-
owners who were financing the Anti-Corn Law League. The
second, on a complicated back-bench amendment to increase
imperial preference for sugar, was even more objectionable to
the Cabinet since it resulted from an understanding, if not an
actual compact, between dissident Conservative Protectionists
and Liberal Free Traders. On both issues the Cabinet came close
to resignation and on both Peel showed a fierce determination
not to compromise. The real point, in his view and that of other
members of the Cabinet such as Stanley and Graham, was not
so much the technical merits of each case but the fact that on a
carefully prepared Government proposal that formed part of a
wider strategic policy, ministers had failed to receive requisite
support from their own party. On the sugar resolutions Peel

unwisely allowed his anger to be seen in the speech he made when moving the virtual rescindment of the previous vote; and Gladstone was not the only one to think he had made a serious error. Peel in fact thought he was going to be beaten yet again and warned the Queen before the division took place that defeat would have serious consequences for the Government.

Though the breach was covered over by a brief conciliatory speech Peel made a few days later, what was at stake was something more than personalities. When the first rumour of a possible resignation of the Government swept London, a party meeting of some two hundred Conservative MPs was held to deplore such a step and to express their 'anxious desire' that the Government should continue in office. But this declaration of confidence was qualified by the statement that the signatories reserved to themselves 'the full exercise of an independent judgement upon all measures submitted to the consideration of Parliament.' Individual MPs clearly tended to interpret party loyalty as implying merely a general duty to sustain their leaders in office and to vote for them on matters of broad principle. But as Lord Sandon, one of the more influential Conservative back benchers, wrote to Peel, 'you cannot expect that upon all points, whether of individual interest or class interest, the whole of your supporters should sacrifice everything to this general but honest allegiance.'

This for Peel was hardly reassuring. Ministers working twelve or fifteen hours a day felt that they had a right not only to the confidence of their party but to their steady support in the division lobbies. As he replied rather dryly to Sandon,

'Declarations of general confidence will not, I fear, compensate for that loss of authority and efficiency which is sustained by a Government not enabled to carry into effect the practical measures of legislation which it feels it to be its duty to submit before Parliament.'[6]

This was the crux of the matter. How was the theory of an assembly scrutinising on its own merits every piece of legislation to be reconciled with the practical needs of the executive for steady and consistent administration? Though the traditional 'independence' which parliamentary candidates claimed when talking from the hustings was less in evidence when they arrived at Westminster, a genuine tradition of independence still remained. A corresponding degree of independence was also assumed by their leaders when they became ministers. For most politicians of Peel's generation, particularly those who had served their apprenticeship before 1830, the concept of 'ministers of the Crown' was not an empty one. 'Government' imposed its own duties and responsibilities; and they were not always those of party.

Lord Ashley described Peel's action over the sugar resolution as 'tending to a dictatorship under the form of free Government.' Peel, on the other hand, thought that for a minister of the Crown to have to subordinate his judgement on what was in the nation's interest to the views of his party rank and file would constitute 'an odious servitude'.[7] In the early stages of the modern party system it was perhaps unavoidable that a considerable degree of independence should be demanded by both sides. Without this margin of tolerance the new party machinery built up after 1834 would scarcely have been workable. It is in any case a problem inseparable from party government for which there is no permanent solution. If it seemed a particularly prominent issue in Peel's ministry it was because he was the first minister to come to office as a result of a party victory and because he was more emphatic than most leading politicians in defining his position. But though he demonstrably failed to come to terms with the party system, much the same could be said of Grey, Melbourne, Russell and Palmerston, the other leading ministers of the period. Before the new party system in politics could be consolidated, leaders had to accept greater limitation on their freedom of action; parties had to show greater discipline in supporting their leaders' decisions when in office. To assimilate these unwelcome truths was a long and uncomfortable process.

III

The Conservative Party finally broke in 1846 because Peel acted on his belief that the potato famine in Ireland required the repeal of the Corn Laws in England. On the surface the two events have no connection. To admit cheap foreign corn would not in itself feed a single starving Irish peasant since they had no money to buy food in any case. Peel's reasons are therefore indispensable for judging his claim that the repeal of the Corn Laws was an act of 'conservative' policy in his sense of the word. There were two links which in his view bound together famine and repeal. The first was the state of British public opinion. Since 1842 the propaganda of the Anti-Corn Law League had made enormous headway. With business money and brains behind it, the League had become the most effective political machine the country had ever known. The famous editorial in *The Times* in November 1843 which dubbed the League 'a great fact', went on to recognise that 'a new power has arisen in the state'. The League, however, was not simply a confederation of industrialists pressing for an isolated point of fiscal policy. Behind that much-publicised issue was a weight of social and religious emotion drawn from the class and sectarian struggles of early nineteenth-century British society. The failure of the Liberal Party to give adequate expression to those feelings and the ineptitude of the Whig Opposition after 1842 created the opportunity for the League; the astuteness of their leaders did the rest. The latent hostility of the new industrial middle-classes towards traditional aristocratic government, Dissenting feeling against the Establishment, the rivalry of Manchester and the industrial north with London and the rural south – all these elements were present in the great movement headed by the League. It was not just a pressure-group, it was a crusade fought with all the class venom, lack of scruple and high moral fervour characteristic of the early Victorians.

With Cobden and Bright preparing for a decisive struggle at the next general election, due in 1847, and much of British middle- and lower-class opinion outside the purely agricultural areas converted to their views, it seemed clear to Peel and Graham that to ask Parliament for a million or more of taxpayers' money to feed Ireland, while still retaining the Corn Laws in operation, would produce a storm of controversy. To suspend the Corn Laws on the other hand would be to concede the League its case and be tantamount to repeal. On this at least Peel's Cabinet were in agreement. If such a controversy

took place, it would involve not merely economic policy, but
the whole position of the landed aristocracy and their control of
Parliament and the other great institutions of the state, including the Established Church. In such a struggle the aristocracy would not only be defeated, as in 1832, but their position
in the country immeasurably weakened. In a confrontation, in
Canning's phrase, between property and population, the latter
would inevitably win. By acting in 1846 so that, whether under
himself or Russell, a parliament of landowners passed repeal,
and by deliberately avoiding a general election on the issue,
Peel ensured that such a confrontation, unlike what happened
in 1831–2, did not take place.

But repeal was not merely a concessionary act. In Peel's
judgement, to identify the preservation of aristocratic influence
with the cause of agricultural protection was a political fallacy
of the worst kind. Though agriculture was a great economic
interest, it was only one of several great interests; and, like
Liverpool, he believed that agriculture, industry and trade were
interdependent. 'Agricultural prosperity,' he told the Commons in May 1846, 'was interwoven with manufacturing prosperity, and depended more on it than on the Corn Laws . . . It
is for the interest of the agriculturalist that you should lay the
permanent foundation of manufacturing prosperity.'[8] As early
as 1834 he had criticised to Croker the ultra-Protectionist
doctrine that the landed interest, because it was important,
should be a favoured class for the benefit of which the other
classes of the community should be taxed. By 1845 agriculture
was in a dangerously isolated position as the only great economic interest still receiving substantial Protection. More important still, Peel had come to disbelieve that Protection played any
effective part in maintaining the prosperity and productivity
of British farming. For him, as for many other improving landlords in both parties, greater efficiency in farming methods and
the creation of a domestic market with greater purchasing
power, seemed the only sound basis for agricultural prosperity.
The success of his budgetary experiments had convinced him of
the essential value of the Free Trade principle; and while he
rejected the extreme prophecies of both Leaguers and Protectionists, he believed that agriculture would be invigorated
rather than weakened by the ending of Protection. The history

of the middle decades of the century, the golden age of British farming, bore out his judgement.

The repeal of the Corn Laws was in no particular sense a surrender by Peel to the industrial middle-classes. Indeed, socially his sympathies lay less with the mill-owners and manufacturers than with the industrial proletariat. Though he came to respect Cobden's personality and intelligence, he never liked the methods or motives of the League. In the disturbed summer of 1842 the resentment of Peel and Graham was directed against the League leaders and agitators, whom they held morally responsible for much of the social unrest, rather than against the starving, striking colliers and mill-hands. They shared the view of the local police and military that economic distress was the prime cause of the disturbances, and that the cotton-masters and colliery owners were more to blame than the men. In handling the riots they drew a sharp line between the restoration of order and any action by their subordinates which could be interpreted as protecting employers against what Peel called 'just and peaceable demands for a rise of wages'. Even the Chartists were handled lightly and no attempt made to single them out for exemplary punishment. Most of them in fact escaped with lighter sentences than the ordinary rioters.

The experience of 1842 was one that Peel never forgot. In 1846 he made it plain that in his eyes the repeal of the Corn Laws was virtually a 'Condition of England' question. The Irish crisis made a review of the Corn Laws imperative; but what made their repeal necessary was a larger consideration. 'The real question at issue,' he told the House of Commons, 'was the improvement and moral condition of the masses of the population.' Materially the repeal of the Corn Laws would protect the poorer classes in time of scarcity against any disastrous rise in food prices. Morally it gave them the assurance that, unen-franchised though most of them were, their welfare was an object of concern to an aristocratic Government and Parliament. As he said in his first speech in the Corn Law debates,

'I have thought it consistent with true Conservative policy to promote so much of happiness and contentment among the people that the voice of disaffection should be no longer heard,

and that thoughts of the dissolution of our institutions should be
forgotten in the midst of physical enjoyment.'

And in his last he affirmed his conviction that

'the greatest object which we or any other Government can
contemplate should be to elevate the social condition of that
class of people with whom we are brought into no direct relationship by the exercise of the elective franchise.'[9]

When in 1848, the year of European revolutions, Britain alone
among the great European powers remained peaceful and un-
scathed, Peel was not the only one to ascribe her immunity to
the social confidence inspired by the action of Parliament in
1846. It was not without some justification that he described
the repeal of the Corn Laws as the most conservative act of
his life.

Yet he failed to convince his party. When the crucial division
came over the Corn Bill of 1846, two-thirds of the Conservative
members voted against it. The defection was even greater than
over Maynooth and this time it was decisive. It is important,
however, to make clear the nature of the split. To see in the disruption of 1846 only the final revolt of the country gentlemen
against Peel is to over-simplify the issue. To repeat the famous
roll-call of family names in the description of the Protectionists
given by Disraeli in his *Lord George Bentinck* is to fall into the rheto-
rical trap which the author intended. An equally impressive list
could be compiled from the 112 Conservative MPs who voted
for repeal on the second reading; an even larger one from the
Conservatives who supported Peel in the division on the Irish
Coercion Bill which Disraeli was describing. Not all landowners believed in protection, any more than all industrialists,
bankers and lawyers believed in Free Trade. Repeal of the Corn
Laws was, after all, passed by a legislature composed largely of
landed gentry and aristocracy. In the House of Lords, which
represented the largest single agglomeration of landed wealth,
the bill went through with comparative ease. Traditional
country gentlemen were found voting for Peel; families, friends
and neighbours were divided on the issue. In the pro- and
anti-repeal sections into which the Conservative Party was

split, the proportions of country gentry were exactly the same. Whether occupation or status is examined, no significant difference in kind between the two groups is discernible.

Moreover, the vote against repeal was a vote against a specific measure. The issue that brought about the fall of Peel's Government was the Irish Coercion Bill, which was defeated primarily by the solid votes of the Liberals and Irish. Though the vengeful group which Bentinck led into the Opposition lobby made the difference between victory and defeat, it represented less than a third of the Conservative Protectionists, only a quarter of the whole party. It is probable that almost from the start, and certainly after Russell's firm language to the wavering Whig peers in May, the Protectionists realised that the repeal of the Corn Laws could not be prevented. All that could be done was to try to ensure that Peel would never again lead the Conservative Party. Bentinck in June 1846 was obsessed by the necessity of evicting Peel, even if that meant joining the official Opposition in voting against a measure which was supported by most Conservatives and for which he himself had voted earlier in the session. It was an act of sheer revenge; but one in which only a small minority of the Conservative members were prepared to participate.

To particularise with confidence at this distance of time the individual motives of several hundred MPs is impossible. But the traditional view that Peel was driven from office by the outraged gentlemen of England is one that does not stand up to the evidence. Even on the Corn Bill the significant feature is not so much the kind of men who voted on either side as the kind of constituency they represented. On this the pattern is highly suggestive. Of the Conservative MPs representing English counties 86 per cent voted against repeal, only 14 per cent for. Of those representing English boroughs, only 54 per cent voted against repeal, 46 per cent for. Given the social similarity of the two groups, it is difficult to account for this differentiation except on the assumption that feeling in the constituencies played a major role in deciding the vote of their representatives. This assumption is strengthened by an analysis of the voting among the Conservative borough MPs as a whole. Among the representatives of the small boroughs with less than 500 registered electors, survivors from the pre-Reform system and likely therefore to be influenced by their rural surroundings, there was a marked preponderance of protectionist votes: 33 against repeal and only 19 in favour. Among the representatives of the larger boroughs the proportion of repealers and anti-repealers was exactly equal: 55 on each side.[10]

It is probable that even without constituency pressure the party would have been divided at least as deeply as over Maynooth. The events of 1844 and 1845 had left an unconsumed legacy of distrust and disaffection; and in proposing in 1846 what to many seemed a sacrifice of the party's main economic interest, Peel as party leader had no remaining capital on which to draw. Tiredness, ill-health, over-work, resentment at the perpetual criticism and opposition from his own party had made him more inflexible than ever. Though he laboured patiently to persuade his Cabinet colleagues in the autumn of 1845, he made no effort to convert the mass of Conservative members. No party meeting was held to explain his change of front. Though compensations for agriculture were envisaged as part of the repeal policy, these were never adequately explained or emphasised. He assumed from the start that the effect on party unity would be disastrous and that repeal of the Corn Laws could only be carried by a cross-party majority in the Commons. This belief was probably justified. The last party meeting, held over the contentious sugar resolutions, had been a complete failure and Peel was in no mood to repeat the experiment. He was determined that the Corn Laws must go and all the evidence suggests that he was prepared to see his ministry break up once his objective had been achieved. He told Victoria and Albert that even before the news from Ireland he had made up his mind to announce his change of mind to the party before the next general election; and there is no reason to doubt his statement. The Cabinet had long been aware of his view that there was no alternative to the 1842 Act except total repeal.

With their leader intellectually committed to one policy and the Protectionist movement equally intransigently committed to another, the party was caught between two irreconcilable extremes. The moderates received no assistance from their leader in their hopes of a compromise; and at the same time many of them were subjected to unprecedented pressure from their rural constituents. Long before the Irish famine the strident propaganda of the Anti-Corn Law League had evoked a counter-movement in the agricultural counties, the so-called 'Anti-League'. The first sign was the growth of local protection societies, largely designed to influence gentry and MPs against further Free-Trade measures. It began with the formation of the Essex Association in November 1843. Within a few months there were nearly a hundred similar organisations, mainly in the southern and eastern parts of England. In 1844 came the formation of the Central Agricultural Protection Society under the presidency of the Duke of Richmond. Agricultural societies and farmers' clubs had already been busy, calling for greater protection, demanding pledges from their representatives and criticising Conservative MPs who preferred the claims of party to the interests of their constituents. But the Protectionist Society movement in 1844–5 marked the final emergence of the tenant farmers as a political class. Though the Central Society was to some extent an attempt to retain aristocratic control and MPs like W. Miles, G. J. Heathcote, Newdegate, Stafford O'Brien, Tyrell, G. Bankes, Blackstone and Christopher had always provided an active Protectionist element in the House of Commons, the movement was fundamentally one from below. It was a movement, moreover, that cut across conventional party lines, and when in the autumn of 1845 it became clear that the Cabinet was considering a change in the Corn Laws, it became a movement against the Government.

The December 1845 meeting of the Central Association was held in London in the middle of the excitement caused by the Cabinet discussions, the redoubled activities of the League, and Russell's *Edinburgh Letter* announcing his conversion to repeal and calling for a nation-wide agitation. The Association responded to the ferment among the farmers by rescinding its rule of non-interference in elections and calling upon its local branches to support only those candidates irrespective of party who supported Protectionist legislation. In January and February Protectionist meetings were held all over the south and south-east to demand that local members should stand by Protection, and in some cases to resign if they were not prepared to do so. Many Conservative MPs returned to London for the start of the session already pledged before they even knew what Peel's proposals would be.

The impact of this intensive farming agitation on the Conservative Party was a decisive element in the parliamentary crisis of 1846. Some members, torn between loyalty to Peel and duty to their constituents, between personal opinions and past commitments, resigned their seats. A few gave a token vote on the second reading and abstained on the third. Many, who left to themselves might reluctantly have accepted Peel's proposals, gave way to local pressures. The committed Protectionists were fortified by the unmistakable feeling of the farming community. For the first time Peel found his control of the party threatened not merely by dissident individuals or minority groups but by a substantial majority backed by a powerful national organisation. Immediately after Peel's announcement of his intentions a special meeting of the Central Protectionist Society began to plan a parliamentary Opposition party. It was only at that stage that Bentinck entered the scene.

What broke the Conservative Party in 1846 was a fundamental clash of will and interest between the leaders in office and a great body of electors mainly responsible for putting them there, represented by a majority of the Conservative MPs in the Commons. To ascribe the central role in the crisis to the attacks of Bentinck and Disraeli on Peel is to personalise, and to that extent trivialise, a great cleavage in the party itself. Whether those two prominent Protectionist spokesmen exercised any decisive influence on the outcome of the crisis is at least arguable. It is possible that the violence and unscrupulousness of their attacks did as much harm as good to the Protectionist cause. Many MPs thought Bentinck miscast in the role of a serious politician and his repudiation by the Protectionist whips in 1847 is evidence of the little hold he had over the rank and file. Disraeli himself, their one man of talent, was for many years after suspect and unpopular. It can hardly be said that he was fully accepted by the party until 1867. What their personal attacks on Peel did, however, was to introduce a note of savagery into the repeal debates of 1846 which made any talk of Conservative reunion unrealistic as long as Peel was alive.

Yet it was Disraeli, with his deadly gift for exposing the weakest point of his adversaries, who stated most clearly the fundamental party issue in the Corn Law disruption. If party since the Reform Act had become the vehicle of government, in turn there was a moral obligation on government to respect the claims of party. It was this which weighed most heavily on Peel's Cabinet in the protracted discussions of November–December 1845. Though free trade in corn had not been an explicit issue in the 1841 election, there could be no disputing that if it had been, the Conservative Party including Peel would have pledged themselves to maintain Protection. Peel came to power as Prime Minister not as the choice of the sovereign but as head of a victorious political party. He had used that power to propose and carry a measure of which the majority of his party and their electors disapproved. He had neither consulted his followers nor allowed the issue to be settled by a general election. In an age when the electorate was becoming more important than ever before, he had broken the bond of trust that should exist between politicians and the public. That protection for agriculture was perhaps inexpedient or unnecessary was irrelevant compared with the fact that his party had stood for the principle of agricultural Protection in 1841 and expected him to stand by it in 1846.

It was true, on the other hand, that the agricultural interest was hardly a party interest in the sense of identifying itself with a political object other than the maintenance of Protection. If the independent ministerial tradition of Pitt and Liverpool was still strong in Peel, much of the old independent 'country party' spirit survived among the ultra-Protectionists. In the first twenty years after Waterloo they had formed a cross-bench grouping embarrassing the leaders of both parties in turn. In 1846, as their language demonstrated, they were concerned only with their economic interest. Christopher in Lincolnshire told his constituents early in January that 'he would not join any political party but associate with those members who would form in the House what might be termed the country party.'[11] Robert Baker, the Essex tenant farmer who had started the Protectionist movement in 1843, said at a meeting of the Essex Protectionist Society in December, that the issue was not 'a question of politics, of whether its advocates were Whigs or Tories, . . . it was a question of protection or not protection.' The *Essex Standard* affirmed that 'we must . . . in future discard the old distinctions of party: these have become obsolete. We are not in this question Tories, Conservatives, Whigs or Radicals any longer, but we are divided into Protectionists and Leaguers.'[12] The Protectionist movement in fact, like the League, was essentially one of the many pressure-groups that emerged in the early-Victorian era. They were a mark of the increased public interest in national affairs but they did not so much seek to strengthen the parliamentary parties as to dictate to them.

The real problem was how these special interests could be assimilated into the party system. Peel's concept of ministerial responsibility, and parliamentary assent as the final sanction of ministerial policy, not only blurred the distinction between parties but discounted the direct authority of public opinion. He disapproved in principle of the resignation of MPs in deference to the demands of their constituents and disliked the demagogic element present in the farmers' societies. Yet, as Disraeli was soon to realise, a political party dominated by one sectional economic interest was equally unsatisfactory. The failure to find a compromise in 1846 wrecked the party; but that did not mean that a compromise was still not the only real solution. The disruption over the Corn Laws, the most spectacular British political crisis of the nineteenth century, was part of the growing-pains of the modern party system: unpleasant at the time but educative both for leaders and rank and file. Peel himself, though he thought the bulk of the party wrong and himself right on the issue of Protection, accepted that party must remain the basis of any stable government. 'A government,' he told his Cabinet in June 1846, 'ought to have a natural support. A Conservative government should be supported by a Conservative Party.' The principle was clear enough; it was over the political implications that the difficulties arose.

Peel's diagnosis of the true interests of Conservatism cannot easily be faulted. After 1846 aristocratic rule seemed stronger than ever. The Church was safer in 1850 than in 1830; radicalism had subsided; Chartism was dead; the country was about to enter on the mid-Victorian decades of harmony and prosperity. The Corn Laws were repealed and Peel was regarded as a hero by the mass of the population, including the agricultural labourers. But from a party point of view his handling of the crisis had been disastrous. It was not that he had tried to carry the party with him but failed; he had ignored party claims entirely. The great Conservative Party of 1841 was broken and in the process many of his followers were left with their careers damaged or destroyed. For Protectionists the offence was unforgivable. Even those who shared Peel's views or respected his judgement had a right to feel hardly treated. 'My criticism on your present measure shall be very gentle,' wrote Sturt, one of the Conservative county MPs who resigned his seat, 'whether it might not have been managed without stranding others and myself.' Many years later Sir John Mowbray, who became Conservative member for Durham in 1853, delivered a similar verdict. He was a supporter of Peel's Tamworth Conservatism in the 1830s, regretted that (as he said) protection 'formed such a prominent *cheval de bataille* in 1841' and became a convert to Free Trade. 'In my judgement no charge of treachery can be maintained,' he wrote of Peel's action in 1846, 'and the change of opinion was honest. But we may regret that Sir Robert had not taken his supporters sooner into his confidence and "educated" his party.'[13]

The Conservative disruption had profound effects on the development of the Victorian party system. It was not only the split but the character of the split that was significant. The talent and experience of the party went one way, the numerical strength the other. With the exception of Stanley (whose attitude in 1846 was more ambiguous than his subsequent leadership of the protectionist party might suggest), the leading men and nearly all the party managers stayed with Peel. The rump of the party was left in almost continuous Opposition for another thirty years. As long as Peel lived he used his influence to maintain the Whigs in office as the only means of preserving stable parliamentary government and the essentials of Peelite policy. Though he made no effort to lead or organise a party and discouraged the efforts of his followers to do so, his mere presence in politics helped to perpetuate the looseness of the party political system. Loyalty to Peel and the issue of Protection itself blocked the tentative efforts made after 1846 to reunite the two sections of the Conservatives. Engrained partisan differences and an intellectual contempt for the shuffling Whig ministry rendered equally abortive Russell's repeated attempts to recruit individual Peelites for his Cabinet. The central coalition, which some of Peel's younger colleagues thought would be the inevitable outcome of the confused political situation created in 1846, did not come until two years after Peel's death. But the Aberdeen coalition did not last and by 1857 the Peelites as a party had virtually ceased to exist. Of the total reckoning of 117 Peelite MPs present in 1846, the majority had melted away by retirement, reabsorption into the main Conservative Party, or conversion to Palmerston's brand of conservative liberalism. Aberdeen and Graham abandoned active politics at the end of the fifties and the remaining leaders made their final choice in 1859 when Gladstone, Sidney Herbert, Newcastle and Cardwell joined Palmerston's Cabinet. The looseness of party ties and the vagueness of party principles had left the Peelites with no clear ground on which to stand.

The decision of 1859 did not represent a choice between definite political creeds. Though in the end the Liberal Party was the residuary legatee of the Peelite disruption, the Peelite tradition was diffused over the whole of public life. 'We are all Peelites now,' observed *The Times* in 1852. Yet if that was even approximately true, it followed that there was no place in politics for the Peelites as such. The choice between Lord Derby and Lord Palmerston, both ironically former colleagues of Peel, was swayed less by principle than by accident, expediency and personalities. But at least it was a recognition that only through party could a politician hope to exercise power. That it was Palmerston who was the beneficiary both of Peel's work of national reconciliation and of the best of Peel's young men, was chiefly an indication of how far the Conservative Party had become, in Bright's words, 'a constant minority', out of alignment with the deeper forces in mid-Victorian society. To regain its position it had to relearn the lessons first taught by Peel; that it must have concern for the condition of the people, that it must hold the balance between the great interests of the country, and above all that it must be a national party. The 're-education' of the Conservatives under Disraeli was in fact a return to Peelite principles; but done by a man of greater political flexibility and more adept in the arts of party management.

NOTES TO PART ONE

Chapter 1

1 Towards the end of his life Burke came close to accepting the name of Tory: cf. his *Fourth Letter on a Regicide Peace*, 'Scarcely had the Gallick harbinger of peace and light began to utter his lively notes, than all the cackling of us poor Tory geese to alarm the garrison of the Capitol was forgot'.

2 Boswell, *Life of Johnson* (1927 edn.), II, 419.

3 *First and Third Letters on a Regicide Peace.*

4 *Thoughts on the late General Election as demonstrative of the Progress of Jacobinism* (1803).

5 *Lord Auckland's Correspondence*, ed. Bishop of Bath and Wells (1862), III, 320.

6 *Life of Romilly* (1842), II, 23.

7 *The Moral and Political Crisis of England* (1820), by the Rev. Melville Horne, p. 12.

8 Denis Gray, *Spencer Perceval* (1963), pp. 258, 273; N. Gash, *Mr Secretary Peel* (1961), p. 108.

9 C. D. Yonge, *Life of Lord Liverpool*, II, 275; Castlereagh's speech on agricultural distress, 15 Feb. 1822, in the H. of C.

Chapter 2

1 Duke of Buckingham, *Memoirs of the Regency* (1856), II, 315.

2 Yonge, *Liverpool*, II, 133; speech on agricultural distress, 26 Feb. 1822.

3 *Life of Romilly*, II, 537.

4 J. E. Cookson, *Lord Liverpool's Administration 1815–22*, p. 143.

5 *Croker Correspondence*, ed. L. J. Jennings (1884), I, 170.

6 H. Twiss, *Life of Lord Eldon* (1844), II, 329.

7 Speech on foreign trade, 26 May 1820.

8 Speech in H. of L. on foreign affairs, 14 April 1823; Yonge, *Liverpool*, III, 316–17.

9 Yonge, *Liverpool*, III, 311.

10 Speech on foreign trade, 26 May 1820.

11 Duke of Buckingham, *Court of George IV* (1859), I, 292.

12 Speech of 26 Feb. 1822.

13 *Rep. Hist. Manuscripts Commission Bathurst MSS.*, p. 584; *Letters of George IV*, ed. A. Aspinall, III, 75.

Chapter 3

1 Yonge, *Liverpool*, III, 197.

2 *Prime Ministers' Papers: Wellington*, I, 283 (Lady Salisbury's diary, 21 Aug. 1833).

3 Either Fullerton or Miller, the two regular writers of political articles at that time; but not J. W. Croker to whom it was at one time customarily ascribed. See M. F. Brightfield, *J. W. Croker*, p. 403.

4 *Report of the Speeches at the Constitutional Meeting . . . Edinburgh 28 November 1831* (Edinburgh & London 1831). John Wilson was the 'Christopher North' of *Blackwood's Magazine* and a colleague of J. G. Lockhart on the

staff of the magazine for many years while holding his chair of Moral
Philosophy at Edinburgh University.

5 C. S. Parker, *Sir Robert Peel from his Private Papers*, II, 186–7.

6 ibid., pp. 212–13, corrected from ms original in Goulburn Papers.

7 *Prime Ministers' Papers: Wellington*, I, 528.

8 N. Gash, *Sir Robert Peel*, p. 125.

9 T. J. Nossiter, *Influence, Opinion and Political Idiom in Reformed England*,
pp. 31, 70–1.

10 Brit. Mus. Add. MSS., 40420 f. 74.

11 *The Times*, 23 April 1835.

12 ibid., 11 August 1837.

13 *The Times* provides much information on the growth of Conservative
Associations in these years. See also, R. W. Davis, *Political Change and
Continuity 1760–1885*, for Buckinghamshire and R. J. Olney, *Lincolnshire
Politics 1832–1885*.

14 The first two quotations are from Peel's Glasgow speech in 1837 and
the last two from his City speech of 1835.

15 27 July 1841.

16 *Croker Correspondence*, ed. L. J. Jennings, III, 113.

17 *Memoir of T. D. Acland* by A. H. D. Acland (1902), p. 76.

18 *Norman Gash, Sir Robert Peel*, p. 718.

19 Olney, *op. cit.*, p. 103.

20 *Dyott's Diary* ed. R. W. Jeffery (1907), II, 370. I would like also to take
this opportunity of acknowledging my debt to Dr Travis L. Crosby for
allowing me to read his unpublished work on 'English Agricultural
Politics 1815–1852'.

21 In the House of Commons, 27 August 1841.

Chapter 4

1 *Edinburgh Review*, art. on 'Present State and Conduct of Parties', vol.
lxxi; *Speeches of T. B. Macaulay MP* (1854), p. 203.

2 Norman Gash, *Sir Robert Peel*, p. 324.

3 ibid., pp. 327, 360–1.

4 ibid., p. 476.

5 ibid., p. 478.

6 ibid., pp. 451–2.

7 cf. his letters to his close friend Hardinge Sept. 1846, Feb. 1847 (C. S.
Parker, *Sir Robert Peel* (1899), III, 472–6).

8 *Speeches*, IV, 685 (4 May 1846).

9 ibid., IV, 581, 696.

10 For a detailed analysis of the voting of the Conservative MPs in 1846 see
W. O. Aydelotte, 'The Country Gentlemen and the Repeal of the Corn
Laws', *Eng. Hist. Rev.*, LXXXII, 47.

11 Olney, *op. cit.*, p. 117.

12 The Essex quotations in this paragraph are taken from Dr Crosby's
'English Agricultural Politics 1815–1852'.

13 Parker, *Peel*, III, 335; Sir George Mowbray, *Seventy Years at Westminster*
(1900), p. 80.

Part Two

From Disraeli to Law

by

Donald Southgate

Reader in Political and Constitutional History
at the University of Dundee

CHAPTER 1

The Defence of
Land and Labour

DISRAELI AND BENTINCK

On May Day 1844 there appeared the prototype of the British
political novel, entertaining but conveying a message. Its writer,
author some years back of light fiction and polemical journalism,
Jewish in origin though Italianate, if pale, in appearance, was
addicted to foppish dress and epigrammatic conversation and
was said to have married an older and rather strange woman for
her money. To Peel and Graham he was a disappointed place-
seeker whom they would rather have seen among their open
enemies than sitting at their backs accompanied by the promising young men from Cambridge, Hon. George Smythe, Lord
John Manners and Baillie-Cochrane, who affected the name of
'Young England' and whose friendships, conversations and
fantasies give the novel *Coningsby* its coherence. Their views
must be recorded, though obviously their strictures on Peel are
too wild for acceptance.

Coningsby was an indictment of 'the condition of the people'
among whom 'governments were hated and religion despised',
in need of a heroic guide to overcome 'the Spirit of the Age'. It
repudiated the Conservative Party as a dexterous contrivance
of Peel but without knowledge, thought, genius, truth or faith,
possessing instead extruded placemen like Rigby and those
figures of true comedy, 'Tadpole and Taper', whose minds and

gossip were confined to the state of the electoral register, the courting of the Wesleyans and the need for 'a good cry', which would mean nothing. At the top, Peel, who might have become 'the representative of a creed [and] supported by earnest and enduring enthusiasm', was instead only 'the leader of a Confederacy' sustained with 'churlish sufferance'. 'A sound Conservative government', says Taper, 'means Tory men and Whig measures.' Nobody could say what 'Conservative principles' were, except resistance to changes until they were demanded, whereupon they were conceded. In his imaginative story of two generations of politics – those described in very different terms in the first section of the present work by Professor Gash – Disraeli attributed to the *laches* of the Liverpool administration the introduction into the constitution of a new principle and power 'which may ultimately absorb all – AGITATION'. After O'Connell's Catholic Association and the political unions had come, *inter alia*, the Chartists and the Anti-Corn Law League, to produce 'that fierce and fatal rivalry that is now disturbing every hearth of the United Kingdom . . . The Condition of England Question.' There was no acknowledgement that Peel was devoting all his energies to dealing with this question by 'making the country cheap for living'.

The political institutions, Disraeli argues, are fragile. Young Coningsby tells his uncomprehending grandsire that under 'the cause of our glorious institutions . . . the Crown has become a cipher, the Church a sect, the nobility drones and the People drudges.' And the *Tamworth Manifesto* is made the villain of the piece, with Peel breaking in office the pledges of Opposition. On 10 April 1843, on the Irish Arms Bill, Disraeli asserted that broken pledges on Ireland had freed his followers from the bonds of party. The hustings of 1841 made clear what the squires and farmers meant by 'Conservative principles', but 'It is another question what they mean now!' At Shrewsbury in 1842 he had asked his constituents not to desert Peel 'because you think he will do a certain act which I think he will not do.'[1] But on 25 April 1843 he warned them that the Government might be compelled to pursue anything pressed by the strenuous Liberal majority in and out of Parliament.[2] When, on Peel's ultimatum on sugar, Disraeli asserted that his conduct was degrading and he ought to deign to consult a little more the feelings of his supporters, he confronted squarely Peel's opinion 'heads see, and tails are blind'.[3]

The mainly inarticulate successors of the eighteenth-century Country Party, who formed two-thirds of the Conservative MPs, found in the Mazzini letters controversy, before February 1845, that they had an exponent of formidable debating skill on their side. After remarking that 'a Tory majority remains', if not a Tory ministry, Disraeli convulsed the House with his picture of Peel as 'a strict conservative' in the garments he stole when 'he caught the Whigs bathing'. Peel, having quoted Canning's desire to be saved from his 'candid friends', Disraeli congratulated him on his 'courageous conscience' in choosing *that* authority. The jibe and the cheers which piqued Peel must have caught the attention of one MP seen more often in the smoking room in hunting gear than on the benches. Lord George Bentinck had been private secretary to Canning, who married his aunt; his association with Disraeli was to prove vital to the latter and probably to British party history. As a Canningite who joined the Whigs with Stanley and Graham in 1830 and left the Whigs with them in 1834, Bentinck could not approve the anti-Maynooth speech (11 April 1845) by which Disraeli, denouncing Peel as 'the great parliamentary middleman', broke up 'Young England'. Nor did he accept Disraeli's statement of 17 March that 'Protection appeared to be in about the same position that protestantism was in 1828', thinking Disraeli's description of a Conservative government as 'an organized hypocrisy' a bit strong. Disraeli complained that Peel's protectionist speeches were the best he had ever heard, but that now he sent down his valet [Sidney Herbert] to say 'We want no whining here'.

The matter ceased to be funny when Peel, having resigned because he could not persuade his colleagues that, if once opened to cheap corn, the ports could ever be closed again, resumed office to do what Stanley felt 'they could not do as gentlemen'. On the Address, 22 January 1846, Disraeli protested. 'What I cannot endure', he said, 'is to hear a man come down and say: "I will rule without respect of party, though I rose by party, and I care not for your judgement, for I look to posterity".' Lord Blake calls this a wonderful speech, without a boring sentence, and in his *Lord George Bentinck*, Disraeli

himself held that, because it was so opportune, it was a great
success, greeted with tumult and cheering.

By December 1845 Peel's successive 'betrayals' and haughty
aloofness had made his party a shell. Yet, convinced by the
Cobdenite argument and the economic and political facts as
he saw them, he felt bound to adopt, as a solution to the Condition of England Question, a prescription intolerable to many
of his back benchers and to the constituency pressure groups of
others. This meant rather more than carrying repeal by cross-
party voting, as he had carried Maynooth. As the months of
1846 passed, it meant, increasingly certainly, his fall from
office. Yet it was a reasonable expectation that, after the *fait
accompli*, the unforgiving Protectionists might be reduced to an
obscurantist rump, and the Conservative Party re-form under
some colleague of Peel. That this did not happen was due to
three men, all in their forties, but as diverse as could be –
Bentinck and Stanley (both of whom would have gained
financially from repeal) and Disraeli.

The key man was Bentinck, 'who could not bear being sold',
and, at the meeting to which Richmond's newly politicised
Agricultural Protection Society invited all MPs responding to
pressure from constituents, urged the utmost prolongation of
debate. An anguished and anguishing speaker, he rose in the
small hours of 27 February to assert that the policy of Protection
was laid down in the Dissolution Speech of 1841 and the House
had no right to be double-dealing with the farmers of England.
He deplored the presence to hear Peel of Prince Albert 'to
give éclat . . . and the semblance of the personal approbation of
Her Majesty to

'a measure which . . . a great majority at least of the landed
aristocracy of England, of Scotland, and of Ireland, imagine
fraught with deep injury, if not ruin to them – a measure . . .
calculated to grind down countless smaller interests engaged in
the domestic trades and interests of the Empire, transferring
the profits of all these interests – English, Scotch, Irish and
Colonial to . . . Americans, to Frenchmen, to Russians, to
Poles, to Prussians and to Germans . . .'

Asked to lead 'the third party', he replied, 'I think we have had enough of leaders', but was soon being treated as one for the purposes of parliamentary business. And he was doing the work, turning from his great interest of cleaning up the Turf and bringing to bear to economic debate a formidable memory for detail and statistics derived from the assiduous study of equine pedigree and form. Disraeli's devastating power in debate made him the obvious lieutenant, but the close friendship developed with Bentinck was a bonus, for Lord George remarked that he did not know much, but he did know horses and men. The benefit was the greater in that Stanley disliked Disraeli and did not deal with him.

Stanley 'had no wish to play the part of leader of any party, or of any combination of parties'[4] but, 'drafted' at Richmond's house – in his absence – to lead the protectionist peers, he presented petitions and made a speech. He also found himself receiving requests from Bentinck and from the Commons whips, Beresford and Newdegate – chosen without Bentinck's knowledge! – who evidently regarded him as the leader of the whole protectionist party. Once the designated political heir of Grey, Stanley had been called by Peel his 'right arm', but the former 'Rupert of Debate' felt he was no longer needed as a Commons front-bench speaker. He went prematurely to the Lords (1844). Unable to commend what he felt should not be done, and certainly not by the Conservative Party, the proud magnate was inclined to acquiesce in the inevitable on this occasion; it was not for him to destroy 'a safeguard against the innovating spirit . . . in matters even more essential' than the Corn Laws.[5] Not understanding that to the county MPs, and still more their supporters, in the mood of 1846, *nothing* was more essential, he was, like Peel, astonished at the length of the conflict in the Commons and genuinely displeased by the upshot. For if a protectionist party did not prove ridiculous, the idea of a government of protectionists would. So his thoughts were all of Conservative reunion. He deplored the violence of Bentinck's vendetta against 'the delinquent Politicians' and 'common cheats', for he looked to a leader's problems of Cabinet-making.

Stanley did, however, come to agree that Russell was likely to prove less radical than Peel. For Bentinck it was a matter of bringing a shady stable before the stewards; 'atonement should be made to the betrayed constituencies of the empire'

whom Peel had intended to consult after an educational process. Bentinck admitted to Stanley that the protectionist MPs
'never meant that I should pursue the Traitor Ministry to
death, but the betrayed County Electors did.' When Bentinck
and Disraeli chose the Irish Coercion Bill, earlier supported by
most protectionists and leading Whig lords, to get Peel out on
25 June, as soon as Repeal was law, 105 protectionists supported
the minister and more abstained than the mere 69 who joined
what Wellington called the 'blackguard combination' with all
sections of Opposition including Leaguers and Irish.

THE TERRITORIAL PARTY VERSUS THE MANCHESTER SCHOOL

In 1831–2 the Whigs had argued that parliamentary reform
would prove conservative, and that to concede sooner rather
than later would limit dangerous agitation. Kitson Clark and
others have argued that 1846 should be viewed in the same
light as an act of political sagacity by which the governing class
retained its power. But there was quoted against Peel in 1846
his warnings of 1832 – that the *vis inertiae* would be forfeited,
the Dissenters strengthened and emboldened, and the Corn
Laws endangered. Had he not been right, argued Disraeli on
15 May, in the speech O'Connell described as 'incomparable' and
Disraeli remembered as 'my great speech . . . followed by the
loudest and longest cheer ever heard in the House of Commons.'[6] Cobden now said (24 April 1846) that the question was
being settled out of doors by 'not the country people, but the
people who live in towns *and will govern this country.*' Peel denied
he cheered that, but, although he spurned Cobden's appeal not
to resign but to govern through the great middle class, he went
out of his way in an otherwise boastful resignation speech to
hail Cobden as the real author of repeal.

Where then, Disraeli was entitled to ask (20 February 1846),
was the 'territorial constitution' whose existence induced men
to put money into the land for other than financial reasons and
secured the people against centralisation? Apparently they were
to be rescued from the alleged power of one class only to sink
under the avowed dominion of another which Cobden alleged
to be distinguished for its intelligence and wealth, led by the
'Manchester School' which Disraeli (2 July 1849) claimed to

have christened as 'a homage due to their deleterious, but not unprincipled, doctrines'. *Sybil*, the sequel to *Coningsby*, published on May Day 1845, depicted the squalid life of the poor in the North, where 'the altar of Mammon has blazed with triple worship . . . until we are startled from our voracious strife by the wail of intolerable serfage.' If the 'Young England' solution to an iniquitous exploitation of the worker by the capitalist – that industrialism should be organised on 'feudal' lines – seemed a fantasy to the 'men of intelligence and wealth', the picture drawn in *Sybil* was no fantasy. It was based on blood-chilling reports obtained under pressure from Lord Ashley, MP, on Chartist correspondence and on observation when Disraeli and his young colleagues went to Manchester in October 1844, staying at Bingley with an MP – Busfeild Ferrand, whose Dantonesque figure and stentorian voice had startled the Commons when he appeared in 1841 as member for Knaresborough.[7] *Sybil* seems to owe more than usually granted to Ferrand and to the writings of Richard Oastler (imprisoned for debt in the Fleet from 1841 to 1844) who stood at the heart of a Northern movement against the 'thraldom of capitalism' and the oppression and *laches* of government. The Tory element in this movement embraced anti-Whig noblemen and squires, philanthropic businessmen, Evangelical parish priests and Conservative Working Men's Associations, sometimes acting in unison not only with humanitarian radicals and nonconformists but trade unionists and Chartists. Their current fight was for a ten-hours factory bill, the parliamentary struggle for which had passed into Ashley's hands when Macaulay, having slated Michael Sadler for his anti-Malthusian essays, beat him at Leeds in 1832.

Sadler and Oastler, Methodists who turned to the Church of England, had worked for Wilberforce in 1807 and Oastler swore an oath in 1830 to do for the English child serf what he had done for the negroes. But when Ferrand, new to the House of Commons, declared (28 September 1841) that every farthing Cobden made was sprinkled with the blood of children and that the boastful cotton lords ought to recognise duties as well as rights, he got little support. For as a representative of northern radical Toryism he condemned not only 'the disgraceful factory system' but also the New Poor Law of which the Whigs were so proud and which Peel supported. It was wholly inappropriate to the northern industrial areas where its implementation was resisted by ultra-Tories and ultra-Radicals. Tories benefited electorally in the North by opposition to the Poor Law. There were southerners too who opposed it, but the Yorkshire operatives justly complained that 'when [the landed interests] were strong, they never really aided us. They took the lure which the New Poor Law offered them to transport their "Surplus Poor" and their families to the regions of "White Slavery", and it concerned them little to amend the factory system.' Neither in *Coningsby* nor *Sybil* does Disraeli spare the rural landlords like the Tory 'Earl of Marney', who revelled in the reduction of rates and low wages. He held that Chartism was the offspring of the Reform Bill and the Poor Law and as early as 16 December 1834, fighting Wycombe as a Radical, predicted that the Tory party would 'yet rue the day' when it approved the system which 'made all England thrill with feelings of horror and indignation.'

The New Poor Law was illustrative of 'utilitarian' precepts – Disraeli's bugbear – and of the social oppressiveness of aspects of 'liberalism', but to old John Walter of *The Times*, a patron of Young England and a good friend of the northern protestors, also involved 'a change in the British Constitution itself'. Disraeli agreed, for (although the terms of current political science tend to frighten the historian disposed to use them) he was quintessentially a pluralist. He always agreed with Oastler that 'the very essence of the British Constitution is self-government [and] the tendency of every plan of the reformers is centralisation . . . despotic power . . . and entire destruction of the present social system.' He believed in power balanced and checked at the top and dispersed through all natural units with community feeling from the family up. He deplored the replacement of the parish by the Poor Law union areas supervised by the Three Kings of Somerset House, and rejoiced that the Church remained 'territorial' – i.e. parochial. Fighting Whigs as a Radical at Wycombe and as a Conservative at Taunton he attacked 'the Whig system of centralisation, fatal to rural property and provincial independence – those Gallic imitations of which they are so fond' and said one had only to recall what the Rump Parliament did when it was despotic (including the imposition on necessities of the excise, 'the tax most odious to Englishmen', strongly attacked by Bentinck on 18 May 1847) to appreciate that all had an interest in maintaining the pre-rogative of the Crown and the privileges of the peers and the Established Church, 'the patrimony of the poor'. Crown, Lords and Commons were not even the most important parts of the Constitution, which lay in that great building up of laws and manners embodied in 'the landed interest'.

Disraeli's admiration for the territorial constitution, as is rightly stressed by the editor of his speeches, Kebbel, predated his becoming 'the leader of the gentlemen of England', just as his devotion to the Crown long preceded a mutually rewarding association with an occupant long prejudiced against him. On behalf of 'feudalism' he struck back at its opponents, for example, at Shrewsbury, 9 May 1843: 'Let me tell these gentlemen that labour has its rights as well as its duties'; fortunes of millions were being made 'by a mode which does not recognise it as a duty to endow the Church, to feed the poor, to guard the land, and to execute justice for nothing.' Perhaps the misery, suffering and demoralisation of a once happy popula-tion was the result of permitting property to be created and held without the performance of duties by those whose attitude to 'the estate of the Church, the estate of the poor, that great fabric of judicial rights, those traditional manners and asso-ciations which spring from the land and the national character' was 'Let it go!'. But that immense element of political power and stability, landed property, had made England a greater power than Sweden or Denmark, able to defy Napoleon. And the English a great people: 'You want to be a great people, because you *are* a great people.' Writing in 1851 he declared that 'in the great contention between the patriotic and the cosmo-politan principle which has hardly begun and on the issue of which the fate of this island as a powerful community depends, Lord George Bentinck appeared to represent the traditional influences of our country in their most captivating form.'

In a sense, this tribute is strange, as Disraeli saw in Bentinck essentially an old Revolution Whig, and Disraeli devoted much time to lambasting such 'who courted the mob in the first instance and in the next the commercial interest' and re-habilitating forgotten and misrepresented eighteenth-century

Tories as 'the landed interest of England who desired to see an honourable, dignified government conducted with order and due subordination.'[8] Disraeli is famous for his strange and tenuous apostolic succession linking mediaeval abbots via the Stuarts to the Bolingbroke of *The Patriot King*, forgotten Wyndhams and Hinde Cottons and thence via Shelburne (in whom he found the crucial missing link) to the younger Pitt, 'forced, unfortunately for England, to relinquish Toryism', and so via only partially uncorrupted associates of the 'Arch-Mediocrity' Liverpool, including Canning, to the 'Young England' critics of Peel the 'Arch-Traitor'. This wild hagiography involved systematic aspersion of the ancestors of Bentinck. His Cavendish grandmother's family, fattened on Reformation pillage, stood high among that Whig 'Venetian oligarchy' which, Disraeli argued, turned the King into a doge and the people into helots. The Bentincks themselves came with William III and a Dutch army, unwanted, according to Disraeli, by the English people, to fasten upon it 'Dutch finance' (the National Debt) and acquired the Portland dukedom in the early years of George I. And George III, fighting the 'factitious oligarchy', received his greatest humiliation when Charles James Fox forced the replacement of Shelburne by Bentinck's grandfather. Bentinck might even be said to have reproduced the attitude of Fox who, when Pitt in the spirit of Bolingbroke attempted to work with France that policy of commercial reciprocity which Disraeli deemed the Tory tradition and the true national policy of England, would not 'see the country sacrificed for the sake of a foreign trade.' But Disraeli and Bentinck found themselves as one in a battle between patriotism and cosmopolitanism and the defence of the territorial constitution against the capitalists and what Oastler called Peel's 'cotton twist' ministry. Till January 1846 they had rarely been at one on anything, for Bentinck, like Stanley, approved so much that was done between 1827 and 1845, including Maynooth. Bentinck had opposed Ashley's ten-hours measure and Stanley was firmly with Graham in Cabinet for reversing it.

Only 61 Tories withstood Peel's ultimatum on that occasion, just before Disraeli and Manners went north to respond to the cry of 'Altar, Throne and Cottage'. A difficulty in squaring the principal demands of the Northern reformers was Macaulay's point that the Sadler–Oastler–Ferrand idol was 'the omniscient and omnipresent state', repudiated by the reformers in the case of the Poor Law. There did exist the tradition of Elizabethan paternalism (which had included wage-fixing), shattered now by the fashionable dictum 'commercial enterprise is a subject directly unfit for Parliamentary regulation'. But the revelations of the roving commissioners, utilitarians all, forced legislation in 1833 and the Whig Charles Wood said that, but for the enfranchisement of the great towns, it would have included ten hours. This was prevented formally for fourteen years, and effectively for more, in the interests of the sort of people who led the Anti-Corn Law League, Bright being, according to Ashley, the most 'malignant' opponent of all. For, while many admitted that children, 'young persons' and women should be protected, the hours of the men depended on their labour.

Naturally a majority of ten-hours Tories (though not Ashley himself) remained Protectionists. The great question was both land versus capital and labour versus capital, and the two causes seemed to go together, as the squire, Colonel Sibthorp, never tired of repeating. He handed oranges to Ferrand while the latter on 14 February 1842 urged the landed interest to aid the operatives. Ferrand. himself undertook a 22-speech tour of Yorkshire and Lancashire at the end of 1843, 'representing a small party in the House of Commons which was pledged never to cease agitating . . . until the working-class of England obtained that protection for their labour which was awarded to every other description of property within the British Isles.' (Bradford, 27 November). When Disraeli makes Sybil say that the Queen reigns over 'two nations – the rich and the poor', he is echoing Ferrand at the Manchester Corn Exchange, 14 December 1843:

'We are now divided, as nearly as possible, into two classes – the very rich and the very poor . . . [No country can long survive with] society broken into such widely distant divisions. We must have the intermediate links, amalgamating into each other, descending with a regular and even gradation; in order that the monarch on the throne and the peasant in the cottage may alike enjoy the privileges and blessings of our free and glorious constitution.'

Oastler long preceded Disraeli in complaining that under Peelism 'principle was deemed folly', explaining in 1841 that it was want of bread and 'a fair day's wages for a fair day's work' which drove people to riots (such as those described in *Sybil*) and these no true English-hearted Tory could deny them. He himself was still 'an old-fashioned ultra-Tory [who] never saw any charm in the word "Conservatism"'.

'A Tory is one who, believing that the institutions of this country are calculated, as they were intended, to secure the prosperity and happiness of every class of society, wishes to maintain them in their original beauty, simplicity and integrity. He is tenacious of the rights of all, but most of the poor and needy, because they require the shelter of the constitution and the laws more than the other classes. A Tory is a staunch friend of Order, for the sake of Liberty; and knowing that all our institutions are founded upon Christianity, he is of course a Christian, believing with St Paul that each order of society is mutually dependent upon the others for peace and prosperity.'

How superior is the Coleridge–Southey conception of the social organism to 'an aggregate of individuals' which was all Harriet Martineau, still arguing against factory inspection in 1855, could see.

Peel ascribed Ashley's victory of 1844, which he rendered abortive, to 'a great body of agricultural members, partly out of hostility to the Anti-Corn Law League, partly from the influence of humane feelings, not foreseeing the certain consequences as to the Corn Laws.' (With Repeal, the argument that Corn Laws and a Ten Hours Act could not co-exist, disappeared.) While Repeal was before the Commons, 117 of the 168 Protectionists present voted for Ashley's bill (now managed by the Radical MP Fielden) while the Peelites were 73 to 7 against. Lord John Manners' speech on the second reading (13 May) circulated in the North, and Bentinck registered his conversion. When Peel, out of office, in 1847 opposed Fielden's bill, seconded by Ferrand, the small majority against it had gone and crucial votes (with Beresford 'whipping' at report stage) were carried by 2:1 before it swept through the Lords. This was fortunate, for in 1847–8 there was a recurrence of Chartism. But defective drafting, seized on by the employers, upheld by the courts, rendered the Ten Hours Act ineffective as a protection for children, and the Whig Home Secretary's Act of 1850 eroded it. This compromise, though approved by Walter and to some extent Ashley, was denounced by Manners as compromising both the rights of the people and the honour of Parliament.[9] Not till there was a Tory government with a majority, with Manners a Cabinet minister for the fourth time, was Fielden's Act fully restored.

Nevertheless, the Tory–Radical movement, embattled with the Peelite–Radical elements, had, in the name of humanity and the interests of social reconciliation, and thus of order, put some check on 'the cruel monster, Unrestricted Competition'. Tory support, before the Corn Laws were seriously menaced, shows that it is far from the whole truth to regard, as Marx and others have, Fielden's Act as a Tory reprisal for the repeal of the Corn Laws. Disraeli's own sympathy for the Chartists, though not for the Charter, preceded his declaration of war on Peel, though it was in 1844–5 that he wrote of the 'two nations' (the sub-title of *Sybil*), mutually ignorant of one another, whom it was the task of statesmen and churchmen to reconcile. What though he closely followed Ferrand? He coined a phrase that will live for ever and was immediately arresting. While doing their best to make merry over 'Young England's' 'Merrie England' ideals, Marx and Engels thought the 'feudal social-ism' of *Sybil* 'struck the bourgeoisie to the very heart's core' (1867).[10]

THE ENIGMA OF DISRAELI

Bentinck in 1847 was 'low-spirited at seeing the party occupying itself about the exclusion of an individual (Rothschild) from Parliament at a moment when the greatest commercial empire in the world is engaged in a life and death struggle for exist-ence.' When West Indian sugar collapsed, he obtained a com-mittee which under his chairmanship sat often and urgently and reported by his casting vote for a six-year 10s differential for the colonies, and wrote over-optimistically, 'We have saved the colonies. It is the knell of free trade.' He mastered the case against the repeal of the Navigation Acts, and organised the temporarily successful opposition which Herries led. The West Indian and shipping interests had deserted him on the Corn Laws, but to defend them he sold his cherished stud (including the next year's Derby winner). When he died suddenly of a seizure, he was planning a committee which he hoped would recommend total abolition of all duties in the colonial empire.

Bentinck was furious when in February 1848 Stanley author-ised Beresford to send round a 'Conservative' whip's letter, for the word had become to him as to Disraeli, Ferrand, Miles 'a byword of reproach', the symbol of hypocrisy and lack of principle. More than a quarter of a century later, Salisbury (Robert Cecil) was to complain that Disraeli had no principle except that of maintaining party unity, and Kebbel admits that after he became leader 'it cannot be said that he imparted any absolutely new ideas into the practical questions of the day.' We must grant that if he had not won an election in 1874 he would not occupy his unique position in the history of the Con-servative Party. It may be that the party would not exist. Disraeli was, of course, bound to be memorable, because of the play of his original imagination; the vilification of Whiggery and the assault on 'Whig' historiography; the political novels; the interesting phenomenon of 'Young England'; the brilliant invective which rattled Peel and steadied the Protectionists; the stratagem that brought Peel down. Then would come the long years of Opposition, wearying work, requiring, as he said, 'the devotion of a life', wearying even for one who loved the great game – twenty-five years of it, interspersed with two very short minority governments, but then by a third in which he baffled and bewildered a large hostile majority and contrived important electoral reform in 1867–8, finally convincing Derby that he must be Prime Minister. But when there is added the sequel of a working majority in 1874, even though it was followed by defeat and gloom (which he shared) the overall picture is changed. The eighteen-forties can be linked to the sixties and seventies as a success story.

Nor is this all! Victorian Liberalism is dead and partly dis-credited. It ceased to be relevant. Asquith and Lloyd George were not for ever quoting Gladstone, and if some have sighed for the Palmerston touch, others have deplored the man's very existence. Liberals today rarely invoke Asquith or Lloyd George.

To Labour MacDonald is anathema, Attlee is unquotable and mention of Gaitskell invites faction. Yet from the days of the Fourth Party, whose antics began before Disraeli died, it has been the habit of Conservatives to go to Disraeli as to a sacred flame. He is unique – the only party leader to whom the young of successive generations turn for inspiration with which to revive flagging fortunes and move the older generation to action. This was notably demonstrated when the Tory Reform Committee arose during the Second World War out of dissatisfaction with the Churchill coalition's response to the Beveridge Report and when R. A. Butler and Harold Macmillan, among others, were refurbishing the Tory image after the catastrophic defeat of 1945. Progressive members elected in 1950 made the debt to Disraeli's ever-relevant themes overt by adopting the name 'One Nation'. And this is the justification for paying so much attention here to Disraeli *before* he became the official leader of the Conservatives in the Commons.

On merits as a parliamentarian he had no rival. Yet he was not considered when Bentinck precipitately resigned the leadership on the personal hint of Beresford on the morrow of the Rothschild debate nor, some months later, after an interregnum. The impediment was not that he had 'risen from the people', as the Queen remarked when he became Prime Minister. His father was a literary man but monied, living in a Queen Anne mansion in Buckinghamshire, preserving game. From him, before he met Smythe, Benjamin had already derived an admiration for the Stuarts. But he had also been 'trained by learned men who did not share the passions and prejudices of our political and social life' so that 'even as a boy' he mused on 'the elements of our political parties' from the point of view of an 'outsider'. Kebbel makes this point with delicacy: 'a singularly original and penetrating mind, surveying English history and politics from a perfectly independent position, outside the hereditary influences and prejudices of our party life . . . brought to the consideration of political theories an understanding . . . absolutely unhampered by the shackles of political tradition.' Here was a handicap. Again and again Disraeli hammered home the theme that in his youth 'no party was national: one was exclusive and odious, and the other liberal and cosmopolitan.'[11] In the process he was, in fact, insulting a great many of the older politicians he aspired to lead, and the disciples of others dead or retired, and he rarely wrote of a fictional bishop except in wounding terms. And it does not seem to have occurred to him that descriptions in *Coningsby* and *Sybil* of unworthy or worthless or even evil Tories, as well as Whig landlords, struck near many a bone and that the peerage was unlikely to appreciate the description in *Sybil* of its disreputable origins. If Peel and Russell thought as he did that the country gentry were 'magnificent asses' (they would probably have omitted the adjective!), Disraeli had to pay the price of inventing the political and social novel. It was that people recognised themselves and their like, depicted often in unflattering terms by a jumped-up literary fella!

Disraeli could not stand the after-dinner talk of the huntin', shootin', fishin' men, after the ladies (among whom, especially the elderly, he shone with his flattery and his epigrams) retired; it bored and disgusted him. But he was determined to be their leader. 'The friend who sate by Lord George Bentinck' became in 1847 MP for the county of Buckinghamshire, redolent of famous political names. With Bentinck money he became the squire of Hughenden Manor. But ill-wishers held up against him his early pot-boilers (which he greatly bowdlerised in the 1853 edition) and his earlier amours with married women, his youthful speculations and current debts (their extent fortunately not known) and the dubious routes by which he had made his way in London society; all were recalled as though he had a monopoly of such imprudences and social climbing – he who had long ago won the patronage of Lady Londonderry and was accepted at Almack's and – more to the point – at the Duke of Rutland's Belvoir as well as the Duke of Buckingham's Stowe (on the brink of bankruptcy). He discarded the chains and rings which had jangled over outré garments under the tight raven ringlets, appearing on the Opposition front bench sombre, black-coated, middle-aged and speaking with gravity enlivened by flashes of wit and gifted phrase – less often now by scathing invective. And yet, to quote André Maurois, whose far from definitive *Disraeli*, written in 1927, is full of interest and perception, he now 'seemed sinister – not a dandy but a potent and malign magician.' Was he sincere? people asked about one of the basically most consistent actors in the political arena.

He played his role superbly and yet, as Blake writes of *Coningsby* and *Sybil*, failed 'to touch the deeper feelings'. Would he play straight? Would the man described when he became Prime Minister as 'impenetrable' continue to say what the squires wanted said, if he could climb the political ladder more quickly some other way?

That he was not considered for the leadership in the Commons when, after an interregnum, Manners' brother Granby was chosen (February 1848), only to resign because conscious of his inadequacy, was explained by Lord Malmesbury, Protectionist whip in the Lords and until the mid-fifties an ally. 'They are puzzled and alarmed by his mysterious manner, which has much of the foreigner about it.'[12] In the intimacy of his diary Disraeli had long agreed: 'My mind is a continental mind . . . a revolutionary mind . . . I could rule the House of Commons, although there would be great prejudice at first.' The prejudice was increased when this exotic, a romantic whose first hero was Byron, persisted in entering into the question of race – *his* race – with the apparent objective of convincing the nobles and squires that he belonged to the most aristocratic branch of the most aristocratic of races, chosen by Jehovah to enlighten the world.

The effort was as foolish as it was brave. To publish *Tancred* in March 1847, to the effect that civilisation flourished in the East when the ancestors of his followers were 'Baltic pirates' or 'flat-nosed Franks' was imprudent. To tell parochially-minded Protestant squires, in the debate on whether to admit to Parliament an elected Liberal de Rothschild (whose family was buying up square miles of Buckinghamshire), that they ought to do so because, their religion being only completed Judaism, they ought to esteem Jews above all others, was to disturb the equable tempers and often slow minds of the weekly readers of first lessons and reciters of the Psalms. Bentinck, rising from his sick-bed out of loyalty to Disraeli to argue for Rothschild on the old Whig ground of civil equality, was unpopular enough for doing it. His resignation was an immediate consequence. But Disraeli was incorrigible. At a time equally vital to his career he published in *Lord George Bentinck* (1851) a wholly irrelevant summary of his own speech on the Rothschild claim. Among men suspicious even of cleverness, he would have been better advised, as he did to the Bucks electorate at Aylesbury on 26 June 1847, to base his claims on proven capacity and cite his brains against the blood of his Cavendish opponent. For, although he said all 'the right things' from a party point of view, about the mission of the Church of England, and even more, about its essential role in the Constitution and the English way of life, the Hebraic theme made it difficult to accept as a true believer a man who had muttered in drawing rooms, 'Allah is great', and is said to have remarked 'it is curious, Walpole, that you and I have just been voting for a defunct mythology.'

By contrast, the earnest High Churchmanship of Gladstone, who was to emerge as his chief adversary, was respected even by Nonconformists. To the latter, however, the Protectionist Party, despite the whiggism of Bentinck and Stanley, could make no appeal except in the crudest of anti-popery terms, which both deplored. In 1847 Stanley expressed no pleasure at Tory victories in Leeds and Lambeth won on Low Church–Dissent alliances, and Bentinck complained that 'No Popery hangs round the neck of the party for evil and must eventually drown it.' More representatively, Beresford claimed that only 'the proper and just old No Popery cry', which had served well in 1841, had stirred the electors. On this subject, and the allied one of the Irish, Disraeli had made speeches and written words in three different *genres* which it was vain to hope would not be raked up. There was, in particular, the remark when launching the 'Young England' campaign in the House (9 August 1843) that it was strange that 'the descendants of the cavaliers should . . . be the advocates for governing Ireland on the principles of the Roundheads', and the *mot* in *Coningsby*, 'I look upon an Orangeman as . . . the only professor and practiser of unadulterated Whiggism.' The surveys of British policy in Ireland which strike the modern reader as enlightened were a positive handicap. So also was the fact that 'Young England' makes no sense except as a socio-political counterpart of that similarly anti-Whig 'Catholick and Apostolical' Oxford Movement with its *Tracts for the Times* and its secessions to Rome. Both were revolts against 'the Spirit of the Age', rationalist, utilitarian, materialistic, latitudinarian, liberal and individualistic, under which the nation drifted astray spiritually, morally, socially and politically. Each appeared to retreat to an archaic, romantic, 'neo-Gothic' mediaevalism. By rehabilitating the social role of the religious houses in *Sybil*, seeming to blame the Reformation for the modern woes of the Industrial Revolution, by venerating Laud and Charles I, and preferring James II to Dutch William, Disraeli cut himself off from the Evangelicals. These included Ashley and Sir Robert Inglis (member for Oxford University) and the leading figures in the Tory northern protest movement, especially in Yorkshire. As he remarked, the Church had not lost the great towns; 'unhappily it never had them'. The ten-hours Evangelicals had little regard for the corporate character of the established Church to which they mainly belonged. When the Duke of Newcastle, before giving his borough of Newark to Gladstone as a 'stern, unbending Tory' gave it to Sadler, it was not because he was a factory reformer but *'a bulwark of the Protestant cause'*. Oastler and Ferrand were furious 'No-Popery' men of the Orange school and the social-reforming clergy of Bradford joined the dissenters against Maynooth in 1845, when Ferrand called Peel the greatest traitor since Judas Iscariot.

Though on occasion describing himself as 'High Church', Disraeli had in fact no Tractarian leanings, and took the opportunity, which Derby found it pointless to resist, of plumping firmly for Protestantism, when the Whig premier, Russell, issued in 1850 his stirring protest against the aggressions of Rome and 'unworthy sons of the Church of England' (the Oxford Movement). But, in extolling the Church as 'part of our history, part of England itself', which 'consecrated society and sanctified the State', as a partner not a creature of the State (the language of the early Gladstone), he professed admiration for its 'catholicism', in the sense of its comprehensiveness. Opposing Buxton on the amendment of religious tests (1863) he had no wish to see it 'so comprehensive that no one can comprehend it . . . a Church without a creed, without articles or formularies'. He preferred to 'stand on the ancient ground', and if society had to decide between physical scientists and theologians, he was 'on the side of the angels' because 'the Church teaches us that man is made in the image of his Creator' and is a being 'born to believe'. The religious principle was the most important that governed man; the Church 'a majestic corporation – wealthy, powerful, independent', was the proper national instrument for the purposes of education as well as spiritual supervision and public worship.

Like many leading Peelites, Gladstone had Tractarian leanings, but moved steadily towards the release of Nonconformists from disabilities, as his liberalism and provincial contacts evolved. Disraeli deplored the tendency: 'our charities are assailed; even our churchyards are invaded; our law of marriage is to be altered . . . Finally, the sacred fabrics of the Church are no longer to be considered national,' he said in the first of three speeches in the early sixties to Oxford diocesan bodies. The last was a reference to the exaction of Church rates which, in the early sixties he considered 'the great domestic question of the day', and on which he leaned to a compromise achieved in 1868, when he was Premier but Gladstone held a majority in the House. Gladstone's spiritual Anglo-Catholicism had tempted him towards disestablishment in the fifties. The prospect of state spoliation, the end of the old English parish and of ministers of all sects state-salaried, horrified Disraeli, regarding the Church as part of the Constitution which the party existed to defend. He would not have minded the later description of the Conservative Church of England as 'the Conservative Party at prayer', because he held that 'where institutions are in question . . . the clergy ought to interfere'.[13]

It has recently[14] been argued that in 1857 'Disraeli was quick to spot the need to revive the rather latent connections of Church and Toryism' on which he could be reactionary in order to balance his edging his party towards greater flexibility in other matters and that from 1860 to 1868 he made the defence of the Church the most conspicuous commitment of his party. Even this sagacious comment seems to the present writer not to take due account of Disraeli's earlier obsession – it was little less – with the Church as part of the territorial constitution he defended and it evades the criticism almost universally made that the institution he least understood was the Church of England. This criticism seems to the present writer – despite the distinction of its exponents – unjustified. That he did not understand it as an 'insider' must, indeed, be granted; that its most spiritually devoted adherents thought he did not understand it may be granted also; that some of his ecclesiastical

patronage was ill-employed is undeniable. But he understood
it a good deal better than the Queen and Albert, and no more
cynically than Palmerston, who left appointments to his Tory
stepson-in-law, the violently evangelical Ashley, Lord Shaftesbury. If he was to find the High Church against him (as on the
Balkan question in the eighteen-seventies) it was because those
who had not gone over to Rome gazed oecumenically upon
inter-communion with the Greek Orthodox, while he was considering the maintenance of Turkish rule, hegemony and suzer-
ainty in terms of the Balance of Power and the highways to
India. Whether or not he understood the Church of England,
he did not understand its failing to do its duty; when and where
it did, Toryism flourished in its wake. It is true that as a majority
Prime Minister in 1874 he condoned an advance from Privy
Council definitions of the creed and permitted ritual (now
understood to be bad in law) to a disastrous parliamentary
interference with the liberty of Anglican priests to preach and
parade a Catholic interpretation of the formularies and cere-
monies. He talked of 'putting down the mass in masquerade'
and, while under Gladstone, gas stokers had been gaoled for
conspiracy, under the Public Worship Regulation Act 1874.
Anglican priests were gaoled for contempt of court. 'Lord
Penzance's Court', established by that Act, did far more harm
than good – except that the discontent it provoked in its attempt
to establish 'order' resulted in the growth of tolerance via dissen-
sion and, ten years after Disraeli died, the abdication of the
Judicial Committee of the Privy Council from an arena for
which it was wholly unequipped. Matters were left to the
bishops, as ever since 1850 the Anglo-Catholics had desired.
But the most Catholic of Anglicans must admit two things –
firstly, that Disraeli acted under extreme pressure from the
Queen and the muddle created by the Primate, and, secondly,
that an attempt to reduce the Church of England to a state of
Protestant order and uniformity was the wish of most Anglican
legislators *and* of most of the *vitally important* Tory constituencies,
to say nothing of non-Anglicans. The man who in middle
age had romanticised the mediaeval monasteries was
recognising the prevalent Protestantism of Britain when he
bowed to it and exploited it. This is quite different from 'not
understanding the Church of England', though he certainly

added to its discords, without the slightest intention of so
doing.

STANLEY STICKS ON PROTECTION

Leaping backwards to the leadership of the Protectionists a
quarter of a century before the Public Worship Regulation
Act, we have to note that in his *Reminiscences* Disraeli frankly
admits that Stanley (before and after Peel's death on the
morrow of the Don Pacifico debate in 1850) had a perfectly
valid reason for denying it to him. The reconciliation of the
Peelites was, Stanley held, 'essential to the formation of a
Cabinet'. And 'I had destroyed their famous leader and covered
them with confusion.'

Yet it was Stanley who, when asked to form a government
early in 1851, repelled the Peelite Gladstone by talk of a fixed
corn duty of 6s a quarter. Palmerston had favoured some such
compromise in 1846, when it represented the secret wish of
most Tory and Whig party leaders, thwarted by the uncom-
promising terms of Russell's Edinburgh letter and the conversion of Peel to the Mancunian doctrine and the aggressive
intent of the Anti-Corn Law League. When Palmerston, dismissed by Russell in December 1851, was approached by Derby
(as Stanley had now become), they having together contrived
Russell's defeat on the Militia Bill, he responded to a similar
proposal with a crisp 'too late'. And it was Derby who (House of
Lords, 24 May 1852) insisted on submitting Protection 'to the
deliberate expression of the electorate', though he was willing
to confess in public as well as in private that he saw no chance of
a favourable response. By contrast, Disraeli, as early as the
1847 election, sought to convince Protectionists that any
attempt to undo the repeal of the Corn Laws was either hopeless or very dangerous (Aylesbury, 26 June 1847) and told the
Commons on 19 February 1850 that he did not look to that
(thereby confirming the suspicions of those who saw him as an
unprincipled adventurer who had merely taken up Protection
to advance himself). As Chancellor of the Exchequer under
Derby his statesmanlike recognition of a *fait accompli* on 30
April 1852 amounted, complained the Prime Minister listening
from the gallery, to 'a eulogy of Peel'. Derby lived until 1869

and was thrice a minority Premier. Among the several who prevented him ever having a majority, the principal was himself – by his refusal to abandon Protection *before* the 1852 election, though he knew he would have to afterwards. Disraeli tried in vain to get him to issue the equivalent of a *Tamworth Manifesto* which would have given the party a chance of power. The party leader remained singularly aloof after the 1847 election, which was supposed to settle everything, settled nothing, being held by Russell before the harvest when nothing in the economy looked good *except* corn prices, so that there was no great Protectionist effort. He dealt directly with the Commons' whips, of whom the chief were hostile to Disraeli, who was, however, after a mammoth but largely barren session asked to deliver the Opposition's parting shot and did so, on 30 August 1848, in a speech labelled by Kebbel 'The Labours of the Session' and described by Disraeli himself as 'the speech that made me leader'.

The Stanleys had at last deigned (July 1848) to dine at the Disraelis', and relations improved until on 21 December Stanley wrote to Disraeli that, although his talents would always give him 'a commanding position in the House and a prepondering influence in the Party', there was lacking that 'general and cheerful approval' requisite for formal acknowledgement of his leadership. Disraeli was an ambitious man, but he was also a proud one. He knew his own worth, and he knew exactly how to reply to this patronising magnate. It was the kind of reply Gladstone was always giving. He thought he could best 'uphold the aristocratic settlement of the country . . . [by] acting alone and unshackled.' If this was a shock to Stanley, it ought not to have been. The riposte, and the knowledge that by his assiduous leadership he was gaining supporters, though perhaps at the same time consolidating opponents in the party, no doubt account for Stanley's adoption (22 January 1849) of Herries's idea of entrusting the Commons leadership to a triumvirate consisting of that undistinguished veteran himself, Granby, the self-confessed incompetent, and Disraeli. Of course, noted Stanley, Disraeli 'should or must be the real leader' and would be so acknowledged when Granby succeeded to his peerage. The triumvirate had an intermittent existence, though not enough to convince Granby that his dignity was being duly acknowledged. Disraeli never acknowledged it at all, dating his leadership of the party in the Commons from 1849.

The crucial fact was that, as long as he was the leader of the Protectionist or Conservative Party, Stanley meant to call the tune. It was not only to the individualist Bentinck, profoundly unsuited for party leadership, that he framed the standing order (as it was in effect) that the language of the Commons' party leader 'must be in accordance with my feelings and opinions'. Addressing a party which existed because it resented authoritarian rule, and had rebelled against it, Stanley took the view, as Peel had done, that he had been 'drafted' and was entitled to obedience (Salisbury was to do the same). Bentinck, who did not lack spirit, replied that business could not be conducted on the basis that 'the leader of a party, being a peer, was to dictate . . . the whole Party's commercial and financial policy.' But Derby proposed to do just that – and Disraeli could not say him nay. He tried, arguing (10 March 1848) for countervailing duties to combine abundance, cheapness and the protection of British labour. Stanley simply wrote that off as a lost cause. Disraeli therefore turned to that 'considerable relief' of burdens on the occupiers of land which, promised in 1845–6 by both Russell and Peel, had initially led magnates, Whig and Tory alike, to consider Repeal, relying on the word of the Duke of Wellington – who let them down!

The Providence which upset Peel's timetable by sending him the rotten potatoes now stepped in with three bad harvests which made a mockery of Peel's predictions as to corn prices; imports multiplied sevenfold in five years. This strengthened Disraeli's case for relieving land, urban property and public utilities of half the cost of services really no more 'local' than some paid for out of taxes and not rates, their administration remaining, however, in local hands. Enough Peelites supported him to reduce the Government majority in a large House to 21 (19 February 1850) and 14 (11 February 1851) and suggest Conservative reunion with perhaps the elderly Peelite Goulburn leading in the Commons. But the agricultural distress goaded the farmers again to political action. The fiery Limehouse colonial shipper George Frederick Young, with his National Association for the Protection of British Industry and

Capital, wanted no Disraelian talk of loans to farmers and rate relief. He demanded a return to Protection, which, Disraeli held, 'no great class in the country itself either desired or deemed practicable.' Disraeli's warning to Young that if the agricultural constituencies ran amuck there would never be a Conservative majority brought a rebuke from Derby, persuaded, Disraeli alleges, by Beresford. It seems that Stanley, remembering Peel, and his own dictum to Bentinck that 'no man in these days can hope to lead a party who cannot make up his mind sometimes to follow it', felt that it would be 'base' to abandon Protection before an election and may have had a sneaking hope of winning one. On 31 October 1849, at Aylesbury, Disraeli came dolefully into line; on 11 May 1850 Stanley told farmers asking for an 8s fixed duty to agitate the country from one end to another – which Disraeli thought 'a pernicious course'. He would remember his relations with Stanley as' 'uneasy' throughout 1849, but more cordial in 1850, though he was 'unable to shake his prejudices on the subject [of Protection] and his distrust of me with regard to it . . .'. Disraeli virtually disobeyed Stanley's instruction to hit Palmerston hard in the Don Pacifico debate, though his co-operation with the Peelite Gladstone in organising it achieved Stanley's now-presumed object of forcing the Peelites (alarmed by Young's movement) into the lobby with him. The Peelites had supported Disraeli in the annual 'distress' debate when he asked for 'such an equal justice for all classes as is possible in an ancient society.'

From June 1850 he was at last Stanley's 'Dear Disraeli' instead of 'My dear Sir' in correspondence. Even Stanley had wondered whether a Protectionist government would not precipitate that conflict between the principles of democracy and aristocracy and monarchy which he expected. He was probably relieved to receive no summons to the Palace till early 1851, when he stipulated for a dissolution or Peelite support and, failing this, told his colleagues and, more woundingly, the Lords that he had not men of sufficient experience to form a government. This was bad for the prestige of the 'Who? Who?' government which he did form after Palmerston helped him turn out Russell a year later. But, as Disraeli writes in his *Reminiscences*, 'every public man of experience and influence however slight declined to act under Lord Derby unless the principle of protection were unequivocally renounced.' But Derby committed himself to a 5s duty some months after his son, another Edward Stanley, at Lynn, remarked that the turnips of Norfolk would soon join the turnip-headed inhabitants in 'crying out against us'.

It is small wonder that Disraeli was a depressed man in 1851 when, however, at the end of the year he received the final title-deeds of leadership of the Opposition in the Commons – the prior copy of the Queen's Speech to read to colleagues. The Government in which he was Leader of the House from February to December 1852 was put by Derby (as by his father's death he now was) in an absurd position. The Prime Minister unfurled the flags of Protectionism and Protestantism (the latter shared with the Whigs and disliked by the Peelites) as its emblems.[15] Yet he put the anti-Protectionist Henley at the Board of Trade and sent to the Treasury Disraeli who had said the autumn before that to reverse Repeal would require 'an almost universal feeling in the country' and after a good harvest was not practical politics. Nor was it in 1852 when the country prospered under Free Trade. After the elections, Protection was officially repudiated by the Commons by 468:53. Disraeli had then to introduce a December budget on which, after a powerful attack from Gladstone, winding up, the ministry fell by the narrow margin of 305:286.

Malmesbury said they had lost the election 'from bad management'. The Protectionists were, indeed, badly managed from the first, having lost with Peel his chief whip Young and the agent Bonham. Derby's interest in politics was intermittent. The requests of the persevering Beresford for assistance were brushed aside. The neglect of the press was glaring. More important in their effects, since the Peelites had constituted themselves the custodians of public rectitude, were the corrupt methods of Beresford as central election manager and of the new whip Forbes Mackenzie, unseated for bribery at Liverpool, and the anti-Popery which constituted the only Conservative appeal in the towns. It seemed the party had no faith, only a hatred of one. It fought with little hope, little talent, little to appeal to ambitious young politicians. Disraeli's talk of the gradual elimination of duties in favour of direct taxation, nearly as universal as indirect had been, might mean taxation of urban interests to the advantage of the 200,000 lesser landed proprietors and the farmers. And that was what Disraeli proposed in his budget. The main relief fell on malt and hops, the new burdens on the £100–150 a year man (to pay income tax for the first time) and the house tax was doubled and extended from the £20 and upwards class to the £10 class. The 'Young England' sentiment of Disraeli's election address (vetted by Derby) – 'a ministry formed on the principles of Conservative progress [might] terminate for ever, by just and conciliatory measures, the misconceptions . . . between producer and consumer and extinguish the fatal jealousy that rankles between town and country' – seemed now to have been meant for irony as well as euphony.

Most Peelites still in politics had rejoined the Conservative ranks and helped to swell the number of MPs Disraeli led. But the leading men – Peel's colleagues and many of his lieutenants who had held junior office – went the other way. The new administration (which lasted from January 1853 to January 1855) was a coalition of Whigs and Peelites with Palmerston and the Radical Sir William Molesworth. It was headed by the Earl of Aberdeen; his thirteen Cabinet colleagues included Graham at the Admiralty, Sidney Herbert as Secretary at War, Lincoln (now Duke of Newcastle) at War and Colonies, the young Peelite recruit the Duke of Argyll with the Privy Seal and, most importantly, Gladstone at the Treasury. Just outside the Cabinet were Young (Chief Secretary for Ireland) and Cardwell (Board of Trade), apart from peers like St Germans and Canning. There were enough Peelite MPs in the administration itself to have given Derby and Disraeli a bare majority if they had voted for the latter's budget, and, of course, they had followers, though not very many. George Frederick Young, Beresford and Newdegate, aided, it must be emphasised, by Derby, had done their work too well, causing resentment where they should have sought understanding and sympathy. Disraeli had tried to project a moderate image, but his personal position as Derby's second-in-command was itself a difficulty, and he was thwarted at every turn by extremists and/or his leader, whose actions would not have been different if they had decided deliberately to forfeit chance of power. And then, ill-advised by unfriendly (and unimaginative) Free-Trade officials at the Treasury, whose predictions of revenue returns were inaccurate, Disraeli had tried to do his duty by the landed interest in the only way it could be done – by spreading the load of income tax and excise. He thereby infuriated what Cobden called 'those centres from which radiate the light and intelligence of the country' and gave Gladstone the chance of a 'great' budget which would appeal to them.

Gladstone retained Disraeli's much maligned £100 income tax base and the extension of the tax to Irish fundholders and salary earners, while projecting the elimination of income tax altogether by 1860. But he delighted the Mancunians by sweeping away many tariffs and some excises and by aiming a blow at the landed interest by extending the succession duties, against which Palmerston, in *domestic* matters the opponent whose views were most congenial to the Tories, protested in vain.[16] Manchester had won! A Liberal chronicler remarked that the budget proved that, predominantly landed though the Commons remained, 'the middle classes now overmatch, or are at least fully equal to, the aristocratic classes . . .' and had as much of their own way as they were entitled to. Which was to say, in effect, that the Tory revolt against Peel had entirely failed to achieve its object. The middle classes still looked to Peel's men, but these were no longer in the Conservative Party. And that party could have no rational prospect of returning to office with power unless it became Peelite again. Bentinck and Disraeli, dragging with them a dubious Derby, had merely succeeded in breaking up the developing two-party system and handing over power to an unpredictable House of Commons on which no government could wholly rely.

CHAPTER 2

Dogdays and Daring

Disraeli had now 'arrived', in the sense that two biographers, one (Francis) fulsome, the other (MacKnight) venomous, took up their pens. But to one ranked (by John Vincent in *The Prime Ministers*) with Fox as a great Opposition leader, it was galling that leading the largest party in the House of Commons offered so little prospect of office, the more so in that Derby, who advocated a 'policy of patience', was now ready to take office only if he saw a chance of keeping it[1] and was almost uniformly wrong in his assessment of political prospects. He was astonished, for instance, at the enormous majority by which the Aberdeen coalition was overthrown for its misconduct of the Crimean War; he then declined office because he thought Palmerston, for whom the country cried out, would fail to form a government. It is small wonder that Disraeli was thrown into 'a state of disgust beyond all control' when it was the considered verdict of Gladstone that this Derby refusal early in 1855 was 'a palpable error' – Disraeli thought it 'almost ruinous'. The suggestion that Derby was merely the voice of Disraeli is the absolute reverse of the truth. Disraeli was the subordinate of a grandee whose sole intimates were the sharers of his outdoor and indoor sports; who could rarely be induced to dine MPs and when, at last, he had Disraeli to stay at his Lancashire mansion, Knowsley, in December 1853, was bored by political talk; who failed to make an adequate financial contribution to the extra-parliamentary party organisation entrusted by Disraeli to his invaluable solicitor Philip Rose, whose commission greatly relieved the new and respectable chief whip Sir William Jolliffe. Derby was always remote, often ill, still more often listless. Addressing a Commons leader, activist and ambitious by nature and interest, Derby dealt largely in vetoes. Thus, when Disraeli wished to discomfort the Government in co-operation with the pure Whig Earl Grey, the Irish Brigade or the Manchester Radicals, Derby wrote that he (the Leader of Her Majesty's Opposition) *was indifferent to the disruption of the party in the Commons*, but it would be bad for England![2] Yet, when his leadership was widely criticised, Derby could be very imperious; on 28 February 1857, when he was trying to get hold of Gladstone, who thought Palmerston the worst of Premiers and would greatly have preferred Derby, the Tory leader told his party: 'Should any member of the Conservative connection attempt to dictate to him the course he should pursue with regard to any political personages whatever, he would regard it as an insult, and no longer recognise that member as attached to his party.' It is difficult to see how this authoritarian attitude differs from that of Peel, revolt against which had made Derby a party leader!

Occasionally Derby, a formidable speaker still, in purist English filled the Lords, with spectators from the Commons gathered round, when some cause, like the defence of Oxford University, whose Chancellor he had become on the death of Wellington, moved him.[3] But he was not a fit, active, regular head of an alternative government, as he was supposed to be, and he was a sore trial to Disraeli, who thought the duty of an Opposition was to oppose and did not accept the impossibility of a majority Tory government. But Disraeli could not fail to be aware that his own record and personality impeded the achievement of that majority. Thus, many years later Gladstone explained his refusal to join Derby on the fall of Aberdeen at the beginning of 1855:

'A strong sentiment of revulsion from Disraeli personally ... was alone sufficient to deter me absolutely from a merely personal and separate reunion; besides which there would have been no power, unless in company, to give Conservatism a liberal bias in conformity with the traditions of Peel.'

Since Professor Gash remarked that the Conservative Party's outlook may have been Disraelian, but its practice has been Peelite,[4] this paradox has become a platitude. None can say how Disraeli and Gladstone would have got on together in a Derbyite Cabinet; it is quite likely that Disraeli, rather than undergoing many years of sterile opposition in which Derby did not give him a free hand, would have welcomed the experiment. But it is far from clear that the opportunity ever existed. For Gladstone had enemies as well as Disraeli. Derby was expert in dealing with party meetings, but when he met 230 MPs on 21 February 1855, the cries of 'No Papists. No Puseyites' (patently referring to Gladstone and other Peelites) and the predictions that from a Derby coalition with Gladstone in charge of the finances and Palmerston of the war there would be a hundred Tory defections indicated clearly that there was no alternative to the Commons' leadership under Derby except Palmerston, who had no difficulty in forming a ministry (though not a very efficient one) of his own.

Meanwhile, Disraeli relieved his tensions by vehement articles in *The Press*, his organ from May 1853 to 1858, conspicuous for the absence of references to Derby. Late in 1856, a very bad year for the party, with Palmerston as Premier carrying all before him, Disraeli succumbed to nervous debility. It is significant that there was no attempt to get rid of him.

On 24 February 1857 Derby, in one of his spasmodic interventions, spoke passionately for 'the feeble defencelessness of China against the overbearing might of Great Britain.' The passivist, economical, non-imperialist role of the Tory party under Derby, barely distinguishable from that of Cobden and Bright, proved unpopular, however; the middle classes were becoming imperialist, the landed gentry remained patriotic. Defeated in the Commons, Palmerston did not resign. He indulged in a 'punitive election' which decimated the Mancunians, especially in their Lancastrian stronghold, and dented the Peelites. The result was mortifying for the Tories. Their hold on the English counties sank to the 1835 level and many scrambled back by clinging to the tailboard of the Palmerston waggon. Sidney Herbert had just noted that Palmerston's popularity was very great with the country gentlemen because of 'his old Protectionist leanings, his unconcealed aversion to Gladstone's financial policy, his objections to Parliamentary Reform ... and his noisy foreign policy', and concluded that many who sat opposite him only failed to sit behind him because the machinery of party was stronger than its spirit – 'the club in London and the attorneys in the country prevent them.'[5] In other words, Palmerston, not Derby, still less Disraeli, was the natural leader of the gentlemen of England, but had somehow got onto the wrong side of the fence, leaving them with no alternative to the strange, though brilliant, Jewish intellectual.

The plebiscitary majority secured by Palmerston in 1857 with chauvinist attacks on 'an insolent barbarian wielding power at Canton' failed him the following year, and on 20 May 1858 Derby agreed to take office since 'if he refused the Conservative Party would be broken up for ever.' His efforts to attract Earl Grey and Gladstone failed. The latter said his unpopularity with the Conservatives would make him a source of weakness, but E. J. Feuchtwanger, in his life of Gladstone (1975), thinks he was motivated by his dislike of Disraeli, the incompatibility of his outlook with that of most Tory MPs, and perhaps an appeal from Bright – 'If you join Lord Derby, you link your fortunes with a constant minority and with a party in the Country which is every day lessening in numbers and in power ...'

Of course, the adhesion of Gladstone would have won the Tories new friends in the country – though probably with a temporary loss to Palmerston of old ones. Derby tried to achieve it by a declaration calculated to disturb many of the latter, and strongly at odds with his private correspondence hitherto, his own *Tamworth Manifesto*. The new Premier told the Lords on 1 March 1858:

'My Lords, there can be no greater mistake than to suppose that a Conservative Ministry necessarily means a stationary Ministry. We live in an age of constant progress, moral, social and political ... in politics, as in everything else, the same course must be pursued – constant progress, ... adapting our institutions to the altered purposes they are intended to serve, and by judicious changes meeting the demands of society ...'

He promised to bring in a measure of parliamentary reform acceptable to all 'moderate, impartial, and well-educated men' and tried to sweeten the pill for the diehards by pointing out that the Constitution was a result of a series of perpetual changes, like the venerable country houses altered for the convenience and comfort of the inhabitants.

The nature of these architectural changes was not to be revealed for a year, and the Government was saved from defeat within three months only by the improper leakage that the Queen, in her hatred of Palmerston, would give Derby a dissolution if the censure on Ellenborough's despatch to the Governor-General of India, Lord Canning, was carried. It was important for the Tories to stay in for some time for, as Disraeli wrote in *Endymion* at the end of his life:

'. . . unless they had dared these ventures [minority governments] they never could have found a body of men competent, from their official experience and their practice in debate, to form a ministry. Had they continued to refrain from incurring responsibility, they must have been broken up and merged in different connections, which, for a party numerically so strong . . . would have been a sorry business.'

The main measure of 1858 was the India Bill, abolishing the Company – as Disraeli and Stanley junior had presciently sought to do in association with Bright, only to be met with the standard jargon of prescriptive rights of chartered bodies – and transforming Stanley from President of the Board of Control to Secretary of State for India. In this and other connections it was noticeable that Disraeli behaved more independently of Derby and the Cabinet than he usually did of Derby when out of office. For he had as Leader of the House the power of making commitments.

By their 1859 Reform Bill the Conservatives staked their claim to have as much right as any other government to deal with the issue revived when Russell renounced, ten years before, the 'finality' of 1832. But it was the product of a Cabinet compromise, attacked – in breach of promise – by Walpole and Herries, who resigned over it. Disraeli introduced it in a speech, Hardy noted, of skill and adroitness, and Derby defended it powerfully to the party meeting at his house.[6] But, although it was anticipated that Beresford and Newdegate would be among eight opponents of the second reading, this did not mean that it met Derby's own tests of being passable and 'final'. It was a partisan measure, reflecting Derby's advice to Disraeli in 1857 that the key was the transfer to the borough registers of those Whig and League assets – the men whose qualification to vote in a county arose from property in a represented borough. The bill was segregationist; it proposed such a change and at the same time envisaged the lowering of the county but not the borough franchise. On these two points, Russell, who wanted reform, and Palmerston, who did not, fixed to scramble back to office with the aid of all the Opposition groups except a few Irish who, on account of the Italian war, obeyed the papal advice to vote Tory. Derby treated Russell's amendment as a question of confidence and, when it was carried by 330 to 291, secured a dissolution.

Every effort had been made to strengthen Derby's Government by securing recruits from outside. Disraeli had offered to yield the lead to Graham and sent a personal entreaty to Gladstone (May 1858). In view of the closeness of the eventual result, it looks as though Aberdeen, by deterring Gladstone, delivered the last conclusive Peelite riposte to the Protectionist desertion of Peel and, by determining Gladstone's political future, determined also Disraeli's. For when the crucial vote was taken in the new Parliament of 1859, on a straight motion of no confidence identical with Peel's in 1841, the Conservatives were defeated by only thirteen. And this although the sectional Opposition leaders, Palmerston, Russell, Herbert and Bright, had previously summoned 'Liberal' MPs to Willis's Rooms in a deliberate effort to re-establish the two-party system destroyed in 1846. The leading men were very anxious to achieve this. Gladstone had long deplored the party chaos, which he blamed on Peel for his attitude 1846–50, agreeing with Disraeli that the transformation from the golden age of the two-party system (1835–45) to that of the private member (1846–59) left the executive too weak. And Derby, announcing the dissolution on 4 April 1859, had dilated upon the same theme. Gladstone had not voted with the Opposition on the motion dictated to the young Marquess of Hartington as a result of Willis's Rooms.

The usually cited explanation of his joining Palmerston's 1859 Government – that he concurred with Palmerston and Russell over Italy – may well ignore his passion for the two-party system and his enthusiasm at the victors' offer of the Exchequer. It was not till March 1860 that he resigned from the Carlton Club.

THE TORY LEADERSHIP UNDER FIRE

'In what sense, and of what, are they Conservatives?' must have been widely asked, and the fact that the elderly eccentric Henry Drummond was both the founder of the Irvingite Church and of a chair of political economy does not mean that he was alone in complaining to Jolliffe:

'Lord Derby and Mr Disraeli have led the Conservative Party to adopt every measure they opposed as Radical ten years ago. They have made their party the tool of their own ambition . . . I do not think it creditable to the intelligence or honour of the Country Gentlemen of England to vote black to be white, or white to be black at their bidding.'

Some still did not accept the new conception of party; others thought the party tie a contract between leaders and led, binding mainly on the leaders. Among these was a man of powerful intellect destined to influence the fortunes of the Conservative Party for over forty years – the son of a member of Derby's first two Cabinets, and known successively as Lord Robert Cecil, Viscount Cranborne and the third Marquess of Salisbury. It was his conviction that only the Radicals had principles, while other prominent men, losing sight of 'a stiffer and less complicated morality out of doors', treated politics like chess 'with mighty principles and deep-seated sentiments as mere pawns.' He thought Disraeli by far the worst of these political gamesters and had accepted the pocket borough of Stamford in 1853 only when the patron, Lord Exeter, assured him that complete distrust of 'Mr d'Israeli' was no bar to being a Conservative MP.[7] Sure that Disraeli's public life had been one of low dodging and purely selfish, he quite misunderstood the relationship between Derby and Disraeli, attributing to the latter not only the welshing on the Corn Laws, Jews and Catholics but on parliamentary reform as well – 'in alternation between womanish spite and Oriental cunning' – whereas it seems, in fact, that the liberal tone in 1858–9 had been set at least as much, if not more, by Derby under pressure from his heir. But Disraeli got the abuse, of the sort employed to keep him from the leadership in 1847–8. The only justification for this is that while young Stanley, though really a Liberal, who found himself in the Conservative Party because his father led it, was seen as a man of principle if not of decision, and long spoken of as its next leader although unrepresentative of its opinions, Disraeli did try to educate his party within the strict limits Derby would allow – and had his efforts ascribed to self-seeking! In so doing, 'he incensed his own friends'.

The second Marquess of Salisbury disapproved of his second son's marriage to the daughter of a Tractarian judge. She saved his sanity and made his career, but the father's sanctions drove Cecil to political journalism, which he hated as long as he was financially dependent on it. He hated the House of Commons too, describing himself as its Ishmael, until, about 1864, he began to feel his power in it. Neither in writing nor speech did he mince words. 'Obstinate Constitutionalists were pulled along the democratic road on which their leaders find it more remunerative to travel.' 'To crush the Whigs by combining with the Radicals was the first and last maxim of Mr Disraeli's tactics.' The enemies of the party 'little knew the deep and bitter humiliation masked by the outward loyalty of its votes.'[8] Similar criticisms are found in ministerial diaries, such as those of Gathorne Hardy, who thought that Disraeli 'has shown himself a shifty and unsafe tactician and we shall never win our way with such guidance.' But these are either criticisms of particular tactical errors (such as all politicians make) or complaints that Disraeli is trimming his sails in order to gain public support. Is this not what shrewd politicians habitually do, and are they not attacked as incompetents if they fail to do it? Disraeli was hard done by. He was a practising, pragmatic, ambitious politician, constantly facing heterogeneous majorities, but forbidden by Derby to try to split them. He had to carry screaming into a society of Free Trade and rising living standards for many – a world for Gladstone to capture! – people whom

Cecil himself described as 'dodos' with 'stagnant minds'. And he was attacked for the attempt by a clever, unhappy young man (whose pen ran away into epigram and vehement denunciation) who differed from the Disraeli who had attacked Peel only in the sense that Cecil's integrity was unimpeachable.

But integrity even when allied to the highest intellect does not guarantee sound judgement. Cecil was failing to understand what Disraeli's experience was teaching him. He was attacking Disraeli as though he had the power that Peel had had; he was repeating, almost to the point of monotony, what Disraeli had said and written earlier about the territorial constitution, local government, corporate rights, equipoise, checks and balances, hatred of red tape and doctrinaire centralisers, the maintenance of Church privileges and the revitalisation of its mission, humanisation of the Poor Law, consideration for the working classes – all, though he did not seem to see it, 'Young England' stuff. Once again the nation was told that its rulers and potential rulers had forfeited respect; once again the Conservative Party was told that, in order to gain the nation's trust, it must cease its fidelity to a leader tried and found wanting. Disraeli recognised the genre and brushed it all aside. But we must take account of a penetrating analysis of the inconsistency of Cecil's views.[9] They were not coherent. Accepting – as Disraeli had done with relish in defence of his 1852 budget – the Benthamite view that the public man must act for the greatest good of the greatest number and that as evils changed so did the required remedies, for old laws get out of gear with modern realities, Cecil, a High Churchman of great devotion, assailed with a withering empiricism both progressive dogmas and obscurantism (brusquely dismissing Disraeli's novels as vehicles for 'mysterious views'). And yet his general line was that of the rankest of diehards – one should offer 'the deadening resistance of a sandbag to the dangerous forces of political fanaticism' (represented at home by John Bright). 'Once the dyke is breached by small concessions all would be lost.' '*Any* parliamentary reform would upset the precarious balance of institutions' (1858). Peel had been right to go to the brink of revolution in his resistance of 1831–2.

Increasingly from 1860 to 1866 the public were treated to trenchant assertions of this kind, delivered in the Commons as well as anonymously but identifiably in the *Saturday Review* and the *Quarterly* after *Bentley's Quarterly Review* (1859–60) perished after four issues. Office was to be 'dreaded' without a majority; at least in opposition Tories could preserve their own honour and restore shaken confidence in public men. But Disraeli must go!

As Disraeli's colleague, Salisbury *père* felt bound to protest at his son's abuse, and got the reply, 'I merely put into print what all the country gentlemen were saying in private.' But although Disraeli wrote to one of these, Sir William Miles, on 11 June 1860, that he must resign, it is doubtful whether Cecil did accurately reflect party opinion at the time. Palmerston had formed a government of Whigs and Peelites and *passé* Radicals (Cobden refused to join and Bright was barred by Palmerston for his attacks on classes). To this administration Derby had been induced by his son Stanley to promise 'independent and generous support' and Disraeli duly received his orders (12 January 1860) to 'keep the present men in and resist all temptations to avail ourselves of a casual majority'. The decision to attack the 'great' budget of 1860 and the allied Cobden commercial treaty with France was a collective one, keenly supported, and on 24 February 1860 Disraeli made a good case. But in June, and again in January 1861, Derby sent Malmesbury to the Palmerstons to assure them that the Opposition would support the more conservative ministers (of whom Palmerston was the doughtiest) against the Radicals and, by implication, the less conservative ministers. This contact helped secure the abandonment of Russell's Reform Bill (a Government measure) and Palmerston enjoyed telling Gladstone in October that Tory MPs were missing divisions on orders from their leaders. Gladstone complained that they 'live[d] in antireforming times.' At Easter-tide 1861 even Cecil admitted that 'Dizzy has behaved like an angel', supporting Palmerston and opposing Bright on all possible occasions. Lady Palmerston led the cheering from the ladies' cage when the Lords defeated Gladstone's abolition of the paper duty, the recurrence of which setback in 1862 he avoided by procedural means, becoming the hero of the radical provincial press, an important Liberal asset.

The understanding with the Opposition made it unnecessary

for Palmerston, for ever embroiled with Gladstone on defence expenditure, especially for ironclads, to take seriously the latter's innumerable draft resignation letters. But there was also a difference of opinion, both on international relations and defence techniques, between Derby and Disraeli, and the former's attempt to explain away the latter's reference to 'bloated armaments' when Gladstone was saying 'the epoch of retrenchment has commenced' led to a major Tory fiasco (June 1862) which overshadowed a Palmerstonian setback. To keep his Cabinet together the Prime Minister had to meet a Radical motion for reduced expenditure with an amendment stating that the House was 'deeply impressed with the need for economy . . .' At what seemed one of his usual successful party meetings, Derby read out an amendment to be moved by Walpole. It had to be withdrawn. As Disraeli said, 'you cannot keep a large army in order without letting them sometimes smell gunpowder'. But a wise commander should be sure of his troops. These at least could utter a cry of triumph when the Church Rates Bill was beaten by 287:286. On this Cecil had complained referring to Derby and Disraeli, that 'Conservatives of the illuminated school, bent on popularising their creed' shook off the question to advance their careers. But *he*, 6 March 1861, with a timetable for ten years delay on rates and another twenty on tithe, and twenty more before the wicked Radicals struck at endowments, cried 'No Surrender' – all the outworks of the citadel must be defended.

While the Disraelis received marks of royal favour and he of social acceptance, Benjamin's stock slumped and the editors of his *Reminiscences* describe them as written mainly in 1862–4, when he was 'treading water and trying to avoid being forced under by the hostility of his own followers and the accomplishments . . . of Gladstone'. In October 1862 Disraeli's objectionable secretary, Ralph Earle, told him that Malmesbury had said 'We shall never get on until we get rid of Disraeli.'[10] From the autumn of 1861 Derby's health deteriorated quite seriously, until early in 1865 he was thought in danger of his life. Palmerston, nearing eighty, seemed immortal. Derby was sixty-five and Disraeli sixty when one of those occasions arose which forces a numerically strong Opposition, however determined to keep moderates in office as the next best thing to enjoying it themselves, to act, especially if an election is not far off. Palmerston and Russell, alienating France over Poland (on which they showed what Cecil called 'quixotism which falters at the sight of a drawn sword') had to admit over Denmark (a conquered country promised by Palmerston on 27 June 1863 that she would not have to stand alone) that as we had no allies we could not act. Derby had attacked Russell for 'meddle and muddle . . . lecturing, scolding, blustering and retreating.' At his house on 28 June 1864 the 'Cabinet of the Opposition' drafted a censure, approved by the MPs at Salisbury's later in the day ('very successful both in numbers and spirits'). The Opposition lost the vote but won the argument put by Disraeli that HMG had failed, that Britain's moderating and media-torial influence in Europe was lowered, that the securities for peace were diminished.[11] Palmerston had failed to take the measure of Bismarck, who in 1866 defeated Austria and in 1870 France, creating the German Empire. Cecil had predicted that, with the Manchester policy of free trade and 'isolation', the establishments were so 'clipped and starved' that statesmen could not act on old-fashioned brave words. Now he said that 'all respect for our national character . . . founded on a belief in its bull-dog characteristics has disappeared'. To find the Germans untroubled by the question 'what will England do?' was humiliating, but our treatment of Denmark 'branded on our nation a stigma of ineffable baseness.' He was not the only future foreign secretary who learned that British diplomacy must be cut to the cloth. The modest garb eminently suited Lord Stanley, whose views on peace, retrenchment and reform much resembled Gladstone's. This parliamentary encounter was a landmark in British foreign policy.

THE MENACE OF GLADSTONE AND BRIGHT

During the years when Palmerston (who said 'We cannot go on legislating for ever') kept Radicalism in check, Tories showed signs of the social responsibility Young England and the Oastler-ites had preached. Gathorne Hardy, born in the latter school, made his maiden speech on a factory bill in 1856. Cecil had told the submissive electors of Stamford that he favoured 'measures tending to social and sanitary improvements and the amelioration of the conditions of the labouring classes' (1853), and he and Stafford Northcote, future rivals for the leadership, supported the Cobbett–Fielden attempt of 1855 to restore ten hours. Cecil harried the dishonest inspectors supervising Robert Lowe's educationally unsound Revised Code in the schools, forcing the minister's resignation (1864). But he also harried mean and harsh Poor Law guardians who looked on unemployed girls as 'hands', not human beings, and those of St Pancras especially. He got a committee in 1864. Derby said that when 10,000 were rendered homeless at a stroke (increasing the over-congestion in the mean streets) so that gentlemen in North London could get to the Bank of England in ten minutes by train, a social and political evil was created – and *he* got a committee.

Cecil identified the incidence of taxation as 'the field upon which the contending classes of this generation will do battle.' He feared that under democracy 'the rich would pay all the taxes and the poor make all the laws.'[12(a)] He explained that he mistrusted working-class domination not because that class was unlike any other but because it was not.[12(b)] 'Taxation ever falls lightly on the depositories of absolute power.'[12(c)] He was there-fore alert to spot fiscal inequity under the existing system of 'equipoise'. He found it monstrous that the Thames Embank-ment should be paid for out of a tax on a necessity – the metropolitan coal dues. Derby, in a splendid speech (House of Lords, 20 June 1860) on 'Manchester finance', attacked Glad-stone for taking duty off French wines and not tea or sugar. He was in line with Cecil, who complained that Gladstone, working blindly to a formula (unlike the empirical Peel) had given the poor a grievance by remitting all the duties on the rich – wine, French silk, gloves, jewellery, watches, plate. Gladstone was defeated when in his 1863 budget he attempted to tax charities, 'the heritage of the poor'. But the behaviour of the Lancashire operatives, thrown out of work by the American Civil War, yet sympathising with the North because of anti-slavery, may have weakened the doubts of Derby, as well as Gladstone, about lowering the borough franchise. For the Tory leader was a working chairman of the central executive committee of the federated relief committees while Gladstone was making 'a vile speech', as Bright called it, to the Tyne-

siders, profiting from the Civil War, to the effect that the South
had made a nation. Of the Lancashire cotton famine era Derby
said: 'It has led the rich to think of the duties they owe the
poor and it has shown the poor that the rich are not unmindful
of them.' On these Sybilline matters Disraeli was inconspicuous.
Cecil drew from Lancashire the moral that there was no
Chartist-type revolutionary threat and therefore no need for a
Reform Bill.

The 1865 election was held so that the Liberals could cash
in on the theme 'Leave it to Pam', who did not live to meet the
new Parliament. Conservatives thought it hard that so sturdy a
champion of the established equipoise should thus imperil it.
For next in line came Earl Russell (aged seventy-three) and a
Gladstone transforming himself into 'the People's William'. A
speech of 1864, for which he was sternly rebuked by Palmerston
on 12 May, seemed to imply that the onus of proving a man
should *not* have the vote lay with what Cecil called 'a constitutional party based upon a love of freedom and resistance to
democracy as its most dangerous enemy', which, he feared, was
'likely to remain the dream of sanguine bystanders'. In a
triumphant tour of Lancashire, Gladstone found the moral
sense of the masses sounder than that of their social superiors,
so that justice required political recognition of their deserts. On
28 March 1865 he told the House of Commons he was no longer
loyal to the Irish Church as an Establishment. There was great
Tory delight when Hardy, backed by the arguments of Lord
Cranborne (as Cecil had now become by the death of his
brother) on the community of interests between the Church
and the Conservative Party, turned Gladstone out of the
representation of Oxford University. But Derby knew that,
although Disraeli cast bait for Roman Catholic voters, the
Tories would lose seats, and thought that 'a purely Conservative
Government is all but hopeless until ... Gladstone tries his
hand with a Radical Government and alarms the middle
class.' Hence the Opposition strategy, inspired, it seems, by
Disraeli,[13] of pretending that the Reform Bill of Earl Russell,
managed by Gladstone as Leader of the Commons in succession
to Palmerston, was more radical than it was.

Cranborne, of course, had no hesitations. The bill reflected
Bright's 'persistent, unyielding hatred of the rural interest.' It

was a step towards household suffrage. The working-class, which had shown through trade unions a vigour and tenacity and power to organise of which the middle and upper-classes were utterly destitute, would alternate between apathy and – when moved by physical privation or some contagious passion – 'a tyrannical recklessness of the rights of others'. The executive would be weak but spendthrift. MPs would be corrupt as well as mediocre and unduly responsive to shifts in public opinion. It was wealth, not numbers, that was under-represented: 'the rich must be protected from the inroads of the mob.'

What happened to the Russell–Gladstone bill depended on the thirty or forty conservative Liberals reckoned likely to rebel, and discussions on how to get them to support a Conservative administration began before the contents of the bill were known. Derby was willing to give up the leadership if Disraeli could achieve a coalition, but if he was to be Prime Minister again Disraeli and not someone 'independent' must lead in the Commons. Disraeli's previous offer to assist coalition by going to the Lords became relevant again when it was found that the thirty or forty would not follow Derby, but might accept Stanley. But Conservatives in general lacked confidence in Stanley, who in 1857 had left the front bench because he differed from them on so many issues. Stanley lacked confidence in himself, more or less acquiescing in his father's verdict that he would be 'a child dealing with men'. Then there was talk of Disraeli or Stanley linked with some Whig magnifico as Premier – Devonshire or Lansdowne, the latter the chief organiser, with Lord Elcho, MP, of Whig rebels who grumbled that 'Mr Bright governs, though he does not reign'. The most articulate spokesman of these Adullamites was Robert Lowe, though his mistrust of democracy was matched by his contempt for the aristocracy, from whom in all but mistrust of democracy he differed radically. But it was Whig heirs, Lord Grosvenor (seconded by Stanley) and Clanricarde's son Dunkellin, who moved the crucial motions.

Defeated on the Dunkellin amendment, Russell resigned. The obvious sequel would have been a coalition headed by Lansdowne, prime organiser of the Adullamite rebellion, or the cynical old Whig Clarendon, or the Duke of Somerset, another Whig minister, with Stanley (to whom Russell in 1865, follow-

ing Palmerston's example of 1857, had offered office) leading the
Commons. The impediments were Derby and Disraeli, neither
of whom would serve under anyone else in his own House.
Derby was on record as determined never again to be a
minister on sufferance. Was Disraeli then to become Lord
Hughenden in some Trollopian arrangement? There were
young men willing to see him shunted off, as well as unrelenting
old-stagers. But even a party as unlucky electorally as the
Conservatives had been since the Protectionist–Peelite break
has its pride. The Adullamites, though importunate, were
heterogeneous, and could not provide either the talent or
administrative experience the Peelites had hawked in the
market where Cabinets are made. Their attitude was resented.
Disraeli argued in his own interest that there would be desertions cancelling the gain of adherents; he persuaded Derby
that it was 'not consistent with the honour of the Conservative
Party' to relegate him. When the Queen summoned Derby,
he consulted twenty-two Conservative leaders. All thought it
his duty to try to form a coalition himself; all but one that, if he
failed, he should form another minority government (28 June
1866). Visibly ill and apprehensive, he told the Lords on 9 July
that, having failed to form a coalition, he had accepted the
'onerous post' for fear that, if he refused, the Conservative
Party, with the largest stake in the country, and constituting a
material element in the strength of the Empire most interested
in peace and prosperity, would be disrupted. So Disraeli's
chance of moving next door from the Chancellor's house at
No 11 Downing Street, remained.

'THE LEAP IN THE DARK'

Derby and Disraeli had, probably with party approval,
repelled boarders. But had they foreseen the article which
Cranborne would be able to write for the *Quarterly* of October
1867 under the title 'The Conservative Surrender', many
Conservatives in Parliament and country would have regretted
not only Russell's resignation (which Derby thought unnecessary) but their votes against Gladstone's bill. For in the
interval Derby and Disraeli had made what the former, in the

Lords on 6 August 1867, borrowing a Palmerston phrase, called 'the leap in the dark'.

If Gladstone's bill had become law, argued Cranborne, the prospects for the British Constitution would have been brighter:

'. . . There was no doubt at all as to the nature of the resistance offered by the Conservative leaders in 1866 to Mr Gladstone's Bill. There was no doubt of the nature of the support they received in doing so . . . Their supporters were fully hood-winked . . . no presentiment crossed a single mind of the utter ruin of their cause . . .'

Even *he* had not been suspicious. His article in the *Quarterly* of July 1866 – he was a Cabinet colleague of Disraeli under Derby by the time it appeared – had been exultant, for he could see no danger except that factious Whigs might bring up a measure liable to democratic amendment. Himself prepared for a measure of working-class 'participation without predominance' and a handful of working men in the Commons itself, he, for all his mistrust of Disraeli, never dreamed that the Conservative Government which he joined as a Secretary of State would bring forward a measure 'in the presence of adverse forces strong enough to engraft democratic amendments', still less that it would accept ones more drastic than Gladstone or even Bright desired.

Many typewriters have rattled at length on the parliamentary epic which produced household suffrage in the boroughs,[14] including some using the red ribbon which seems to suggest that, however progressive a measure may be, its virtues are not in any circumstances to be acknowledged if a Conservative presides over its passage. At least one colleague, who remained loyal amid much heart-searching (for he, like Cranborne, was an earnest High Churchman much given to such exercise), felt that 'a great measure ought not to be in the hands of a minority, but with those who can mould, and resist the moulding of others.' In other words, Disraeli ought not to have done it! But only Disraeli could have done it – or would have done it!

A Liberal journalist would write 'Politics are to him a game in which the rules are not very strictly defined – in which a large latitude is enjoyed by the player who is not particularly scrupulous . . .' Cranborne saw that Disraeli was uniquely dangerous because he alone could 'forward Radical changes in a way that no other Minister could do – because he alone can silence and paralyse the forces of Conservatism. And in an age of singularly reckless statesmen he is I think beyond question the one who is least restrained by scruple.'[15] From what Derby and Disraeli said *after* the coup, Cranborne came to believe they intended a 'democratic' Reform Bill from the moment they took office in 1866. We know that no single minister contemplated any such thing. When Derby told the Lords on 22 July 1867, 'I determined that I would take such a course as would convert, if possible, an existing minority into a practical majority' and not be made for a third time 'a mere stop-gap until it should suit the convenience of the Liberal Party to forget their dissensions', he did not say he had intended the bill he now commended; he admitted that he did not relish two of its provisions imposed by opponents and said nothing of a third – Disraeli's crucial and gratuitous concession on the compounder. Replying to Cranborne's motion to reject the bill at third reading, Disraeli said 'We greatly objected to the Praetorian Guard' (i.e. the artisans who had accepted the Victorian middle-class ethos of Samuel Smiles's *Self-Help* and looked to Gladstone and Bright) and thought it less perilous to appeal to the sympathies of the great body of the people. Between his speech of July and his writing of 'The Conservative Surrender', Cranborne passed from the charge that 'the leaders kept their counsel . . . certainly from their colleagues in office . . .' to the allegation of 'a project of Tory Democracy . . . long and sedulously concealed . . . from their colleagues in opposition' since 1859.

Cranborne's devoted daughter and biographer, Lady Gwendolen Cecil, long ago dismissed the conspiracy theory. We must likewise reject the notion that Derby and Disraeli envisaged the bright future which lay before their party, which proved able to tap unknown or long-neglected wells (Lancashire textile towns and London slums as well as suburbia) by representing itself as peculiarly the national party confronting a motley of organised sectional groups such as those whose aspirations were included in the Liberal shopping-list at Newcastle in 1891. Having consistently refused to accept that the settlement of the electoral system was a Whig monopoly, they were simply out to 'dish the Whigs'.[16] The Reform Act of 1867 is a classic symptom of the regime of 1837–68, when every House of Commons expressed no confidence in at least one government. But, although the principles of the Act were in substance *not* the same as the principles of the bill as approved by the Cabinet, ministers claimed credit and tried to believe, with Hardy, who came to prominence in the debates, that they would 'enter an unknown world . . . more safely, or at least as safely, and more permanently than a £5 franchise would enable us to do.'

As between Derby and Disraeli, the responsibility for what happened is fairly clear. Derby had never intended a bill *for 1867*; Disraeli, on 11 February, promised to outline one in fifteen days' time. And on 17 May, in an almost empty House, Disraeli conceded to the obscure Hodgkinson what he had twice succeeded in defeating after major debates – the enfranchisement of what Bright delicately called 'the residuum' and others 'the dregs of the people', those who had not passed those tests of worth based, as Disraeli himself had put it, on 'their industry, their intelligence, their integrity.' Neither of these fundamental concessions had the authority of Derby or the Cabinet behind them, and the second was irretrievable.

On the other hand, Disraeli had initially resisted Derby's conviction that the Cabinet must tackle Reform because 'there is a genuine desire *now*'. Derby had said publicly that a moderate measure might not stop agitation. On 9 October 1866 he informed Disraeli he would raise it in Cabinet on 1 November. Gladstone complained, of household suffrage, that 'the Government bowled us over by the force of a phrase, and forced us to make the phrase a reality' beyond the wants and wishes of the time – a charge repeated against Disraeli by Cranborne's son Lord Hugh Cecil in his *Conservatism* (1912). But among the ministers it was Derby who first said he could not see how they could leave £10 and stop short of household suffrage, which he put to the Cabinet on 6 February. What he had in mind, however, was parliamentary *discussion* in 1867, possibly leading to defeat and an election. There were to be resolutions, from which the term household suffrage was omitted because it made General Peel see red. And there was to be a commission, to act

as a buffer to prevent precipitate action. But, having introduced
the resolutions with patent indifference, Disraeli on 11 February disrupted the Prime Minister's timetable. Together they
thrust household suffrage (or, rather, personal payment of
rates) through the Cabinet on 23 February, but temporarily
abandoned it in the face of threats of resignation organised by
Cranborne over the weekend, and substituted 'the ten minute
bill' – so-called from the speed of its composition rather than the
shortness of its life. This was a bill of the all-too-familiar type.
Disraeli was determined to smother it, and was delighted
(as a convert to personal payment of rates) when a party
meeting, and growing talk at the Carlton, showed a wish for
something bolder. But it was Derby who exercised the option
on 1 March, carried in Cabinet the next day, Cranborne,
Carnarvon and Peel walking out.

The bill as it was introduced contained all sorts of checks and
balances, such as the 'fancy' franchises for income tax payers,
fundholders and savings bank depositers (features of Russell's
bills), a two-year residence requirement prior to registration of
the new ratepaying voters, and the dual vote for the more highly
rated of the householders. Paupers and migrants would be
excluded most effectively. But Derby must have known that
most of these would be struck out by the Radicals unless
Gladstone stood by the Government. The 'dual' vote was
already only a shadow of the original 'plurality'; it was on the
basis of a householder having one, two, three or even four votes
according to the rateable value of his dwelling that Derby had
told Disraeli in December 'we might safely go as low as Household Suffrage for single votes'. But as early as 19 February he
had spoken in Cabinet of 'dual', not 'plural', and contentions
in Cabinet on 9 March caused him to pass Disraeli a note,
'Duality will defeat us – abandonment of it will destroy us.'
On the 18th Disraeli, moving the second reading, said he would
not recommend this concession to protect the middle-classes
against the invasion of their political power and act as a
counterpoise, as the new voters proposed would number no
more than under Gladstone's bill. (The force of this argument
collapsed the moment the concession was made in May to Mr
Hodgkinson, the solicitor from Newark to whom Disraeli
assured fame.) Losing the 'fancies', Disraeli claimed they were

not needed now that, as he had thought likely at the second reading, the £10 lodgers were put in (as in the 1859 bill). The two year residence rule described to the party on 15 March as one of two essentials, with a hint of dissolution if it were defeated, was rejected by a large majority, one year being substituted. The county franchise figure was lowered from £15 to £12 in response, Disraeli claimed, to representations from the gentry.

It had been accepted that the half million English householders who 'compounded' for their rates in their rent must be given the option of becoming voters by taking the trouble and expense of becoming personal payers of the poor rate. It was imagined that few would bother, and they the fittest. 'Under our Bill you will get all those men you say you wish to get,' Disraeli told Gladstone and Bright when the former moved a major amendment on 12 April. And then, suddenly, on that May afternoon, he 'let in the mob' – an event, to quote Cranborne, 'of startling magnitude' which he ascribed to 'sheer panic'. But on 9 May, *after* the Hyde Park affray to which so much has been ascribed by so many, but which the present writer, in agreement with Professor Ward,[17] thinks had no more effect than to break the health and spirits of 'Weeping Walpole' (replaced at the Home Office by the tougher Hardy) and furnish ministers with the argument that 'something' must be passed, Disraeli had defeated by 322:256 a Radical amendment to enfranchise *some* compounders. Under Hodgkinson's amendment the compounder, described by Disraeli on 12 April as the creature of jobbing vestries, rapacious landlords or indigence, would become a personal ratepayer and could, on meeting the one year residence requirement, become a voter, provided he had paid his poor rate and not been in receipt of poor relief.

No one knows why Dizzy did it, for all his subsequent explanations must be taken with many grains of salt. There had been little talk of the masses as a Tory asset, though in the eighteen-fifties Malmesbury and Stanley thought they might be, and it was always part of Disraeli's theme that 1832 was an anti-working-class measure of the magnitude of 1688 – a calculated alliance of the Whig oligarchy and the middle classes to put the former in power, or at least in office, for a generation. Many, including both admirers and critics, have

ascribed to him – and some at least of his party – a combination
of intuition and calculation which explain the party's continued
existence. Cranborne – by then third Marquess of Salisbury – in
a *Quarterly* article entitled 'The Past and Future of Conservative
Policy', written in 1869 – referred to 'the clear conviction of
the mass of the Conservative Party that in a Reform Bill more
Radical than that of the Whigs they had discovered the secret
of a sure and signal triumph.' This conviction was based on

'. . . a vague idea that the poorer men are the more they are
influenced by the rich; a notion that those whose vocation it
was to bargain and battle with the middle class must on that
account love the gentry; an impression that the ruder classes
of minds would be sensitive to traditional emotions . . .'

What is clear is that it *was* Dizzy who did it. The Queen's
secretary had already told her he had become 'the directing
mind of the ministry'. It seems that he could have consulted
Derby, but did not; the Cabinet, but did not; a party meeting,
but did not. Rejoicing in his newly-achieved freedom from
Derbyite thraldom, he 'felt the pulse of many in the course of
the morning.'[18] And perhaps the pulse *did* register something
of the attitude described by Cranborne; perhaps echoes of
Sybil and 'Young England' did inspire the audacious act. For
if he was not always straight with others, he was always true
to himself and what he deemed the party interest. On the other
hand, there was no follow-up in electoral appeal when in
1868 Disraeli, by now Prime Minister, dissolved. Many of the
bodies incorporated in the National Union of Conservative
and Constitutional Associations (formed before the bill was
passed) had 'working-men's' or 'operatives' in their title. But
NUCCA could find no impressive sponsorship and Hardy had
to suggest the addition to Disraeli's election address of 'the
hope that time may be given for legal and social improvements
so long laid aside'.

From Derby had come at the outset of the Commons proceedings on the bill one 'advice' which Disraeli vastly enjoyed
obeying. The line was to be that ministers were 'willing to
consult the opinion of the *House* but refuse[d] to submit to the
dictation of one assumed Leader of a Party.' The willingness to

accept almost anything from anybody, but nothing from Gladstone, was long attributed to Disraeli himself. Certainly he relished a gladiatorial contest with the Leader of the Opposition, who failed to understand how precarious was his standing in a multifarious majority which included Adullamites and was accustomed to be led by Whigs, which found Gladstone far from comprehensible and also lacking in the social arts of parliamentary management. He wished to divide on the second reading, but dared not. The 'tea-room mutiny' managed by the Radical Clay, a youthful booncompanion of Disraeli in the Mediterranean, later saved the Government – Disraeli was in touch with Clay. Gladstone had to withdraw a proposed instruction to the committee to draw a line (£5) above which all houses would qualify the ratepayer and below which none would. Then on 12 April came what he himself called 'a smash perhaps without example'. His motion to strike out the requirement for personal payment of rates was rejected at 2 a.m. by 310:289. Disraeli had hinted in *The Times* at a dissolution and argued that Gladstone had already had his innings in that same House. To Cranborne's disgust, country gentlemen rushed to shake the leader's hand and, before going home to Mary Anne's pie and champagne, Disraeli was acclaimed at the Carlton on the toast of Sir Matthew Ridley. Lord Blake writes of 'a decisive step in Disraeli's career'. The Queen thought it made him Prime Minister. Certainly, in Feuchtwanger's words, he 'had at last established an unequivocal claim to succeed to the leadership of his party'. F. B. Smith quotes the *mot*, 'Why is Mr Gladstone like a telescope? Because Disraeli draws him out, sees through him and shuts him up.'

In committee Disraeli showed a marvellous patience and a vast virtuosity. He let the members talk away, quietly calculating the odds on amendment after amendment before preferring one to another – such as Bright's to Torrens's on the lodgers (only 4,000 of whom were registered in 1869 outside Westminster and Marylebone). But every opportunity was taken to undermine Gladstone, who on 11 May at last desisted from attempts to find a value. He was thunderstruck when he heard the next week of the acceptance of the Hodgkinson amendment. It was a personal humiliation, and Disraeli described it as 'a step which would destroy the present agitation and extinguish Gladstone & Co.' The master-parliamentarian watched. He enjoyed it all – 'the great game' – the next best thing to ruling an empire.

In July the bill passed up to Derby to coax the Tory peers on the 19th into believing that, whatever the Whig Earl Grey might say, this was not only a 'large and extensive' but a 'conservative' measure and to warn them that Government and Commons would stand no nonsense from them.

As to whether the Act was 'democratic', the problem is partly one of semantics. It is easier to answer questions such as whether it squared with –

(1) Disraeli's stated ideal of 'an aristocratic government in the proper sense of the term – that is, a government by the best men of all classes' *as contrasted with democracy* (Commons, 8 May 1865).
(2) Disraeli's Bucks. election address, 1866, promising that any solution would not be of a foreign type, but 'in the spirit of the English Constitution', which recognised not the rights of man or of numbers but orders and classes.
(3) The Queen's Speech of 1867 which spoke of the franchise being 'freely extended' without the balance of power being 'unduly disturbed'.

On all these points Disraeli, denying that he had introduced democracy, could make a case more convincing to us than to those such as Cranborne, immersed in the study of America and France since their revolutions and predicting similar trends in Britain 'once the dyke was breached'. There are studies which show how real, if not superficially apparent, were the checks on political democracy even after the great changes of 1885 – checks which lasted till 1918.[19]

In the days of his political romances, Disraeli had regarded the poor, but free and independent, as an 'order' or 'estate of the realm'. He now claimed that the need for Reform arose because in 1832 Parliament 'abolished the relations between the labouring classes and the Constitution' – the relatively few popular boroughs, such as Preston, which had returned Orator Hunt and Cobbett and defeated Lord Derby, in those pre-1832 days, proved mighty useful. Now what had the 1867 Act done?

Of four million householders it had added half a million to the million qualified already. Was this not giving representation to a nation, rather than preponderance to a class? The vote had not been made a personal right – it remained attached to the ownership or occupancy of property. The county householder under £12 value did not have it, nor the transient urban householder, nor any man recently on poor relief, nor the householder of under £10 value in a borough without separate representation. And there was substance in Disraeli's claim that 'popular principles' were quite distinct from 'democratic rights', since the former 'are consistent with a state of society in which there is great inequality of conditions ... I trust it will never be the fate of this country to live under a democracy.'

This last quotation, delivered when introducing the bill on 9 March 1867, might have been directed straight at Cranborne, who never ceased to expound the evils to come. He did not accept Disraeli's claim that the bill at introduction had no democratic tendency; he had first threatened to resign when a weekend over Baxter's figures convinced him there would be a working-class majority in two-thirds of even the smaller boroughs. Lord Hugh Cecil in 1912 was echoing his father when he ranked 1867 with 1829, 1832, 1846 among the great events on which party struggles had hinged which were disastrous to the Conservative Party. In the first two cases 'resistance was kept up till the mischief done by resistance was already in being' but Disraeli, 'in defiance of the previous attitude and old traditions of his party, ... hurried forward an extension of the franchise before public opinion required it and to the scandal of Conservative sentiment. He was too quick where Peel had been too slow ... The disasters of the elections of 1868 and 1880 were undoubtedly the consequence of *the long step towards democracy**.' To Cranborne, all Disraeli's explanations were a mere smoke-screen raised by one who neither believed in nor dreaded democracy, who belonged to 'a school of politicians who raised surrender to the dignity of a principle.' 'An extension of the suffrage to the working-classes means that upon a question of taxation, or expenditure, ... or vitally affecting commerce, two day-labourers shall out-vote Baron

---

* Present author's italics.

Rothschild,' Cranborne had written in 1864. He believed that
in 1860 they had already begun to descend the sloping path
of popular finance at the end of which lay confiscation, and that
'the struggle between the English constitution and the forces
labouring to subvert it was, in effect, 'between those who have,
to keep [it], and those who have not, to get it'. He had earlier
pronounced that 'the bestowal on any class of a voting power
disproportionate to their stake in the country must infallibly
give to that class a power *pro tanto* of using taxation as an
instrument of plunder.' When universal suffrage was reached,
it would be simple despotism. Already in 1865 he discerned a
new school of ultra-Radicals who believed in the supreme
power of the State and the divine right of the multitude. He
welcomed Fitzjames Stephen's lament in 1873 that 'the
approaching advent of universal suffrage' was widely welcomed 'with something approaching religious enthusiasm' as
a sign that 'Whig' intellectuals were beginning to see the light,
though there was no comfort in Stephen's conclusion, 'The
waters are out and no human force can turn them back, but I
do not see why . . . we need sing Hallelujah to the river god'.[20]
Salisbury had been deeply appalled by the episode of the Paris
Commune, feeling sure its doctrines would cross the Channel
and strike not only at inequality and property but religion and
family and all those features of English life which gave it a
bare chance of being led by its 'natural leaders': 'Always
wealth, in some countries birth, in all intellectual power and
culture, mark out the men to whom, in a healthy state of
feeling, a country looks to undertake its government . . .' Such
men would have leisure, be without taint of sordid greed,
watched closely by the neighbours among whom they were
prominent, and possess a high code of honour. This is a self-
portrait of a high-minded Cecil. But even such 'must be checked
by constitutional forms and watched by an active public
opinion, lest their rightful pre-eminence should degenerate
into the domination of a class.'

It goes without saying that Salisbury saw little hope of such
élitist rule surviving 'the long step towards democracy'. We
have seen his opinion of his former colleagues; 'one or two' had
'shown a freedom from scruple beyond all former example and
others a feebleness of conviction difficult to understand.' He

felt that his own connection with the party, having been 'purely one of principle', was severed. Parties, which ought to be based on mutual confidence between leaders and followers, had become 'nothing but joint-stock companies for the attainment and preservation of place.' His ex-colleagues naturally resented the allegations of political and personal chicanery. Hardy, who could not see that he had violated principle 'as our accusers say', responded very sharply to Cranborne in the House on 31 March 1868. But much may be forgiven to burning sincerity and formidable intellectual power even when, as Disraeli complained, he spoke as though he were the only sane man among lunatics. Nor was it sensible to enter upon government in the sure and certain fear of reading those *Quarterly* articles attacking whatever they did. They needed him, and they asked him back, the less unwillingly because, despising the petty artifices other men used to serve a good cause, he had not embarrassed them by forming a 'Cave'. He had merely moved that their bill do not pass.

CHAPTER 3

Elijah and his Mantle

OPPOSITION TO GLADSTONE (1868-72)

The Cabinet which sent Northcote as an intermediary to invite Cranborne to join was a Disraeli Cabinet. Derby, chronically ill, at last resigned in February 1868, recommending Disraeli to the Queen, saying that he had 'fairly and most honourably' won his way to the highest rung of the political ladder, and writing of twenty years' unreserved and unbroken confidence – which was polite if not true.

Thus ended the partnership between the two utterly diverse characters whom some enemies called 'the Jockey and the Jew' and others 'the Derby and the Hoax'. Partnership between Disraeli and Cranborne there could not yet be. Cranborne told Northcote that 'I had the greatest respect for every member of the Government except one – but that I did not think my honour was safe in the hands of that one'. The concept of Disraeli as still an 'outsider' emerges blatantly in a further comment: 'If I had a firm confidence in his principles or his honesty, *or even if he were identified by birth or property with the Conservative classes in the country*, I might ... work to maintain him in power. But he is an adventurer and as I have good cause to know he is without principles or honesty.' Similar qualms afflicted a young widower who had entered the Commons in 1864, was ambitious, and eminently fitted by his work with Archdeacon Denison among the London poor for the junior office to which he was invited: 'One doesn't want to be committed to the support of other possible Radical measures,' wrote Hicks Beach, known from his appearance as 'Black Michael'.[1] Disraeli was already enlisting material for a strong future Cabinet as he congratulated himself on having reached the top of the greasy pole. The last few feet of the climb had involved, as we have seen, acrobatics of no mean order.

Disraeli inherited business: Scottish and Irish Reform Bills, a most important Act transferring disputed election petitions from partisan Commons committees to judges (much against their will) and a controversial Education Bill. On this last Derby and Disraeli had disagreed, but at Edinburgh on 29 October 1867 Disraeli had stressed the importance of 'study[ing] to make every man the most effective being [possible]' because of 'our limited population' and 'the great imperial position which it occupies'. He had not missed the significance of continental conscript armies and economic advance and protectionism abroad. He also inherited anxieties far and near – a war in Abyssinia and Fenian atrocities in Britain; at Clerkenwell an inept attempt to breach the prison (12 December 1867) had killed twelve and injured over a hundred innocent people. Derby had kept his head, sure that the people would not stand for the suspension of habeas corpus in Britain itself, but fearing 'indiscriminate proscription of Irish Roman Catholics'. And well he might, when he was negotiating with Archbishop Manning for a return to the policy of 'concurrent endowment' favoured by Pitt and Castlereagh, Peel and Graham – and by the Whigs, too, until blown sky-high by Russell's gaffe. It seemed by far the best means of warding off the attack on the Anglican Church in Ireland to which Gladstone 'was no longer loyal as an establishment'. Gladstone sabotaged this by declaring for both disestablishment *and* disendowment of the Irish Church.

This Opposition move was not, at first sight, an election-winner, and Disraeli wrongly thought the Fenian outrages and the toughness of 'Hanging Hardy' might see him through, especially as a moderate line was taken on the Church. In February he (and Cranborne!) had accepted Gladstone's method of abolishing compulsory Church rates in England and now the compromise party in the Cabinet decided to accept the proposition that a modification of the temporalities of the Irish Church might be expedient – though a matter for the

new Parliament – and *Stanley* was deputed to move an amendment to that effect. Derby blazed with anger. And there rose in
majestic wrath after Stanley's speech – described by Hardy as
'the cry of a whipped hound' – Cranborne, making, as it turned
out, his last speech in the Commons. Evidently he had been
right to predict that ministers 'would no doubt give up the
Church too for sake of office'. Such taunts, Hardy noted, were
'felt because deserved'; he, returning from dinner, found the
party 'dismayed, [with] all the symptoms of disorganization
aggravated by ... Cranborne, sneering as regards us all,
venomous and remorseless against Disraeli.' The amendment,
said Cranborne, was 'too clever by half'. He doubted if the
party could restrain their erratic leader, whose intentions were
as unpredictable as tomorrow's weathercock. 'I have seen the
process once before, and I do not wish to see it again', he said.
'Instead of accepting the ambiguous utterances of a more than
Delphic oracle ... if you wish to support the Church you must
come forward and fight in the light' (30 March 1868).

Only a few months earlier Gladstone, a prentice leader of
Opposition outmanoeuvred by Disraeli, had fled to Italy, discredited and humiliated. Now, told in effect by Earl Russell
that he was the leader of the Liberal Party, he reunited it in
the Commons, won a majority of 61 (4 April) and was greeted
outside and in, as Palmerston had sometimes been, and Disraeli
on 12 April the year before. The elections, held as soon as the
new registers were ready, were conducted in the old-fashioned
way by the Tory managers under Col. T. E. Taylor (chief
party whip since 1859) and Gerard Noel, the taint of corruption
afflicting even the ejection of John Stuart Mill by one who was
to be known as 'Old Morality'. W. H. Smith of the bookstalls,
born 'over the shop' in the Strand in 1825, the new member for
Westminster, appeared as a portent of the switch from
Palmerstonian Conservatism to the Conservative Party of
moderate Liberals afraid of Gladstone, including the middle-
class commuters on the suburban lines – 'professional men,
tradesmen and clerical employees' – to whom another future
Cabinet minister, Lord George Hamilton, attributed his
victory in Middlesex.[2] In England, the election had its usual
result. The Tories took the whole net increase in the county
seats effected by the redistribution; this gain of nearly thirty

was exactly cancelled by the effect of the borough redistribution. The extent to which the Tories were an *English* national party was emphasised by 220 of their MPs again coming from English constituencies. But now it was 220 (of an English total of 467) out of a party total of 276, for in Wales, Scotland and Ireland there was a net loss of 31, Scotland out of its 60 seats giving them only 8 (none in a burgh) and Wales 8 out of its 30.[3] Gladstone owed his majority of 100 less perhaps to his relatively recent contacts with Nonconformist leaders and the Liberation Society than, as he said, to Scottish Presbyterians, Welsh Nonconformists (partly motivated by feeling against their Anglicised landlords) and Irish Papists. He ought to have excepted from the first category many members of the official kirk, and recognised that the connection with the Irish Catholics was counterproductive in Lancashire, where even in Preston the Tories had easy victories and Cobbett failed at Oldham by six votes; that, here, each of the four candidates for the two seats polled between 6084 and 6140, combined with the expectations of neo-Palmerstonian support not only growing but redistributing itself into new suburbs in county seats, would stack the English constituencies against the Liberals. On the surface, the Conservatives did not seem to have gained much from 'the policy of legerdemain' which Cranborne (now Salisbury) had denounced. But there were promising growth points, and soon a brilliant young barrister, John Gorst, was employed by Disraeli to identify and exploit them.

Meanwhile, Disraeli did something far more democratic than his acceptance of Hodgkinson's amendment. He recognised *vox populi* and resigned without waiting to be defeated in the new Parliament. Gladstone, more orthodox, thought this rather unconstitutional, but reluctantly (in 1874) accepted the precedent and it became the norm, when the result of an election was clear-cut, broken only by Salisbury in 1892.

Salisbury had declared that 'hostility to Radicalism, incessant, implacable, hostility, is the essential definition of Conservatism' and it had been remarked that he spoke like a Legitimist Bourbon. He now revealed that he was not to be the kind of diehard whose views disqualify him from the offices for which his talents fit him. He would not sit on the front bench with the Ulsterman Cairns who had recommended the Stanley amendment. Cairns resigned the leadership in the Lords (1869) after contriving in secret with Granville a compromise on the Irish Church. Stanley, now by the death of the former Premier on 23 October 1869 14th Earl of Derby, fortunately declined the succession. When the duty fell on the humdrum Duke of Richmond, Salisbury consented to sit alongside him, though still refusing to participate in party counsels. He said the future lay with a Tory–Whig coalition, though he did not see how he would fit into it, let alone be qualified to lead it. He began to write on subtly new lines. If it was true that 'the party of movement lives on discontent and, as each successive cause of discontent is removed ... [it] must find some new object of complaint', was it not also true that, shying away from 'a vista of perpetual subversion', the moderate men of property who had been the major support of Palmerston would move away from them? After all, there was now much more of a common interest between the classes than had previously been the case. And, a point to be emphasised in the next century by Quintin Hogg, and too frequently forgotten by political historians and political scientists, 'the vast mass of every nation is non-political'. Salisbury began not only to hope for but to believe in 'the swing of the pendulum', since the army of Reform at every stage converted a detachment of its followers into opponents. So often accused, and not unjustly, of lacking a sense of proportion, he made, as he approached his fortieth year, that crucial graduation from the over-logical, over-vehement polemicist, demanding of leaders impossible standards of consistency, to the potential leader, the potential statesman. Conservatives should 'make up their minds what is worth struggling for', he now said. 'Let them maturely decide, before the conflict begins, what is essential and what is of secondary importance'. And, further, 'concessions made before a contest are no sign of weakness.'[4]

This was Salisbury's *Tamworth Manifesto*! Indeed, he did what his son and grandson, also leading their party in the Lords, also did – perhaps with little choice, but not necessarily to the nation's advantage. When in his very first speech to the peers he denounced Gladstone for planning the spoliation of a great corporation, the Church of Ireland, for 'party expediency', he asked the Lords not to agree to it until 'the firm, deliberate, sustained convictions of the nation' had been tested at an election. Did he foresee that this was an invitation to parties to issue lengthy manifestos and then propose measures, however inappropriate to the circumstances of the time, on the basis of 'We've got a mandate'? On 17 June 1869 he urged surrender on the Irish Church because the nation had spoken. But what had it spoken for? A massive majority of peers would have been willing to uphold the old policy of 'concurrent endowment' rather than the 'lay appropriation' on which the dying Derby had his replay of the battles of 1834–7 with Russell. Henceforth Salisbury's maxim (as when the Opposition abstained but he opposed the Government on the secret ballot, 1872) was 'We yield only to the nation at the polls'. He deplored the failure of the Lords to insist on their amendments to the Irish Land Bill and the measure to abolish University tests, partly on the merits, and partly because 'otherwise our position in the Constitution will be purely decorative'. He joined with Russell in an attempt to secure the appointment of a limited number of life peers representing commerce and industry who knew about the health and morals of the people – inadequately studied by their Lordships – and, when taunted with the moderation of his proposals, made the uncharacteristic reply that 'all change to be wholesome must be gradual ... I do not like ... a policy which produces a transformation scene once every two or three years'.

Salisbury was, however, still ambivalent. His closest friend Carnarvon, still feared his 'wild elephant' moods. Everything the Liberals proposed he opposed – the Irish Land Act 1870; the abolition of the purchase of army commissions; open competition for the civil service; the abolition of University tests without safeguards to prevent teaching which would make the places 'citadels of infidelity'; even Forster's Education Act of 1870, establishing school boards only where the voluntary schools were manifestly inadequate, on which there was a good deal of concert between Forster and the Tory front bencher Lord Sandon, aided by W. H. Smith. On university reform he made a 'blazing speech'. On the Irish Land Bill he made the very good point that for Ireland to live under a free constitution was very dangerous, since Irishmen would not listen to argument or allow 'remedial measures' to take effect until they had been taught that, whereas in Britain one could guide, 'there you must govern' (Lords, 29 March 1870).

Meanwhile, at Hughenden, Disraeli had been writing *Lothair*, published the day after May Day 1870 and selling well, as it deserved. While Salisbury held that the fiscal question was the key one – 'democracy' allowing the poor to rob the rich by legal means – Disraeli contended in his *Reminiscences* that 'it will, generally, be found that all great political questions end in the tenure of land. What is the nature of that tenure is the first question a Statesman should ask himself'. To this question, in relation to Ireland, Gladstone on 1869–70 addressed himself for the first time, thirty years after Disraeli had made (9 August 1843) a penetrating analysis of the Irish Question as not one of politics or religion but of over-population and tragic sub-tenure. This achieved a European reputation (for the problem was a continental one) and is rightly quoted in almost every book on the Irish Question. Then the Irish land problem had been partially solved by what Trollope called 'the Famine, the Pestilence and the Exodus' and the Peel-inspired Encumbered Estates Act 1849, unfairly called by Disraeli 'the Act of Confiscation'. Now, twenty years later, the Tories contended that the Liberals, wrongly diagnosing as 'national' a conspiracy emanating from the United States and Rome, had recognised, in relation to the Church of Ireland, 'principles of socialism' equally applicable to the estate and the park. After all, it was landlords and their agents who were being murdered and assaulted, not Church of Ireland clergy, who walked in peace and safety. Though making the point that the Tories had supported all the proposals of the Devon Commission of 1845, which by 1860 were law – apart from compensation for tenants' improvements, which he supported – Disraeli opposed both 'compensation for disturbance' and the Bright clauses intended in 1870 to advance peasant ownership of tenancies.[5] By contrast, Salisbury applauded these virtually inoperative provisions, his studies of post-Napoleonic France having convinced him that the widespread ownership of land made for stability and social cohesion. In this rather roundabout way Salisbury may be identified as the author of the twentieth-century Tory concept of the 'property-owning democracy'. He had switched from arguing that only those with a stake in the

country should vote to, at least in germ, the idea that all
entitled to vote should be encouraged to take a stake in the
country, which would tend to make their voting habits conservative. It is notorious that in the twentieth century home
ownership, even with a heavy mortgage, has proved as strong a
Conservative electoral asset as council house tenancies, often
granted to those who do not need them, and at the expense of
those who do, have been for Labour.

It was, however, that Liberal opponent of democracy,
Robert Lowe, who said 'We must educate our masters' and the
way in which this should be done never ceased to be an issue
during, and for some time after, Salisbury's life. At his resignation Derby believed that 95 per cent coverage could be achieved
in a few years by state aid to any religious body which provided
schools. Gladstone's special contribution to Forster's Act of
1870 – large increases in state grants to voluntary schools,
mostly Anglican, but also Roman Catholic and Wesleyan,
combined with the principle that rate-sustained school boards
should come into existence only where the voluntary schools
manifestly failed to meet the need – made a special contribution to his defeat in the next election. It led to a serious rift in
the Liberal Party and the rise of Joseph Chamberlain's
National Education League to press for free, compulsory and
secular education. Its failure, though turning Chamberlain
into a national figure, led to Liberal apathy and abstention
in the 1874 election. Disraeli at Manchester (3 April 1872) was
able to express mortification that Nonconformists worthy of
respect should have become from envy or pique partisans of a
merely secular education.

DISRAELI'S SEMINAL SPEECHES (1872)

In *The Prime Ministers* John Vincent remarks on how sparingly
Disraeli, operating in the age before the political leader moved
from platform to platform, 'used his great talent for making
the kind of speech that achieves a sweeping redefinition.'
The famous speech at Manchester's Free Trade Hall and the
shorter one at the Crystal Palace on the following 26 June
have ever afterwards constituted the *locus classicus* of the Tory
faith.

Disraeli had maintained Derby's 'policy of patience', which he now imposed upon himself, almost too long, so that it looked like Derbyite lethargy. And, indeed, the leader was afflicted with gout and other woes, culminating in the death of his wife from cancer. In January 1872 five of the MPs who had been in his Cabinet met Cairns and Marlborough at Lord Exeter's mansion, Burghley, and agreed that Disraeli 'has not the position in the House and country to enable him to do what others might.' Only Manners denied knowledge of such a feeling out of doors and only he and Northcote dissented from the view of the chief whip, Noel, that Derby (the former Stanley) would be worth forty or fifty seats. They seem to have overlooked the fact that, by entrusting the central agency to the indefatigible John Gorst in 1870, Disraeli had ensured that the party machinery in the constituencies was far better than ever before and in crucial seats superior to that of the Liberals. It was Gorst who, with much difficulty (partly due to the Stanley lobby and partly to controversies as to venue) contrived the Manchester visit. The speech was the culmination of a vast parade and the presentation of two hundred addresses from the county divisions, boroughs and townships of the whole country.[6]

It is in this context that the form and balance of the speech have to be assessed, and criticism that only a relatively small part of it was devoted to the theme *Sanitas sanitatum, omnia sanitas* overlooks this. It was, in general, the standard speech familiar to the electors of Shrewsbury thirty years before, spiced by attacks on the Gladstone Government – 'the first avowedly formed on the principle of violence . . . proceeding like a body of men under the influence of some deleterious drug' and now reminding him of 'a range of exhausted volcanoes'. The personal influence of the monarch and the value of the nation being 'represented by a family' were defended against critics of its cost (the Queen was not publicly active). At the Crystal Palace Disraeli would say that 'the advanced guard of Liberalism [had] flatly announced itself Republican'. At Manchester the peers, worth, according to Gladstone, £9 million, were declared representative of the 30 millions of men, women and children who did not have the vote; only 2,200,000 did. They represented property, 'visible . . . and therefore responsible property . . .

generally territorial' and were the more responsible because hereditary. At the Crystal Palace, Disraeli added that they possessed all the virtues required of a senate – 'independence, great local influence, eloquence, all the accomplishments of political life, and a public training which no theory could supply. The liberty of England was declared to depend much upon 'the fact that there is a class which can alike defy despots and mobs, around which the people may always rally, and which must be patriotic from its intimate connection with the soil.' The gist of the Edinburgh speech of November 1867 was repeated – the Whigs' 'abolition of those ancient franchises which the working classes had exercised from time immemorial' had been the origin of Chartism and thirty years' electoral un-ease. This the late Lord Derby had dealt with by an act described at the Crystal Palace as 'founded on a confidence that the great body of the people were Conservative.' The existence of the established church constituted 'a national profession of faith', the combination of which with 'unlimited enjoyment of private judgement in matters spiritual' was 'one of the triumphs of civilisation.' Its comprehensiveness was a virtue. Disestablishment would probably strengthen the Church and weaken the State.

'In political institutions are embodied the experience of a race,' said Disraeli, so it was due to the institutions that an island intended by Nature to be the appendage of some Continental Empire had been 'the only inviolate land', attract-ing all the capital of the world, its flag floating on many waters.

The agricultural labourers were told that the farmers could not afford higher wages, but that they were entitled to form responsible trade unions. The poor in general were told that the increase in means and leisure – 'the two civilisers of men' – assisted by locomotion, cheap postage and an unshackled press, should be further assisted by 'judicial and prudential legisla-tion' and with practical sanitary objects like pure air and water, the inspection of unhealthy dwellings, protection of food and drugs. 'It is impossible to overrate the importance of the subject', avowed the Leader of the Opposition; '*the first con-sideration of a minister should be the health of the people.*' At the Crystal Palace the NUCCA representatives – receiving signifi-

cant recognition at last, because of the pressure of Gorst, who
had nursed their movement – heard from Disraeli that one of
the three great objects of the Tory Party was 'the elevation of
the condition of the people.' The Liberals had 'opposed the
Tory Party when, even in their weakness, they . . . introduced
and supported those Factory Laws, the principles of which
they extended, in the brief period when they possessed power,
to every other trade in the country' (a reference to Spencer
Walpole's Acts of 1867, which covered even small workshops).
A rising Liberal politician had scoffed at 'a policy of sewage'.
But this, to 'one of the labouring multitude of England . . .
[was] a question of life and death. The hereditary, the traditionary policy of the Tory party, that would improve the conditions of the people, is more appreciated by the people than the
ineffable mysteries and all the pains and penalties of the Ballot
Bill . . . Why, the people of England would be even greater
idiots than the Jacobinical leaders of London suppose, if . . .
they should not have long seen that the time had arrived when
social and not political improvement is the object which they
ought to pursue.'

Disraeli went to Lancashire well briefed by Gorst on that
uniquely fertile soil for a composite Conservatism that played
on hopes and fears. Here the Conservatives were working 'with
the grain' of social and religious influences; here the two parties
met, as they rarely did elsewhere in so large an area, on equal
terms. Manners thought in 1849 that 'Oastler was the one
great engine by which the Manufacturing Districts could be
worked'; only four years later the young Lord Stanley saw in
Oastler's sworn foes 'these Lancashire manufacturers, material
for Conservative principles to work upon.'[7] By 1872 the Conservative Party had enough middle-class support 'to put it on a
parity with the Liberals.' In some places where the Liberals
'seemed the instrument of the rich and powerful', the Tories
were the popular party, their candidate F. S. Powell (just
returned for the West Riding North division, a Tory gain)
attributing his defeat by 156 at Stalybridge, in the 1871 by-
election, to the absence of the ballot, which he supported.
But many Conservative and Liberal employers alike were
accepted as pillars and benefactors of the local community and
prospective MPs. They reciprocated by declaring sympathy

with trade unions, co-operatives and friendly societies, as well as factory legislation. Disraeli would find such a one in W. R. Callender, MP for Manchester. 'Class' had become, for a time, less important. 'The two nations' of *Sybil* had grown together in defiance of the rubric of Engels (a Lancashire businessman) and Marx, the former complaining to the latter on 7 October 1858 that 'the English proletariat is actually becoming more bourgeois.'

Religion was the opium, though no word could be less appropriate to Lancashire's singularly muscular brand of Anglican Evangelicalism, which attracted converts from the Wesleyans and Congregationalists – and from Liberalism similarly – like Callender. Here the Church of England had risen to the challenge as Disraeli in speech and novel long ago, and in the Oxford diocese 1861–4 had cried out that it must. Here, too, the Roman Catholics, always thicker on the ground than in most parts of Britain, but reinforced by hordes of indigent Irishmen (though Ulster Protestants came over too), vied with the Anglicans in building churches and schools. Sectarian differences, especially between Catholic and Protestant, and most of all when allied to economic and social competition dragging down standards, have their nasty aspect, seen at its worst in the Stockport riots of 1852, and long institutionalised in Liverpool, from trade unions upwards through every stratum of society. P. F. Clarke, on whom we depend for the rounded picture, writes:

'In Lancashire the working class was characterised by Conservative politics and aggressive Churchmanship; by a certain racial and religious intolerance; by acceptance of good Tory principles of hierarchy, loyalty, and a solid unquestioning patriotism which could slide into jingoism.'

Disraeli's Manchester speech should be read in the light of this verdict, with the defence of institutions coming first, and the Church praised, though no colour given to religious intolerance. For the Roman Catholics hated the school boards set up by the Liberal Government under the pressure of Liberal Nonconformists, and some of the boards which were set up – because the voluntary schools simply could not cope with the demand – were run by Anglican–Papist coalitions, as was Manchester's for twenty years under its sometime Tory MP, Hugh Birley.

One should add that the Oastler–Ferrand tradition still had the power, in an area with some of the oldest and most powerful craft unions, of producing influential Tory trade union leaders – such as the two chief officials of the Manchester Trades Council at the time of Disraeli's visit. Among the spinners, the Mawdesly family, father and son, spanned the era from Ashley's act via Disraeli (through the Tory Democracy which Lord Randolph Churchill attributed to Disraeli) to partnership in the Oldham by-election of 1899, with the young Winston Churchill as a Tory.

EMPIRE BECOMES AN ISSUE

The last phrase of the quotation from Clarke is seminal. There was among the workers of Lancashire 'a solid unquestioning patriotism which could slide into jingoism'. The Manchester School's vision of a world civilised by Free Trade and international arbitration has for us a quality of unreality, but when Disraeli went to Manchester in 1872 the full peril of Britain's adoption of Free Trade as a religious dogma had not yet become apparent, though within ten years Farrer Ecroyd would win Preston as a Protectionist. When Disraeli said that nobody was interested in foreign affairs, however, he knew very well that in an area so dependent on foreign and imperial trade this simply was not true. In the China War election of 1857 Rochdale had defeated Bright and Manchester had sent its passivist MPs away to pastures new. '. . . that newer Conservatism of which Benjamin Disraeli was the great apostle', says Clarke, was 'no democratic creed but an outgrowth of Palmerstonian Liberalism'. He is referring to the conversion of the ultra-Radical William Houldsworth, and such men were at least as interested in 'opening up' the undeveloped markets of the world as in the maintenance of the domestic status quo. The retention of profits by a fiscal system bearing mainly on articles of general consumption (Gladstonianism) and the opening of new markets in which there would be, if not advantage, at least fair competition with the foreigner (Palmerstonianism) was bound to be popular in Lancashire and – whether the British Government was Conservative or Liberal – blot the copybook of British rule in India.

Imperialist *expansion* was not yet a prime issue. But a potential belligerence repugnant to the late Cobden and the current Bright (recently resigned from Gladstone's Cabinet) lay dormant. At Manchester Disraeli, while knocking the Liberals for their diplomatic humiliations over the *Alabama* claims and the Russian repudiation of the 1856 treaty – of particular interest to the local Roebuck Conservative and Sick and Burial Society, for it was Roebuck who had proposed the motion which led to the replacement of Aberdeen by Palmerston in 1855 – denied that he had ever favoured a turbulent and aggressive diplomacy. Britain's policy in Europe should be one of reserve, but of *proud* reserve. The Empire he mentioned only in his peroration: 'I believe that [the people were] never prouder of the Imperial country to which they belong . . . I now deliver to you . . . the cause of the Tory Party, the English Constitution, and of the British Empire'. Less than three months later, at the Crystal Palace, 'to uphold the Empire of England' had become the *second* great object of the Tory Party, following the defence of the Constitution and preceding the elevation of the condition of the people.

When the Protectionists first broke from Peel, it was Bentinck rather than Disraeli who talked of obligations and duty to the Empire, and, though Disraeli said it would one day have to be reconstructed, the tendency had been for almost every leading politician to be either a pessimist or fatalist as to the future of imperial ties, with an important smattering of separatists who actively willed what the others thought, in the course of nature, or on the American precedent, inevitable. Radical separatists, Disraeli complained in 1849, held the Empire up to hatred as maintained for the benefit of rapacious aristocratic families – *their* system of outdoor relief, as Bright called it. They complained – and Lord Robert Cecil had agreed with them – that the burden of imperial defence and the need to extricate 'the black sheep of our colonial flock' (i.e. the Whites of South Africa and New Zealand) from native wars brought on by their impolicy, constituted a very bad financial bargain for the privilege of indulging in the sentiment that 'the sun never sets

on our Empire' (a Palmerstonian boast). But the majority were
pessimists, concerned, if at all, with the problem of how separation could be accomplished with mutual goodwill. Gladstone
was of their number, and often Disraeli. He had said at
Shrewsbury in 1843 'I, for one, am not prepared to sit under the
power of a third-class if I can be the citizen of a first-class
Empire.' As Chancellor of the Exchequer, he complained
(privately) of 'these millstones round our necks' and 'these
colonial deadweights which we do not govern'.

So great had been the emigration to North America and
Australasia that many a British citizen had kith and kin there,
and few villages had not seen off some young man or family
for such parts. Yet the public seemed to show little interest in
'colonial ties' until the Gladstone Government of 1868 appeared
to wish to break them. It had been agreed to reduce colonial
garrisons, but under Lord Granville the tone of the Colonial
Office towards New Zealand seemed unduly querulous, and it
looked as though he wished to be rid of Canada (federated in
1867 under Carnarvon). At once dormant senses of solidarity
bestirred themselves, and the public men's mood of a quarter of
a century was challenged. Disraeli grasped the opportunity. He
had, Lord Hugh Cecil would write (1912) in another context, 'a
penetrating power of judging the dominant tendencies and
movements of his time and whither they were likely to lead.'
Sensing the resentment induced by the combination of an
apparently ineffective foreign policy and a 'Little England'
attitude towards the empire of British settlement, he decided
that at the Crystal Palace he would elevate this into a major
Conservative theme.[8]

There was a good hook to hang it on. Consistently he had
contrasted 'national' with 'foreign' or 'cosmopolitan' principles,
traditionary manners with abstract principles. So, at the Crystal
Palace, he held that the first principle of the party was to
maintain the institutions of the country against those 'influenced
in a great degree by the philosophy and politics of the Continent'
who 'endeavoured to substitute cosmopolitan for national
principles' under 'the plausible name of "Liberalism".' But the
great body of the people were 'Conservative':

'I mean that the people of England, and especially the working-

classes, are proud of belonging to a great country and wish to
maintain its greatness – that *they are proud of belonging to an
Imperial country, and wish, if they can, to maintain their Empire* . . .
They are English to the core. They repudiate cosmopolitan
principles. They are for maintaining the greatness of the
Kingdom and of the Empire and they are proud of being
subjects of our Sovereign and members of such an Empire . . .'

Then, after an interlude on the Church, to be encouraged
by 'the National Party', comes the major innovatory statement:
that it is 'the second great object' of the party

'*to uphold the Empire of England*. If you look into the history of
this country since the advent of Liberalism – forty years ago –
you will find that there has been no effort so continuous, so
subtle, supported by so much energy . . . ability and acumen,
as the attempt of Liberalism to effect the disintegration of the
Empire of England.

'And, gentlemen, of all its efforts, this is the one which has
been nearest to success . . . I confess that I myself thought that
the tie was broken . . .

'Well, what has been the result of this attempt during the
reign of Liberalism for the disintegration of the Empire? It has
entirely failed. But how has it failed? Through the sympathies
of the Colonies with the Mother Country. They have decided
that the Empire shall not be destroyed, and in my opinion no
minister in this country will do his duty who neglects any
opportunity of reconstructing as much as possible of our
Colonial Empire, and of responding to those distant sympa-
thisers which may become the source of incalculable strength
and happiness to this land.'

The apparent attempt of the Liberals to hasten separation, the
effect of which could not have been to pacify the world but to
provoke infinite international complications – difficult enough
to deal with in Fiji (which Gladstone annexed), Samoa and
New Guinea (to say nothing of Africa) without adding Australia
and New Zealand to the list – was to provoke at home a mood
of disquiet at rebuffs to that 'determination to maintain the
closest and most affectionate relations with the Mother

Country' professed from the colony of Victoria by Gavin Duffy who had left his mother country (Ireland) as a rebel in 1848. Disraeli seized upon it. At Edinburgh in 1867 he had merely made a ritual reference, appropriate to Scotsmen, who specialised in expatriates to the colonies, to 'a circle of domestic settlements which watch us for example and inspiration'. Now he sensed a revived feeling of solidarity between the far-flung subjects of the Queen and spoke wistfully of lost opportunities of imperial consolidation. In less than twenty years Lord Rosebery, a Liberal Imperialist, was christening the 'British Commonwealth' in a speech in the Antipodes. But to unite the Empire of settlement without affronting the growing autonomy of its members proved easier said than done and Cobden and Bright, Peel and Gladstone, had done their work too well to enable the British to restore the preferential trading ties which principally interested the self-governing colonies. But it is *Imperium et Libertas*, not *Auctoritas et Sanitas*, which appears on the banners of the Primrose League, formed to keep Disraelian attitudes alive.

VICTORY AND SOCIAL REFORM

The clarion had sounded, with what effect we cannot tell, as the Tories had a net gain of about six a year in the by-elections of 1871–3. While impatient followers chafed, the leaders felt it was a matter of waiting for the victory that had so long eluded them. When Gladstone resigned after his grotesque Irish Universities Bill of 1873 was defeated by three votes on 16 March 1873, Disraeli declined to form a government on the advice of colleagues to wait for the fast-maturing Conservatism of the country to ripen; '. . . if we appeal to the country before the breach in the Liberal ranks is fully made, and before the policy of the extreme men is fully developed, we consolidate them . . . ,' Northcote advised, referring to 'hallucinations which have attached a great mass of moderate men to the Liberal cause', now disintegrating (14 March 1873).

Gladstone had offended interest groups pillaged, harassed or menaced – though some felt that the exaggeration with which Disraeli stated this lost Bath for the Tories in October. The Liberal Premier had certainly cooled the ardour of his active

party workers, the Nonconformist chapel folk over education
and licensing and temperance, and the trade union politicians
(also often chapel folk) over the labour laws. He had lost his
way, his nerve and his touch; perhaps even his interest.
Scandals forced the resignation of ministers; what looked like
sharp practice over an ecclesiastical and a legal appointment
scarred even his own personal rectitude. The arbitrators'
award to the United States on the *Alabama* claims – though in
general supported patriotically by the Conservatives – was felt
to be humiliating and unfair. Everything was going wrong for
Gladstone, who, conscious of his own integrity, blamed his
party and his colleagues as unworthy of him and precipitately
sprang upon the nation an election (January 1874) in which it
was apparently to decide – without knowing that it had to do
so – whether it was to abolish the income tax, reduce local
burdens and the duties on consumer goods, which the service
ministers said was quite impossible.

The result was a famous Conservative victory, the first since
1841 and due not merely to Disraeli's thirty-year struggle but
to his franchise and redistribution of 1867–8. He secured a
majority of over 50, although Irish losses to Home Rulers partially offset the twelve gains in Scotland, where he had been
well received as the student-elected Rector of Glasgow University a few months before. The Conservative Party was still
very much an English Nationalist party with 288 of its 352 MPs
elected there, and 68 of its net 78 gains collected there.[9] The
cheers which greeted Disraeli at the service to celebrate the
recovery from illness of the heir to the throne (March 1872)
proved to have foreshadowed eight gains in the deliberately
under-represented metropolis. Lancashire and Cheshire were
already so Tory that they could provide few gains. But outside
these two areas came 27 gains in the larger boroughs, and the
Tories held a higher proportion of the seats in the English
'industrial counties' than in the English counties as a whole
(where their tally was 145 out of 172; (net gain 18)). There was
evidently a considerable middle-class movement against a
radical government, a garnering of the votes of which the Tories
had been deprived by Palmerston. Education was an important
issue: Manning had told Hardy the Nonconformists expected
the Roman vote but would not get it as 'we do not want to pull

down anything in England'. Nearly 200,000 compounders having got onto the register, Gladstone chose to blame 'the residuum' and, having come second to a Tory brewer at Greenwich, spoke of being borne down by 'a torrent of gin and beer'. There is nothing to justify this except that many a working man had 'no social centre except the public-house' and the Liberal temperance advocate Sir Wilfred Lawson admitted the power of the Tory jingle, 'We've shortened the hours of labour, and lengthened the hours of drink.' The new Home Secretary, Richard Cross, who had ousted Gladstone from his Lancashire constituency in 1868, at once restored Fielden's Factory Act (substituting a 56½-hour week for a 60-hour week) and amended his Liberal predecessor's Licensing Act.

The smallest Cabinet between 1832 and 1916 contained nine departmental heads, of whom six were able or more than able, and the rest, other than Derby at the Foreign Office, adequate.[10] Only one of these – Manners – had been with Disraeli in the 'Who? Who?' Cabinet of 1852 or, indeed, in Parliament at the time of the 1846 disruption. These were 'modern' men who took Free Trade for granted. The oldest, Hardy, was only sixty; he represented the northern tradition of social reform by an enlightened business family, and also the Oxford Movement, having sat at the feet of Newman at Oriel. The man with whom he was most likely to quarrel was the Ulster Lord Chancellor, Cairns. The youngest members, at 43 and 44, were the other Anglo-Catholics, Carnarvon and Salisbury, the resigners of 1867. The only man raised straight to the Cabinet with no official experience was Lancashire's Richard Assheton Cross, aged 51. Destined to join or supersede them in Cabinet were a strong reserve, including W. H. Smith (49), Financial Secretary to the Treasury, Lord Sandon, Hicks Beach, Colonel Stanley (important mainly as Derby's brother) and Lord George Hamilton (in 1874 aged only 29). Some mistakes were, almost inevitably, made. It was thought wise to exclude from the Cabinet the noted colonial and social reformer, Adderley, and his conduct of the Merchant Shipping Bill, 1875, made the Liberals' champion of the imperilled seamen, Samuel Plimsoll, 'dance with rage'. (Plimsoll got his Act the next year.) Sclater-Booth, who in view of his numerous legislative chores probably ought to have been in the Cabinet, was so unfortunate as to encounter in 1878 the lashing tongue of Randolph Churchill (aged 29) who, regardless of the fact that his family name was sometimes Spencer-Churchill, remarked 'how often we find mediocrity dowered with a double-barrelled name'. Churchill had chosen to rise by the Disraeli and Cecil technique of flaming denunciation of leaders for 'desertion of Tory principles . . . violation of political honesty' etc.[11] and, in the new era of platform oratory in the early 1880s, drew crowds rivalling those of Gladstone and Chamberlain – and amused them a great deal more.

Disraeli's great catch in 1874 was, of course, Salisbury, who said that 'the prospect of having to serve with this man is like a nightmare' but could find no justification for refusing except 'intense personal dislike', and wrongly believed that Disraeli did not want him. He insisted on the India Office. Disraeli would have given him anything he asked, for it was true, despite what the clever young men say, that Disraeli, of whom Bulwer had remarked that he was the only man he knew who preferred power to fame, achieved power too late – twenty years too late, he said, remembering the 'days when, on waking, I could move dynasties and governments'. A visit to Spartan Balmoral (only once repeated) guaranteed a chill, bronchitis and gout. Within a few months there was talk of his retirement. Gouty, asthmatic, weary, lonely – despite the attentions of Monty Corry – he had to retire (August 1876) to the Lords as Earl of Beaconsfield, 'dead, but in the Elysian fields'. His life, imperilled by the side effects (nausea, headaches, aggravation of gout and acute depression) of 'orthodox' treatment for asthma and Bright's disease, was prolonged only by a homeopath discovered for him by Cairns in October 1877. In choosing his successor as leader in the Commons, Beaconsfield made what was only later, when Gladstone (who had resigned the Liberal leadership in 1875) became Prime Minister again, seen as a gross error. He passed over the man he had called 'my sword-arm' and had indicated as his successor (1872) on the ground that, being at the War Office, 'our best speaker, and never happier than when you make a party speech' had 'not been prominently before the House'. This was Gathorne Hardy who, ambitious and badly treated, perhaps as a result of pressure from a very high quarter, lost his zest and insisted in the spring of 1878 on becoming Earl of Cranbrook. This deprived the Cabinet in the Commons of 'our strongest man in debate' and the party in the next election (in which it was not etiquette for peers to take part) of its fiercest high-level combatant, and left it in the next House under the inefficient leadership of Sir Stafford Northcote, who drew the lucky straw in 1876. Blake suggests as reasons for passing over Hardy his hot temper, his habit of going home to dinner, and the dislike of Lord Derby, who certainly represented Lancashire (and the Queen) in suspicion of Hardy's High Churchmanship. This was displayed in action in alliance with Gladstone in the Commons and Salisbury in the Lords over the Public Worship Regulation Bill of 1874, an amalgam essentially concocted by Disraeli and Cairns when the Archbishop, strongly prodded by the Evangelicals under Shaftesbury, had made a sorry mess of things. Hardy (July 1874) had found 'the greater part of the House, and especially our own side, hot for the measure ... our friends are mad – and show a profound ignorance of what a Church is'. Salisbury said the bill would cause civil war in the Church – and it ·did.

In office with power, the Conservatives redeemed Disraeli's promise of social reform, though to speak of 'a package' would be misleading, and of a package masterminded by the Premier grossly misleading. Cross, expecting to find Disraeli full of legislative schemes, found him 'above or below mere questions of detail'. But we learn from Feuchtwanger how much Gladstone, personally immersed in the measures that were to 'pacify Ireland', left to his departmental chiefs in 1868–74. Bills come out of departmental pigeon-holes or result from official inquiries such as that instituted and chaired by Adderley from 1868 on the sanitary laws which led to the Liberals' Public Health Act, improved in 1875 and 1880 by Sclater-Booth, who also passed the Sale of Food and Drugs Act and the River Pollution Act, both of 1875, showing that Manchester and the Crystal Palace had meant something. Cross set up a royal commission which led to the consolidation of factory legislation in 1878. The criticism that Cross's Artisans' Dwelling Act 1875 was not widely adopted Disraeli met in advance: 'permissive legislation is the characteristic of a free people.' A go-ahead authority like Birmingham under Joseph

Chamberlain found Cross helpful in securing it the necessary powers by local Act. Even the Chancellor of the Exchequer, Northcote, got into the social reforming action with a Friendly Society Act pressed on Disraeli by Callender.

Cross's greatest problem concerned the law relating to trade unions, whose contact-man with parliamentarians, irate that the Liberals' Trade Union Act 1870 recognised the right to strike without making it at all safe to do so effectively for fear of their new Criminal Law Amendment Act, the old Masters and Servants Act and the common law, had got the TUC at Sheffield in January 1874 to call on working-men to oppose candidates who would not denounce the status quo. He expected action from the new Government for whose victory working-class support was partly responsible – and rightly, for Disraeli had on 10 August 1873 asked Hardy for a memorandum 'on the Law of Conspiracy, and the Statutes which regulate the relations between master and men' adding 'the subject will press us'. Cross's proposal of a royal commission was therefore regarded as 'an adroit move' for evasion and delay, which labour men should boycott. But Cross promised legislation for 1875 and, finding the draft report would uphold the Liberal point of view, furnished Howell (who had assisted the Liberal victory in 1868) with the means of issuing a simultaneous critique. When bills appeared, Cross, backed in Cabinet by Disraeli, 'did an 1867' on them. And so the Conspiracy and Protection of Property Act repealed the 1871 measure; nothing done in combination would be illegal unless it would have been unlawful for one person to do it and peaceful picketing was protected by the removal of obnoxious and obscure phrases, one of the new clauses being Howell's own. The Masters and Servants Acts gave way to the Employers and Workmen Act, a significant recognition of the existence of a mature capitalist society. It put the two sides on parity over breach of contract. The specially privileged position accorded to the unions constituted a settlement for a generation, when the courts began to erode it. Howell's official report to the TUC said that Cross had conceded more than all the demands of successive congresses.[12]

Disraeli told the Queen he did not remember 'so many important and truly popular measures' carried in any session.

His own public contribution was to bring the squires to heel on the Agricultural Holdings Bill at 'a most satisfactory meeting of the party . . . Disraeli never spoke better.' In view of the record it seems captious of Lord Blake to hold that the Government had no programme and 'Disraeli had little idea what to do', especially as he admits that this was the biggest instalment of social reform in the nineteenth century. Disraeli hoped that social reform was 'a policy round which the country could rally', even that the Conservatives would 'retain . . . the lasting affection of the working-classes.'[13]

And why not? Here was a basis for 'Tory Democracy', sustained by Lancashire's church bells. Northcote was a more sympathetic figure than that anti-democrat Lowe, who had brought the match-girls out on strike against his tax on a necessity, and Cross more sympathetic than Bruce, the Home Secretary with whom the TUC had such trouble, a leading light of Powell Duffryn. Meanwhile, in Ireland, Hicks Beach got a pound for pound grant for draining the Shannon; made it possible (1875) for the ratepayers to support the 'national' elementary schools – undenominational only in name; promoted the Intermediate Education Act 1878 under which inspected schools would receive a 'float' of £1 million from the surplus funds of the disestablished Church (with a conscience clause accepted by Cardinal Cullen and the Presbyterians). He also paved the way for his successor, Lowther, to pass the Act creating the Royal University of Ireland (1879), which would examine students from any college or none, including the Jesuit-dominated University College, Dublin, founded by Newman, to which the State refused direct recognition but to which it would award fellowships! In England also there was university reform, and Lord Sandon's Act, virtually establishing compulsory education (1876), brought free education nearer than Forster had contrived. Cynics said the intention was to keep school boards out of the country districts. Cynics are perfectly entitled to argue that it was politic for the Tories to distract the country 'from this fever for organic change', as Bismarck was doing to ward off Socialism by social reforms from which the British Liberals were, rather belatedly, to crib, and for the same purpose. But, as Disraeli said on 19 May 1874, when opposing the enfranchisement of county householders, 'the disposition of the country [was] favourable, beyond any time I can recall, to the successful consideration of the social evils of the great body of the people.' The Tories were certainly better entitled than the Liberals and old-school Radicals of the *laissez-faire* school to take on this task, in which Gladstone showed no interest, as he lived in retirement to 'make his soul' and counter the Vatican Decrees of 1870, which stimulated English Protestantism. Disraeli himself, when in opposition, had dealt with this theme, in a very different way, in *Lothair*, 1870, with an interesting general preface to a new edition of his works. As usual, *Lothair* and his current parliamentary speeches had echoes of one another. Both spoke of an international revolutionary conspiracy, *imported into Ireland*, where it did not 'take', and a Roman conspiracy to convert Ireland (in the novel, not Ireland only) into 'a Popish Kingdom'. But, in office, the Tories, allied with the Papists of England against secular education, did their best to achieve a *modus vivendi* with a hierarchy frightened of Fenianism and infidelity, not wholly happy about the Home Rulers and terrified of losing its hold on the peasant priests so strongly tempted to solidarity with their parishioners. This problem became acute when the European agricultural depression struck the British Isles with full force. A series of bad harvests simply meant lower farm incomes and pressure on rents – Beach's were halved and his poorer land became unlettable. This was due to the flood of cheap American grain. It was what the Protectionists had prophesied in 1846, though they got their time-scale woefully wrong. Nothing is more pathetic than the speeches of Beaconsfield in the Lords on 28 March and 29 April 1879 in reply to Huntly's motion for agricultural relief and Bateman's for reciprocity – the causes he had fought for in vain so long ago. There was, alas, nothing to be done. Parliament had 'not precipitately, but determinedly, adopted' Peel's prescription of fighting hostile tariffs with free imports. Practically speaking, reciprocity, whatever its merits, was dead: there were only twenty-two articles on the tariff and more than forty most-favoured-nation treaties. That was the legacy of Peel, Cobden and Gladstone. Northcote had effected some transfer of charges from the ratepayer to the taxpayer – e.g. lunatics and the police – but it would be bitter mockery to tell the farmer that anything further on these lines could remedy his distress. That state of affairs 'long threatened ... has arrived'.

Poor Northcote! He had begun by taking the tax off sugar and reducing the income tax. But there had arrived the Great Depression of 1873. At first it involved not a loss of production but lower prices and profits, and the revenue fell. Then every European country except Britain and Belgium resorted to tariffs, export bounties, dumping etc. and to falling British revenue was added the call of industrial towns particularly stricken, with Bradford as the storm centre and (bitter retribution) a Cunliffe Lister (whose family had fiercely opposed factory Acts) crying out for Protection, soon to be joined by landlords and farmers – and a Government offering no more hope than the Opposition, despite the ingenious linking of the Protectionist and imperialist themes, in Disraelian terminology, in Farrer Ecroyd's *Policy of Self-Help* (1879) which became the bible of the National Fair Trade League founded in 1881. And the revenue fell, and the poor rates rose, until in 1879 twelve per cent of union members were unemployed. This was a very poor prospect for a ministry involved by distant viceroys – Lord Lytton and Sir Bartle Frere, both in defiance of instructions – in wars in Afghanistan and Zululand.

GLADSTONE VERSUS DISRAELI AGAIN

Most Prime Ministers give major attention to the conduct of diplomacy, and the loss of British prestige under Gladstone and Granville had undoubtedly contributed to Tory victory in 1874. Disraeli wished to cut a figure on the world stage and, on the strength of his youthful visit to the Near East, his musings on semitism, and his fascination with India as the source of Britain's world role, found the bankruptcy of the Egyptian Khedive and Balkan disturbances, which brought a Russian army to the environs of Constantinople and another pointing through Asia Minor to the Persian Gulf, an enthralling, if perilous, conjunction of events. The first he dealt with in an original way. If Whigs could suspend Peel's Bank Act and then come to the Commons for an indemnification of their illegality, why should he not borrow Rothschild money overnight to buy the Khedive's holdings in the Suez Canal (though this would give control neither of the company nor the waterway)? It was therefore natural that when the Queen insisted on being made Empress of India in the following year (1876) and Disraeli justified the necessary bill on the ground that 'the imagination of nations [is] an element which Governments must not despise', the idea, which aroused unforeseen opposition, was thought to be his.

It is no part of Conservative Party history to dwell at length upon the handling of the Eastern Question, on which Disraeli seems to have had no pre-conceived ideas against either a Russian alliance or the partition of Turkey – only the desire to break up the League of the Three Emperors. He believed (what Salisbury, for instance, doubted) that Constantinople was the key to India. Certainly the armistice terms and Treaty of San Stefano between Russia and Turkey after their war were intolerable. He also liked moving fleets and armies and brought Indian troops to the Mediterranean. For a year a British fleet lay off Constantinople. What *is* important for our story is the knowledge acquired fifty years later that the Foreign Secretary, Derby, still spoken of in mid-1876 as the destined successor, was not the incompetent he seemed nor the alcoholic he became when 'rumbled' but the active collaborator of the Russian envoy (to whom he conveyed Cabinet secrets), under the impression that Disraeli 'believes thoroughly in prestige, *as all foreigners do*, and would think it in the interests of the country to spend £200 millions on war if others would think more highly of it as a military power' (to Salisbury, 23 December 1877). After his resignation, his revelations in Parliament of what had happened in Cabinet were disgraceful. It was left to Salisbury, who succeeded him on 27 April 1878, to pick up the china which Derby had broken (as he modestly put it), though Rosebery thought his first three months at the Foreign Office the most brilliant period of his career. Beaconsfield relied on his clarity and courage; Salisbury recognised the Prime Minister's spunk. Animosity died away. It is clear that Beaconsfield wished Salisbury to be his successor and maintain the aristocratic tradition; he had remarked to him at the Congress of Berlin (whence they returned, with San Stefano torn up, to receive heroes' welcomes and the Garter) of the panic of which they heard among ministers at home, that they were all, especially Northcote, middle-class men afraid of responsibility – a splendid comment from a self-made Jewish adventurer to a Cecil!

A second effect of the Eastern Question was to add to Disraeli's defence of the Empire of settlement a new glorification of the dependent Empire in Asia – the more important as it occurred on the eve of the carve-up of Africa, so that a reluctant Salisbury who had tried to get out of Egypt found himself committed to controlling the Nile from Alexandria to Uganda. Unlike Beaconsfield, Salisbury did not believe in any imminent danger to India from Russia and spoke of the peril of using small-scale maps. But the Great Depression would make it essential to see that Britain was not excluded by Protectionist powers from any undeveloped market, and Disraeli helped to create the spirit of a new imperialism – especially but not uniquely associated with his party – by speeches to the effect that 'We have a substantial interest in the East; it is a commanding interest and its behest must be obeyed' (Lords, 8 April 1878); 'We shrink from the responsibility of handing to our successors a weakened or diminished Empire' (ibid., 18 July); 'the Empire was no mean heritage'. Feasting Beaconsfield and Salisbury at Knightsbridge after Berlin, the audience therefore (27 July 1878) heard the Crystal Palace theme expanded and updated. In getting Parliament to vote credits in January; in activating the first stage of Cardwell's new system of mobilisation in March; in announcing the arrival of the Indians in Malta in April; in acquiring Cyprus and a commission to reform the government of Turkey-in-Asia, the two ministers had been striving to pick up the broken thread of England's old Imperial traditions against men who thought all the past history of England a mistake, 'who disdained empire, who objected to colonies, and who grumbled even at the possession of India.'

A third effect of the Eastern Question, or, rather, of Disraeli's attitude towards it, was to bring Gladstone barn-storming back into the political arena to the acute embarrassment of his Commons successor Hartington, who essentially agreed with the Premier as to the defence of 'the permanent and important interests of England.' As the prime authority, Shannon, has

shown, Gladstone did not at once join the agitation which
Disraeli ascribed to a 'Hudibrastic crew of High Ritualists,
Dissenting ministers and Liberals', joined (with conspicuous
exceptions) by most intellectuals, some of whom, especially the
historian Freeman, were strongly anti-semitic. But Disraeli
chose first to be incredulous, and then flippant, and then
dismissive of protests at Turkish atrocities in the Balkans
(June to August 1876); he had no sympathy with the rising
spirit of nationality, whether in Ireland or Bosnia or Bulgaria.
He was concerned only with the interests of England. As an
Anglo-Catholic inclined to the Greeks, and on that ground
anti-Turk *ab initio*, Gladstone was disgusted, and poured out
his indignation in a pamphlet which enjoyed a vast sale and
then another which did not. Lacking, as Blake notes, Disraeli's
'acute, though sporadic, comprehension' of the material needs
of the working-classes, he found himself once again in rapport
with their 'virtuous passion'. He resolved that his Satanic rival
be brought to judgement. It did not matter that Tory majorities
were high because Gladstone's interventions in the House split
Liberals three ways. Disraeli had the London mob, with the
music-halls ringing to 'We don't want to fight, but by *jingo* if
we do . . .' and, his Harley Street windows broken, Gladstone
needed police protection. Disraeli had the Irish Catholics, who
disliked the Orthodox Church. He had, despite Shaftesbury
and Evelyn Ashley, most Evangelicals. He had most of 'the
Upper Ten Thousand', the clubs, the gentry, the City, when he
condemned the exploitation of 'noble sentiments by designing
politicians for sinister ends' (Aylesbury, 20 September 1875)
and repeated Palmerstonian talk of Britain's resources being
inexhaustible in a righteous war (Guildhall, 9 November 1876).
But he did not, Gladstone was convinced, have God on his side.
And '*Vox Populi . . .*'

DEFEAT AND CONFUSION 1880–4

Gladstone's crusade probably did not win the Liberals the next
general election; it did make him, rather than Granville or
Hartington, Prime Minister. The Liberal Party workers,
apathetic and resentful in 1874, either responded with him
against the Turk and the acquisition of Cyprus and the wars

against Africans and Afghans or decided quite blatantly to *use* Gladstone, as did Joseph Chamberlain with his National Liberal Federation – the *caucus* which Salisbury had always feared would come over from America with democracy. There has been much discussion as to whether the Tories would have won an election on the morrow of Berlin; the judgement of Professor Hanham that they would not, 'on balance' endorsed by Lord Blake, does not convince the present writer. By early 1880 the prospects were, of course, much gloomier, and Beaconsfield was much alarmed at the rise of the pro-Liberal *Farmers' Alliance* founded in July 1879, in which month both the Chief Whip Hart-Dyke and the (incompetent) principal agent Skene advised a dissolution in January. On 14 February the Cabinet decided unanimously against an election; on 6 March they (with Beach and Manners dissenting) decided with the concurrence of the whips and Central Office to hold one, on the strength of what proved a striking but maverick by-election gain at Southwark.

A pacific Foreign Secretary, Salisbury, addressing 100,000 at Manchester, hailed the new Berlin–Vienna axis as 'glad tidings of great joy' (7 October), but Gladstone in Midlothian in November and December shrewdly linked the heart with the pocket, 'immorality' in diplomacy with 'profligacy' and, thinking this over, Salisbury wondered whether it was indeed true that people ignorant of foreign policy required only 'repose'. Back in Midlothian in the spring, Gladstone, who had seemed to blame the industrial and agricultural depressions on ministers (as Disraeli predicted he would) talked of 'a great trial now proceeding before the nation' with the aristocracy, landed interest, clergy of the established churches, the wealth and rank of the country on the side of the villainous defendant. (When Gladstone said 'trial' he meant 'trial' not 'contest'.) But it was not what the defendant called the drenching oratory of 'a sophisticated rhetorician inebriated with the exuberance of his own verbosity' that won the country – or even Midlothian, where dark arts prevailed. Beaconsfield was almost certainly right to blame defeat on 'Hard Times'; it had fallen to his lot 'to govern England . . . with a decaying commerce and the soil stricken with sterility.'[14] But the Tories made a sorry show of it. Chamberlain kept asking what had happened to the social reforms on which even Cross was strangely silent. As Vincent says, there was 'no theme, no co-ordination, no serious fight "at the general level of utterance"', nobody to answer Gladstone. Beaconsfield's manifesto, an open letter to the Lord Lieutenant of Ireland on the dangers of Liberal complicity with Home Rulers, was prescient but at points barely intelligible, the product of a doped old man.

Cross took on Hartington, but in Lancashire and Cheshire, especially hard hit by the decline of international trade, the losses were the worst – in the largest boroughs, where half the seats were lost, far worse than 1868. In English boroughs with over 17,500 electors the Tories won but 13 of the 57 seats. Other criteria give 24 out of 114 (for boroughs with over 50,000 inhabitants) or 36 out of 159 (a net loss of 36). With 41 elected out of 118 in the smaller boroughs, the net loss there was only 19. Outside England only 35 Tories were returned for 196 seats, the Scotsmen sinking from 20 to 7 and the Welsh (where the farmers' revolt was well and truly under weigh) from 11 to 2. It was a dreadful result, and obviously owed something to Disraeli's strange neglect of constituency organisation once Gorst had gone in 1877. This has never been explained.

Had the fruits of thirty years' labour been simply to leave the Tories as the Country Party, with 137 of its 238 MPs sitting for counties and even more for quasi-counties, and threatened there by the revolt of the farmer against the squire, with the enfranchisement of the labourer looming?

The picture was not quite as gloomy as that. Hanham estimates that this reversal of forces had been brought about by a mere five per cent swing; Dunbabin would put it rather lower. Concealed in the net loss of 27 English county seats were gains in the commuter-belt, including three in well-organised Kent. That denoted urban middle-class support. The metropolis, perhaps responsive to imperialism, held up well, with only two net losses, giving a better result than 1868. Moreover, in the 62 seats with electorates of over 17,500 in 1880, if only 19 seats were won, that was two more than in 1868, and the Conservative share of the vote had *risen* by seven per cent.[15] So, although Beaconsfield was very pessimistic about the political as well as the economic future of the landed interest, now that 'an

intelligent and persevering party avowedly hostile to it' had
Chamberlain in the Cabinet, it might still turn out that, as he
had said at Edinburgh in 1867, 'the Tory party is the national
party of England ... formed of all classes. But an awful lot
would hang upon the next redistribution of seats – and who
planned it.'

Beaconsfield was now forced to admit what a mistake he had
made in the choice of Northcote, a respected parliamentarian
capable enough as chief ministerial spokesman until everything went wrong for him at the last, but, as Salisbury's
nephew Arthur James Balfour remarked, 'no more a match for
Mr Gladstone than a wooden three-decker would be for a
Dreadnought.' He was mild and deferential, but, though he
suffered from chronic heart disease, there was no question of
easing him out, for he was ambitious, and the Queen gave
him to understand he would be the next Conservative Prime
Minister when Disraeli died. But when the time came, in
1885, she quite rightly sent for Salisbury as a matter of course.
In 1881 the Commons men had refused to acknowledge Salisbury as Beaconsfield's successor in the leadership of the party
as a whole, feeling that the battle would be fought in their
House and that he, outside it, and never visiting it, might well
commit them, proving another Derby – and quite likely a very
vehement one, out of tune with the public mood and the MPs'
mood. But the dual leadership was hardly likely to be a success
when the Government was headed by a great, determined,
though now ailing, man like Gladstone. Lord Randolph
Churchill, now aged thirty-one, finding things drab under the
presidency of Northcote, whom he called 'the Goat', decided
to liven things up even before Beaconsfield died, and on 25
August 1880 Balfour took the old leader to see 'the Fourth
Party' in action below the gangway. The party consisted of
Churchill, Gorst, Sir Henry Drummond Wolff and, somewhat
ambivalently (one suspects he was always acting primarily in
his uncle's interests), Balfour himself. The four, and the forty
or so of the Home Rulers who acknowledged another man,
Parnell, as their leader, made life hell for ministers, and not
very pleasant for Northcote or for Smith and Cross whom
Churchill, a snob who really yearned for an alliance of aristocrats and masses against the respectable bourgeoisie, called

Marshall and Snelgrove. Beaconsfield approved of 'the light cavalry', adept at leading Gladstone off into side issues, and let them know it: 'I was never respectable myself.' He told the Queen they were 'a safety-valve and tend to disorganise the ministerial ranks.' He pointed out to them, indeed, that prudence was required as well as enterprise; Northcote represented the respectability of the party and was trying to draw away moderate Liberals from Gladstone. But Northcote wrote to Cross on 29 November that he feared the Fourth Party were getting 'a little too much encouragement' from Beaconsfield.

As for the moderates, they hardly seemed to need drawing away. Doctrines were being preached – by Henry George, by Parnell, by Jesse Collings and soon by Chamberlain, Cabinet minister though he was, with his argument that property owners owed ransom-money to the community from whom its land had been stolen – which applied, logically, not only to land, but to minerals and urban ground rents. They turned from the defence of liberty as guaranteed by property – Disraeli's persistent theme – to the defence of property in the name of liberty. And though this involved the acceptance of *laissez-faire* as the bastion of estates, mines, London squares and Liverpool docks, and stocks and shares alike, the Conservative Party turned with them, or ahead of them, into acceptance of Professor Dicey's dictum that 'if you once desert the solid ground of individual freedom, you can find no resting place till you reach the chasm of Socialism.' Not that they ever accepted it fully; Dicey regarded the factory Acts as the beginning of socialism, and the extreme dogmatism of Lord Elcho's *Liberty and Property Defence League* and the book he wrote as Earl of Wemyss in 1883 – *Socialism at St Stephens 1869–85* – were unacceptable for their strictures on Tory reforms. This chimed in with the dire predictions of Lord Robert Cecil, but Salisbury was now a wiser, more pragmatic, statesman, who would extract from the Liberal Government a royal commission on the housing of the poor and horrify the Liberal Goschen by his 'socialism', besides informing Lord Wemyss that if a case for practical improvement was made out, Parliament never enquired from which doctrinal stable it ran. But, initially, Gladstone devoted himself to separating farmer from squire and parson. He abolished the malt tax and by the 'Hares and

Rabbits Bill' gave the farmer protection for his crops. This was so just that Beaconsfield called it the most devilish of the 'A(rch)V(illain)'s schemes'. But the remark of the Farmers' Alliance MP, James Howard, that the Irish Land Act of 1870 was a precedent, put people on their guard, Young Whig MPs from famous families – Brands and Greys – began to put down fierce amendments to Liberal bills. A temporary Compensation for Disturbance Bill for Ireland, of three clauses only, occupied thirteen Commons sittings and would have been defeated in the Lords if no Tory had voted: the figures were 282:51, Whiggery agreeing with Beaconsfield – who left the running to Earl Grey – that it was 'a reconnaissance in force' to test opinion on tenure and the position of the landed interest in *England*. The permanent Irish Land Act 1881 introduced a cumbersome dual-ownership, with rent-fixing tribunals. Partly for fear that this also might 'cross the water' it consumed thirty-three days in committee. Though its opponents knew they were confronted by 'a blunderbuss', they at one point reduced the Government majority in the Commons to five. The Lords abstained from a hopeless fight, the Tories, however, taking pleasure in the statement of the Whig ex-minister Dufferin:

'to speak plainly, the tendency of the extreme section of the Liberal party is to buy the support of the masses by distributing among them the property of their own political opponents, and it is towards a social rather than a political revolution that we are tending, at least if what is taking place in Ireland is any indication of the future, and a precedent established there is almost bound sure to be applied elsewhere.'

They were delighted that Lansdowne had resigned over the Disturbance Bill in 1880 and Argyll over the Land Bill in 1881. Smith and the Irish Tory lawyer Gibson (later Lord Ashbourne) grasped that the knell of proprietary right in Ireland had tolled and began to work the party round to the transfer from landlord to peasant ownership, with a moderated support from Salisbury under whose first premiership the Ashbourne Act was passed.

Beaconsfield died on 21 April 1881 and thenceforth hung at the Carlton a large portrait, sardonic and inscrutable in death as in life, bearing the ironic legend, 'He alone is wise; the rest are fleeting shades' – ironic because no biographer professes to understand him, or what he really believed, if in anything but his star. 'All display, without reality or genuineness', said Gladstone. But are not parliamentarians actors on a particular stage – and 'the play's the thing'? The elements of mystery attaching to so colourful a figure meant that much could be made of his memory. People do not crowd to the unveiling of a statue (by Northcote, to Churchill's disgust) with primroses (on the Queen's word, his favourite flower) for an ordinary man. When they did it gave Drummond Wolff the idea of a commemorative body whose draft rules Churchill sent to Salisbury (who *hated* flummery) on 22 December 1883. By 1891 the Primrose League, with a million members (more than the TUC) was serving that vital Conservative purpose of bringing together at rallies and garden parties people of all classes, especially the upper and middle, in common obeisance to the legend of a maestro which they certainly did not all interpret in the same way. Disraeli had become 'a religion to the party he led', wrote a Primrose League dame.

To the most conspicuous of the young men who surveyed his party, finding it 'a not very competent body with an opposition mentality', the maestro's memory was a card to be conjured with. As Vincent says, Disraeli had conferred on his party the priceless advantage of making the Liberals 'look left wing and dangerous to men of property', while also, to quote G. M. Young, propounding the 'audacious paradox' that the Tories were 'the party of the people'. The then Sir Edward Boyle, writing in 1953 that Disraeli 'established a tradition of Conservatism that is still the inspiration of our own day' adds that 'it stretches through Lord Randolph Churchill to be still vital.'[16]

Churchill, stressing the destructive radicalism of the enemy, made his mark by refusing to treat Gladstone as an Olympian figure; he convulsed vast midland and northern audiences, to whom he became an oracle, by treating the giant figure of British politics as a figure of fun. But he also converted Disraeli into the founder of 'Tory Democracy', which, however, he was careful never to define consistently except by the use of phrases such as 'Trust the People' (Birmingham, 16 April 1884), which, says Winston, 'I learnt in my father's house'. The phrase had been used by the Churchillite Arthur Forwood, a Liverpool shipowner, in his *Contemporary Review* article entitled 'Democratic Toryism', February 1883. Randolph's Liberal friend and racing companion, Rosebery, opined in 1906 that 'Tory Democracy was . . . an honest and unconscious imposture . . . a useful denomination or resource for anyone who found himself with Radical opinions inside the Tory Party, and who did not wish to leave it . . . simply Liberalism under another name . . .' Significantly, both Gorst, who wrote to Beaconsfield on 4 April 1878 that the party managers were hostile to him because of his 'steadfast adherence to those popular principles in politics, which you taught me, which won the boroughs in 1874 . . .' and Winston Churchill fought in 1906 as Liberals. Randolph remarked that the appointment of Balfour as Leader of the Commons in 1891 meant the end of Tory Democracy.

We may quote Rosebery on the quite remarkable effect on Tory fortunes in an age of mass meetings of 'a stripling come to stir the dry bones of party' whose very moustache, on the platform, seemed to live a life of its own:

'He was supremely interesting . . . He leaped into renown. He soon became the principal platform speaker in the country . . . He . . . plunged into the fray with the keen enjoyment of an undergraduate on 5 November, giving and receiving hard knocks with almost equal pleasure . . . He was brilliant, courageous and unembarrassed by scruple; he had fascination, audacity, tact . . . and an almost unrivalled skill in attraction on the platform . . . He had also the vital mainspring of zest . . . Popular audiences delighted in the pungent flavour of . . . personal attacks . . . [on] "these children of revolution, these robbers of churches, these plunderers of classes, these friends of the lawless, these foes of the loyal . . .".'

The difficulty for the dual leadership was that by these orations Churchill was building himself in the great centres of population a constituency vital to party electoral recovery but smarting under neglect by the Disraeli Government. The provincial leaders were justly contemptuous both of the *ad hoc* committee of whips and others which had 'run' – or rather, failed to run –

the 1880 campaign and of the investigatory committee under Smith appointed at the last meeting of the Conservative Cabinet, which became a permanent 'central committee' representing the leaders and whips.[17] With Gorst, reappointed on a part-time basis never properly defined, but simultaneously an MP contemptuous of the leaders, there was bound to be trouble; and there was, at all levels from Smith and his deputy Stanhope down to the minor people from Central Office whose local activities were often deplorable. Gorst urged most strongly against 'The Old Identity' (the 1880 committee controlled by money-raisers like Lord Abergavenny – formerly Lord Nevill – and Lord Henry Thynne, and their creatures who practised the old corrupt ways) that the Conservatives stood to gain by an efficient Corrupt and Illegal Practices Act (eventually passed by collusion between the front benches in 1883), though it would not be popular with the party. Smith opposed him, arguing for paid agency since 'our supporters only want to be left alone' while the enemy had 'the Trade Unions, the Dissenting Chapels and every Society for the abolition of property and morality.'

In October – December 1882 there occurred a series of incidents which showed the poor shape the party direction was in. The *Quarterly* published an article signed 'Two Conservatives', one known to be Churchill, saying that there stood in the way of the mission to gain the confidence of the working-classes a narrow land-owning class which half-feared and half-despised the common people (and, added Lord Charles Beresford in a congratulatory note, 'treated them like scum'). And so the mantle of Elijah bequeathed by Disraeli had been rent in twain. A Manchester delegation asking Churchill to be their candidate was told that the duty of an Opposition to oppose had been for three sessions 'either systematically neglected or defectively carried out'. This Salisbury knew very well, since the explicit agreement made at his house that wrecking amendments to the Irish Arrears Bill would be insisted on had been sabotaged, to his vast indignation, when the peers, threatened with an appeal to the people, ran away like wet hens (10 August).[18] In the Commons on 1 November Churchill had asked how 'the great Tory Democracy, which Lord Beaconsfield's party constructed' was to prosper when it was the secret conviction of its leaders that the best they could hope for was short spells of minority government. In November, also, the *Contemporary Review* published an article, thought to be by Gorst, critical of the treatment of the borough members and voters under Disraeli and since, for the party must become popular or impotent. On the 17th Gorst, censured by the Chelsea Conservatives under the guidance of the Establishment figure Lord Claud Hamilton, resigned his agency. The following month Smith resigned the chairmanship of the Central Committee, to be succeeded by Stanhope, while Bartley, formerly of the National Penny Bank, replaced Gorst.

In the spring of 1883 Churchill gave great offence by two letters to *The Times*. The first said that the Opposition did not need a policy, but did need a leader, and that if it was in a negative frame of mind it would stick to Northcote, if in a cautious frame of mind choose Cairns, but if in an *English* frame of mind would choose Salisbury. In the second he said that the party leader must be 'a statesman who fears not to meet and who knows how to sway immense masses of the working classes and who either by his genius or his eloquence, or by all the varied influences of an ancient name, can "move the hearts of households".' In the *Quarterly* in May he indicated that if Salisbury declined the Disraelian inheritance of Tory Democracy, he would assume it himself.

Salisbury had an over-modest view of his power to 'move the hearts of households' but, much against his inclination, made seventy speeches in the country 1880–5, not as the master of jibes and flouts and jeers but as one sustaining the faithful and appealing to the centre with the language of commonsense. That he showed no interest in mobilising potential Tory voters is the reverse of the truth. He saw the need to mobilise villa Toryism and suggested as his epitaph 'died of writing inane letters to empty-headed Conservative associations.' But, although he would have been the choice of the National Union as successor to Disraeli, he was, inevitably, as one of the two party leaders, associated with 'the Old Identity' – the Central Council, the organ of the leaders and whips, and the less official group of 'managers' headed by Abergavenny and Thynne. If these were to be put down from their seats, it must therefore be with his assistance or in his despite. The obvious solution – a Salisbury–Churchill alliance – eventually achieved, was not easy to come by, though it had the advantage for both of deposing Northcote.

A bitter conflict between Churchill and Gorst on the one hand, and Salisbury and Northcote on the other (the last normally ignored by the rebels and kept in touch by his colleague only so far as courtesy demanded), broke out. The two former, knowing the resentment of the provincial Conservative leaders and agents at their lack of status, decided to issue at the National Union conference in October 1883 a declaration of war on the leaders, the whips and 'the Old Identity' in general. After Churchill had delivered a violent attack on these, the conference demanded for its executive, dominated after the elections by Churchill, its 'legitimate influence in the party organisation'. The leaders' man, Lord Percy, was booted out of the chairmanship of the Organisation Committee and in February 1884 resigned the chairmanship of the executive. Churchill now had two roles in either of which he could, and did, write to Salisbury (ignoring Northcote), often in pretty sharp terms. The wrangle was a long one. It mainly revealed two things. Firstly, Salisbury was a brave man, not at all afraid, as was Northcote, of a Churchill campaign in the country exposing the issue, although, as Percy Mitford pointed out, 'if the masses comprising the Conservative Associations throughout the country were, at any time, to realise that their representatives on the Council' (of NUCCA) were being thwarted by the Central Council, a 'deplorable . . . impression might . . . arise that the party organisers in London were indisposed to trust the people.' After all, Churchill wanted to beat the Liberals, not split the Tories. Secondly, that for all the rudery which passed between Churchill and Salisbury, the former regarded the latter as the party leader and was not fighting the sort of battle Chamberlain and his 'caucus' were fighting to determine the *policy* of the party. On 16 April 1884, indeed, Churchill gave a broad hint that all was far from right in the party. 'I have no fear of democracy', he said. 'The English Constitution will endure and thrive . . . as long as the Tory party is true to its past, mindful of its history, faithful to the policy that was bequeathed to it by Lord Beaconsfield,' adding that 'there are still a few in the party . . . who have yet

to understand that the Tory party of today is no longer connected with that small and narrow class . . . connected with the
ownership of land.' This was a very natural point to stress in
the stronghold of Joseph Chamberlain and John Bright. But it
was a defiance and a threat, and Salisbury did not yield to
threats. He yielded to facts. All hands were now needed to man
the pumps against the extension of the vote to the village
householder without a redistribution of seats. Late in June all
was suddenly sweetness and light – except for Gorst, who did
really care about Tory Democracy and regarded the détente
between Salisbury and Churchill as 'the great surrender'.
Beach, the member of the Commons front bench most friendly
to Churchill, was to be Chairman of the National Union,
flanked by Vice-Presidents Balfour (representing Salisbury),
Akers-Douglas (the brilliant young whip from Abergavenny's
'Kentish Gang' selected by Northcote for rapid promotion at
the expense of the diehard chief whip Rowland Winn), and
Gorst, with Bartley as Treasurer (who, finding he did not
count, quickly resigned). The controversial Central Council
disappeared. Churchill was assured, unless his demands were
too unreasonable, of important Cabinet office. Northcote was
merely informed of the settlement.

Sir Michael Hicks-Beach now assumed a considerable importance. The great issue was the extension of the vote to the
county householder. Churchill was so frightened of it that he
had opposed it at Edinburgh, to be countered by Balfour from
the same platform (19 December 1883); probably the municipal representatives on the National Union changed his mind.
Salisbury and Winn hoped to use the Lords to force an election
on the existing franchise. This the party funked. And so, while
Chamberlain campaigned on the peers versus the people, and
Gladstone promised Hartington (worried about the Irish mud-
cabiners) that he would preside over redistribution as well as
enfranchisement, the question narrowed to the absolutely vital
question of the nature of the redistribution. And Black Michael
produced proposals shocking to Gladstone and Hartington,
though acceptable to the Radicals. The Liberals proposed that
boroughs of under 10,000 inhabitants lose their member. Let
it be 25,000 said Beach, with the smaller towns grouped (as in
Scotland and Wales) to reach that total. Let boroughs with

under 40,000 lose a member, said the Liberals. But why, asked Beach, keep in general to the old rule, ancient though it was, of two-member constituencies as the norm? The Liberals proposed single-member constituencies only in the great cities of Yorkshire and Lancashire and London. Why, asked Beach, except to facilitate alliances between Whigs and Radicals? Let there be single-member constituencies of up to 80,000 inhabitants.

A Tory was proposing the biggest major surgical operation ever imposed on the electoral system – the substitution of single-member constituencies for the traditional doubles *and* the determination of their boundaries with 'regard to the pursuits of the population'. This Tory adoption of Chartist 'equal electoral districts' combined with the proposition that the carve-up should not be purely arbitrary, but environmental, was altogether too radical for Gladstone, in many respects a very old-fashioned man (though a special visit from Lady Salisbury was needed to save the university seats). Over tea at No. 10, with Salisbury and a mute Northcote visiting a bewildered Gladstone and Hartington and a delighted Dilke, a compromise was arranged. The Tory proposals for the reduction of the over-representation of Scotland and Ireland (included in the Acts of Union) and for the special representation of Irish minorities were dropped. Some two-member constituencies were preserved. But the single-member constituency based on numbers and delimited according to economic character became the norm. No borough with less than 15,000 inhabitants would be separately represented; none with under 50,000 would retain two members. The counties and cities would be split into individual constituencies, the former often taking their name from a previously represented borough.

Salisbury, while willing to risk an election on the old basis, had feared a Radical Commons distributing the constituencies at its will, according to the advice of the National Liberal Federation's expert Schnadhorst. Instead, in December 1885, he found after a few months as Premier, with Beach as Leader of the House and Churchill Secretary of State for India (with Northcote relegated to the Lords as Earl of Iddesleigh and a purely honorific office), that only the farm labourers let him down. The Tories won half the votes and half the seats in the

English boroughs, and did better than that not only in the smallest but the largest. The 39 Lancashire and Cheshire MPs included 29 Tories; the North-West's 70 MPs, 46 Tories. And gone was the old Tory fear of a London behaving like Paris; of the 62 metropolitan MPs, 37 were Tory. Even bearing in mind the built-in Tory assets (plural voting, complex registration rules and so on) Salisbury as the pacifier of the moderates and Churchill as the stimulator of the enthusiasts had, in alliance, proved, under the fairest electoral system so far tried, that the Conservative Party *was* a national party, at least in England. It could poll almost as well in London slums as in Belgravia. It could take in large city districts not solidly working-class. It could take, or have a sporting chance in, boroughs large enough for separate representation. It polled surprisingly well in divided cities, even where it gained no seats, including Glasgow, where the spread of its votes between nearly 40 per cent and nearly 50 per cent must have surprised practically everyone.[19] Ironically – since it seems that Jesse Collings' three acres and a cow project may have been directed primarily at the urban voter, ignorant of countryside conditions and specifically urban cows, such as attacks on the Church and free education, converted none and repelled some – it was the counties which let the Tories down. But how long would it take for the farm labourer to grasp that the Liberals were a dogmatically Free-Trade party, essentially urban as well as essentially Nonconformist?

THE LOSS OF CHURCHILL

The Conservatives fought the 1885 general election as a Government because, after Northcote had (perhaps fatally to his prospects) failed to defeat Gladstone over the Sudan in February 1885, although most of the Irish supported him, control passed to Salisbury and Beach joined, after his return from abroad, by Churchill. As it was in connection with the Irish 1885–6 that the only serious attacks on Salisbury have been made, it must be admitted at once that the Chief Whip saw Parnell during this debate and reported, without undue haste, to Salisbury. Probably no material communications at that level took place until Hicks-Beach, with Irish aid, had defeated the budget (9 June 1885) and provided Gladstone with an excuse to offer the resignation of a Government hopelessly divided as to what mixture of Spencer's 1882–5 Coercion Bill, devolution of some kind, and land purchase should constitute its Irish policy. It seems clear that Beach's coup was the last stroke of the Fourth Party, not the decision of the Shadow Cabinet, as Salisbury was unready for the summons and Northcote for his humiliation. Whether the Liberal absences were due to the contrivance of the Whig whip Lord Richard Grosvenor or the 'Birmingham' Radicals (the resignations of Chamberlain and Dilke having been tabled) is still uncertain. What is clear is that the Tory leadership, taken by surprise, did not know what to do, until eleven days later Churchill was converted to taking office under Salisbury (or Salisbury into accepting him as a secretary of state), it having meanwhile been contrived that Northcote (*not* an enthusiast for the Elysian fields) should be elbowed away.

The full story of Conservative-Irish intrigues from early 1885 to January 1886 will probably never be known. Nor does it matter very much what Carnarvon, the Chief Secretary (known to be favourable to Home Rule) said to Parnell when he met him secretly in an empty house on 1 August (with Salisbury knowing of the meeting, but not that Carnarvon would be unaccompanied), or what Churchill was saying to Nationalist MPs. There is nothing strange in Churchill turning from seeking Salisbury's approval to 'intrigue with Archbishop Walsh' over money for Irish university purposes (in effect Catholic ones), which might have appeared in the Tory Queen's Speech of January 1886 had Churchill and Ashbourne got more support, to his preliminary arrangement with the strong Orangeman Colonel Saunderson from Ulster for the visit of February 1886 and the cry 'Ulster will Fight, and Ulster will be Right' which led to riots in Belfast. Gladstone's son complains that 'between the attitude of the Conservative Government before and after the General Election of 1885 is a deep chasm of inconsistency.'[20] But the essential point is that Parnell, for a price, was willing to help the Tories win seats, in order that *he* might hold the balance in the next Parliament – an objective he narrowly achieved. He therefore, in the words of Lord Gladstone, issued a manifesto which was 'an offensive, provoca-

tive and unqualified philippic against the Liberal party'.
Churchill hoped as long as possible that the understanding
could be preserved or that in some other way the Conservatives
could remain in office, but this hope was dashed when young
Gladstone himself revealed his father's conversion to Home
Rule for Ireland. This was to lead to a Gladstone Government,
a Home Rule Bill defeated in the House of Commons, a general
election in which Conservatives allied with Liberal Unionists
of both the Hartington and Chamberlain wings beat the Liberal
and Irish Home Rulers, and Salisbury's second administration,
which lasted from 1886 to 1892.

In this administration the leadership of the House of Commons was given to Churchill, instead of Beach. How long he
lasted depended on how the champion of Tory Democracy
behaved – the man of whom Balfour had always thought he
meant to get the premiership in one step or two. He turned out
to be an intolerable colleague. Salisbury showed exemplary
patience, telling protesting colleagues demanding a showdown
'The time is not yet.' He parried with his straight utilitarian
bat a shower of ferocious complaints, and then, suddenly, at
Christmas accepted as a resignation what Churchill may have
meant to be simply part of a rough bargaining process. Lord
Randolph was *not* kicked out because he was a Tory Democrat;
he saw his Dartford programme (virtually Chamberlain's
purloined) enacted over the years by the colleagues he left. It
is true that he had wanted to do a lot quickly and had burst
out to Salisbury that it was an idle schoolboy's dream to think
that the Tories could legislate under a democratic constitution,
and that he had not the patience to go on struggling against the
cliques as poor Dizzy had done all his life. But that was the
characteristic petulance which alternated with the brilliant
charm of the man. The proposed budget on which he resigned,
though containing an item or two mildly irritating to the landed
interest, was essentially a symbol of the peace and retrenchment
which he had preached in Cabinet and wished to carry, as
Salisbury observed, further than was wise in either the patriotic
or party sense. He resigned because the service ministers could
not in conscience make the cuts he demanded; he resigned on
Gladstonian Liberal grounds.

Such was the spell which Churchill had wielded in and out of

Parliament from 1880 to 1885 that the old hands wondered if they could go on without him, for he was not likely meekly to fade away. In practice, it proved quite easy; much of his power had depended on the circumstances of that particular House of Commons. But no doubt, though he proved to have but a handful of followers in the House, with whom he quarrelled one by one as he moved pathetically towards his death from general paralysis of the insane, the ministry, and therefore the party, suffered by his going. It had lost its spice!

Imperium et Libertas
1886-1923

Salisbury and his Scottish nephew Balfour led the Conservative Party for twenty-six years, for seventeen of which one or other was Prime Minister. The former was perhaps the most intelligent man who ever led it, the latter the most cultured. They led it to a disaster that might have been permanent. After Balfour had lost three elections in a row, the party turned to a superficially unimpressive man of business experience, who had never sat in the Cabinets christened 'The Hotel Cecil'.[1] Bonar Law was not chosen because of his origins, but because of his gift for fighting hard on a basis of clear, factual argument. But it required a strange concatenation of circumstances to make him in 1922 the first Conservative Prime Minister since 1905. By this time, Balfour had acquired an enviable reputation as a servant of the state, to which he was, after Law's death in 1923, to add. But he well-nigh ruined his party for good and all in the years from 1899 to 1910.

THE DEFENCE OF THE UNION

Two misconceptions prevail about Salisbury. The first is that he was unambitious and treated Northcote with scrupulous fairness[2]; in fact, with Balfour at his elbow, displaying the ruthlessness only later exposed to the public, the Marquess was quite determined to get the better of both Northcote and Churchill. It is true that after 1867 he was in principle a 'fusionist', devoted to the gathering in of what Winston Churchill was accustomed to call 'men of good will' to fight Radicalism. It is true, also, that he set little store by the office of Prime Minister, the power or potential of which he under-rated and failed conspicuously to exploit except for vetoing purposes. He would probably have served happily at the Foreign Office, his London base, under Hartington, the Whig to whom the authors of one of the strangest and most mis-leading books ever written,[3] attribute a desire for the premier-ship wholly alien to his character. Hartington did not like being cheated of the highest office by Gladstone in 1880 and expected to succeed him in 1884, 1885, or 1886. But he ex-perienced only relief when the offer came on unacceptable terms from Salisbury after the 1886 election (he could not accept the exclusion of Chamberlain) and after the resignation of Churchill, when the Conservative whips indicated that their MPs and supporters in the country insisted (unlike the Tory leaders) on Salisbury's premiership. This confidence Salisbury acknowledged with gratitude because it guaranteed him the Foreign Office, from which he had eventually, when incap-able of meeting a crisis without a recurrence of the psycho-somatic troubles of his youth, to be prized in 1900 by a conspiracy between his colleagues, his family and the Queen. What, unlike his predecessors Beaconsfield and Balfour, he did not neglect, was the party leader's responsibility for organisation. He was very well served by the incomparable partnership of Aretas Akers-Douglas as Chief Whip (spotted by Northcote but progressive enough to be thought a Churchil-lian) and 'Captain' Middleton – both from Abergavenny's 'Kentish Gang' but in a different class altogether from the Taylors, Noels and Hart-Dykes and Winns on the one hand and the Skenes and Bartleys on the other – not least in the harmony of their operations, ambitious though these were (the distribution of literature to every household). But Central Office was the only deviation on his daily journey, Hatfield – Foreign Office – House of Lords – Hatfield, and it was due to his personal influence that there were so few contests between Conservatives and anti-Home Rule MPs (the whole christened

Unionist by Churchill) in the 1886 election which made him
Prime Minister for the second time.

The other misconception about Salisbury is that he even
considered Home Rule for Ireland. The only basis for this is
Gladstone's own view that it would be very convenient if the
Tories repeated their performances of 1829, 1846 and 1867,
and the thesis of his son Herbert that 'for five months up to
1885 December, the question of Irish autonomy, that is to say
Home Rule, was under the serious consideration of the Conservative government.' 'Lord Salisbury', he wrote, 'considered
that Home Rule was not only not wrong but that it was the
duty of the Government to explore the whole ground . . . ' He
concluded that 'though, like Peel, Lord Salisbury saw what
was wanted, he would not, like Peel, divide his Party.' But
this is all nonsense, brought out at the last moment in 1886
by Parnell in an effort to sway the vital Commons vote, which
Gladstone lost by 341:311. Salisbury himself could never
understand how anyone could think he would stage a transformation scene like 1829 and 1846 and break up his party
for the benefit of Gladstone and, prospectively, Chamberlain,
who had held him up as an example of a class that neither
toiled nor spun and owed the community ransom. Perhaps his
greatest fault as leader was his over-concern for the prejudices
of the faithful, out of a strange fear (perhaps induced by the
1868 result) that they would abstain at the polls. There never
was a leader who so strictly regarded the relationship of leader
and led as one of mutual contract, binding on the former. How
otherwise could he justify the attacks on Derby and Peel,
repetitive of Disraeli's on Peel? And what were Salisbury's
views on Ireland? They were consistently those of a strict
Tory and of a Foreign Secretary steeped in the history of
Ireland's connections with Britain's enemies. Thus he wrote
in the *Quarterly* of October 1872:

'. . . The optimist view of politics assumes that there must be
some remedy for every political ill. Is it not just conceivable
that there is no remedy that we can apply to the Irish hatred
for ourselves? . . . At present we are, or believe we are, fixed
in our resolve that no kind of separation shall take place. . . .
But [the Irish peasant] knows enough of recent history to

disbelieve it. The one impression our policy has left in his mind is a firm belief in the efficacy of turbulence. . . . On Tory principles the case presents much that is painful, but no perplexity whatever. *Ireland must be kept, like India, at all hazards, by persuasion if possible, if not by force!'**

The agrarian war having been resumed, in ghastly form, as Disraeli foresaw, as a result of the Great Depression, it was met by the Liberal Government with a mixture of coercion and concession, culminating in a three-year period of strict coercion under Spencer after the Phoenix Park murders of mid-1882 (with which the Salisbury Government in 1889–90 ineptly tried to implicate Parnell). Neither these atrocities nor the temporary success of Gladstone's rent-fixing Act of 1881 shifted Salisbury, who in his last *Quarterly* article, October 1883, entitled 'Disintegration', wrote robustly:

'. . . One issue there is which, in the judgement not only of the Conservative Party, but in that of the great majority of Englishmen, is absolutely closed. The highest interests of the Empire, as well as the most sacred obligations of honour, forbid us . . . to concede to the majority in that country licence to govern the rest of Irishmen as they please . . .'

Gladstone may possibly have been misled by Salisbury, in his deliberately delphic pre-election speech in 1885, saying that the 'integrity of the Empire' was more important almost than any other political consideration, for the Liberal leader always spoke of Home Rule for Ireland as compatible with 'the integrity of the Empire'. But *he* had begun to envisage Parnell as a potentially conservative devolutionist leader, and Salisbury never believed that such a one would survive under Home Rule. Even in 1885 he specifically linked the retention of Ireland with the imperial theme, and it was on the basis that 'any political power conceded to an Irish assembly will be made the fulcrum by which more will be exacted, until complete independence is secured,' that he joined with Whig notables led by Hartington at the anti-Home Rule rally at the Royal Opera House, Covent Garden, on 16 May 1886. He never believed that the issue was devolution; he knew it was separ-

* Present writer's italics.

ation – and, moreover, an anti-British tariff, if not an anti-British foreign policy as in days of yore. He told the National Union on 16 May 1886 that Hottentots, Indians, Greeks, Russians and Irish were unfitted for self-government. Apparently only Teutonic races were so fitted. He dwelt on 'sacred obligations [to] all that is Protestant – nay all that is loyal – all who have land or money to lose' in an Ireland that had never been one nation but two. He approved Churchill playing 'the Orange Card' in 1886, and in May 1893 followed Balfour to Belfast to hail Ulster as 'a rampart of Empire' and tell the Londonderry Prentice Boys that an 'ancient, arrogant, hostile, lawless spirit' sometimes masqueraded in ecclesiastical garments. A pessimist ever, he feared that John Bull might be tempted to get rid of the Irish from Westminster, as Radicals feared no effective work could be done with them there. 'The instinctive feeling of an Englishman is to wish to get rid of an Irishman', he said, though Gladstone's proposal of taxation without representation was Chamberlain's excuse for the breach with the Liberal leader who so fatally undervalued him and paved the way for the defeat of Home Rule in 1886.

Similarly, Salisbury did not think the O'Shea divorce in 1890, which led Gladstone, mindful of the Nonconformist vote, to insist on the deposition of the co-respondent, Parnell, would be a Unionist electoral asset, though it counteracted the effects of the foolish Unionist Commission on 'Parnellism and Crime' based on forged letters. But he deprecated, amid wild cheers, at Leeds on 18 June 1886, Irish immigration into Britain, which dragged down wages and housing standards, so that his opponents labelled his policy 'manacles and Manitoba'. This line patently assisted the Tory–Liberal Unionist alliance both in Lancashire and the West of Scotland; in the latter Conservatism had been weak but Unionism, based on religious prejudice and economic competition among the working classes, was strong.

Salisbury, however, both as a cautious Foreign Secretary and a party leader willing to exploit, but not exacerbate, imperialist sentiment, also emphasised the strategic and diplomatic importance of Ireland. Its coast, in unfriendly hands, 'would be something more than a pistol held to the mouths of the Clyde and the Mersey and the Severn.' (This mattered the more when Peel and Gladstone had made Britain dependent on foreign food.) And there were other subject-races assessing the resolution of the British: 'If you fail in this trial', he told the primrose-badged audience at Exeter in April 1892, 'one by one the flowers will be plucked from the diadem of Empire and you will be reduced to depend on the resources of this small, over-peopled island.' Moreover, 'the great game' to Salisbury was not, as to Disraeli, parliamentary politics but diplomacy, the balance of power in Europe, accommodation in Africa and the East, and he regarded the firm maintenance of the union with Ireland as a test of British will-power which would be noted in St Petersburg, Berlin and Paris.

On these interwoven themes against Gladstone and his successors, who sidled away as fast as they could, some with decency and some without, from his Home Rule commitment, Salisbury, allied with Hartington and Chamberlain, never failed to carry the British people with him.

But Unionist policy towards Ireland was not merely negative, as Salisbury's speech to the National Union on 16 May 1886 seemed to imply:

'My alternative policy is that Parliament should enable the Government of England to govern Ireland. Apply that remedy honestly, consistently and resolutely for twenty years and at the end of that time you will find that Ireland will be fit to accept any gifts in the way of local government or repeal of coercion laws that you may wish to give her. What she wants is government ... that does not flinch, that does not vary; government that she cannot hope to beat down by agitations at Westminster ...'

This seemed to suggest a permanent Spencerian regime, with nothing more than county councils at the tail. In fact the latter, vastly pleasing to the Roman hierarchy, came in 1898 (and nearly in 1892). There was, indeed, a permanent Crimes Act, giving the executive the widest powers (the use of which Salisbury sometimes restrained) prepared by Beach but, to the general astonishment, entrusted to the delicate and apparently dilettante Balfour. The Irishmen and Gladstonians prepared (1887) to 'make a meal of him', but in Dublin and at West-

minster he showed a toughness which made him Salisbury's
obvious successor. To Irish MPs and a few turbulent priests
incarcerated at his command the man mocked as 'Clara' or
'Pretty Polly' became 'Bloody Balfour'. When he left the Chief
Secretaryship to become Leader of the Commons in place of
W. H. Smith (who died of the strain) in 1891, coercion was
being hardly applied at all. For Balfour added to the recipe of
'twenty years of resolute government' the policy of 'killing
Home Rule by kindness'. The unpopularity with the landlords of his Land Purchase Act of 1891 and that of his brother
Gerald, 1896 – the larger-endowed successors of the Ashbourne Act of 1885 – made them less radical than he would
have wished, and therefore less effective; coercion had to be
reactivated in the South-West at the end of the century. But
when Balfour was Prime Minister, his brilliant colleague
George Wyndham, by an Act of 1903, which at state expense
bribed landlord to sell and tenant to buy, enabled Balfour in
his old age to claim that the Ireland inherited by the Free State
(1922) was a peasant democracy which 'we created' as a substitute for the 'radically rotten' system of Gladstone's 1881 Act.
While, under Treasury guarantee, the landlords were being
bought out, governmental guarantee and grant were achieving
positive improvements which constitute the first experiments
in public aid to 'depressed areas'. After assistance for drainage
and light railways came the Congested Districts' Board, grant-
aided but independent, to provide not, mainly, relief but the
revival of fishing, cottage and light industries, assisted emigration and livestock improvement. Though it was felt that
the ambit of the Board ought to be extended and the graziers'
land made available to the peasant, the Roman prelates of
Connacht paid tribute to Gerald Balfour, whose policy Sir
Horace Plunkett described as 'the most fruitful . . . which any
administration had ever devised for the better government of
Ireland.'

In Ireland the Unionist policy of 'no nonsense' combined
with goodwill deeply alarmed extremists, for it was bringing
together people thought irreconcilable. Thus the savage
Orangeman, Colonel Saunderson, who led a splinter group in
the House of Commons, was elected chairman of the Financial
Relations Committee, a body of Irishmen determined to ex-

ploit the evidence of the Childers Report (1896) to the effect that Ireland was over-taxed. The Parnellite Redmond sat on the Recess Committee proposed by Plunkett which led to the establishment of the important Department of Agriculture and Technical Instruction, under Plunkett, which enjoyed considerable goodwill among the Roman priesthood. The Wyndham Purchase Bill, and its accompanying development grant, emerged not from Whitehall but from a Land Conference in Ireland. 'I want to smash the agitation, introduce a Land Bill, get money for a Harbour and Fishing policy in the West and float a Catholic University', wrote Wyndham on appointment. In all but the last he succeeded. Given the support of the Irish and English Catholic hierarchies for Balfour's (English) Education Act of 1902, a détente with all Irish public men except the wildest on either side seemed in the cards, and the appointment of the Indian administrator, Sir Anthony Macdonnell, a Roman Catholic with devolutionist leanings, as Permanent Secretary at Dublin Castle seemed propitious. But Irish divisions, not crudely Protestant versus Catholic, killed the scheme, and in January 1904 Londonderry, the Ulsterman who was Lord Lieutenant, made it clear that nothing would be done. Within a year he had been joined as Chief Secretary by the pro-Ulster Walter Long, remembered, if at all in Ireland, as the man who stopped the money for Gaelic teaching. Wyndham, a Tory reformer, had gone – his offences two-fold. His speech of April 1904, based on the report of a Royal Commission on the National (Elementary) School System, was too like Arthur Balfour's English Act to be tolerable to the hierarchy, horrified at the role proposed for local and central government, displacing the priest as the effective overseer. And no one would believe his denial that he had encouraged Macdonnell in working with Lord Dunraven (a Plunketteer) on behalf of the Irish Reform Association for 'devolution' and an Irish financial council. Wyndham, for whom a great future had seemed indicated, resigned in March 1905, a victim of the Orangemen.[4]

THE DEFENCE OF CAPITAL

The party most associated with the doctrine of *laissez-faire* in the nineteenth century was the Liberal, and its attacks were increasingly levied against landed property, whether rural or urban. The latter, with its potential of 'unearned increment', began to take precedence as agriculture declined, though Lloyd George, after his 1909 assault on real property (in practice ineffective and repealed when he was Prime Minister), planned for the next election (stopped by the war) a Land Campaign.

This radical movement against the owner of real property was of far greater political than economic significance. Gladstone chose allotments, with an amendment by Jesse Collings to the Queen's Speech, as the occasion for bringing down Salisbury (January 1886) without committing himself on Ireland. But good landlords were already practising what radicals preached. Gladstone disliked compulsion as much as Salisbury. The permissive legislation adopted by the Salisbury Government of 1886–92 under implicit pressure from Chamberlain, upon whose goodwill the administration depended, was not widely implemented. Similarly, the Housing of the Working Classes Acts of 1885 and afterwards had little effect. Yet Salisbury, to whose initiative they were due, was regarded by Goschen as well as Wemyss as a dangerous radical for his suggestion that property for rehousing be acquired at less than market value. The genuineness of his horror at the human squalor in the cities which he blamed for 'the great plague of intemperance' and impeding education is not in doubt; it was right to 'be forward in defence of the poor; no system that is not just between rich and poor can hope to survive', he said, and they must deal with the conflict of capital and labour and widespread poverty.[5] There was nothing wrong with the analysis, though in time the Marquess lost his 1880 fear that 'the hurricane which has swept us away ... may be the beginning of a vexatious war of classes'.[6] But in the 'Disintegration' article of 1883 he wrote of 'the slow estrangement of the classes' in a democracy where the civil war was fought with gloves on. He argued that the Liberals' aim was to split the nation 'into a bundle of unfriendly and distrustful fragments' and that the Conservatives ought to concentrate the united force of the nation on objects of general importance. This is a reiteration of the Disraelian theme that the Conservatives were the 'National Party' (Salisbury suggested the name might be 'Constitutional') which they have faithfully symbolised with their Union Jacks and national anthems at their meetings. But the truth is that the nation was moving, under the impact of the Depression, into a division as threatening as that of the 1830s and 1840s.

Soon after Gladstone took office in 1886, unemployed demonstrators looted in the West End; under Salisbury armed troops were deployed in Trafalgar Square and insubordination spread among the police, the postmen and even a famous regiment. There were strikes galore, including the celebrated London dock strike, and new 'mass' unions seemed a fertile field for socialist agitators of various kinds, other than the Fabians who hoped to advance collectivism through Chamberlain or the Liberal imperialists. So far from minimising the threat to social order Salisbury declared that something must be done. 'Unemployment was a constant anxiety to the benevolent and a peril to the State'; that so many quacks gathered round a bed showed the existence of a patient. But, unlike Peel, Salisbury did not know what to do about it all, except to express sentiments which have been part of Conservative philosophy ever since – that the remedy lay not in the redistribution of existing wealth but in the creation of new. 'What is important to [the poor] is that capital should flow, that employment should exist.' Such speeches butter no bread; they are essentially negative and Goschen's 'sound system of finance based upon a pacific policy' was simply Gladstonian Liberalism with a Tory gloss to the effect that this should enable the Conservatives to devote their energies to social issues. When the Liberal Harcourt with his death duties (1894) and his dictum 'We are all socialists now' trumped, Salisbury in the general election of 1895 overtrumped, surrendering, the Liberal leader Rosebery alleged, to 'the Birmingham clique'.

There was some truth in this. The Salisbury Government of 1886–92 had performed good works in Britain as well as Ireland, but when Chamberlain boasted of this, Salisbury reproved him, partly because the old Tory faithfuls would say he had yielded to Liberal Unionist pressure and partly because he disliked the suggestion that he had done anything other than his duty when a practical case had been made out for a reform. He was almost apt to top the error of Beaconsfield and Cross in the 1880 election, when they failed to stress their

social reforms, by adopting an apologetic note. This was partly
because he feared abstentions by the old faithfuls and partly
because of his contractual view of the duty of the leader to the
led, already discussed with regard to the Union. C. T. Ritchie
would not have passed or survived his Act of 1888, creating the
county councils elected by ratepayers, in the face of the indignation of thousands of old faithfuls whose public service on
the old local boards had supplemented or created their status
as local notables, without strong support from Salisbury, who
said that if they did not keep control in the hands of their own
class (as in the rural counties they did) it would be their own
fault. With the greatest reluctance, persuaded by the Cowper
Report that Irish tenants could not afford the judicial rents
fixed under Gladstone's 1881 Act (which made no provision
for continually falling agricultural prices), he persuaded the
Lords (1887) to join him in reversing his own refusal to accept
this argument from Parnell the previous year. It was, he said,
part of the heavy price they had to pay for maintaining the
Union to allow downward revision of rents. In 1891 he was busy
explaining to the old faithfuls the proposition that if one made
education compulsory it was only fair to make it free. He usually
sounded as though he was trying to convince himself as
well as his followers.

Having decided, despite defeat in the 1892 election, to meet
the new Parliament, Salisbury rejected as dishonourable the
proposal of Chamberlain and Balfour that they should put
into the Queen's Speech (on which they would be defeated)
'an ambitious social programme' in order to embarrass the
incoming Gladstone Government, which would be weighted
down by its leader's Irish obsession and the patchwork Newcastle Programme. So it seemed a new Salisbury who told the
Lords on 6 July 1895, on resuming office but before the election,
that they must put an end to a generation of 'muffled civil war'
and attend to 'the restoration of prosperity and the decrease of
suffering among the poorer classes of the population.' Much
could be done 'in alleviating the conditions of those who, by
no fault of their own . . . are cast into misery.' And then, as
victor, heading a Unionist Government but also the first
Conservative majority since 1874, he told the peers that instead
of the Liberal recipe of 'uproot, uproot and uproot' and tamper

with the unity of these kingdoms, Parliament had the blessed
task of securing 'the improvement of the daily life of the struggling millions.' The lyrical note survived in a speech at Watford
in October:

'We have got to make, as far as we can, this country more
pleasant to live in for the vast majority ... Is it not more
important that we should save men, well-to-do men from ruin
and working men from starvation, instead of bringing forward
measures whose only effect can be to hound class against class,
and creed against creed. . . ?'

Yet little action followed. There was always a deadening
caution. The Unionists, as Christopher Hollis once said, were
becoming 'sodden with Whiggery'. Previously defending
property in the name of liberty, they were now defending
property and liberty as inseparable. The real attitude at the
top comes out in an exchange between W. H. Smith and
Salisbury. 'Men who are strictly honest in their transactions
with their neighbours have come to regard Parliament as an
instrument by which a transfer of rights and property may
equitably be made from the few to the many', writes the
former, and back comes the gloomy reply: 'We are in a state
of bloodless civil war ... To loot somebody of something is
the common object, under a thick varnish of pious phrases. So
that our lines are not cast in pleasant places.' Salisbury 'rather
looked', to the London County Council created by Ritchie's
Act, 'to play the drunken Helot for our benefit', and when its
pressures for extensive collectivist powers confirmed his expectations, its potential was curbed (1899) by the creation of
the twenty-eight metropolitan boroughs. As to public expenditure, profits were not to be mulcted to provide what Sir
Alec Douglas-Home in an off-guard moment in 1963 called
'donations' to the needy – except that the Poor Law survived
and was somewhat relaxed and the distressed 'old faithful'
squires, parsons and farmers received rate relief. The Gladstonian fiscal system of income tax and duties on a very few
articles of common consumption survived, but the central
contribution to local expenditure increased.

This is not to say that the Salisbury Governments did nothing in the way of social reform. It is sometimes claimed that his second did more than any in the nineteenth century, by development along traditional lines, so that, for instance, shops came under surveillance on Factory Act lines; free elementary education became virtually universal and full-time, except where (as in Lancashire textiles) employers and unions conspired to keep half-timers; Goschen's 'whisky money' could be used for technical education. A host of 'minor' measures involving no expenditure except for criminal prosecutions – such as that for the protection of children from cruelty – were passed.[7] Chamberlain sent Salisbury in November 1894 a nine-point programme (significantly avoiding references to land!). With the first, especially important in East London and confusingly involving Jewish Tory candidates in a policy somewhat tainted with anti-semitism, the Premier had dealt in July when, with reference to alien immigration (especially from Tsardom), he said 'the state has a right to say that our poor law and our social system is for ourselves'. To most of the others Salisbury had no objection. Industrial arbitration courts, instituted by the Conciliation Act 1896, were little used. He was all for the encouragement of local authority slum clearance, but the ratepayers were not, and for cheap workmen's trains. Technical education he favoured. Chamberlain's proposal for labour exchanges was tried on a modest scale under Balfour but left for Winston Churchill as a Liberal to generalise. In temperance legislation, regarded as a residue of Chamberlain's Liberalism, Salisbury had no faith, and party supporters varied from members of the United Kingdom Alliance (mainly consisting of Liberal Nonconformists) to those who regarded the possession of a licence (though technically requiring annual renewal) as if it were freehold. Salisbury 'doubted the largeness of the principle' of allowing local authorities or a trade association to fix shop hours. The Liberal Government's Employers Liability Bill had been wrecked by the Unionists in the Lords and, on this item of Chamberlain's programme, he characteristically remarked that 'parties are always liable to the suspicion that ... the leaders may, in their anxiety to obtain new support, be inclined to hold cheaply the material interests of those whom their legislation affects'.

Presumably it was for this last reason that he made the doleful remark that, 'I fear that these social questions are destined to break up our party'.[8] For this he must be condemned. It is surely the duty of a party leader not merely to maintain party unity but to transmit to his successor the prospect, or hope, of triumph. Salisbury, with his *après moi le déluge* attitude, seems to have acknowledged no such obligation, for if his fears were justified a sustained process of 'educating his party' would seem to have been indicated. Perhaps he thought this was up to Balfour, the obvious successor, but he should have used the magisterial authority which he enjoyed in the country for the purpose of prodding the party in the Commons, which knew him not and refused to be overawed by someone so out of touch as to keep Henry Matthews at the Home Office for six years, although he was patently incompetent, and to appoint Sir James Fergusson as his Commons Foreign Affairs spokesman (1891) because he did not wish to offend the right-wing on the eve of an election. Every excuse to keep Matthews, upon whom Churchill had stumbled in Birmingham and recommended as a Roman Catholic ex-Home Ruler, was accepted; every excuse for not raising to high office the tetchy and aggrieved, but able, articulate and progressive Gorst was equally accepted – including his tendency to make it known that he sympathised with the grievances of underpaid public servants. This was regarded as disloyal. This was symptomatic of a failure to take into account the changing character of the party in the Commons at the same time that Salisbury, with infinite boredom, was wooing a changing party in the country. Yet when the Commons' ministers on two occasions told him that the sessional programme would have to be abandoned, he became very angry, imagining that the reforms in procedure (easier closure, the guillotine, regular closing time except for exempted business) ought to make anything possible.

That major legislative break-throughs were possible was shown by the passing of the Workmen's Compensation Act 1897, piloted nominally by Ridley but in practice by its begetter, Chamberlain. Technicalities on the basis of which two-thirds of claims under the Employers' Liability Acts had been rejected were swept away. Employers were compelled to insure against liability; the legal onus would in future favour the injured workman. Salisbury weighed in by informing Wemyss

(29 July 1897) that even if individual property should be regarded as an idol, it was 'the duty of the state to see that those interests which are represented by safety of life and limb for all its citizens' were protected. How, indeed, could it be otherwise when the alternative was poor relief? But this, surely, applied equally to the uninsured old, whether 'worthy' or not so. In 1891 Chamberlain raised the issue of old age pensions, suggesting State facilities to encourage self-provisions; Salisbury talked of it in the 1892 election; commissions heard evidence; committees conferred, and one presided over by Goschen made proposals. But nothing was done. By 1899 the Labour and humanitarian groups had 'given up' Chamberlain. In December of that year Salisbury told the Chancellor, Beach, that a scheme would be both just and wise, but that it was not urgent. The money raised by taxes and loans went to the Nile and the Niger, the sands of the Soudan and the South African veldt. Late in 1901, Chamberlain raised the question again, but Beach ruled it out, identifying heavy taxation as 'the great social danger' (16 September).[9]

No one now defends the folly of the Unionists in leaving to the Liberals the great basic social reform, the only one that proved universally popular among the working classes. It was too much to expect Salisbury to 'act in the spirit of democracy', though aristocratic paternalism, intellectual utilitarianism and the same sort of calm, realistic appraisal of facts which he brought to foreign policy, had carried him a long way from the 'pure squire Toryism' which, he saw in 1867, was played out. He lived essentially from day to day. He imparted no impulse. He developed no doctrine – except one of caveats. He left no legacy, except his brilliant, eccentric sons. His merits as Foreign Secretary in the period 1887–92 (Iddesleigh had been discarded simultaneously with Churchill) were rated high, and still are; possibly they are overrated. This was an asset to his party. But how it is possible to rate him a great, or even a competent, Prime Minister the present writer is unable to see. In effect, he was, in that role, no more than a Cabinet chairman, and aspired to be no more. He had criticised Beaconsfield for not being sufficiently master of his Cabinet, but was himself even less effective in this respect. This was partly because, as himself the head of a great department, increasingly subjected to criticism by his colleagues and from 1895 to 1900 increasingly overruled by them, he felt he must leave other ministers the autonomy he desired for himself.

The Treasury is always potent, and in Salisbury's time (after his dismissal of Churchill) it tended (outside the fields in which the Foreign and Colonial Secretaries and their agents imposed large and almost inescapable expenditures, and the naval programme based on the two-power standard – to counter the French and the Russians) to become omnipotent under Goschen, Beach and Ritchie, all of whom (despite the earlier Protectionism of Ritchie) may fairly be described as 'Peelite' in their attitude to domestic questions. And in that sphere of inter-departmental co-ordination which requires that a Premier be strong *as Premier*, Salisbury was hopeless. His foreign policy being based on the defence of Constantinople, he dismissed as chicken-hearted the realistic Admiralty view that this was impossible, though leaving his Liberal successor Rosebery (in effect chosen by the Queen and himself as a sound imperialist) a note that the disagreement between the two departments was serious. Report after report revealed the need for radical reforms in the War Office and army, and effective liaison between the service departments. Salisbury acted in the spirit of none of them, and the Cabinet Defence Committee which he set up under Hartington (from 1891 Duke of Devonshire) had a miniscule impact.[10]

Although at last induced to leave the foreign secretaryship in 1900 – his son Cranborne became Under-Secretary to keep father in touch – Salisbury thought it his duty to retain the premiership (with the office of Lord Privy Seal) until the end of the South African War in 1902. Although Balfour had his bad patches – as, for instance, when, after Black Week in South Africa he had to make a series of public speeches in January 1900, unable to blame the generals (as he would have liked to do) he blamed the public, which on the whole thought the ministry might reasonably shoulder some of the odium – the Unionists might hope for better leadership under nephew than uncle. Salisbury had never held a domestic office; as party leader he had never even visited the gallery of the House of Commons, in which the new Prime Minister had sat for nearly thirty years and led his party for eleven – an expert on procedure, a master of debate, and, judging by his Irish and educational legislation, altogether a more 'modern' man, despite his air of languor and intellectual sophistication.

Balfour had just forced the great Education Act of 1902 through the Cabinet. This brought all education, other than that in the public schools and universities, under the Board of Education created in 1899 in lieu of the Privy Council com- mittee, which gave direct grants to some high-status schools and subsidies to special committees of county, county borough and some large non-county borough councils. These managed the old 'board' schools of the 1870 Act and secondary schools, which were to be generally provided for the brighter pupils in the elementary schools (who could gain scholarships to them) or fee-payers. They were given minority representation on the management committees of the voluntary schools, which were to be rate-aided as well as state-aided. This evoked a great outcry from militant Nonconformists and Welsh county councils, for here was not only Lambeth but 'Rome on the rates'.

Balfour seemed a man who might hope to outwit the hetero- geneous Liberals, divided by personal rivalries and political differences accentuated by the Boer War. In 'Joe's election' of 1900 most Liberals were labelled pro-Boer and the Unionists contrived to maintain their parliamentary strength. It had been difficult to get Salisbury to issue any appeal to the electors, as he had nothing to say. Characteristically, the old man was alarmed at the lack of the 'swing of the pendulum', in which he had believed since 1867, hoping the cause was 'accidental and temporary' and not indicative of some new deep-digging factor.[11] There was, in fact, such a factor: economic, intel- lectual and emotional trends were working in favour of a 'progressivism', as P. F. Clarke calls it, to which the Unionists failed to appeal. In Lancashire the Tory peak was reached in 1895; there was a falling-off in 1900, and though the Education Act helped there, it was the last straw for Nonconformist, Church of Scotland and Free Kirk Liberal Unionists elsewhere (these were dying off anyway).

IMPERIALISM AND TARIFF REFORM

Salisbury's years of office saw imperialism in all its guises burgeon. Africa was partitioned between the European Powers;

China divided into spheres of interest for each European Power, including Germany, the ports, navigable rivers and potential lines of rail like the Trans-Siberian indicating an appropriate target. The Japanese joined in, becoming Britain's ally in 1902, despite Salisbury's protests – for her enemy was Russia.

In his European policy, the reign of 'public opinion' was used by Salisbury as a reason, or excuse, for refusing to turn his association with the Triple Alliance (Germany, Austria-Hungary and Italy), expressed in the Mediterranean Agreements, into a military alliance which the country might not, if occasion arose, be willing to honour. National self-assertion outside Europe, though repugnant to him, who did not believe Europeans, especially resident ones, would ever treat coloured races fairly, had to be recognised as a fact of the age. It was an unhealthy fact from Britain's point of view, since her traders were likely to be excluded from, or handicapped in, the areas acquired by Protectionist powers. The dividends from earlier British investment abroad added to the profits of current trade were failing to conceal Britain's comparative industrial inefficiency, as German and American industry grew apace and British money was tending to be invested abroad again instead of applied to the modernisation of plant and the development of new processes at home. So the British must have their share of the markets that were being partitioned, and the areas chosen must take account of expected profitability and also of strategic communications. Even the projected unification of South Africa *vis-à-vis* the rest of the world – *de facto* if President Kruger of the gold and diamond producing Transvaal was reasonable, *de jure* and in the last resort to be imposed by force if he was not – owed as much to the importance of the routes to India as to the resources of Africa.

There were, however, powerful pressure groups ranging from Scottish missionaries and their subscribers, determined to keep the papist Portuguese out of Nyasaland, to speculators seeking company charters out of lust for land, the minerals under it, and trade, who acquired political leverage in high places and were able to appeal to the vanity of many who believed that Britain had a providential imperial mission. This belief could derive either from national or racial vanity or genuine humanitarianism, which often conspired, producing a form of romanticism to which Rhodes appealed with his notion of painting Africa red on the map from the Cape to Cairo. Tales of adventure and discovery attracted adults and children alike, whether the hero be an honourable Livingstone or a dubious Stanley. The very term 'Missionary Road' up to Rhodesia tingled the conscience even though the British South Africa Company's charter of 1889 was to bring death to the bewildered Lobengula, servitude to the British (instead of to the Matabele) for the Mashona, and gold and land (with rich copper deposits to the north discovered later) to the predecessors of Ian Smith – though the Company was never able to pay a dividend until relieved in 1923 of its governmental responsibilities. The great companies operating in East and West Africa had had to be bought out within a very few years of their chartering because they could not afford the governmental responsibilities imposed upon them by a Treasury insisting on 'empire on the cheap'. Rosebery had the greatest difficulty in 1892–5, as Foreign Secretary, and then as Prime Minister (regarded by the Queen and Salisbury as a caretaker until Salisbury returned to power), in keeping the Uganda railway project alive.

The activities of other powers made it impossible for Salisbury to wait till the Uganda Railway was built before re-occupying the Soudan. This had to be done from Egypt and was followed by the removal of a small French party under Marchand from Fashoda, on the Nile south of Khartoum and Omdurman, where Kitchener had won his decisive battle (1898). This gave the Government a much-needed boost, but perturbed Salisbury, for where there is a victor there is a resentful vanquished. No such inhibitions deterred Chamberlain, in whom the militant imperialist had taken precedence over the social reformer. It was not without bloodshed that he secured for Britain so large a Nigerian Protectorate, at the expense of the French. His choice of the Colonial Office in 1895, in preference to the War Office, was significant; his staying there under Balfour, instead of asking for the Treasury (he was injured and in hospital when the change-over occurred), was to be fatal to the Unionist cause for many years because his adoption of Tariff Reform as the only practicable means of securing imperial solidarity (1903) found Ritchie, the erstwhile Protectionist but now a strong Free Trader, ensconced as Chancellor.

Salisbury was a reluctant imperialist, most concerned to achieve colonial agreements with other powers with the minimum of friction. Of these the most important seemed the Anglo–German agreement of 1890, which secured Kenya, Uganda and Zanzibar for the price of Tanganyika (and the Cape to Cairo aspiration), and useless Heligoland in the German Bight (which upset the Queen). But probably more important (as paving the way to the Anglo–French entente of 1902, which in turn led to the Anglo–Russian entente of 1907, and settled the line-up in the First World War) were an incomplete series of Anglo–French colonial agreements. Salisbury's European policy was based less on the Palmerstonian maxim that England must 'count for something' in the transactions of the world than the fear that, if she did not, she would be despised, as under Gladstone, by the powers, and they might gang up to treat the British Empire as 'divisible booty', it being a fact, as he told the Primrose League in Darwinian terms, that the world was divided into growing and declining empires. Chamberlain's private intrigue (known to Balfour) in 1898 for an Anglo–German alliance, publicised with talk of the worldwide supremacy and solidarity of the Anglo-Saxon Powers (the British Empire, Germany and the USA) offended him, for his answer to every German approach, by Bismarck or his successors, had been 'your price is too high'. This is characteristic of the gulf between Birmingham and Hatfield, immortalised in the contrast between Chamberlain's boast, 'I am a Jingo' and the declaration 'We are all Imperialists now', with Salisbury's petulant complaint that Africa was created to be a plague to the Foreign Office. Yet it is true that Gladstone, as Salisbury said, 'awoke the slumbering genius of imperialism' by the 'surrender' to the Boers after the skirmish of Majuba (1881), the massacre of Gordon and his men at Khartoum owing to dilatory decision-making (1884) and, indeed, the offer of Irish Home Rule.

While historians quarrel as to how deep and lasting was the hold of imperialism upon the British masses who, Marxists argue, were its victims as (under the Gladstonian fiscal system) they paid for it while a minority of entrepreneurs and investors profited, there is no doubt of two things. First, that in the South African War the news of the relief of Mafeking sent the East End of London as crazy with jubilation as the West End and, when it was thought the war was won, 'Joe's War' was followed by 'Joe's Election', in which the Government, for the only occasion between 1865 and 1955 (excepting the unusual coalition circumstances of 1918 and 1931) maintained or increased its majority. If there were warning signs from Lancashire, and the emergence of David Lloyd George from the status of an anti-landlord Welsh nationalist solicitor to an eloquent and fearless spokesman of pro-Boer Little Englandism, Scotland, which contributed hugely to the regiments at war, returned the first anti-Liberal majority since 1832. Second, imperialism infected the Liberal Party as well as the Unionists, so that the Webbs, for ever hopeful of 'debunking Gladstonian Liberalism in order to clear the way for Fabian Collectivism', alternated between looking to Rosebery and his associates Grey, Haldane, Asquith, Acland and Fowler for 'national efficiency' and condemning their faction as standing on 'a broad and shallow ground' and its Little Englander opponents for pure negativism. The majority of Liberal MPs appear to have moved with their new leader, the humdrum but shrewd Scots glutton, Sir Henry Campbell-Bannerman, from viewing the South African War as inevitable (while Grey said it was 'just') to condemning as 'methods of barbarism' the concentration of Boer women and children into insanitary camps when their men, not knowing when they were beaten, resorted to guerilla warfare; also to protesting subsequently in the name of humanitarianism and/or the interests of white labour, against 'Chinese slavery' – i.e. the employment in the mines of the Rand of volunteer yellow-skinned workers under indenture under barrack-like conditions and discipline.

Nevertheless, the personal and political divisions in the top Liberal echelon had seemed so wide that in November 1905 Balfour (perhaps knowing via Balmoral of the compact of Grey, Asquith and Haldane not to serve under 'C-B' if he stayed in the Commons) suddenly resigned, in the hope that Campbell-Bannerman would fail to form a strong government. It is never wise to underrate a politician's ambition and Balfour miscalculated. He could, however, take comfort in the appointment of Grey to the Foreign Office, which guaranteed continuity of foreign policy as in 1886 and 1892, though Haldane's radical army reforms (justified by him as the only means of averting compulsory military service as advocated by Lord Roberts and an increasing number of Unionists as it became evident that the growing German navy had no *raison d'être* other than to challenge the British Empire) do not appear to have been welcomed by Tory leaders, except perhaps Balfour himself privately, who retained even in Opposition a connection with the Committee of Imperial Defence.

The establishment of this committee of the Cabinet, in which service chiefs mingled with ministers in a network of sub-committees, with a secretariat and agenda and minutes (providing the prototype of postwar Cabinet government), was one of Balfour's achievements as Premier. The 'War Book', which was prepared to secure the stream of orders which issued in August 1914, was a reflection of his horror at the state he found the War Office in during Black Week 1899. The incompetence there and in the field were mercilessly exposed by a series of investigations which told adversely upon the Unionist ministers as well as the War Office 'experts' and the commanders (especially the Liberal General Buller, whom Balfour promptly replaced by Roberts, to whom Salisbury added the younger Kitchener), while the proposals for army reform of Brodrick (later Lord Middleton), one of the errant ministers, and of his critic and successor, Arnold-Forster, were laughed out of court, not least by young Winston Churchill, Tory MP for Oldham.

It is explained that Balfour remained in office for over three years of mounting unpopularity because there were certain things he was determined *as a statesman* to accomplish before he lost the general election, as Chamberlain had warned he was bound to do if he persisted with the education and licensing legislation (the latter recognised the right of 'the Trade' to compensation on the basis of the investment, when a licence was not renewed). These things included the establishment of the entente with France, the constitution of the CID and the decision as to the calibre of artillery to be used in Flanders in the Great War.[12] Whatever the judgement on these decisions, there is no doubt that, in and out of office, he was disastrous as Conservative leader. He was negligent. If it be said that he failed to reverse by legislation the Taff Vale judgement of the courts, which removed some important elements of trade unionist protection thought to have been assured by Cross in 1875, because he recognised that the business interests which had come over from the Liberals since 1870 were strong and unsympathetic to the unions (especially the new-style post-1890 sort), there is no excuse for failing to oversee Central Office effectively when Akers-Douglas was put into the Cabinet and Middleton resigned.

Balfour was too detached to be a good chief. The spread from Manchester, one division of which he represented, *of progressivism* under the impetus of C. P. Scott and L. T. Hobhouse of the *Manchester Guardian* – Liberal editors and writers were more important than MPs and most Shadow ministers and, later, ministers – was to him simply 'interesting', if noted at all. His followers were not even interesting. But what turned probably inevitable defeat into a catastrophe in terms of seats (the percentage swing was far less dramatic than is often thought) was his failure, lest decision split the party, to come to an intelligible decision on the issue of tariff reform raised by Chamberlain in public in May 1903 at Birmingham. Balfour half-enjoyed the two years of word-games such as Oxford philosophers now play. On one occasion the ministerialists left the chamber to avoid taking a stance on the issue. It was magnificent, and, as a parliamentary performance, long sustained, and has been much admired by Winston Churchill among others. But being 'too clever by half' is not leadership; Churchill himself crossed the floor in mid-1904 and thus qualified for a long ministerial career and intense Unionist animosity.

Unlike Balfour, Chamberlain liked to be positive and trenchant. Salisbury privately and Campbell-Bannerman publicly regarded the Boer War as 'Joe's', and so did the public. In fact it was Milner's war, and Chamberlain often advised restraint while Salisbury, strangely, sometimes did not. But Chamberlain was accorded the acclaim – and the odium. He adopted a positive attitude not only to Anglo-Saxon expansionism but to the development of the existing 'imperial estate', including the West Indies, ruined originally by free competition with foreign slave labour and now by subsidised European beet sugar. Provision was made for research into tropical agriculture and tropical diseases. Even Salisbury had deplored (1889) the application to the self-governing colonies of the 'most-favoured nation' clauses of commercial treaties, especially those with Belgium and the Zollverein, and co-operated with Chamberlain in getting rid of them (1897). The dominions (as they were soon to be called) of the British Com-monwealth of Nations (a phrase coined by Rosebery in Aus-tralia in January 1883) had since 1859 asserted the right to impose differential duties and horrified Gladstone by adding later the right to institute preferences one with another and negotiate treaties with foreign powers (as well as escaping from British ones which bound them). They did not see why rigid Gladstonian finance should dominate their very different circumstances. Generally, they were willing to grant preferences to Britain and at home only six dissented from Howard Vincent's motion at the National Union conference in favour of extended imperial preference in November 1891. At the Ottawa Conference in mid-1894 the colonies formalised their demands and the Canadian representatives passed on to Paris to negotiate after the Colonial Conference of 1902, making it clear they expected shortly to receive the offer of British preferences. The preferences till now had all been one-sided.

The difficulty of reconciling growing autonomy with imperial consolidation constituted the great problem in Britain operating as an imperial power. The 'colonies' – as they still were in law – at the jubilee conferences of 1887 and 1897 and that of 1902, intended to coincide with the coronation of King Edward, proved unwilling to make a 'due' contribution to the imperial defence on which they relied, and despite the French–Canadian Laurier's appeal to Chamberlain to 'call us to your counsels' felt that in any Council of Empire such as Chamber-lain desired Britain was bound to call the tune. The projects of 'organic union' advocated by the Imperial Federation League, founded in 1881 and for some years supported by Free Traders such as Forster and Rosebery, were not a practicable starting-point for closer and fortifying relations; having nothing to propose, Salisbury refused a call for a conference in 1889. By the end of the century Chamberlain had come, if only by a process of elimination, to the conclusion that the closer union all sentimentally desired, but of which the former dependencies were constitutionally afraid, could be achieved only by mutual imperial trade preferences. As the only impediment lay in British attachment to Cobdenism, with tariffs for revenue only and most-favoured nation clauses in commercial treaties, Chamberlain challenged this positively, under the soubriquet of 'tariff reform', in the Birmingham speech of 15 May 1903. The time seemed apt, as there was a growing cry, not only from Rosebery, for 'national efficiency', strengthened by every report on an aspect of the South Africa War, and revelations of German and American industrial progress calling for a reappraisal of British sloppiness.

If the Unionists had offered the people the Chamberlain line, appealing as a united party both to imperialist and efficiency sentiments with a programme enabling them to finance both defence expenditure and social reform, they would probably still have lost the 1906 election, for Chamberlain admitted to Lloyd George in the House that his policy involved food taxes, the produce of the dominions consisting of cereals and minerals rather than manufactures. Although the Liberals (in a limited electoral alliance with the new Labour Party negotiated between their whip Herbert Gladstone and Ramsay MacDonald in 1903) won on the whole on religious and moral issues raised by the education and licensing laws and 'Chinese slavery', they were able to add the spectre of 'black bread and horseflesh', calling in aid survivors from the 'hungry forties', Peel and the most popular aspect of Gladstone's career to the marginal effect of trade-unionist and class-orientated appeals. In any case, as has so often been said, the doctrine of free trade had come to attract an almost religious veneration. It was quite unnecessary for the Liberals to have a positive programme of any kind when, for the first time since the one-issue election of 1868, they could enter the contest visibly more united than their opponents; though Lord Rosebery stood aloof, attacking Home Rule, his Liberal Imperial League lieutenants, and Asquith most prominently, had participated as vigorously as Little Englanders in the defence of free trade. On the other side, all Balfour's brilliant equivocation had failed to prevent desertions, even of MPs, and open hostility to Chamberlain's programme among others, including the great houses of Cecil, Stanley and Cavendish, to say nothing of engendering popular suspicion that he himself was more deeply committed to Chamberlain than was the case.

While Chamberlain resigned, to become a proselytiser, Balfour extruded from his Cabinet the Cobdenite element led by Ritchie and including (to his regret) Devonshire, whom he had tried to separate from them. Chamberlain's son Austen became Chancellor of the Exchequer and clearly the Chamberlains thought Balfour had reneged on an agreement, for Austen's letter to Balfour of 24 August 1904, saying that in the circumstances it was futile to delay an election, clearly indicates that his father would not have resigned had he not expected Balfour to come out clearly for imperial preference, including food taxes. Was the party unable to move because of forty Free Fooders? he asked. Did Balfour not see that the party, 'timid, undecided, vacillating', without a constructive policy, beaten already, must be brought together on a common policy 'for the future' to awaken its enthusiasm for the necessary two election campaigns? 'Cannot you make a bridge for us all', he asked, to enable his father's enthusiastic supporters 'to unite with you?' Balfour replied that he hoped what Joseph Chamberlain fought for – imperial union, fiscal, military and naval of every kind compatible with self-government – would one day be national policy. Meanwhile, Protection would remain, 'as it had long been, a doctrine largely held in the Party, but with no place in its official creed', and in the next Unionist Parliament there would be no bread taxes, but a full and free and private discussion with the colonies, any resultant agreement to be submitted to the electorate by referendum.[13] 'If this is your last word, I do not see how I can possibly come into line with you at the next election', replied Austen tartly. But Balfour declined to lay down the upper limits of a corn tax (there had been one of 1s. a quarter during the war, repealed by Ritchie in contravention of a provisional Cabinet decision before Joseph Chamberlain left for South Africa in 1902) and a tariff on manufactures to impose 'retaliation' on foreign competitors, with anti-dumping provisions.

Retaliatory duties on foreign luxuries had been mentioned with approval by Salisbury in the early eighties and was thought by Chamberlain at the time to have attracted artisans in the 1885 election.[14] Randolph Churchill had said at stricken Bradford on 18 September 1881 that the opening of foreign markets, like oysters, required 'a strong clasp knife instead of being tickled with a feather', and the National Union in November 1887 called for measures against the influx of foreign goods and people. Salisbury had refused to be committed and took steps to see that the conferences of 1888 and 1889 did not pass similar motions. However, at Hastings on 19 May 1892 he had named the luxuries that might be taxed – wine, spirits, silk, gloves, lace, hops. But Chamberlain came to tariffs out of enthusiasm for imperial solidarity and defence, holding that Tariff Reform was just as vital as the navy, for which it would help to pay. This approach muffled the alternative or complementary theme that Protection (a word many a Unionist fought shy of) would create profits, investment, employment and revenue by 'taxing the foreigner'. Even to this there was a powerful reply – that all taxes fall on the ultimate consumer and that the Unionists, in a sordid alliance between landowners and capitalist entrepreneurs which, in operation, might well be corrupt, were trying to divert Britain from a road which would involve 'soaking the rich'. The old Conservative Party 'of religious convictions and constitutional principles' had given way, alleged Winston Churchill, to a new party 'rich, material and secular'.

Campbell-Bannerman said the real enemy of free trade was retaliation, as any greater scheme 'runs against free food and breaks its neck.' Joseph Chamberlain virtually admitted this to a minister, acknowledging Balfour's problem. 'The first political duty of a Prime Minister is to keep his party together,' he wrote (Balfour constantly said that he would never be a Peel). 'The part of our programme which has strong popular support is retaliation and reciprocity. The part that is weak, is Preference to the colonies and its attendant tax' (on food). He himself switched from talk of tariffs raising money for such things as old age pensions to talk of balancing any rise in the cost of living by reducing taxes on tea and sugar.[15] This switch of emphasis discouraged social reformers in the party and absolved the Opposition from having to present the image of 'a body of men with life and energy and a new outlook on the problems of the State', which Haldane as well as the Webbs deemed necessary. McKenna's heir remarks that in 1906 neither party had decided 'whether social reform was a duty or an unwelcome necessity'. The mammoth Liberal majority (the Unionists were reduced to 157) produced not only the first House of Commons without a clear majority committed to the Anglican Church and the first with substantial Labour representation (due in all but two cases to the Gladstone–MacDonald Pact or, as in South Wales, to Lib–Lab arrangements with the miners), but the first patently middle-class one, including a number of *laissez-faire* Liberals. But it took the Unionists very nearly ten years after Chamberlain raised the Tariff Reform issue to decide that Balfour's attitude to food taxes had been right after all.

In the interval Liberal ministers turned their attention to what Churchill in the *Nation* on 7 March 1908 called 'the untrodden field' of the 'corrective and constructive role of the State'. He assiduously cultivated Lancashire (he sat for a Manchester marginal until defeated in a by-election in 1908, when he entered the Cabinet) – Lancashire whose huge Unionist losses were attributed to Free Trade rather than the growth of 'progressivism' – even after he became member for Dundee, though it was at Glasgow, in a speech of 1 October 1906 published under the title *Liberalism and the New Social Problem*, that he enunciated a creed which, against a different foe, he still expounded as Conservative leader 1940–55. There was a great gulf fixed between the constitutionalist and the socialist, but no fixed line between individualism and collectivism. 'I look forward', he said, 'to the universal establishment of minimum standards of life and labour, and their progressive elevation as the energies of production may permit'. Asquith had talked of the Fabian national minimum years before and on the eve of his premiership, 1908 – admittedly during what Lloyd George called 'an electoral rot', which showed 'it is time that we did something that appealed straight to the people' – introduced on a modest scale old age pensions paid for out of taxes. The Unionists welcomed this as a temporary step to a full-scale contributory scheme and deplored, and in some cases excised, its limitations, though in the Lords there was some old-fashioned Gladstone–Salisbury talk about 'demoralising charity'.

The Opposition that year – the free trade ministry having naturally given the latest conference with the dominions the brush-off on preferences – put down an amendment to the King's Speech calling for the broadening and rationalising of the basis of taxation and the adaptation of the fiscal system to 'the present conditions of national and imperial trade'. But when Lloyd George succeeded Asquith as Chancellor, he declared that the sick, infirm and unemployed were 'problems the State has neglected too long' and added ominously, 'I have no nest egg . . . Next year I shall have to rob somebody else's hen roost and I must consider where I can get most eggs easiest and where I shall be least punished.'

Battle was about to be joined, essentially between two rival systems of financing the armaments required by the nature of the new but growing German navy, and social reforms involving more than inspection and mandatory or permitted local authority action, though the State subsidies in aid of rates would grow too. Although Lloyd George's 'People's Budget' of 1909 was, as Austen Chamberlain said, 'certainly great . . . a regular election manifesto', probably he did not expect the Lords to reject it. Even if Balfour's astonishing statement that whether in office or Opposition 'the great Unionist Party . . . [would] still control the destinies of this great Empire' was foolish, the more so in that he was without a seat till the City of London provided one, the Lords in general defeated only ministerial measures of the old kind – education, licensing, Welsh Church disestablishment and disendowment – while passing the Trade Union Bill as amended by Labour with the approval of 'C-B' (it reversed Taff Vale) and old age pensions. But the tactics of the Upper House were determined by the Shadow Cabinet, so that Lloyd George called it 'Mr Balfour's poodle'[16]; it was less the peers than the Opposition leadership which determined to take advantage of the constitutional nicety that, while it would be unconstitutional for a money bill to be introduced or amended in the Lords, no such certainty (whatever the Commons might say) prevented the Lords from defeating one. The Finance Bill of 1909 was defeated. The

explanation for what turned out to be folly was neither the
land and capital gains taxes (both of which disappointed the
revenue authorities while impeding housing), distasteful
though they were to an assembly of landholders, nor the
increases in taxes on whisky and tobacco, the one resented by
the Irish, the other by Labour. It was the insistence of the
Conservative Chief Whip, Acland-Hood, that 'all our people
are spoiling for a fight'.

A majority of the depleted Unionists in the Commons were
Tariff Reformers, looking for guidance to Austen Chamberlain
as the public voice of his father, incapacitated by a stroke in
1906 but following affairs keenly till his death in 1914. Ill-
content with the *Valentine Letters* of 14 February 1906 (a joint
production of Austen and Balfour's confidant Sandars, which
at the last moment averted a complete breach between Joseph
Chamberlain and Balfour), they thought that the masses (as
distinct from merchants, bankers, shippers and manufacturers
with cosmopolitan interests) were being converted to their
cause. In a time of rising unemployment and short time,
industrial disputes and a fall in real wages due to rising prices,
the pendulum appeared to be swinging satisfactorily. Urging
everyone to stress that, because of its anticipated effect on
investment and employment, Tariff Reform was 'the first and
greatest branch of social reform', Austen and Wyndham had,
with some difficulty, persuaded the Shadow Cabinet before the
Lloyd George budget to put down an amendment to the
Address on those lines, as well as one on Home Rule (of which
there was, in that House, with its independent Liberal majority,
no prospect). They remembered Joseph Chamberlain's penetrating remark that the danger lay not with the Liberals but
with 'Labour working through the Liberals'; by sheer hard
luck for the Opposition in this very year the Osborne Judgement declared trade union subscriptions to party funds illegal,
and the Lib-Lab miners' MPs joined the Labour Party.

Austen understood from 1906 that democracy wanted two
things: '. . . imperialism and social reform. We were successful
just as long as we combined the two ideals. We lost when we
failed to satisfy their aspirations on the second.' But a party
led by Balfour, with Joe speechless, could not match the cru-
sading tone with which Lloyd George advertised his budget as

'a war budget' to 'wage implacable war against poverty and squalidness.' Many a Unionist understood that his leader understood neither the 1906–10 House ('C-B' had flattened him with his 'Enough of this foolery; let us get down to business') nor ordinary mortals; after his defeat in Manchester he hardly ever met any, and could not enter into their inner minds. While at one level deeply disturbed by the crisis in the Cabinet – it was the year of 'We want eight [Dreadnoughts] and we won't wait', as Wyndham put it – he still thought electorally in 1885, or pre-1885, terms of old issues, old connections, old communities. Thus, though he had regarded the 1906 result as a dreadful portent, a pale reflection of the Russian revolution and the growth of continental socialism, he was afraid that if education was out of the way, Free Trade would carry Lancashire. It was only when he was told 'We are going to win largely in London and recover Lancashire. We shall reverse the position in the Midlands' that he stiffened on Tariff Reform, cheered Wyndham's assertion in the House that effectual preferences meant taxing corn and meat, and even at a Tariff Reform League meeting rebuked the Free Fooders for impairing the unity of the party.

Unfortunately for the Unionists, in the January 1910 election only the Midlands and Southern Counties came up trumps; the London and Lancashire gains were merely enough to put Unionists on a par with Liberals, with over eighty Irish Nationalists and over forty Labour MPs holding the balance and insisting on the abolition of the Lords' veto, which would *inter alia*, make Home Rule possible. This election – when in face of the menace to property, Liberal businessmen opposed to Tariff Reform voted Unionist (but who were they among so many?) – seems, if Lancashire is any guide, to indicate a marked secularisation of politics among the electors, to be reinforced by years of industrial disputes followed by the Great War.

The year 1910 was consumed by debates over the Parliament Bill, designed to replace the veto of a hereditary chamber by a delaying power for two sessions to be exercised by a body reformed in composition at some time in the future. The Opposition tried in vain to ensure that grave constitutional questions such as Home Rule could not be settled by the fiat of the Commons, elected perhaps on other issues, but must be submitted to a general election or referendum. After the Lords defeated the bill, another election in December produced no net change. The Opposition was reduced to a shambles as the 'diehards' were prepared to die in the last ditch, even if swamped by newcomers whom the new King, George V, had had to promise to ennoble if necessary, and the 'ditchers' were prepared to bow under protest; the division cut across that between full-blooded Tariff Reformers and Free Fooders and persisted when the diehards formed the Halsbury Club (named for the aged ex-Lord Chancellor whose partisan judicial appointments under Salisbury had done much to alienate Labour), though some who joined it denied that they were 'BMG' ('Balfour Must Go') men mustering at the call of Leo Maxse of the *National Review*, a strong Tariff Reformer. Indeed, Austen Chamberlain thought that, having got the party into a great mess, Balfour 'should help to extricate us before he left us.' For Lansdowne the Lords leader, who had joined him in urging surrender before 37 Unionists and 13 bishops gave the Government a majority of 17 for the bill, 116 opposing, might go too. And how could the diehard Selborne (brother-in-law of the Cecils) and the prime 'ditcher' Curzon (former Viceroy of India) be expected the one to serve under the other, and similarly Austen and Long in the Commons. The party was the more befuddled because, largely in response to a *cri de coeur* from the Tariff Reformer Bonar Law, whom he had persuaded to fight the Manchester seat which had elected and then turned out Churchill, Balfour, at the Albert Hall in the December election, promised that a Unionist Parliament would not introduce Tariff Reform without a referendum. Austen, who was away in Scotland when Balfour and Lansdowne decided this should be said, was furious as well as saddened. For, though Balfour purported to be answering Asquith's question why the Opposition insisted on a referendum on Home Rule while unwilling to assent to one on Tariff Reform, this was an Asquithian trap. What had been under discussion had been the right *of the Lords* to force a reference to the electorate. Since the Lords would defeat Home Rule but, presumably, not Tariff Reform, the parallel was, to say the least, not exact!

Balfour went, in November 1911, with the party so befuddled

that its MPs nearly elected in his place the dim, if peppery, squire Walter Long, of far less intelligence and parliamentary proficiency than Northcote, to confront the most talented Government front bench in our history. Nearly all the Shadow Cabinet, the Chief Whip, Lord Balcarres, and the machine at Central Office – taken over in July by the Birmingham MP, Arthur Steel-Maitland, holding the new post of Conservative Party chairman, in the leader's gift – preferred Austen Chamberlain, who ached to lead a ministry 'which would do great things in imperial and social affairs'. But the facts that he was technically a Liberal Unionist, a determined Tariff Reformer and food taxer, a diehard over the Parliament Bill, unconnected with the land and not a reactionary, offended enough back benchers to make it certain that if he beat Long when the Unionist MPs voted at the Carlton Club, it would be by a narrow margin and would not secure the unity of the Opposition as Long would indulge in the same sort of subterranean intrigues he had employed against Balfour. Despite his background – which told against him both because it was Birmingham and he was regarded by some, on the whole unfairly, as simply his father's voice – Austen was more of a gentleman than Long; 'he always played the game and always lost it', Churchill was to write.

All the canvassing authorised by a candidate was on the side of Long or the dark horse Bonar Law. Balcarres had arranged that the election should be on the earliest feasible day, which told against Long and in favour of Chamberlain, but his strongest wish was that there be no contest, especially if Long might win. And Austen got Long to promise to withdraw if he did, so that on 13 November 1911 Bonar Law was unanimously elected leader of the Unionists in the Commons (but not of the party) proposed by Long and seconded by Austen. The dualism of 1881–5 was thus resumed, for if the Government fell, the King might send for either Lansdowne or Law. This was not unimportant, as the major issue in 1912–14 was Irish Home Rule, to which Lansdowne, with large estates in Kerry, was totally opposed, whereas Law, born in an Ulster manse was, in the last resort, prepared to concede if an Ulster – the historic nine counties of Ireland's thirty-two, failing which six (which became in 1920 'Northern Ireland')

or even, at the pinch, four counties plus two-thirds of another
and half of a sixth – remained, as the Protestants wished, an
integral part of the United Kingdom. But the odds were that,
if the question arose, the King would send for Law.

THE LEADERSHIP OF LAW IN WAR AND PEACE (1911–21)[17]

Law, who had been a junior minister at the Board of Trade
1902–5, after a surprise victory in a Glasgow constituency in
1900 put him in the House (of whose business methods he
thought poorly), owed such status as he possessed to the stroke
which debilitated Joseph Chamberlain, making Austen the
principal Opposition speaker on fiscal matters, with Law
as his second string. A morose widower, raised in a dank
Canadian maritime manse and educated partly by Glasgow
High School and partly by his own reading, which made him
a quoter of Carlyle and an addict of Disraeli, he learned about
men and affairs as an iron and steel broker and banker, had a
memory for statistics rivalling Lord George Bentinck's and
never, unlike Disraeli, relished country house visits. A convinced Chamberlainite – the Chamberlain family's verdict that
he was a Protectionist rather than a Tariff Reformer was not
just, despite his advice to Balfour about the food taxes in
December 1910 – he resembled Balfour only in being a 'Hedger'
on the Parliament Act, believing that 'time . . . is worth something'. He totally lacked aesthetic sensitivity and, where
Balfour was detached, complex, equivocal, Bonar Law, even if
apparently pedestrian, was committed, partisan and clear.
'Where Balfour hesitated, Law struck.' Respected for his quiet
hammer-blow speeches on taxes and economics before he
became leader, he adopted a new style of rasping invective
at the Albert Hall and in the House in January 1912, damning
the Government as 'a revolutionary committee' of 'gamblers
who load the dice' and had no convictions. It was very difficult
to get such a man to 'run away' – he had the inner ruthlessness
that Austen lacked. Austen had bravely – for his ambitions,
fatally – repudiated Balfour's referendum pledge during the
leadership struggle.

Law got the Shadow Cabinet (which, finding cumbersome,
he consulted as little as possible) to agree in April 1912 to

repudiate, in due time, both this and Lansdowne's plan for the reform of the composition of the Upper House. He recognised that food taxes were an electoral handicap, but believed in them both as necessary to preferences for the dominions and a help to smallholders and Ireland, and saw in the issue a means of diverting contention from industrial conflict which threatened to end in revolution. But the 4th Marquess of Salisbury wrote that Tariff Reform with food taxes would prove the most costly policy in history if it made possible 'the dissolution of the constitution, the prostitution of the Prerogative, the Repeal of the Union and the Disestablishment of the Welsh Church' (1 May 1912), and Bonar Law, an agnostic who objected to the disendowment rather than the disestablishment, had to recognise that to many MPs (enthralled by the rhetoric of F. E. Smith, returned for Birkenhead in 1906 and admitted, like Law, to the Privy Council in the Coronation Honours List of 1911) the disestablishment of an Anglican Church was more important than even Home Rule, to say nothing of food taxes. Himself devoted to Tariff Reform and Ulster – 'the rest was only a game' – he, with Lansdowne, resolved on resignation when it transpired that Lansdowne's announcement to the National Union (11 December 1912) of the repudiation of the Balfour-pledge and the Lansdowne proposals for Lords' reform no longer bound 'the party' (in 1911 the Conservatives and Liberal Unionists had amalgamated) did not receive general endorsement.

After a campaign against 'stomach-taxes' by the press magnate Lord Northcliffe and *The Times* was, in effect, reinforced by the Lancashire Tories, probably (despite his assurances) reinforced by Lord Derby, all but six (the six including Law's bosom friend from Canada, Max Aitken, and also Leo Amery) signed an appeal, instigated by Carson, requesting the leaders to remain while repeating Balfour's pledge. They assented on the ground that only by so doing could they maintain the unity of the party, in the interests of which Austen had withdrawn in 1911. Law was convinced 'that if we are united we can win on the faults of our opponents'. By-election results showed that Lloyd George's scheme of national insurance, married to Churchill's system of benefits for a minority category of unemployed, was not an election winner. Not having divided against the third reading, the Tories were embarrassed by Law's impulsive pledge in the House to repeal the Act, a pledge he withdrew in *The Times*. But social-reforming Tories such as Worthington-Evans and Stanley Baldwin had an alternative scheme to hand, and the by-elections showed that it was not only with duchesses and doctors that the new scheme failed to 'take'.

The main issue by now was Home Rule. Once the Parliament Act 1911 was law, this could be enacted in the lifetime of the existing Parliament without the assent of the Lords. But the failure of the Liberals to reform the Upper House in accordance with the preamble to the Act enabled the Unionists to claim that the Constitution was 'in suspense' and that, pending Lords' reform, the royal prerogative of requiring a dissolution by dismissing ministers who refused to advise one (tried, and discredited, in 1834) was reactivated. On the other hand the King was entitled to reply that a general election would solve nothing, as the Ulster Unionists, led since early 1910 by a Dubliner of granite appearance and forensic brilliance, Edward Carson (succeeding Long), would not submit to a Dublin Parliament even if the Unionists lost the election. Essentially, Law and Carson, and the latter's lieutenants F. E. Smith and James Craig, were moderates, in that, unlike Unionists such as Long and Middleton (the former Brodrick) and in lesser degree Lansdowne and the Cecils, they were prepared to see Home Rule granted to most of the thirty-two counties provided an Ulster remained an integral part of the United Kingdom. But it was their tactic to sound immoderate, in order, ideally, to secure another general election or, at worst, to secure the exemption of Protestant North-East Ulster from rule by a Catholic Dublin Parliament. Bonar Law's speeches at Belfast on 9 April and at Blenheim on 29 July 1912 were arguably more provocative and dangerous than the disciplined operations of Carson and Craig, with their announced plan for a provisional government in Ulster (September 1911), their (perfectly legal) drilled Volunteers, their Covenant of September 1912 and even their gun-running of arms from Germany to Larne in April 1914. It was very serious to have the leader of the Conservative and Unionist Party, professedly dedicated to union between classes and the pursuit of the national interest by all men of goodwill, saying that there were 'things stronger than parliamentary majorities' and that he could 'imagine no length of resistance to which Ulster can go in which I would not be prepared to support them'.

Asquith called this Blenheim declaration 'a complete grammar of anarchy'. In truth it was a game of bluff and counter-bluff, with Asquith and his colleagues caring for Home Rule only because of their dependence on Redmond's Irish, while some Unionists hoped passionately to prevent any Home Rule at all and others, including Law and Carson, the inclusion of the North-East in Home Rule. That, they assured King and Government, would mean civil war. After talks with the Prime Minister, initiated because Law told the King that, whatever the constitutional rectitude, 'half of his people would think that he had failed in his duty', Law concluded and at Cardiff in January 1914 stated publicly that Asquith had reneged in deference to Redmond.

The Opposition now seriously considered amending in the Lords the annual Mutiny Act (which authorised a disciplined standing army) so that Ulster could not be coerced; Field-Marshal Lord Roberts would state that in civil war conditions normal rules of discipline did not apply. Such a plan disturbed even Lansdowne and Curzon, and Sir Henry Wilson, the Ulster-born staff officer, who from the War Office kept the Opposition better informed than the Government. The Unionists were let off the hook by what ministers called a 'misunderstanding' between the War Office and the officers at the Curragh. When Churchill used the word 'misunderstanding' in the House on 30 March 1914, Bonar Law cried 'rubbish'. He was convinced – on strong circumstantial evidence – of a ministerial plan both to occupy and provoke Ulster. This ministers denied while repudiating pledges given to the cavalry general Gough (who with the majority of his subordinate officers had accepted a stupid ministerial invitation to resign rather than coerce Ulster).

A month of bitter parliamentary wrangling followed, with the House of Commons sometimes resembling an ill-kept zoo, and Churchill comparing Law's vote of censure to one 'by the criminal classes upon the police', until on 5 May Asquith saw Law and Carson and ruled out the coercion of Ulster. But even a palace conference failed to agree what was meant by 'Ulster'. On 30 July, in view of the international situation, Law, who had proposed the exemption from a Dublin Parliament of the Six Counties until they were willing to come under it, requested the postponement of the bill, acceptable neither to Carson nor Redmond, which would give option to these counties now and also at a later date. He was very angry that ministers, after the world war began, insisted on putting through the Home Rule Bill (as well as the Welsh Church Bill) under the Parliament Act procedure, though accompanied by bills postponing their operation till after the war.

If the discordance over Ireland, threatening civil war, combined with industrial unrest and socialist and syndicalist propaganda and the antics of the militant suffragettes, strengthened the German hope that Britain would not intervene in the defeat of France by invasion through Luxemburg and Belgium, enabling the Central Powers to switch their might against Russia, the blame, as far as Ireland is concerned, must be shared between Conservatives and Liberals, both indulging in brinkmanship. But for the international conflict, 1915 if, as predicted, a depression year, might have tested severely the durability of Britain's democratic institutions; Austen thought 'our prospects, if we do win, alarming'. But Law had offered concessions to Asquith in October 1913 whereby 'our best card for the election will have been lost'. And he remained willing, as a Coalition minister after the Easter Rising in Ireland in 1916, to work with Asquith and Lloyd George (provided Irish representation at Westminster was reduced) to see Home Rule go into operation outside Northern Ireland, telling the party at the Carlton meeting of 7 July that since the war began he and Lansdowne had felt 'bound to do what we think right in the national interest without regard even to the interests of our Party' – as in the spring he had told the Unionist War Committee, 'largely representative of the Party', when it demanded universal conscription.

Though Carson as well as Balfour were with him on Ireland, Lansdowne, Long and Selborne were not, and he could not carry his followers. Indeed, since the first setbacks of the war, his prestige had fallen, because 'patriotic opposition' is a very difficult role to fill, and most of the party was ahead of him in concluding (as he did by the spring of 1916) that, in Sir Henry Wilson's words, Asquith was 'mentally and physically incapable of going to war heart and soul'. Having resisted the idea of Coalition, he virtually forced it when his voluble correspondent Admiral Fisher, brought back as First Sea Lord by Churchill, but now unable to work with him, resigned on 15 May 1915 and notified Law that 'a very great national disaster is near us in the Dardanelles' – an expedition unfairly attributed to Churchill, especially by the 'westerners' among the military men, to whom Law was over-deferential.

On 19 May Coalition was announced, but the party felt that Law, in the disposition of offices, did not fight hard enough for himself or his colleagues. The cultivated Asquith despised him as 'a gilded tradesman with the mind of a Glasgow bailie' when he might have made a suitable Minister of Munitions (a post given to Lloyd George) and was to be an efficient and (as the Governor of the Bank of England, Lord Cunliffe, found to his cost) firm Chancellor of the Exchequer. Asquith gave him the Colonial Office and accepted the exclusion of Haldane and Churchill, the one from office, the other from importance, and the inclusion of Carson and his 'galloper' F. E. Smith, though not of Campbell, a signatory of the Covenant. In the first coalition Cabinet, though the Unionists were now the largest party in the House of Commons, they secured only eight members to the thirteen Radicals (including Labour's Henderson), unless one reckons Kitchener as a Tory, whose appointment to the War Office the Unionists and the country had applauded at the outbreak of war, all unaware of how unsuitable he would prove. On the other hand, six of the eleven members of the War Committee of the Cabinet were Unionists. But this, as Carson told the Commons in November, after his resignation, was an inefficient body. Coming to the same conclusion, because a decision to evacuate the Dardanelles was delayed, Law proffered his own resignation. Admission to a reduced War Committee not leading to decision, Law, tangling with Curzon, forced the Cabinet on 23 November to take the decision.

The year 1916 was an awkward one for Law, conscious that

he was growing further away from his followers, who looked more and more to Carson. He shared their conviction that the machinery of government under Asquith was defective, even after Kitchener was drowned and Lloyd George took the War Office (offered Law after he had promised to support George). But he was reluctant to resign and risk a general election, leading to campaigning and subsequent Commons debates on party lines, squeamish of being accused of intrigue, convinced that Asquith, though unsuited to head the decision-making machinery, was the best Prime Minister from the point of view of national unity. How, with the press raging, Law and Carson came together with Lloyd George, and how Asquith, convinced of his indispensability, made and withdrew concessions to Lloyd George running the war, causing the latter's resignation; how Law was offered the premiership but turned it down after a palace conference showed that Asquith, sustained by the Liberal ministers, was as unwilling to serve under him as under Lloyd George, who then became Premier more and more dependent on the Conservative Party,[18] involve details not germane to the present subject. But the result was of the very greatest importance in party history. Conducting the war with a small War Cabinet in which he was the only Liberal and Law the only departmental minister (at the Exchequer), George and Law developed one of the most perfect partnerships in history, the more surprising in that their temperaments were utterly different and that Law's mistrust of George as a self-seeker had grown rather than diminished when they both served under Asquith. This partnership very nearly did not come into existence, for in 1915 Law had said he would cease to be a minister the moment 'the party to which I belong has lost confidence in me' and, stating that the vote on the disposal of enemy assets in Nigeria (on 8 November 1916) was one of confidence, he carried only 73 Unionists (including ministers) against Carson's 65.

Three weeks later he failed to persuade the other Unionist Cabinet ministers that a small War Council with powers, headed by Lloyd George, was necessary, and that he should threaten to resign in order to get it. To the last the attitude of the '3 Cs' (Curzon, Austen Chamberlain and Lord Robert Cecil) and of Long to the ministerial crisis was critical of Law's handling and very hostile to George, whose criticisms of Balfour at the Admiralty had just caused Balfour to resign. But an offer of the War Cabinet to the ambitious Curzon (instead of to Carson) broke the line, and all entered Lloyd George's Government, with Derby at the War Office and Carson at the Admiralty. Law proved an effective leader of the House (which Lloyd George rarely visited, except on very great occasions, till the second half of 1919). Law was gentle but firm. He surmounted the crisis caused by Lloyd George's offer (early 1918) to the Irish Convention – at which moderate Irishmen agreed, though moderate Irishmen were unrepresentative – which caused the resignation of Carson and Craig. The proposal, during the serious German attack in France in spring 1918, to extend conscription to Ireland ended all hopes of a peaceful settlement; the Irish Nationalists abandoned the House of Commons and very few ever returned, for in the general election of 1918 most of their seats were taken by the republican Sinn Fein.

It was not the fault of the Conservative leaders that this 'khaki' election was fought with the Liberal Party split, and 'coupons' awarded to Unionists and Lloyd George Liberals and 'patriotic' Labour candidates to the detriment of the Asquithians (only thirty of whom were returned, as compared with sixty anti-Government Labour). For Law was willing to have Asquith and some of his colleagues back, though they had voted against him and Lloyd George in the notorious Maurice debate of the spring which followed the publication of a letter from Gen. Maurice, based on confidential information acquired *ex officio*, accusing them of lying in Parliament. Nor is it true that the Unionists, eager to cash in on Lloyd George's popularity as 'the man who won the war', treated him badly in the negotiations of the whips over the allocation of coupons; if a large majority of these went to Unionists, it was for lack of Lloyd George Liberal candidates.[19] But the result was a clear Conservative majority (won on a low poll on a register for whose defectiveness a Conservative minister, Hayes Fisher, was sacked). The Unionists had 360 seats, the Ulster Unionists 25, the Lloyd George Liberals 130 and the National Democratic Party (chauvinist Labour) 10. To secure an agreed programme, the Unionists had had to accept concessions to Liberal policies, but the war had made increased state intervention familiar, and when Law made speeches in favour of greatly increased public provision for housing, for example, he seems to have been sincere. The same cannot be said of all, perhaps the majority, of his followers.

In the retrenchment that came with the slump of 1920 'homes fit for heroes' became a sick joke about which the Liberal Dr Addison, who went from the Ministry of Reconstruction to become first Minister of Health, but was, it was alleged, elbowed out of that office (1921) and then out of the ministry by the Tories, wrote bitterly in the *Scandal of the Slums* (1922).[20] Baldwin and Asquith agreed that this was a 'bad' Parliament; the former, who with Worthington-Evans had belonged to the Conservative Social Reform Committee and approved of the Liberal aspects of the 1918 programme (always saving the ban on extensive Protection), spoke of 'hard-faced men who looked as though they had done well out of the war'. Law himself favoured a once-and-for-all capital levy to reduce the swollen National Debt, interest on which consumed so much of the revenue. It was not imposed, because too many public men would be hit by it and feared it as a precedent for a Radical, perhaps a Labour, government. Despite Labour by-election gains in 1919, coinciding with industrial unrest which blossomed among socialist agitation in a world in which the word 'Bolshevik' was now a household one, the Conservative leadership was not 'reactionary'. It had to be realistic and relatively unadventurous at home, because of a widespread desire for a return to 'normality'. From 1920 seats were being lost to independent Conservative candidates promoted by the press-Lord Rothermere and independents promoted by the rascally demagogue Horatio Bottomley, all on the cry of 'anti-waste', and Bottomley's on the cry of 'anti-party' as well. There were widespread calls, echoed by the righteous Cecil brothers, for cuts in expenditure at home and abroad, where Russia and the Middle East ate up money – and there was rebellion in Ireland. When in March 1921 Law left the Government because of blood pressure, he left a nasty inheritance to Austen Chamberlain, elected leader of the Unionists by acclamation at the Carlton.

THE CONSERVATIVE DECLARATION OF INDEPENDENCE (1922)[21]

When Austen Chamberlain at last became leader of the Conservative and Unionist MPs, he called for 'a wider outlook and a broader union than can be found within the limits of a single party.' But, just a year earlier, the weathercock, Derby, had seen that if there was to be fusion between Unionists and 'National Liberals', urgently desired by Balfour and F. E. Smith of the former and Winston Churchill of the latter, it must be now or never. Lloyd George had put it to the Liberal ministers. He thought 'Liberal labels lead nowhere; we must be prepared to burn them', but most of them, and still more the Ll.G. MPs, disagreed, some hankering after Liberal reunion, others unwilling to be swallowed up in an overwhelmingly Conservative Party even under Lloyd George's leadership. It was they who doomed themselves, and Lloyd George with them, by their attitude in 1920. Highly vulnerable they were, having no deep roots or effective organisation in the constituencies, outside Wales, when at the Liberal conference in the middle of that year the split between the supporters of Asquith and of Lloyd George was confirmed; the only assets they brought to the coalition ranks were Lloyd George's prestige and energy and an attachment to Free Trade (displayed in their hostility to the Safeguarding of Industries Act 1921, which fell within the 1918 election programme, imposing a $33\frac{1}{3}$ per cent duty on foreign goods dumped or subsidised by currency depreciation), so that any by-election or future general election vote could not be taken as a mandate for general Protection, let alone food taxes. They took the fearful risk that if the Government which they existed to support became too unpopular, and especially if it became unpopular with the Right as well as the Left, the Conservative majority of the Government's supporters would repudiate them and turn them into scapegoats.

This is precisely what happened after a year and a half of Austen Chamberlain's leadership, when on the morning of a famous meeting of Unionist MPs and ministers at the Carlton Club, it became known that the electors of Newport, Monmouthshire, had made a mockery of the ministerial belief that division between Conservatives and Coalition Liberals would tend to let Labour in on a minority vote. The unofficial Tory won; the 'Coalie' polled less than 9,000 of some 34,000 votes cast. At the Carlton (19 October 1922) the Unionist MPs repudiated the Coalition by 187 votes to 87, even though it meant repudiating the advice of all the leading Conservative ministers. The size of the majority reflected the news from Newport. It also reflected the feeling expressed by a relatively new (and by Lloyd George and the other 'peacocks', Birkenhead and Churchill, who now appeared to be running the Government, ill-considered), Cabinet minister, Baldwin, that they must not allow the dynamic force of Lloyd George ('a terrible thing') to break up the Conservative Party after breaking up the Liberal Party. Finally it reflected the speech, but still more the presence, of Bonar Law. This indicated the availability of a Conservative Prime Minister even if the official leader, Chamberlain, the elder-statesman and ex-leader Balfour, and Lloyd George's cronies, the swaggering and intemperate Birkenhead and the brilliant self-indulgent Chancellor Sir Robert Horne (frequently tipped as a future Premier, but lacking party roots), proved un-amenable to the sentiments of the MPs who were influenced by the more hostile sentiments of their constituencies.

This dash for freedom from the burden of the Coalition's record imposed upon Austen Chamberlain an even deeper humiliation than was suffered by Edward Heath when he was replaced by Margaret Thatcher in 1975. He was not surprised at the antagonism of Bonar Law, for his thought was tinged by memories of 1911 (when Law had behaved as Austen said he never could himself have behaved). At the end of 1921 (when Lloyd George was airily dismissing the notion that Law had any desire to supplant him) he (unjustly) jaloused that Law was still 'a very ambitious man . . . itching to be back in politics where he is disposed to think that the first place might and ought to be his.' Law was, in fact, shortly before the Carlton meeting – though after delivering a shot across the bows which Austen would have done well to heed – thinking of complete retirement from politics. Austen was not the victim of Law, though he and Baldwin struck the public blow in the party forum. He was the victim of a fatal aloofness, not only of mannerisms and contacts but of understanding, from the party he led. At the final issue, he had both the party machine at

Central Office *and* the Chief Whip against him. This was a
record. He moved in an exactly opposite direction from those
he led.

It is said that in the fusion discussions of 1920, Law conveyed
to Lloyd George an opinion which *he* only marginally approved, and this is confirmed by Law's correspondence with
Balfour after the 'Coalies' had made their fatal mistake. On
24 March 1920 Law wrote that though he had become convinced that fusion was 'really inevitable' if the Coalition was to
continue, 'it always seemed more important from Lloyd
George's point of view than ours' and he was not sorry that the
'Coalies' had ruled it out. And we are told that in the decision
to seek fusion Austen 'acquiesced'. Lloyd George therefore
viewed the replacement of Law by Chamberlain with some
anxiety. This was justified as far as the capacity of the new
leader to control his followers was concerned, but not at all as
regards Austen's loyalty to Lloyd George. Sufficiently responsive to party feeling to defend the publication by the influential
treasurer, Younger, of his privately-accomplished sabotage of
the plan that the Coalition should go to the country at the
beginning of 1922, Austen Chamberlain thereafter was found
by Lloyd George easy to manipulate. On 27 February the
Premier offered to retire in his favour (after some by-election
defeats at the hands of Labour and Asquithian Liberals) but
suggested that he consult his Conservative Cabinet colleagues
first. They, as Lloyd George knew they would, said that Lloyd
George was indispensable and the Premier was therefore able
to vet Austen's speech to the Oxford Carlton Club where,
while not excommunicating Conservatives who stood independently, he urged the continuance of co-operation with the
National Liberals whether in or out of office. This was at a time
when Law, returning from the Continent, found among the
Conservatives a marked increase of anti-Coalition feeling. But
Austen, obviously over-impressed by the disappointments of
1910, wrote to the retired minister and rival, Long, on 27
April, that coalitionist feeling was strong among Conservative
members in the industrial districts of the North, the Midlands
and Scotland. A few days before disaster overtook him at the
Carlton Club, he wrote (11 October) to an old colleague of his
father, Parker-Smith: 'The danger which threatens us comes

from Labour. . . . Those who think that the Conservative or
Unionist Party, standing as such and disavowing its Liberal
allies, could return with a working majority are living in a
fool's paradise.' The event was to show that it was those who
met at No. 10 who dwelt in the fool's paradise, and that Law,
from outside, advising Lloyd George to resign while he could
do so with dignity, was the realist.

Lloyd George may be excused his delusions of continuing
grandeur. After all, except on the odd question such as the
payment of Addison as Minister without Portfolio after his
extrusion from Health, Conservative revolts in the Commons,
usually by Col. Gretton's diehards, had been defeated by
large majorities, even on the issue of negotiations in the
second half of 1921 with the Sinn Fein rebels who rejected the
Home Rule solution to the Irish Question imposed (in law in
two Irelands, in practice only in the Six Counties, where Craig
became the first Stormont Premier) by the 1920 Act envisaged
in the 1918 programme. No hero could be found to try to
work it in the South. The 'treaty' with the Sinn Fein delegates
led by Arthur Griffith and Michael Collins of December 1921,
was, arguably, the greatest achievement of the Coalition, the
most prominent British negotiators being Lloyd George,
Birkenhead, Austen Chamberlain and Churchill. It followed
an 'undeclared war' between the British occupying forces and
'the Republic of Ireland' proclaimed in Dublin early 1919 by
the minority of Sinn Fein MPs elected to Westminster who
were not in prison, in hiding or abroad. The conduct of this
war, on the British side – with first the 'unauthorised' reprisals
by the army and police, but especially by the 'Black and Tan'
volunteers and the Auxiliaries, and the authorised reprisals
that followed – offended a minority of Christian Tories
like the Cecils and progressives like Mosley as involving
'methods of barbarism' disgraceful to a civilised people. Even
more accused Lloyd George's Liberal chief secretaries, the
nervous Macnamara and the brash Canadian Hamar Green-
wood, of being too 'soft' with the rebels (simultaneously
misleading the Commons by evasive or lying replies to
questions).

When the Government found itself in a blind alley, it
initiated talks with the rebels (to their astonishment) which

were unpopular with many Conservatives, and the suggestion that ministers were 'pressurising' Northern Ireland in order to get it into a United Ireland with dominion status (but a large autonomy for the Six Counties) brought Bonar Law out of withdrawal and threatened alliance between him and Gretton (who had repudiated the whip because negotiations started). It is not quite clear whether we should regard his intervention as the cause of Lloyd George in November 1921 switching from pressure on the Ulstermen to pressure on the Sinn Fein delegates, but the threat that he might appear in an anti-Government stance at the Party Conference in Liverpool must have strengthened Lloyd George's hand by enabling him to argue to Griffith that unless De Valera's representatives made concessions the Government would be defeated at Liverpool and give place to a 'reactionary' Bonar Law Government. This enabled him to extract from the bemused leader of the Dublin delegation a pledge (intended to be provisional and related to the Liverpool conference) which, at the crisis of the Downing Street talks in December, Lloyd George whipped out as an engagement of honour. This had what we have learned from American experience in South-East Asia to describe as a 'domino' effect on the other Dublin delegates, who all signed the Articles of Agreement for a Treaty between Great Britain and the twenty-six counties, to be known as the Irish Free State, a dominion within the British Commonwealth, with provision for the exclusion of the North (which had had Home Rule thrust upon it), but also for a revision of the border which the Southerners thought would make the North unviable. It was the avowedly reluctant support of Law for the agreement which enabled it to pass through Parliament with no more than the usual diehard dissent, and it was a serious moment for ministers when he said at the end of June 1922 – after Republican extremists had been for some time in occupation of the Four Courts in the centre of Dublin and Field-Marshal Sir Henry Wilson, MP, military adviser to the Northern Ireland Government, had been assassinated on his London doorstep – that he doubted whether he would have voted for the agreement if he had understood that the Southern signatories did not mean to stand by it in good faith. This speech reinforced the ultimatum of Churchill, the responsible minister, to the Southern Government whose subsequent action, in concert with the British, led to civil war between it and de Valera's Republicans.

Probably 'the Irish surrender' and its consequences through 1922 provided the most important single impetus to the Unionist revolt against Lloyd George. In his warning of November 1921 to stop pressure on Craig, Law described the ministerial line as 'the greatest and most obvious breach . . . of the whole political life of every Unionist.' But on all domestic and foreign issues, as well as imperial, such as the Indian and Egyptian, which merged into the foreign, there was Tory criticism of the Coalition. There were, of course, also Tory divisions. Some hard-faced men without historical connections with the party opposed the capital levy which was mooted, regarded Austen 1919–21 as a prodigal Chancellor and welcomed the 1921 appointment of the Geddes Committee to apply the axe to public, including social, expenditure. On the opposite extreme was a minority, represented by Lord Henry Bentinck (who resigned the whip as an anti-coalitionist in 1918 and wrote *Tory Democracy*) and Sir Oswald Mosley (who resigned the whip in 1921). They were sympathetic to Labour and did not relish the way the pledges of social reform of 1918 were being torn up, in obeisance to the 'anti-waste' movement as Chamberlain succeeded Law. The Cecil brothers between them represented the whole gamut of Tory opposition to Lloyd George. Lord Hugh remained an old-fashioned champion of Church and State who in 1912, in his *Conservatism*, had developed a moral defence of private property, but did not consider morality a strong point of the ministry, and Lord Robert, while concurring in retrenchment, thought there was too much consideration for property, or, at least, ill-gotten wealth, and was deeply attached to the League of Nations and social reconciliation at home. He was a progressive. The 4th Marquess of Salisbury (out of office 1905–22 but influential in the party up to 1940) was a High Tory, early against fusion and then Coalition; he was for retrenchment, but, like his father, deplored the growth of class war and thought the ministry partly responsible for its bitterness. Each Cecil brother exposed sensitive Conservative nerves which ministerial action irritated in 1921–2, and their brother-in-law Selborne forced a Royal Commission on the Distribution of Honours, 1921. But it was above all the Marquess who, circulating to constituency associations a criticism of the Coalition as materialist, pluto-cratic, corrupt and prodigal, prepared the soil for its destruction by giving respectability on the one hand to Gretton's diehards and on the other to those who deplored every kind of con-frontation, whether with Labour or with Kemal, the Turkish nationalist leader with whom, on the eve of the break-up of the Coalition, ministers seemed to be on the brink of war.

The most prominent issue of 1922 was evidently foreign affairs, still pre-eminently, to the indignation of the Foreign Secretary, Lord Curzon, Lloyd George's personal business. The Prime Minister, having advertised his intended achieve-ments, failed to produce the hoped-for results of discussions with, especially, the French. But he persisted with a very per-sonal policy, even after the disastrous German–Russian rap-prochement of the spring, and the quarrel with the French about reparations: the policy of assisting the Greeks in their invasion of Asiatic Turkey, embarked upon when the pro-Allied Venizelos was in charge of Greece and strangely per-sisted in when the allegedly pro-German King Constantine returned in 1920. Lloyd George, having in the end vetoed Churchill's policy of continued activity against the Bolsheviks in Russia (which would have involved a renewal of the class war at home), continued to encourage the Greeks against the Turks, until the latter stood eye to eye with the British on the Asian shore of the Bosphorus, all prepared to invade Turkey-in-Europe.

War was avoided only by the rare intelligence of General Harington. The Government was discredited by an appeal to the Dominions, ineptly contrived by Churchill (it was published before they had decoded it), which drew a minimum response lost among the protests. This crisis on the Asiatic shores of the Dardanelles produced a crucial letter in the press from Bonar Law on 7 October, reminding Britishers that their troops were in this tricky position *vis-à-vis* the Turkish Nationalists because of agreements with Allies (including America) on which the Allies had reneged. Law indicated that however desirable it was to prevent Turkish massacres in the Balkans (a Glad-stonian Liberal aspiration) and hostile control of the Straits (a Disraelian Tory one, somewhat impaired by the 1915 agreement that Tsarist Russia should have Constantinople), it was not right that the burden should fall alone on the British Empire, which included more Mohammedans than any other State. There was wide support for his view that 'We cannot alone act as the policemen of the world. The financial and social condition of this country makes that impossible.' The traditional Tory pro-Turk Right and the Liberal–Labour self-determination Left agreed with many of the centre, especially as the French demanded assistance in extracting reparations from Germany while refusing to fulfil their commitments under the Treaty of Sèvres (1920), ratified by the Turkish Sultan but denounced by Kemal and his Nationalists, and were, indeed, actually assisting the Turkish nationalist leader. The bald assertions of the former leader of the Conservative and Unionist Party as to the realities of post-war international relations severely injured the Coalition, because they reflected general opinion in Britain as well as the Dominions. Lloyd George did himself only harm by combining in his Manchester speech an anti-French and anti-Turkish line; the latter had become unpopular, its advocacy regarded as a quaint survival of phil-Hellene Gladstonian Liberalism.

The country was ready for Bonar Law's call to 'restrict our attention to the safeguarding of the more immediate interests of the Empire.' In January Davidson, who on Law's retirement had become Baldwin's parliamentary private secretary instead of Law's, conveying Baldwin's view that 'our own people fervently desire to know where they stand and what they stand for', had suggested honest government, drastic economy, national security and no adventures at home or abroad, adding that 'the Tories must go separately to the Country.' By late July the junior ministers, mustered by the Chamberlainite imperialist and social reformer Leo Amery, were saying the same to their seniors; the rude hectoring of them by Birkenhead increased their conviction that the Coalition must end. Of course, they were the men whose official careers would be advanced by the installation of a purely Unionist administration, but it is impossible to hold guilty of pure careerism a group which included, as well as Amery, Edward Wood (later Lord Irwin, and later still Lord Halifax). And if back benchers were mustered by the ambitious Sir Samuel Hoare, he was assisted by the elderly privy councillor Ernest Pretyman and the archetypal landed back bencher George Lane-Fox, the mover and seconder of the Carlton resolution which slapped down, to their intense anger, the 'peacocks' of the Cabinet, whose reactions were always made public by the brilliant but obstreperous Birkenhead. The weathercocks were the 17th Earl of Derby, politically as well as socially influential (though not very bright), and the brilliant 1st Marquess Curzon, 'the very superior person' who, at the crucial moment when a successor to Law had to be chosen, was to be deemed lacking in popular roots and lose the game to the apparently humdrum Baldwin. By the beginning of September Derby was ready to join 'Salisbury and his new party'; this divided the trio, Derby, F. E. and the Protestant Liverpool brewer Salvidge, who was accustomed to preside over the Unionist effort in Lancashire and had manipulated the party conference of the previous November against Gretton and Salisbury over Irish negotiations. Curzon defected, to make his number with Law, two days before the Carlton meeting, for Lloyd George had humiliated him too often and he could hope under Law to enjoy at last a normal control of the Foreign Office.

The Cabinet decided on 16 September to appeal to the country as a Coalition. Younger was 'frankly appalled'; Birkenhead later described him as the cabin-boy who seized control of the ship. An announcement having been delayed by the Turkish crisis, Wilson, the Chief Whip, pleaded in vain at the Cabinet on 10 October that it should not go ahead without consulting the party. Only Baldwin supported him; the object of the others was to pre-empt the party action, likely to go against them at the annual conference on 15 November. The party managers, knowing that the party would be dangerously split by a continuance in the election of a coalition *under Lloyd George*, who now attracted such hate and whose unorthodox methods of government and meddling but ineffective foreign policy were unpopular, warned the party leader that unless party endorsement was sought they would publicly repudiate him and his Cabinet colleagues who clung to Lloyd George. This left to Austen the choice of means of consultation and date; he chose a meeting of MPs and ministers who were peers at the Carlton Club on the day the Newport result was due to be declared. There the MPs would be told bluntly they must 'either follow our advice or do without us'. This was élitism with a vengeance! It reaped a due reward. Birkenhead, on entering, was booed; Austen received some cheers but Law many more. The size of the majority was determined neither by the speeches of Law nor Baldwin but by the consciousness even of MPs personally inclined towards the Coalition that an electorally disastrous split would be the consequence of either a ministerial victory or a small anti-ministerialist majority. Those with a hankering for a return to 'normality', to clear party lines, a return if possible to a two-party system if the tiresome and now largely irrelevant Liberals, Lloyd George or Asquithian, could be squeezed out of an important role in the body politic, were of Law's opinion: 'I do personally attach more importance to keeping our Party a united party than to winning the next election.'

Immediately after the Carlton vote Lloyd George resigned, but Bonar Law, summoned to the Palace, refused to go until he had consulted 'the whole Conservative Party'. He chose to be elected leader *of the party* at a gathering of its MPs, candidates and peers, ironically summoned to the Hotel Cecil. His election, moved by Curzon and seconded by Baldwin, was unanimous.

Very conscious of the weakness of his Cabinet material – 'Do you think that I or Curzon imagine we can rule the country with the sort of people that will be left? . . . I must have Austen and F. E. back at the first opportunity . . .' – Law did not initiate mud-slinging between his followers and the Coalitionists. But Lloyd George and Birkenhead did, to the great benefit of the new Prime Minister in the election. To the taunt of second-class intellects levelled at the new Cabinet came the Cecilian response, 'better than second-class characters', and to Lloyd George's description of Law as honest to the point of simplicity, Baldwin retorted that by God that was what they were looking for. Nor did the clever and brash succeed in convincing men of the centre that the Carlton vote represented the revolt of the West End and Clubland, and that Law's policy, admittedly unexciting, was intolerably reactionary, even though the Asquithians (privately delighted at the humiliation of Lloyd George) felt bound to echo the charge.

What Law said in his election manifesto was basically what he had said in the famous letter during the Turkish crisis: 'The crying need of the nation ... is that we should have tranquillity and stability at home and abroad, so that free scope should be given to the initiative and enterprise of our citizens ...' These claimed precedence over 'many measures of legislative and administrative importance ... in themselves ... desirable.' Here was the old Salisbury–Whig specific, now directed especially against Labour, of trying to increase the national cake rather than concentrating upon how, in this overtaxed post-war society, the cake should be divided between the classes. The old and fatal dispute between Protectionists and Free Traders was avoided (and, as it transpired, left for Baldwin to manage or mismanage in 1923). The manifesto spoke of an imperial conference on the best way of promoting trade and economic development in the Empire, but during the campaign Law (with Derby, Salisbury, Devonshire and Novar in his Cabinet and a surprisingly wide press support) resorted, probably with crucial effect, to the old technique of promising that there would be no decisive change in the fiscal system without a further resort to the electors. And at the Carlton meeting Law, assured of the support of the diehards, had, most astutely, made a statement which gives a certain unity to the part of this volume contributed by this particular writer. He had looked back to 1846, this pragmatic, Peelite admirer of Disraeli, and declared that, if Austen Chamberlain's advice were followed, 'what is left of the Conservative Party will become more reactionary' and if that were to be the sole element in it 'our party is absolutely lost. ... It will be a repetition of what happened after Peel passed the Corn Bill ... it will take a generation before it gets back to the influence which the party ought to have.'

By virtue of three- and four-cornered contests – some of them due to Beaverbrook's intrusion of Independent Conservative candidates against Coalitionists whom Law, with his eye on reunion, made no effort to oppose – the Conservatives won at the end of 1922 their first avowedly independent majority since 1874, their second since 1841. With some 40 per cent of the electorate behind them, they took 344 seats to Labour's 138 and the Liberals' 117 (almost equally divided between Asquith and Lloyd George) giving them (counting Unionists supporting a defunct coalition and 'others' as opponents) an overall majority of 77. As the decisive results came from the counties, it is evident that the fission at the Carlton had enabled the Tories to heap the blame for the betrayal of agriculture on Lloyd George. It is equally evident that the indecisive borough results, compared with 1910, reflected the plutocratisation of the Conservative and Unionist Party, to which now adhered Liberals attached to private enterprise and the mainly middle-class women enfranchised in 1918 (women have ever since been more conservative than their menfolk), though still also an important minority of the working-classes in work, with old-fashioned ideas of worth and self-help who in the days of Gladstone versus Disraeli might have adhered to either of the rival leaders. Baldwin, succeeding Bonar Law, with even stronger Disraelian emotional loyalties had to decide how to appeal to these middle-class adherents and working-class loyalists, once it had been decided that he, rather than Curzon (a proud peer lacking, conspicuously, the common touch) should carry the Conservative banner and also reconcile Austen Chamberlain, Birkenhead and others, to the party leadership which, through their folly, had by-passed them in 1922. But Bonar Law too had clearly seen that, with a democratised electorate (quadrupled in 1918, though the grant of vote to *some* adult women only probably helped the Tories), the party must avoid a reactionary image. His speech at the Carlton gives the period 1846–1922 a unity often overlooked.

NOTES TO PART TWO

Chapter 1

1 9 April 1842; see p. 14 of Robert Stewart, *The Politics of Protection – Lord Derby and the Protectionist Party 1846–52*, Cambridge (1971), used in this chapter as the main source for Stanley (from 1851, 14th Earl of Derby).

The main source for Bentinck, apart from Stewart, is Disraeli's *Lord George Bentinck* (1851), in which the author consistently refers to himself as 'one who sate by Lord George Bentinck'. The main source for Disraeli (other than Hansard and Kebbel and, of course, Disraeli's own writings) is Lord Blake, *Disraeli* (1966).

2 Except where otherwise indicated, quotations from Disraeli's speeches are from T. E. Kebbel, *Selected Speeches of the Earl of Beaconsfield*, 2 vols. (1882).

3 Professor Gash does not think Peel hoped that 'the gentlemen of England', after deserting in droves on Maynooth and then coming to heel, would have been willing to do the same under *his* leadership once he had gone in for Repeal.

4 Stanley to Geo. W. Hope (Peelite), 7 April 1847, quoted by Stewart, p. 107.

5 Stanley to Rutland (father of Granby and Manners), 7 March 1846, ibid., p. 67.

6 Disraeli's *Reminiscences*, ed. Swartz (1975), p. 41.

7 The main source for this section is J. T. Ward, *The Factory Movement 1830–55* (1962).

8 Kebbel's preface. Shelburne had thought the early eighteenth-century Tories misrepresented.

9 See Ward, p. 387, on the defeat by 181 to 142 on 14 June 1850 of the amendment to end the protected persons' working day at 5.30 p.m.

10 ibid., pp. 310, 406, 415–17.

11 General preface to the 1870 edition of Disraeli's writings.

12 Malmesbury's *Memoirs of an ex-Minister* (1885) are a valuable source to 1869.

13 Kebbel rightly thought Disraeli's speeches to Oxford diocesan bodies in Nov. 1861, Oct. 1862 and Nov. 1864 worthy of inclusion in his selection.

14 John Vincent in *The Prime Ministers*, vol. II (1975), ed. H. van Thal.

15 Publicly, at the Merchant Taylors' Hall dinner, 2 April 1851 (Stewart, pp. 182–3); privately to Croker, 22 March: '. . . If I can consolidate with them the newly awakened spirit of Protestantism, and at the same time keep the latter within reasonable bounds, I can go to the country with the strong war-cry "Protestantism, Protection, and down with the income tax". . .' (ibid., p. 181).

16 See D. Southgate, *The Passing of the Whigs 1832–86* (1962), pp. 248–50, 294. E. M. Whitby, *History of the Session 1852–3* (1854), p. 219.

Chapter 2

1 Wilbur Devereux Jones, *Lord Derby and Victorian Conservatism*, Oxford (1956), pp. 213–14; this is currently the main source for Derby after 1852.

2 ibid., p. 195, Derby to Disraeli, 30 June 1853.

3 e.g. July speech in line with Disraeli's in Commons of 27 April 1854; attack on Gladstone's succession duties, 1853; attack on the elective principle in the Canadian upper house, 1854, bemoaning that the spirit

of democracy was the same everywhere; 31 May 1854 on 'fusion and confusion' as causes of the Crimean War; the China War speech, 24 February 1857.

4 Norman Gash, *Mr Secretary Peel* (1961), p. 14.

5 Donald Southgate, *The Most English Minister – the Policies and Politics of Palmerston* (1966), pp. 423–8.

6 From about this point the diary entries and later interpolations of Gathorne Hardy, as given in *Gathorne Hardy, First Earl of Cranbrook – a Memoir*, 2 vols., ed. Alfred E. Gathorne-Hardy (1910), become important, especially for their accounts of debates and of party meetings as, for instance, this one (vol. 1, p. 128).

7 For sources for Robert Cecil, 3rd Marquess of Salisbury, see Further Reading in *The Conservative Leadership 1832–1932*, ed. Donald Southgate (1974), pp. 249–50, to which should be added *Salisbury on Politics*, ed. Paul Smith (1972), and *Lord Salisbury* (1975), by Robert Taylor, in Allen Lane's British Political Biography series.

8 Gwendolen Cecil, *Life of Lord Salisbury*, vol. II, p. 90.

9 Michael Pinto-Duschinsky, *The Political Thought of Lord Salisbury, 1854–68* (1967).

10 W. D. Jones, op. cit., p. 271.

11 For a summary of the debate and its consequences see Southgate (op. cit., note 5, supra.), chapter XXVI.

12 (a) *Quarterly*, April 1860, 'The Budget and the Reform Bill'; (b) House of Commons, 27 April 1866; (c) *Quarterly*, April 1866. On the Embankment, Commons speeches 4 July 1862 and 22 June 1863.

13 Lord Blake, *Disraeli* (1966), pp. 437–42.

14 For bibliography, see J. T. Ward in *The Conservative Leadership 1832–1932*, p. 249, last paragraph.

15 Wemyss Reid (ed., *Leeds Mercury* 1870–87), *Politicians of Today* (1879).

16 Lord Blake, *The Office of Prime Minister* (1975), p. 36.

17 J. T. Ward in op. cit., note 14, supra, p. 73.

18 Gathorne-Hardy, vol. 1, pp. 208–10; Disraeli to Hardy 18 May 1867.

19 See especially P. F. Clarke, *Lancashire and the New Liberalism* (1971), chapter 3.

20 Fitzjames Stephen, *Liberty, Equality and Fraternity* (1873), chapter V, a riposte to John Stuart Mill's *On Liberty*.

Chapter 3

1 The two-volume life of Beach (later Lord St Aldwyn) by his daughter, Lady Victoria (1932), though dated, is still of use.

2 For Smith, who started as a Russellite Nonconformist and was a Palmerstonian Liberal when he received official Conservative support in Middlesex in 1865, see Lord Chilston, *W. H. Smith* (1965); and for suburban Conservatism, James Cornford, 'The Transformation of Conservatism in the late Nineteenth Century', in *Victorian Studies*, 1963.

3 Ormond, in *The Lord Advocates of Scotland*, gives a breakdown of the clerical vote for one of the two Scottish University seats just created,

which shows the ministers of the established kirk to be almost as solidly
Tory as those of the Free Kirk were Liberal.

4 *Quarterly*, Oct. 1871; Taylor, op. cit., pp. 35 and 38.

5 The best book on the Irish land question as a *land* question in this period
is B. L. Solow, *The Land Question and the Irish Economy, 1870–1903* (1971).

6 Gorst's long struggle to organise the visit is recounted in E. J. Feucht-
wanger, *Disraeli, Democracy and the Tory Party – Conservative Leadership and
Organization after the Second Reform Bill* (Oxford, 1968). The Burghley
House conclusion as stated is Hardy's; his son's *Cranbrook* is useful here.

7 Lord John Manners to his brother Granby, 18 Dec. 1849, quoted in
Ward, *The Factory Movement*, p. 374; Stanley to Disraeli, 1853, quoted
in P. F. Clarke, *Lancashire and the New Liberalism*, p. 33, a book the present
author has found invaluable.

8 Both Bodelsen and Knaplund, *Gladstone and Britain's Imperial Policy*,
published in the 1920s, have been reissued, and should be compared.

9 The figures as compared with 1868 would seem to be: industrial counties
15 of 18 (+5), quasi-counties 5 of 8 (no change), other English counties
129 of 154 (+14). There seem to have been 16 gains in non-English
counties and three in universities. Blake (p. 537) finds that Gorst raised
Scottish contests from 21 to 37 and registered 12 gains.

10 Malmesbury (67) and Richmond (56), with the Privy Seal and Privy
Council respectively, are ignored. Perhaps Carnarvon ought to pass
from the 'adequate' list. Chosen for the Colonial Office as a dedicated
federationist with an eye to South Africa, he chose bad agents and nine
months after his resignation the Prime Minister wrote to Lady Bradford
'Every day brings forth a new blunder of Twitters' (Blake, p. 668). He
was very troublesome on the Eastern Question.

11 Though Winston's biography of his father is a great work, it is obviously
preferable in most cases to rely on Robert Rhodes James, *Lord Randolph
Churchill* (1959). Randolph made a violent attack on the Government's
Irish policy at Woodstock in September 1877; the quoted remark on
Sclater-Booth in committee helped kill the County Government Bill,
which he called 'that impossible mixture of Radical principles and
Conservative precautions' – which it was!

12 Carnarvon also complained of Disraeli that 'he detests details; he does
no work' (Blake, p. 643). For the 'permissive' principle see ibid.,
p. 554. On the trade union legislation see especially F. M. Leventhal,
Respectable Radical – George Howell and Victorian Working-Class Politics,
pp. 179ff.

13 Disraeli to the Queen, 5 August 1875; and to Lady Chesterfield, 29
June; quoted Blake, p. 556.

14 See Blake, pp. 650, 719 and 721–7, including the letter to Lytton from
which Beaconsfield's quotation is taken.

15 See H. J. Hanham, *Elections and Party Management in the Age of Gladstone
and Disraeli* and Cornford in *Victorian Studies* (op. cit., note 2, supra).

16 The verdict on the state of the party, as well as on Disraeli, is by John
Vincent in *The Prime Ministers*, p. 107. G. M. Young (writing in 1937)

and Boyle are cited by J. T. Ward in *The Conservative Leadership 1832–1932*, ed. Southgate, pp. 98–9.

17 On the state of the party Feuchtwanger's book, cited in note 6, overlaps with and supplements Hanham's, cited in note 15, and is the principal source for the disputes of the early 1880s on which, of course, there is much in the biographies, such as that of Akers-Douglas by his descendant Lord Chilston, *Chief Whip* (1961). R. T. Mackenzie's *British Political Parties* (1955) is, of course, relevant and his *Angels in Marble* (1968) of some interest. On Churchill, see note 11 supra, Lord Rosebery's biography of Lord Randolph is of particular interest as being that of a personal friend and political opponent; they were contemporaries and both proved for reasons of health and temperament unsuitable for sustained public office.

18 For Salisbury's deep indignation at this retreat see the present author's article in *The Conservative Leadership, 1832–1932*, ed. Southgate, pp. 107–8.

19 It certainly surprised the present writer, when preparing an article for the Glasgow volume of *The Third Statistical Account of Scotland*, to find the Conservative vote in the seven seats allotted to that Liberal stronghold all lying in the 39–49 per cent range. Many later went Unionist.

20 Lord Gladstone's *After Forty Years* is cited because in defence of his father he makes the strongest attack on the Conservative behaviour 1885–6, his object being to show that the Cabinet, and Salisbury himself, might have adopted Home Rule but for the certainty of splitting the party. For his father's whole case for his own behaviour rests upon that assumption. But Salisbury found Gladstone's approaches to him via Balfour (late December), offering to support a government measure, insulting, not believing Gladstone could so misunderstand him.

Chapter 4

1 For which see Jas. Cornford, 'The Parliamentary Foundations of the Hotel Cecil', in *Ideas and Institutions of Victorian England*, Essays in Honour of G. Kitson Clark, ed. Robert Robson (1967).

2 This misapprehension is unfortunately reaffirmed, at least by implication, in the latest study of *Salisbury* by Robert Taylor (1975) in Christopher Cook's British Political Biographies series, from which some of the quotations from Salisbury's speeches in this chapter are taken.

3 *The Governing Passion*, Cabinet Government and Party Politics in Britain, 1885–86, by A. B. Cooke and John Vincent (1974). Their peculiar thesis is that everybody except them has got this crucial period wrong, because of concentration on the Liberal split over Home Rule. They depict the period as one in which Gladstone, in January 1885 'marked for the axe', carries out 'the most successful party purge in British history.'

4 For the Unionists and Ireland, see especially Barbara L. Solow, *The Land Question and the Irish Economy 1870–1903* (Harvard, 1971), which effectively strips down Hammond's admiring account of Gladstonian policy; David Q. Miller, *Church, State and Nation in Ireland 1898–1921* (1973), equally objective. With which compare Reginald Lucas, *Col.*

Saunderson, M.P. (1908), and John W. Mackail and Guy Wyndham, *Life and Letters of Geo. Wyndham*, 2 vols.

5 Salisbury, House of Lords, 22 Feb. 1884 and 31 June 1885; Taylor, op. cit., pp. 183–5; Enid M. Gaudie, *Cruel Habitations – A History of Working Class Housing, 1780–1918* (1974).

6 Contrast Salisbury with Balfour, 10 April 1880, with his letter to Alfred Austen (the political journalist whom he was guilty of making successor to Tennyson as Poet Laureate – some say because nobody else applied!), 2 Dec. 1889 to the effect that the next election would turn on Ireland as 'Socialism' was apt to blow up and disappear as in 1839, 1848 and 'I think, 1880'.

7 For the legislative reforms, year by year, see R. H. Gretton, *A Modern History of the English People 1885–1910* (2 vols., 1913); for verdicts, and Salisbury's views, see the unfinished biography by Gwendolen Cecil, the biography by A. L. Kennedy (1953), and Robert Taylor, see note 2 above. Also Lord Chilston, *W. H. Smith* (1965).

8 For the Chamberlain 'programme' of 1894, see Robert Taylor, pp. 151–2; for the pessimistic letter to Balfour about social questions 1892, ibid., p. 147.

9 On Matthews, see Southgate in *The Conservative Leadership, 1832–1932*, ed. Southgate (1974), pp. 133–5; on Gorst, see Cornford article cited in note 1; on old age pensions see Bentley B. Gilbert, *The Evolution of National Insurance in Great Britain – The Origin of the Welfare State* (1966) and Julian Amery (see note 11 below) who has (vol. V, pp. 5–8) Beach's letter to Salisbury in effect threatening resignation (16 Sept. 1901); Salisbury to Beach, 31 August and 18 Dec. 1899, are quoted by Robert Taylor, p. 160.

10 Salisbury was particularly incensed by what he regarded as the chicken-heartedness of his colleagues towards the United States over the Venezuela question 1895–6. His disparagement of the office of Premier is made very clear by Lady Gwendolen. For his failure over military re-organisation see W. S. Hamer, *The British Army – Civil and Military Relations 1885–1905* (1970).

11 Salisbury to Cranbrook, 19 Oct. 1900, seeing evil times ahead if the Reform Bills, digging down had 'come upon a layer of pure combativeness' is quoted by Robert Taylor, p. 164; for the Education Bill, including the narrow division at the Cabinet of 13 Dec. 1901, see Julian Amery, *The Life of Joseph Chamberlain*, vol. V, which is of much use in the next section on imperialism.

12 For Salisbury's European policy see, in addition to Gwendolen Cecil, C. J. Lowe, *Salisbury and the Mediterranean* (1962), Lilian M. Penson, *Foreign Affairs under the Third Marquess of Salisbury* (1962), and J. A. S. Grenville, *Lord Salisbury and Foreign Policy* (1964), which contains a character study based on Lady Gwendolen's privately printed *Biographical Studies of the Life and Political Character of Robert, Marquess of Salisbury*.

Amidst the large literature on late nineteenth-century imperialism special mention may be made of W. L. Langer, *Diplomacy of Imperialism* (1956), and G. W. Monger, *End of Isolation* (1963).

For Balfour see A. M. Gollin's essay in *The Conservative Leadership 1832–1932*, ed. Southgate, and the further reading he recommends (including his own longer works), ibid., p. 250. To these should be added P. Fraser, *Joseph Chamberlain; Radicalism and Empire 1868–1914* (1966); W. A. S. Hewins, *The Apologia of an Imperialist* (2 vols., 1929); and G. R. Searle, *The Quest for National Efficiency . . . 1899–1914* (1966).

13 Quotations from Austen Chamberlain 1904–14 and some letters to him are taken from his *Politics from the Inside* (1936), a particularly reliable source, Austen being a peculiarly honest politician.

14 B. H. Brown, *The Tariff Reform Movement in Great Britain 1881–95* (1943, reissued 1966), is important.

15 This letter of Chamberlain to Halsbury, quoted by Julian Amery, is dated 15 Sep. 1903; for divisions in the party later, see especially Neal Blewett, 'Free Fooders, Balfourites and Whole-Hoggers 1906–10', in *Historical Journal*, XI (1968), and R. A. Rempel, *Unionists Divided . . .* (1972).

16 Thus giving Roy Jenkins a ready-made name for his book on the constitutional crisis; see also Blewett, *The Peers, the Parties and the People; the General Elections of 1910* (1972).

17 See Robert Blake, *The Unknown Prime Minister* (1955); Jack Grainger in *The Conservative Leadership 1832–1932*, ed. Southgate; A. J. P. Taylor, *Politics in Wartime* (1964); Cameron Hazelhurst, *Politicians at War* (1971); H. Montgomery Hyde, *Carson* (1953).

18 Beaverbrook, *Politicians and the War 1914–16*, (2 vols., 1928; one vol. edition 1960); Barry McGill, 'Asquith's Predicament 1914–18' in *Journal of Modern History*, XLII (June 1970); P. Lowe in *Lloyd George, Twelve Essays*, ed. A. J. P. Taylor (1971).

19 Beaverbrook, *Men and Power 1917–18* (1959); A. J. P. Taylor, *Beaverbrook* (1972); Trevor Wilson, *The Downfall of the Liberal Party 1914–35* (1966), criticised by Chris Cook, 'A Stranger Death of Liberal England' in *Lloyd George, Twelve Essays*, ed. A. J. P. Taylor (1971), where see also K. O. Morgan on 'Lloyd George's Stage Army: The Coalition Liberals 1918–22' and D. D. Cuthbert on 'Lloyd George and Conservative Central Office'; J. M. McEwen, 'The Coupon Election of 1918 and Unionist Members of Parliament' in *Journal of Modern History*, XXXIV (Sep. 1962); Roy Douglas, 'The Background to the "Coupon" Election Arrangements' in the *English Historical Review*, LXXXVI (April 1971); David M. Close, 'Conservatives and Coalition after the 1st World War', ibid., XLV (June 1973).

20 Though not specifically directed to the subject of Conservatism, Addison's *Politics from Within 1911–18* (2 vols., 1924), and *Four and a Half Years* (2 vols. 1934), are important because unusually detailed. See, in addition to works cited in notes 19 and 21, Maurice Cowling, *The Impact of Labour 1920–4: the Beginning of Modern British Politics* (1971); K. O. Morgan, *The Age of Lloyd George – the Liberal Party and British Politics* (1971); Winston S. Churchill, *The Aftermath* (1929) and Oswald

Mosley, *My Life* (1968). Also D. G. Boyce, *Englishmen and Irish Troubles . . . 1918–22* (1972).

21 Beaverbrook, *The Decline and Fall of Lloyd George* (1963); Thomas Jones, *Lloyd George* (1951); Michael Kinnear, *The Fall of Lloyd George: the Political Crisis of 1922* (1973). Useful memoirs, which go back some years before 1922, are L. S. Amery, *My Political Life*, vol. II (1953) and J. C. C. Davidson, ed. R. Rhodes James, *Memoirs of a Conservative* (1969). The most informative biographies not previously mentioned are Birkenhead, *F.E. . . .* (1959); R. S. Churchill, *Lord Derby, 'King of Lancashire'* (1959); Middlemas and Barnes, *Baldwin* (1969); Chas Petrie, *The Life and Letters of Sir Austen Chamberlain* (2 vols., 1939–40); S. Salvidge, *Salvidge of Liverpool* (1934). See also F. W. S. Craig (ed.), *British General Election Manifestoes 1918–66* (1970), and his *British Parliamentary Results 1918–49* (1969), and *British Parliamentary Statistics 1918–68* (1968).

Part Three

_____

Baldwin and Chamberlain

by

David Dilks

*Professor of International History and Chairman of the School of History
at the University of Leeds*

CHAPTER 1

The Rise of Baldwin

In the evening of his life, after fifty years of public service, Lord Balfour was stimulated into a discussion of Toryism by his niece and biographer, Mrs Dugdale, who asked him to define its principles. After she had brushed aside the characteristic question 'Do you think that a profitable speculation?', Balfour said: 'I suppose the principles of common sense, to do what seems to be the right thing in a given case.' Pressed to say whether there is a common element in the outlook upon politics of all the different groups which have been called Tory over the centuries, he adroitly skirted round the question. If an intelligent young man were to come along and request advice about which party to join, Balfour would tell him to go back to history and judge for himself. 'But if you ask me to give him principles to guide himself, I will answer that men have been asking for those ever since history began. They have been asking for clear simple rules – but the more effort has been made to produce those abstract rules, the greater has been the confusion and the controversy. So I should decline.'

In a party which prides itself on respect for the past, attention to unchanging human nature and reverence for proved methods, the attempt to establish some continuity in values, and perhaps in practices, is nevertheless natural and inevitable. Much depends upon the level of definition. Judged by the broad precepts laid down by Disraeli in 1872 – to maintain the institutions of the country, to uphold the Empire and to elevate the condition of the people – both Baldwin and Chamberlain would count as Conservatives. Some of the external similarities are manifest. Both were brought up in the Midlands, the one in west Worcestershire and the other in Birmingham. Neither came from the long-established landed aristocracy. Both espoused the policy of Tariff Reform, which had convulsed the Conservative Party before the war. Neither held high office before middle age. Yet the differences of up-bringing, temperament and political style, some of which this essay seeks to explore, are at least as worthy of attention as the similarities. Although Baldwin reigned as leader of the Conservative Party for fourteen years, and Chamberlain for little more than three, it would be a mistake to treat the latter's term of office as a mere appendix. From 1923 to 1937 their activities and fortunes interlocked to an exceptional degree. Each brought to politics qualities which the other lacked, and recognised the fact; and conservatism as a creed, not to mention the Conservative Party as a political force, would have been markedly less strong in the inter-war years had the two of them not run in an effective double harness.

So much has been published in recent times about the truce of twenty years which separated one great war from the other that it is not necessary to describe in detail here the general strike, the collapse of the Labour Government in 1931, the Abdication, or the Munich settlement. Those very events seem to betoken nothing but a series of crises at home and failures abroad. Baldwin, who retired in a glow of public goodwill, found himself cruelly abused, and something of the same fate befell Chamberlain in 1940. No doubt both are deserving of criticism, as must be every figure who holds public office; and in the days when it seemed convenient to read the history of those times in terms of wise men and simpletons, when the war was regarded as an unnecessary catastrophe which could have been prevented by the exercise of common prudence, when the collapse of France ruined the whole basis of British strategy and made the search for scapegoats essential, there was a scant hope of any fair judgement for Baldwin or Chamberlain. Even today it is commonplace to read that in a parliamentary speech of 1936 Baldwin confessed that he had deliberately misled the people at the general election of the preceding year, or that Chamberlain was wholly ignorant of the world outside England and imagined Hitler to be somehow akin to the people with whom he had dealt in the business life of the Midlands. Once legends or half-truths of this stamp become ingrained, they are not readily dispelled. However, the opening of all the British official papers for the inter-war years and of private archives helps to establish a more just perspective; careful examination of German and Italian sources has led historians to pronounce with much less confidence about the intentions of Hitler and Mussolini, and therefore to understand more readily the hesitations and fumblings of those who had to negotiate with them; and it is perhaps easier now to sympathise with the difficulties of ministers who had to face industrial unrest and high unemployment, or who came to the conclusion that Britain's commitments all over the globe outran her capacity to fulfil them. These chapters therefore seek neither to slur over failings nor to search for demons, but rather to transmit a flavour of the personalities, and to set down some of the assumptions and conditions upon which policy was made.

In Stanley Baldwin's ancestry there were on his father's side Methodist and, in earlier times, Quaker connections; and his mother was one of the celebrated Macdonald sisters, the other three of whom married Sir Edward Burne Jones, Sir Edward Poynter and J. L. Kipling. Although he prided himself upon an almost intuitive knowledge of the feelings of the English people, Baldwin was therefore half-Celt. He once confessed, perhaps a little in jest, that his love of the classics, and especially of the Odes of Horace, had made him the slave of fine language and beautiful expressions. Certainly he was acutely sensitive, like Chamberlain, to beauty in form, in colour and in language; and unlike Chamberlain he possessed both the facility and the inclination to reveal these tastes in public. Baldwin idled at Cambridge, to his later regret; and after that he joined the family firm, in which the fathers and grandfathers of the men employed had worked before them, and where nobody was ever sacked. All his life Stanley Baldwin loved and respected his father and the example of high standards which he had set; he had a firm conviction that one day they would be reunited; and when the opportunities for service in high office came, unexpectedly, he derived comfort and support from the reflection that his father would have rejoiced, perhaps did rejoice.

Baldwin had been an early convert to the cause of Tariff Reform and fought the General Election of 1906 upon that platform. The England which Baldwin loved, which he could recreate in moving and arresting language, was essentially the rural England of small farms and comparatively small industries, an England fast vanishing. As an undergraduate he had thoughts of entering the Church. There is no sign that he ever showed any special aptitude for his life in business, but the sense of public obligation ran deep and carried him naturally to the Worcestershire County Council and upon his father's death to the representation of the Bewdley division, where he had for the next thirty years a secure base. As he used to remark, there was not a village or hamlet he did not know, not a Friendly Society with which he had not dined. Baldwin's sense of being used for some divine purpose remained with him to the end. For all his good jokes, his toughness and his skill as a manager of the Conservative Party, he was a mystic and a romantic, with a literary and spiritual permeation and not merely with leanings in those directions. The sense of being called by God to a lifetime of service was enhanced by Baldwin's high conception of the duty which those lucky enough to survive owed to the missing generation fallen in Flanders.

As the family firm flourished, and especially on munitions contracts, he feared to become 'tame in earth's paddock as her prize'. He thereupon decided to give away about £200,000 or, in the values of the 1970s, somewhere between one million and two million pounds, and felt the better for doing it:

'as though I had pulled my sweater off for a race, though I did not see where the race would be or how long the course. And gradually after much thought it seemed to me that all this bloodshed would be wasted if the world could not be made a better place; I felt that the men who had made such sacrifices and in such a spirit were capable of rising to any height, and I began to think out the kind of leadership the country would want when the peace came.'[1]

Almost of an age with Baldwin, Neville Chamberlain reached office by a different route and much more swiftly. Even after

Joseph Chamberlain and the Liberal Unionists joined Lord Salisbury's Government in 1895, the Prime Minister continued to deal with him on the basis that he was the leader of an important but separate faction. Since the elder son, Austen, was being groomed for a career in public life from his youth, it was natural enough that Neville should make a career in business. It was a clannish, affectionate and argumentative family. There was a strong tradition of politics and social work, and among the great Unitarian and non-conformist families of the Midlands much inter-marriage had produced a certain community of outlook not unlike that of the Quakers. On the Chamberlain side there was an inheritance of nonconformity dating from the persecutions under Queen Mary, and on the side of Florence Kenrick, Neville's mother, a similar record dating from Cromwellian times. She died in childbirth when he was a small boy.

Partly because Austen was destined to be the family's standard-bearer in politics, and partly because like other families of similar background the Chamberlains heartily mistrusted a university system so long identified with the Church of England, Neville Chamberlain did not follow his half-brother to Cambridge; but he did for a time attend Mason College in Birmingham and it is possible that Stanley Baldwin was a student there in the same term, though there is no evidence that they knew each other so early. At all events, a good part of Chamberlain's later life was shaped quite unintentionally by his father's desire to recruit the family's fortunes. As a shy young man of twenty-two, Neville Chamberlain was sent out to the Bahamas in order to take charge of an enormous plantation on which Joseph Chamberlain aspired to grow sisal. In a span of five or six years, something like £50,000 was spent before the great man was convinced that good sisal will not grow in that region. Neville, who felt this reverse deeply, had striven his hardest to make a success of the venture, living a life of loneliness, hardship and self-sacrifice. Amidst these disappointments he learned to be unusually self-reliant and determined to make good in some other sphere. It was this life of privation that bred in him a special fondness for Joseph Conrad's stories of romantic places, of seafaring men and of solitary struggle against the elements.

On his return to England Chamberlain began a successful career in the business life of Birmingham and, anxious to prove himself and to follow his father's example, he entered municipal politics. His work was characterised not only by promptitude and efficiency but also by a keen sense of the practical and a distaste for empty sentimentality. His record as Lord Mayor fully matched Joseph Chamberlain's example; his activities ranged from the provision of defences against air raids to parties and comforts for those bereaved by losses at the front, the creation against much good advice and the opposition of the City of London of the Municipal Savings Bank, the development of Birmingham University, the establishment of the Birmingham Symphony Orchestra and of Queen Elizabeth Hospital. All these interests retained their hold upon Chamberlain's attention to the end of his life. He played a central role in the organisation of the party in Birmingham and more generally in the Midlands, and especially in bringing together by diplomacy and good judgement the Conservatives and the Liberal Unionists. This is not to say that Chamberlain ever regarded himself as being no more than a Conservative of the old school. On the contrary; and indeed, he referred to himself during the summer of 1939, in a private conversation with an American friend, as being at heart a Liberal. Nevertheless, he was in no doubt that the differences which separated the Conservatives and Liberal Unionists were trifling by comparison with those which separated them from the more extreme Left. Chamberlain prided himself with some justice upon the cohesion, efficiency and discipline of the party's organisation in Birmingham. To hold all the Birmingham constituencies, which was done with hardly a break in the half century between Joseph Chamberlain's departure from the Liberal camp and the last general election fought by his two sons, constituted a remarkable achievement and one to which no other great city in Britain could show a parallel. He felt an almost physical satisfaction when all twelve Birmingham seats returned Unionist MPs at the General Election of 1931, and when that record was retained in the more difficult circumstances of 1935.

Chamberlain, during his career as a member of the City Council and then as Lord Mayor, had consistently refused to consider entry into national politics. Ironically enough, it was

Lloyd George who brought him to London and then, because of the outcome of that experiment, confirmed Chamberlain's reluctant resolution to enter Parliament. The story of his unhappy and unprofitable time as Director General of National Service has often been recounted. The office itself was ill-constituted and the very principle of compulsory National Service had been accepted with deep misgivings by most Liberals, a few Conservatives and almost all the Labour Party. The business of Chamberlain's new office ran counter to all his instincts and training. Prompt and methodical upon paper, he discovered that Lloyd George was neither. Patient in listening to difficulties and trying to reconcile the conflicts of interest and demarcation between the departments, he found that Lloyd George was impatient of all such niceties. As for the Prime Minister, he came to the conclusion that Chamberlain was a man whose national reputation had been much inflated and who bothered himself too much with trifles. As he once said, 'Neville has a retail mind in a wholesale business'. At any rate, both sides soon thought the position intolerable. Chamberlain came to the conclusion that Lloyd George was slapdash, chaotic as an administrator and devoid of all but the haziest principles, skipping nimbly from one policy to another as the needs of the moment or his latest mood dictated. Nothing could be further in every particular from Chamberlain's own habits. Not only did this episode in 1917 set up an antagonism which lasted for more than twenty years, with profound consequences for both men and perhaps sad results for the country, but it also intensified Chamberlain's determination to redeem himself in more fair conditions. The Prime Minister for his part showed that he was glad to be rid of an embarrassment. It was remarked of Lloyd George that he had an almost animal aversion from any sick member of the herd; or as Mr Bonar Law put it a little more prosaically, 'If a man is not successful he never stops to enquire the reasons but gets rid of him at once. He would do that with me if he thought I was damaging the Government, although I believe he likes me.'

It is not uncommon that significant changes in politics pass with less notice than events which excite momentary passion but leave little lasting mark. The election after the First World War was fought on a franchise which perhaps trebled the electorate and admitted some adult women to the vote. On the whole, the record appears to show that the extension of the franchise to women has been to the benefit of the Conservatives; but in 1918 there was another more immediate advantage. The redistribution of seats was of the first importance. Despite the many movements of population, there had been no re-distribution since 1885 and the result was a net gain to the party of about thirty seats. Moreover, the Sinn Fein members did not take their places at Westminster and the introduction of Home Rule for Ireland finally put paid to the Southern Irish representation which had bedevilled British politics for many years, had sometimes rendered Parliament almost un-manageable, and had almost always worked to the disadvantage of the Conservatives. The combined effects of the new franchise, redistribution and Home Rule probably meant a net Conserva-tive gain approaching 100 seats; and the redistribution of 1918 not only created constituencies which the Conservatives were able to win at that moment but, what signifies in the longer run, more safe Conservative seats.

Austen Chamberlain's increasing identification with the Coali-tion posed obvious problems for his half-brother, who recorded at the end of 1921:

'I feel less and less inclined to take office even if it were offered and I certainly shall never go out of my way to get it. Sometimes I wish I were out of the House altogether but I am not sure that I should be any happier if I were. But it is a great handicap to be the son of my father and the brother of my brother, for every success is discounted and every failure is counted double. More-over, when one's brother is Leader all independence goes unless one is prepared to quarrel and I am nowhere near keen enough about politics for that.'[2]

Meanwhile, Stanley Baldwin had recently been taken into the Cabinet. In March 1922 a new Secretary of State for India had to be found. It was a post which, as the Prime Minister put it, did not call for energy but for decision and judgement and common sense:

'I am not sure whether Baldwin has decision, but I should have thought he had a considerable share of good sense . . .

'I have always felt that Baldwin was disappointing. I am sure that a good deal more could be done to recover the confidence of the business community than has been accomplished, or even attempted.'

Austen Chamberlain replied: 'It is precisely Baldwin's lack of decision that makes me doubtful of his fitness and Curzon agrees with me that Peel would be much better in that respect.'[3]

For his part, Baldwin had come to entertain much more serious doubts about the Prime Minister. He used afterwards to describe how he sat in the Cabinet as a new boy, saying little but wondering whether the government of England would ever be clean again. The Coalition, he concluded, was incapable of healing the country's wounds. To make the people realise the brotherhood of the human family was simple and obvious enough to state, but hard enough to do. No one in the world of high politics seemed to understand or care about the bitterness in the country:

'One thing was clear to me, that under the then government which was Lloyd George, F. E. Smith, and Winston, buttressed by the respectability of Balfour and Austen Chamberlain, things would get rapidly worse, until you might pass quickly into a condition little short of revolution. I felt that it was essential to break up that government, but it looked impregnable.'[4]

The issue of foreign policy enabled Bonar Law to write his celebrated letter to *The Times* and plead, with general Conservative acceptance, that Britain had neither the resources nor the opportunity to play policeman to the world. Baldwin, summoned like other members of the Cabinet because of the Near Eastern crisis, determined that enough was enough. He expected failure ('I am resigning from the Cabinet. I shall never get a job again.') and the Prime Minister himself, not unnaturally, did not take a threat from Baldwin seriously: 'Does little Baldwin think he can turn us out?' Baldwin however had close contacts with the junior ministers who had been putting pressure on Austen Chamberlain. It was the emergence of Bonar Law, who feared a deep fissure in the Conservative Party, which enabled many back benchers to show allegiance to a former leader and so to avoid, at least in their own consciences, the taint of revolt.

The local supporters and the National Union were more clearly in favour of detachment from Lloyd George than were many members of the parliamentary party. The party managers one and all voted at the Carlton Club against the Coalition, as did every future chairman or Chief Whip who was present. This was the background to Baldwin's celebrated speech, artful in its simplicity, accepting the description of Lloyd George as a dynamic force and saying that the Liberal Party had been smashed to pieces by it. 'I think that if the present association is continued, and if this meeting agrees that it should be continued, you will see some more breaking up, and I believe the process must go on inevitably until the old Conservative Party is smashed to atoms and lost in ruins.'

Many of those who voted to fight the election independently did not expect a clear Conservative majority. The fact that they won one, and then won again in the autumn of 1924, made Coalition unnecessary. Bonar Law, who had known before he decided to appear as an alternative leader that the Foreign Secretary would abandon Lloyd George, retained Curzon in that office; Stanley Baldwin became Chancellor of the Exchequer, and the new Prime Minister reverted to the traditional conception of a Cabinet composed of ministers with departmental responsibilities. He promptly sent a message to Neville Chamberlain offering him the position of Postmaster General, whereupon Chamberlain, imagining the headship of a department to be far beyond his measure, begged to be given an under-secretaryship instead. However, the Prime Minister persisted; and after coming nearer to a quarrel with his brother than ever before or after, Neville Chamberlain entered upon his first spell of office at the age of fifty-three.

During the next months, with the Prime Minister in obvious ill health, Baldwin rose quickly to a position of public prominence. Until the speech at the Carlton Club, he had been hardly known to those outside the political circle at Westminster. That intervention, and the American debt settlement, made him a public figure almost overnight. In mid-February, in the debate on the address, Baldwin uttered the first of the speeches which more than anything else created the basis of his political power, speeches which breathed reasonableness, affability, desire to encourage people to appreciate the best in each other. For no Prime Minister of recent times except Churchill has mastery of speech done so much. Baldwin used to avow rightly that his tongue, not his pen, was his instrument. 'The English language' he said on this occasion

'is the richest in the world in monosyllables. Four words, of one syllable each, . . . contain salvation for this country and the whole world, and they are Faith, Hope, Love and Work. No Government in this country today which has not faith in the people, hope in the future, love for its fellow-men and which will not work and work and work, will ever bring this country through into better days and better times, or will ever bring Europe through or the world through.'

When, a few weeks later, Bonar Law had to resign, he apparently felt little inclination to recommend either Curzon or Baldwin, and was therefore glad to be told that a Prime Minister is under no compulsion to recommend anyone. The exact reasons for Baldwin's accession are still somewhat mysterious[5] but it appears certain that his candidature was promoted by J. C. C. Davidson, L. S. Amery and perhaps W. C. Bridgeman. The first-named occupied a position of special importance, because he and his wife were intimate friends of Baldwin and he was now Bonar Law's private secretary. It seems equally clear that the Prime Minister did not know what was being done in his name. The handling of the whole business was overshadowed by the seriousness of Law's illness and it may well be that those who wanted no truck with Austen Chamberlain, Birkenhead and others of that stamp feared that if Curzon became Prime Minister he might at once attempt a reunion, which indeed he did intend to do. This course would doubtless have offended the majority who had stood by Law and Baldwin at the Carlton Club. We do not know, and are unlikely now to discover, how fully Baldwin was informed of what was happening in those few days. It is perfectly possible that no matter what advice had been tendered to the King, he would have felt obliged to ask Baldwin to lead a government, since the Labour Party had no representation in the House of Lords. Neville Chamberlain, whose first preference had been for Curzon, was most favourably impressed with Baldwin's confidence and determination, judging him to be the nearest man the Cabinet had to Bonar Law in qualities of straightforwardness and sincerity. Baldwin was in excellent spirits, pleased with himself. The press suggested that Neville Chamberlain might move to the Treasury, which he had not the least desire to do even though it would be considered promotion: 'it is an office which I should particularly dislike, quite apart from my objection to being continually pulled up by the roots.'[6]

Baldwin seems to have shown little skill or tact in his dealings with Austen Chamberlain, though every allowance must be made for the latter's natural sensitivity. Alas, this was to be only the first of a number of occasions upon which their interviews fared badly. The new Prime Minister apparently explained to Austen, quite simply, that a number of members of the Government had said that they would resign if he joined. The latter retorted, 'If you wanted unity, why didn't you send for me, even if it was only to say what you have said today so frankly, that you wished to include me but could not, but that you still wished to heal wounds and asked my help with my friends – why, why did you not send for me?' Baldwin answered 'I am very sorry. I never thought of it. I am very sorry.'[7]

Austen Chamberlain said in private that while deeply upset at the way in which he had been treated, he found it impossible to remain angry with someone so naif and ingenuous as Baldwin. Offered the Washington Embassy, Austen Chamberlain asked the Prime Minister whether he was aware that he had already refused not only that but the Embassy at Paris and the Viceroyalty of India; to which Baldwin replied, with commendable candour, that as he was a comparatively young man and now blocked the way, he thought Austen might like to take something outside politics. When Neville Chamberlain let Baldwin know how sorely his half-brother had been offended, the Prime Minister said that though he had taken the utmost pains to treat him tactfully, Austen had been 'just raw'. Neville sensibly rejoined 'that if he ever did wish to approach A. again he might remember that I was at his service, that I understood A. and might perhaps save such needless wounding of feelings again.' Baldwin cordially accepted this suggestion, saying that he felt sure the time would soon come when reunion would be attempted and that before approaching Austen he would consult his brother. This was very much how matters developed in the early part of 1924.

In many respects, Baldwin must have seemed a welcome relief to members of the Cabinet after Bonar Law who, though loved by many, had in the last phase of his political life sunk into an inspissated gloom. Irreverent younger ministers amused themselves by counting how many consecutive sentences the Prime Minister would begin with the phrase 'I am afraid that . . .' On the other hand, Baldwin came to 10 Downing Street with far less experience of high office than any Prime Minister of recent times save Ramsay MacDonald. In addition, there was in him a strong strand of diffidence and reserve. He was apt to brood long, and to reach his conclusions slowly, consulting many colleagues and friends. Never overwhelmed by his unexpected elevation, Baldwin wrote to his mother, 'I am not a bit excited, and don't realise it in the least.' But he did soon discover the essential loneliness of the position.

Although not equipped for the office of Prime Minister by penetrating intellectual powers or by executive genius, he found that the quiet years in the family's business had given him a knowledge of working people possessed by few men in politics, and by practically none on the Conservative side. Deficient as he might be, and indeed was, in some of the administrative skills which a Prime Minister needs if the machine is to work well, he had the immense strength which comes from an inner conviction of obedience to higher command. This was one of the few subjects upon which Baldwin, when the shell of reserve was penetrated by a close friend years later, expressed himself in unambiguous terms: 'The lines of my policy grew clear, and I *knew* that I had been chosen as God's instrument for the work of the healing of the nation. But you can understand how puzzled I was that He should choose such a specimen of His creatures to work through!'

During the summer of 1923, Baldwin wrote in complimentary terms to Neville Chamberlain, saying how reluctant he was to suggest a move but that the Treasury was of vital importance and Chamberlain was the 'one man' to whom he felt he could safely entrust it. Chamberlain at once declined, but realised that the Prime Minister might press the point so hard as to make it difficult to hold out: 'And yet I believe it would be a mistake to accept. I should be a fish out of water. I know nothing of finance; I like spending money much better than saving it; I hate blocking other people's schemes and – I only thought of this after I had written – I should have to live in Downing St instead of Eaton Square!'

The Prime Minister did press the point, saying that he felt the need of a colleague with whom he could discuss affairs as he had formerly discussed them with Bonar Law. It would be an immense help to have someone close in whose judgement he could trust and hitherto 'it had been as though he were deprived of one of his hands'. Moreover, in the absence of the Prime Minister the Chancellor was leader of the Government bench and it was essential that he should carry weight with the House. Everyone there respected Chamberlain; if the Prime Minister had to be away there was no one he could leave in charge with the same assurance.

While unimpressed by Baldwin's arguments about his fitness for the office in the departmental sense, Chamberlain felt that he could not, consistently with ordinary standards of loyalty to his chief, refuse such an appeal. Accordingly he told Baldwin that though very miserable he was going to accept. Chamberlain went to the Ministry of Health to take leave of the officials, with whom he had been planning a programme of reforms for the next two years. 'Perhaps after all', he reflected, 'I may still go back to the Ministry some day, but it will be difficult, as Austen knows, to get away from that beastly Treasury.'[8]

At the General Election of 1922 the Conservative Party had been saved from the need to face the crucial issue of tariffs and protection by a pledge of Bonar Law, to the effect that there would be no fundamental change in the fiscal arrangements of Britain during the lifetime of that Parliament. In his first summer as Prime Minister, Baldwin ruminated about all this and by early October was disposed to go far in the direction of new duties, with preferences designed to help the Dominions and to develop the industries of the Empire, especially sugar, cotton and tobacco, all of which were then bought in great quantities from the United States. The new Chancellor gave warm support to this policy, which he believed would prove the salvation not only of the country but of the Conservative Party.

There was a good deal of disagreement amongst ministers about the timing. Some wanted to declare at once that a tariff was the only solution and that after the scheme had been worked out it would be put to the country. Chamberlain preferred not to frighten too many people by talking about an election, but to begin with a broad outline. It was believed that both Lloyd George and the Labour Party were toying privately with the idea of tariffs. Opposition in the Cabinet was not thought to be very serious; Lord Robert Cecil might make a fuss but carried little weight, and Lord Salisbury would probably not like it but would be handicapped because his friends were all die-hards who would be the strongest supporters. At first, Baldwin reached the conclusion that it would be premature to embark on food taxes, although he seemed to be convinced that they must come in the end. He and the Chancellor were agreed that a good deal of education was necessary before they could appeal to the country safely on those grounds. Chamberlain recorded on 21 October 1923 that Baldwin now shared his opinion that it would not do to rush an election in the next month. 'He would be accused of slimness in evading the issue of unemployment by drawing a red herring across the trail.' Baldwin appeared to be very worried and said that he was vacillating horribly. He thought of pronouncing for a general tariff and holding an election in January. It was not until the last week of October that the Prime Minister discussed these prospects with the Cabinet. The essence of his thinking was that as Europe recovered, the position must get worse. Only tariffs could provide the Government with a more than tem-porary shield against unemployment. Bridgeman, an intimate friend and trusted adviser of Baldwin, told him that if a speech were made on these lines an election campaign would begin the next day, whatever the Prime Minister might intend. Much the same view was offered in the Cabinet by others.

In his speech at Plymouth on 25 October, Baldwin therefore

reminded his audience of the pledge given by Bonar Law and undertook that in the lifetime of that Parliament there would be no fundamental change. He described unemployment as the most critical problem for Britain and said that it could be fought, but not without weapons:

'I have for myself come to the conclusion that . . . having regard to the economic environment, having regard to the situation of our country – if we go on pottering along as we are, we shall have grave unemployment with us to the end of time. And I have come to the conclusion myself that the only way of fighting this subject is by protecting the home market.'

Prime Ministers, however, can scarcely afford the luxury of saying 'for myself'. It proved impossible to delay the election by more than a few weeks. The campaign on the merits of Protection and Free Trade began at once and the cry of Free Trade was the sole platform upon which the Liberal Party could unite with an almost religious sense of righteousness. But it was also a cry which, despite many anxious moments in Baldwin's Cabinet, did enable him to draw closer to some of those who had gone out of office with Lloyd George, and especially to Austen Chamberlain and Lord Birkenhead. Both supported the Government during the campaign. Most members of the Cabinet, when they discussed the issue in early November, preferred an election in January; Baldwin rather favoured December; surprisingly, the party chairman wanted to hold the election at once and so did one or two leading ministers. At one time, Baldwin had hoped to take Austen Chamberlain and Birkenhead back into the Cabinet before the election campaign began. He found, however, that the feeling within the party against Birkenhead was so strong that it could not be done and Austen Chamberlain would not rejoin without his comrade. Naturally enough, the Liberal and Labour parties exploited for all they were worth – which was a great deal – the cries of dearer food and extra taxation.

In many respects the business had been badly managed and Baldwin's action does not accord in the least with the picture of a calculating, tough party manager. It is more than likely that his later caution derived in part from this experience of

1923. After all, he had been Prime Minister less than six months; he had inherited a handsome majority; his position was by no means secure; and in the new House the Labour Party and the Liberals had together a majority of ninety-one over the Conservatives.

There followed a long period of bustle and intrigue. Baldwin was prevailed upon by some of his colleagues not to resign at once but to meet Parliament, for no party had a majority. Chamberlain, who had expected the Government to win, advised strongly that the responsibility of carrying on the King's Government should lie not with the Conservatives but with Labour or Liberal parties and wished to see Labour take office, too weak to do much harm, but not too weak to be discredited. Had there been a generally acceptable successor, it is probable that Baldwin would have lost the leadership. In a phrase of the time, however, 'they won't kill Baldwin to make Austen King'; Asquith refused to entertain the idea of a coalition; and the responsibility for placing the first Labour Government in power, and for turning it out later in the year, therefore fell upon the Liberals. After some momentary hesitations, Baldwin handled all this shrewdly, not least because he would take no step to nullify the democratic process by preventing Labour from coming to office. There remained the question of the former ministers, towards whom feelings were becoming more gentle:

'What I have striven for', Neville Chamberlain wrote to his sister, 'is to get a united party with a definite attitude on the question of Protection and to do that it is necessary to overcome S.B.'s disinclination to take a decision. But it looks more hopeful at this moment than it has been hitherto and I believe it may prove possible (thanks to Asquith) to achieve it. It would be a curious tit-for-tat if, as a result of S.B.'s uniting the Liberal Party, Squiff were in turn to reunite us!' To bring Austen Chamberlain and Stanley Baldwin together was no easy task. To undertake it called for a good deal of courage on Neville Chamberlain's part, for the risk of personal embarrassment was great and his brother had not concealed his poor opinion of Baldwin's abilities. It was also a selfless act, because the policy if successful was bound to bring back into the central counsels of the party figures clearly senior to himself. At all events, he invited them both to dine with him, having gone over the ground carefully with Baldwin. After a little hesitation, Austen agreed to join the Opposition front bench: 'After that, all went like clockwork and very soon it was "my dear Stanley" and "my dear Austen" as if they had ne'er been parted. They left me about midnight, walking off together . . .'⁹

When the Shadow Cabinet met the next day, Balfour, Austen Chamberlain and Birkenhead were present. Baldwin had sent a note of warning to Lord Salisbury, who had expressed himself with particular vigour against Birkenhead's drunkenness, lack of ideals and crude attachment to the interests of wealth. Both Salisbury and Curzon attended this meeting and no one resigned. Even Austen Chamberlain acknowledged that the former ministers were treated with marked affability and did more than their share of the talking. He still felt unhappy and did not think Baldwin fit to be leader. 'But unless he comes to understand that himself, it would be worse than useless to try to displace him. Balfour, whom he has been consulting, said to me that he couldn't quite gauge S.B.'s intelligence (I suggested one can't gauge what doesn't exist) but that he could not understand why S.B. did not retire.'¹⁰

However, Baldwin with Neville Chamberlain's approval asked Austen to act as deputy leader. Prolonged soundings within the party had indicated that to many members of the party Protection was synonymous with a general tariff, the issue upon which numerous candidates had gone down in the election. There was, on the other hand, strong support for Imperial Preference and for the principle that individual industries should not be allowed to perish because of foreign competition. It was agreed in early February that general tariffs must therefore be dropped until the mood of the country was ripe for a change. Baldwin spoke in that sense to the party meeting which endorsed his leadership, and of the volatility of the immensely enlarged new electorate. For the moment, the verdict had been given; the Conservative Party must learn the lesson; and if it were taken to heart, they would regain office. He appreciated also the genuine and honest ideal in the Labour Party which appealed to the young, and pointed out that Labour offered a career to the able and ambitious:

'in these days no party that cannot equally offer a career to a man who has ability, the desire for service and power inside him to render that service, can possibly compete with a party that does. Now there has always existed in our Party a desire to choose a rich man as candidate. And if you must have a candidate who can water his constituency with £1,000 a year you are going to have a choice of about half percent of the population, and if you are going to fight a party that has the choice of the whole population, you will never beat them in this world, and, more than that, you will never deserve to beat them.'

During this short spell in Opposition, Baldwin established a new machinery for political research and education. It depended on committees composed of Members of Parliament and outside experts, and had a paid staff. All this activity was co-ordinated by Neville Chamberlain, who brought together the results in the manifesto *Looking Ahead*. Meetings of former ministers were now serviced for the first time by a professional secretariat which shared accommodation at the Central Office with Baldwin's staff. It appears that the structure was largely abandoned after 1924, as readily happens when a party gains office and finds itself provided with all the resources of the Civil Service. The members of the secretariat protested against this, on grounds which showed foresight. They argued that the need for such a body gathering information and promoting political education within the party was greater when the Conservatives held office than when they were in Opposition. A party in Opposition naturally thinks of the next election, of framing attractive new programmes. A government is overwhelmed with administrative business and may easily fail to measure the electoral consequences of its policies; only the closest liaison between the leader of the party and its organisation, the rank and file of the members, and the press, can overcome these dangers. Moreover, there is always the question of the manifesto for the next election, for the party should be fertile in preparing ideas for the future based not upon the notions served up by the departments but upon broader political considerations. 'The idea that the party in office can rely for its materials for preparing a political campaign upon department officials or upon the Cabinet's secretariat is, we think, wholly erroneous.'

These judgements were found in 1929 to be prophetic and were taken seriously to heart thenceforward.

Baldwin's warmest admirers would not have claimed for him that he relished or adorned the role of leader of the Opposition. He worried much over his speeches and seemed tired and low in spirits. He knew little of parliamentary procedure. Austen Chamberlain, whose showing in all these respects was much superior, assured Baldwin that he did not wish to be leader of the party, though if Baldwin gave up the position and it were offered, he would probably accept it. On this as on other occasions, and perhaps because he found other methods wholly ineffective with Baldwin, Austen Chamberlain addressed him with emphatic frankness, begging him not to take any notice of those in the Shadow Cabinet who would not forgive the past and who regarded the recent recruits as rivals rather than colleagues:

'If you allow the latter to sway you and if you open your eyes to all their gossip, your life will be miserable, and hearty union will be impossible. There is, I am convinced, no "intrigue" against you among men that are worthy of your notice; but there is much discontent in the party as always happens after a great electoral disaster. But all this will die away if you show yourself to be a fighting leader, always on the alert and capable of seizing such opportunities as the Government gives you . . . Stand on your own merits and prove yourself a leader and don't bother about the rest.'

Baldwin replied simply: 'I thank you sincerely for your letter which I welcome in the same spirit as that in which it was written. I believe that good will yet come out of this unhappy time.'[11]

The position of the Labour Government in 1924, lacking a majority and kept in office only on sufferance by the Liberals, was bound to be a perilous one. MacDonald felt acutely the lack of ministers of suitable calibre, and attempted a near-impossible task in combining the functions of Foreign Secretary, in which field his main successes were secured, and of Prime Minister. The domestic legislation of his Government was of necessity cautious, and often ill-prepared. In the autumn, MacDonald had no choice but to hold an election. By then another member of Lloyd George's Government, Winston Churchill, had rejoined the party which he had abandoned more than twenty years before. The Conservatives were able to campaign unitedly, without a resurgence of awkward disagreements about Protection. Baldwin wrote shortly before polling day: 'The feeling everywhere that I have been is good: confidence, not of a boastful kind, enthusiasm and a spirit of hard work. But it is impossible to prophesy with this unwieldy electorate. However, we shall soon know.'[12]

It was only by the skin of his teeth that Neville Chamberlain held the constituency of Ladywood at that election against Sir Oswald Mosley. Since he was not an ambitious politician in the ordinary sense, Chamberlain had no desire to return to the Treasury: 'I might be a great Minister of Health but am not likely to be more than a second-rate Chancellor. I suppose my friends would be disappointed and think I had gone downhill if I returned to Health but that would soon pass off and I should be very happy to find myself there again.'[13]

And again, when it became known that the Conservative Party had triumphed handsomely at the polls, whereas the Liberals for whatever reason – but almost certainly in part because they had turned out first the Conservatives and then the Labour Government, and because many of the Liberals to the right of their party had become almost indistinguishable from Conservatives – had crashed, so that for the first time in many years Britain was approaching a two-party system, Chamberlain wrote:

'What alarms me now is the size of our majority which is most dangerous. We shall never keep discipline, and jealousies and intrigues will have a grand run. Unless we leave our mark as social reformers, the country will take it out of us hereafter, but what we do will depend on how the Cabinet is made up. Poor S.B.!'[14]

The Cabinet-making proved to be a painful business, and it has to be admitted that Baldwin's record of personal disagreement in such matters with Austen Chamberlain is a long and rather sorry one. Austen advised the Prime Minister that Winston Churchill had no claim, but that Baldwin should consider whether Churchill might not be dangerous if left out 'He is becoming so Tory; he might lead a diehard cave!' This thought had indeed occurred to Baldwin, who at first proposed to offer Churchill the War Office or the Admiralty. Chamberlain thought Baldwin a good deal changed and stiffened by his victory, perfectly courteous and anxious to please him on personal grounds, but not inclined to accept advice unless it chimed with his own ideas. For instance, Baldwin told Austen Chamberlain in terms that he was taking Birkenhead only as a favour to him. Baldwin's interview with Sir Robert Horne, to whom he offered the Ministry of Labour and with whom Austen Chamberlain was much associated, led to a series of misunderstandings so complicated that Austen Chamberlain began one of his accounts to his wife 'Beloved, S.B. is mad!'

Meanwhile, Baldwin had suggested to Neville Chamberlain a return to the Treasury, saying he had decided that Churchill should be taken in at once ('He would be more under control inside than out'). Chamberlain replied that he would like to go back to the Ministry of Health. Baldwin mentioned Churchill as a possible Chancellor, but said he supposed there would be a howl from the Conservative Party; to which Chamberlain rejoined that there would be an outcry if Churchill came into the Government at all and he did not know that it would be much louder if he went to the Treasury than if he went to the Admiralty. He thought the idea worth further consideration. Presently the Prime Minister said that he had another visitor. However, Chamberlain chanced to see the unmistakable hat and stick of Churchill upon a chair. Offered the Treasury, the astonished and delighted Churchill accepted at once. Legend has long had it that when Baldwin said 'Would you like to be Chancellor?', Churchill thought that he meant Chancellor of the Duchy of Lancaster.

CHAPTER 2

Baldwin's Second Government

Within a year or two, Baldwin had emerged from a position of obscurity to one of national leadership, creating far and wide an impression of understanding and patience. There was something comfortable and comforting in his recalling of the intimate life of village or small town, in his robust distaste for theories and tidy constitutions. He made no secret of his sympathy with the aspirations of Labour, or of his conviction that the wilder solutions would do no one any good. Baldwin displayed an artist's skill in representing the Conservative Party's interest as the national interest, and the Conservative Party's mental habits and spiritual values as the distillation of the best of English history. His gaze was apt to fix upon the middle distance or even upon the far distance and there were few matters in which he had either the aptitude or the inclination to take a detailed interest. The habit grew on him with the years; but it meant at every stage that Baldwin was heavily dependent upon a high degree of efficiency in his ministers, and rather prone to make the kind of mistake certain to be made by a man who will not concentrate upon the fine print.

Baldwin never tired of proclaiming his faith in the British genius and individuality, or his mistrust of exotic solutions. 'Let us be content to trust ourselves and to be ourselves.' Since each human soul had its own value, the wise Conservative statesman would cherish individualities and peculiarities, even eccentricities. The British, he sincerely believed, were characterised by a love of justice and truth, a broad humanity and good humour. If those qualities were allowed to flourish, all the asperities would be softened and the obstacles reduced. Many of Baldwin's best-loved speeches, dealing with subjects far beyond the bounds of politics, appealed deeply to many people of no party, the people of whom he once said that he would like to be leader were he not leader of the Conservatives; and of all his themes there was one which he treated with a sureness and sensitivity matched by no other Prime Minister:

'To me, England is the country, and the country is England. And when I ask myself what I mean by England, when I think of England when I am abroad, England comes to me through my various senses – through the ear, through the eye, and through certain imperishable scents. I will tell you what they are, and there may be those among you who feel as I do.

'The sounds of England, the tinkle of the hammer on the anvil in the country smithy, the corncrake on a dewy morning, the sound of the scythe against the whetstone, and the sight of a plough team coming over the brow of a hill . . . The wild anemones in the woods in April, the last load at night of hay being drawn down a lane as the twilight comes on, when you can scarcely distinguish the figures of the horses as they take it home to the farm, and above all, most subtle, most penetrating and most moving, the smell of wood smoke coming up in an autumn evening, or the smell of the scutch fires: that wood smoke that our ancestors, tens of thousands of years ago, must have caught on the air when they were coming home with the result of the day's forage, when they were still nomads, and when they were still roaming the forests and plains of the continent of Europe. These things strike down into the very depths of our nature, and touch chords that go back to the beginning of time and the human race, but they are chords that with every year of our life sound a deeper note in our innermost being.

'These are the things that make England, and I grieve for it that they are not the childish inheritance of the majority of people today in our country.'[1]

Baldwin was setting out, in his quiet, deliberate way, to instil a conception of ordered liberty, with rights and obligations held in a just balance, and to inculcate a conviction of pride in British achievements. When the Cabinet had to decide its attitude towards a bill brought forward by a respected Conservative back bencher, the essence of which was to make trade unionists contract into, rather than out of, the political levy, Baldwin asserted himself in a decisive way against strong pressures. The Prime Minister said that he had striven to breathe a living force into his party. Conservatives had won the election with a great majority, not by promising to bring in a bill of this stamp but because they had created the impression that they stood for peace between all classes of the community. Suspicion had prevented stability in Europe and was the one poison preventing stability at home. Baldwin therefore asked the Conservative Party to say:

'We have our majority; we believe in the justice of this Bill which has been brought in today, but we are going to withdraw our hand, and we are not going to push our political advantage home at a moment like this. . . . We know we may be told that we have gone back on our principles. But we believe we know what at this moment the country wants, and we believe it is for us in our strength to do what no other Party can do at this moment, and to say that we at any rate stand for peace.

'. . . Although I know that there are those who work for different ends from most of us in this House, yet there are many in all ranks and all parties who will re-echo my prayer "Give peace in our time, O Lord."'

On the economic front, Churchill's first budget speech was a masterly performance; but in retrospect, the financial measures of 1925 have generally been thought insignificant by comparison with the decision to return to the gold standard. It is probable that any government of the time would have taken this step, and plain that it was taken only with considerable misgivings on Churchill's part. The Governor of the Bank of England was especially anxious to secure stability in international prices. For a variety of reasons, most of which were unforeseeable, the strategy went wrong. When eventually the pound had to be devalued, it was done not because of the depression or unemployment, but because of failures in the credit and banking system of the United States and continental Europe. Since the return to the gold standard cheapened British imports and made British exports expensive in relation to those of other countries, it rendered the position of the major exporting industries rather more difficult; but there is no reason to believe that the bulk of British unemployment in the 1920s derived from this act of economic policy. Much nearer the mark was the conviction that certain industries which had flourished before the First World War – for instance, coal, cotton and shipbuilding – could not regain their former prosperity in the conditions of the post-war world. In other words, the unemployment could not be cured by any expedient or cosmetic exercise, by public works or by putting half a million men on the land. It was structural, was bound to last for a considerable time and could be met only by the diversion of resources into industries which could compete. But that policy was certain to involve many difficulties, not least the psychological problems of men who had to face the near-certainty that they would never again get jobs in the industries for which they were trained, and the physical problems of mobility. Baldwin's administration, indeed, went beyond the bounds hitherto accepted by British governments of all parties in giving assistance to some of these processes, especially in industrial retraining; though by the standards to which we have become accustomed in the last thirty years, its efforts were trifling. At the time, however, this was a new phenomenon. As Baldwin did not fail to point out, MacDonald's Government of 1924 had not only failed to cure unemployment but failed to show that it had any serious idea what to do about it. And yet, since in the middle 1920s about ten per cent of the working population were out of work, any government was bound to regard this as its most serious domestic problem and one which, moreover, might easily bring consequences far beyond the purely economic.

During the summer of 1925 the Cabinet had to deal with two serious crises. The Chancellor, who was apt to take on the colour of the department which he represented for the time being, treated the armed services with a parsimony which would scarcely be anticipated by those who read only his speeches of the 1930s. Churchill had weighed in vigorously with the Prime

Minister from the outset about the follies of naval building on any substantial scale, and had quite ruled out, at any rate in his own mind, the prospect of serious difficulties with the Japanese. After several weeks of altercation between Churchill and the First Lord of the Admiralty, W. C. Bridgeman, it became clear that no agreement would be reached at that level. Despite numerous entreaties, Bridgeman refused to give much ground. According to his own account, the whips and party managers, who realised what it would mean to sacrifice the First Lord and the Navy for the newly-recruited Churchill, went to Baldwin and shook him (in the figurative sense).[2] The Prime Minister thereupon reached a compromise which gave the Admiralty most of what it wanted.

Undoubtedly he was influenced by the threatening industrial situation. An imminent strike by the miners seemed likely to bring many industries to a standstill within a matter of weeks, to inflict prolonged hardship and to embitter that very class warfare which Baldwin was doing his best to diminish. The Cabinet were told that the miners would be followed immediately by the railway unions and probably by the dockers, that stocks of fuel, while fairly abundant, were not well distributed, and that although the skeleton of a voluntary organisation had been created no volunteers had been enrolled. The Prime Minister explained that the only means of stopping the strike would be a subsidy to hold matters while an inquiry was held. Baldwin indicated, but only in a tentative way, that he favoured the plan. Churchill and Neville Chamberlain both spoke in favour of it. The majority of the Cabinet blessed the idea, though none knew that Baldwin had but a few hours earlier told the miners no subsidy would be granted. This sequence of events caused much embarrassment and it was naturally said that the Government had surrendered from fear. Announcing the subsidy, Baldwin gave a plain warning that if the time came when the community had to protect itself, its response would astonish 'the forces of anarchy'. He said afterwards, and no doubt with some truth, that it was essential to buy off the strike because the Government's preparations were not ready; but in all probability the chief motive was the need to persuade the people that every expedient had been tried.

In the field of foreign policy, the Government fared better. Austen Chamberlain was convinced that until France felt more secure, she would neither deal more generously with Germany nor allow Britain a more substantial share in the framing of policy in Europe. The withdrawal of French and Belgian troops from the Ruhr, the presence in office of the conciliatory Briand, the adoption of a more reasonable scale of reparations and a proposal from Germany to accept freely the permanence of the western frontiers, including the demilitarised status of the Rhineland zone: all this offered better prospects of a settlement than had existed at any time since the war. Austen Chamberlain's first instinct was to conclude a direct agreement with France and to negotiate from that position. To this most of his Cabinet colleagues would not agree. No sooner had he left for Paris than the Permanent Under-Secretary at the Foreign Office reported a discussion among ministers which appeared to upset the basis upon which he thought he was proceeding. The Prime Minister sent simultaneously a short letter which gave little guidance, information or support, and Chamberlain at once telegraphed that if such conditions persisted he would have to resign. Baldwin hastened to assure him that what had been said at an informal meeting by individual ministers must not be taken as constituting a decision of the Cabinet. He realised that there were different trends of thought, and hoped it might be possible to get the French to indicate the lines upon which they would be prepared to move. When this was known, the Cabinet would discuss what Britain could do and Baldwin felt confident that he would be able to sustain his Foreign Secretary strongly. He did not expect serious difficulty in obtaining assent to the policy of a pact as Chamberlain understood it. Sir Eyre Crowe, through whom these messages were sent, added 'I have the impression that he means to stand by you loyally and oppose Birkenhead, Churchill and Amery with determination.'[3]

On Chamberlain's return from Europe, he saw Baldwin privately and they had a satisfactory talk. The Prime Minister promised to insist that the Foreign Secretary should have his way about his own business. This was duly done and after some six further months of negotiation, in which Chamberlain displayed resource, skill and goodwill, the Locarno Treaties were signed. It is not easy to recapture, over a distance of more than fifty years, the intense emotions which they aroused. Britain did what she had refused to do before the First World War by committing herself to military intervention in Europe, on the side of France and Belgium if they should be invaded by Germany and on the side of Germany if she should be invaded by France and Belgium. Austen Chamberlain declined, with general assent, to give any guarantee of Germany's frontier with Poland, which the German Government showed they did not regard as permanent. That guarantee was given in very different circumstances by Neville Chamberlain's Cabinet in 1939. But in 1925 it seemed that the prospect of a major European war had been banished for the foreseeable future. Enmity between France and Germany, the cause of great wars in 1870 and in 1914, had been assuaged. Germany was to enter the League of Nations on equal terms. By her own free will, rather than by dictation, she had accepted that the Rhineland zone must be free of troops and military installations; and France and Belgium had in effect undertaken that there should be no repetition of the occupation of the Ruhr. During the next four years, Austen Chamberlain received solid backing, though little by way of detailed guidance or initiatives, from Baldwin. The League of Nations attained for a brief span a position of high importance; and if the nations failed to reach any agreement to disarm, there developed nevertheless a mood of helpfulness and co-operation in European politics which was never recaptured after 1929.

When Neville Chamberlain had arrived at the Ministry of Health for the second time, he told his principal civil servant, Sir Arthur Robinson, that he wished to see a programme of legislation for the next four years. This Robinson drew up and before Chamberlain left the ministry in May 1929 every measure but one was on the statute book and others had been added as the need arose. There existed an acute difference of method, in addition to the obvious difference of temperament, between Chamberlain and Churchill. The latter once sketched out to Chamberlain a housing campaign to touch the imagination of the country, and to be based upon a vast national organisation. In his calm, almost prosaic way Chamberlain, to Churchill's visible disappointment, said that he preferred to revive the ordinary building industry, so that it would produce houses at prices which most people could afford; then the working man would have the incentive to save, the self-reliance and the sense of happiness in owning his own property which he could derive from no other possession. Housing, public health, the provision of parks and facilities for sport, the new cities, the effort to make municipal estates into genuine communities, the reform of rating; all this was in Chamberlain's mind at the outset. He had the immense advantage, possessed by very few ministers at any time, of knowing as much about many of the subjects as did his civil servants. Good contacts with the local authorities helped him greatly in Parliament. Chamberlain was resourceful in ideas, excellent in negotiation and in the transaction of business. His habit was to read up each important subject thoroughly and not to commit himself to a line either in the Cabinet or in committee or in Parliament without deciding upon the essentials. Once he had made up his mind what mattered, he knew where he might be able to give way. He also knew how to extract the maximum of value and public effect from every concession.

Chamberlain had occasion to call on the Chancellor at the Treasury to talk about pensions for widows. Although he had been in office less than three weeks, Churchill explained how keen he was to reduce direct taxation in order to relieve the burden upon industry, to bring down the income tax, and to show a clear benefit to the working-classes in the shape of better pensions. Chamberlain, who liked this idea and said he would consider it favourably, noted that all through the conversation Churchill was thinking of personal credit. It almost seemed that he regretted not to have been Minister of Health. '*You* are in the van. *You* can raise a monument. *You* can have a name in history.' Mr Churchill then orated about housing, and he hoped that it would be possible in four years to build seven or eight hundred thousand houses. 'A man of tremendous drive and vivid imagination', Chamberlain recorded that night, 'but obsessed with the glory of doing something spectacular which should erect monuments to him.'[4]

Churchill had said to Chamberlain 'You and I can command everything if we work together.' There was, of course, an element of rhetoric in the remark. Nevertheless, it was from the partnership between Baldwin, Chamberlain and Churchill that most of the reforms of this Government derived. Churchill had to provide the money, in addition to which he produced ideas in plenty. As his colleague Bridgeman observed, Winston brought forth ideas as rapidly as a partridge laying eggs, and, like a partridge, he quickly went off to make a new nest if disturbed. Baldwin, with his avowed opposition to socialism but his determination to lead the Conservative Party from left of centre, his realisation that the Conservative Party had to have a policy which amounted to more than a mere defence of the existing order, his conviction that the extinction of party signals the birth of faction, his frequent reference to Disraeli's fostering of social reform, provided the right mood and atmosphere. Chamberlain knew how to take advantage of the mood and how to sift Churchill's many unpractical ideas from those which could be made to work. As a social reformer, he was not a founder of the welfare state. He would have been dismayed by the universal nature, the apparent permanence and the soaring cost of the reforms put into effect during and after the Second World War. Rather, his special skill was to take up practical possibilities and to establish the connections between them not only in his own mind but also in the consciousness of others, so that the policy could be represented not as a series of spasmodic or ill-conceived responses to immediate crises, but as a coherent set of linked plans. It is hardly possible to follow his letters and diaries, and his public speeches, without feeling an admiration for his knowledge, lucidity and grasp. He knew how to delineate the connections between, say, Poor Law reform, rates, pensions and housing, by reference to assumptions and conditions which his hearers could understand and recognise. He knew how to appeal to common sense; and the purpose of most of the social reforms of the second Baldwin Government was to help those who could not help themselves, not to distribute benefits regardless of need. The system was to provide a framework within which individual energy and initiative could be rewarded. It involved the intervention of the State on a substantial scale, a process not inimical to Tory traditions; and it also entailed, given the stamp which Chamberlain and Churchill placed upon the reforms, a policy which accorded with a Conservative dislike of a central, as distinct from local, bureaucracy, a distaste with deep roots in the history of the party and going back at least to the eighteenth century. The purpose of this intervention was not radically to redistribute income or to destroy incentive, or to substitute the whim of government for the experience and knowledge of business.

In both his spells at the Ministry of Health, Chamberlain found himself in close sympathy with the permanent officials. He knew how to get the best service from them, and they from him. Neville Chamberlain was a man of powerful emotions, which he hated to reveal for fear that he should break down or be judged weak. As his brother once put it, 'He is my Uncle Arthur Chamberlain and George Kenrick in one – very sensitive at heart and very *boutonné* on the outside.' From the point of view of the Ministry of Health, Chamberlain's desire to return there was of the highest importance. He did for that department what his father had done for the Colonial Office thirty years before, namely, raised it to a position of the first rank. Perhaps it is not unduly fanciful to imagine that both Chamberlain and Churchill were conscious during this ministry of a sense of destiny, of family piety and of fulfilled romance. Their fathers had once worked together; and each was resuming an earlier spell of service, Chamberlain by drawing upon his municipal experience and Churchill upon the reforms which he had initiated as a young member of Asquith's government some fifteen years earlier.

The Party Conference that autumn (1925) passed off well, with little sign of discontent and abundant demonstrations of loyalty to Baldwin. Indeed, when it is remembered that less than twelve months had elapsed since the former members of the Coalition were brought back into a Conservative government, his achievement becomes the more remarkable. A price had to be paid, and not least because Churchill believed in Free Trade with all the passion of a genuine Liberal. Baldwin said in private that there were two essential things if Churchill was to merge successfully into the Conservative Party: an office which would keep him so busy that even he had no time to interfere with other people, and an office which would keep him out of contact with the working man. The Treasury was the only department which would satisfy both conditions and satisfy Churchill, and Baldwin felicitated himself on having broken up a dangerous alliance between Lloyd George, Churchill and Birkenhead. As for the Chancellor, he felt confident that the hostility of the Beaverbrook and Rothermere press, which pursued Baldwin unrelentingly for most of his political life, for the ten years of his retirement and beyond the grave, would be repulsed neither by speeches nor by disdain, but by events: 'What about that Roman – Fabius Maximus Cunctator – was there not some famous quotation about him? Did he not give his country a chance to pull round and realize its mighty strength and let the deep long forces work for him – instead of being lured into desperate and premature struggles?'[5]

The events of the General Strike have been recounted in such detail that there is no need to recapitulate them all here. The report of the inquiry had been produced by the end of March 1926 and would have involved a good deal of legislation. Proposals for the reorganisation of the mining industry and the nationalisation of mineral rights were linked in the report with a temporary cut in wages. Baldwin was prepared to pledge the Government's support for its recommendations, but only on condition that both the miners and owners did likewise. The miners were adamant that they would not accept a cut in pay or the lengthening of hours which might have been an alternative. The coal owners were almost equally intransigent and Lord Birkenhead was once heard to remark that he would have imagined them to be the stupidest people on earth if he had not met the leaders of the miners' union. Under considerable pressure, the owners were induced to make certain concessions, but late in the day and grudgingly. Had Baldwin been able to convince either the miners' union or the members of the General Council of the TUC, many of whom privately dreaded the idea of a general strike, that he had received from the owners satisfactory assurances about reorganisation, he might have succeeded in dividing the leadership of the miners' union, or at least in dividing the TUC from the miners. Whether any amount of flexibility could have averted a strike must always remain a matter for dispute. Certainly this is the point upon which Baldwin's handling is most open to criticism. By the beginning of May, the coal owners had come to the point of a lock-out; the TUC, having agreed to support the miners, had virtually taken over control of the negotiations. The last talks to find a formula took place under threat of a general strike. Both sides were by then preparing for it, though at one moment it did appear that a peaceable resolution might be reached.

It is important to distinguish between the occasion and the causes. There is no reason to think that Baldwin regarded the prospect of a general strike with anything but distress, for it ran counter to all he had been trying to accomplish. He had probably come to believe that whatever the leaders of the TUC might say, they could no longer hold their troops back and that until the issue had been fought out, and the primacy of the elected Parliament established beyond peradventure, there was little more to be done. A state of emergency was duly proclaimed at once and debated in a restrained and apprehensive way by the House of Commons. For the first few days the upshot remained uncertain. Churchill was allowed to edit the *British Gazette*, the language and tone of which were far from tactful and calming. Baldwin is supposed to have said that he thought this a brainwave because it prevented Churchill from doing more mischief elsewhere; but it would have been better if the Prime Minister had exerted his much-increased authority to curb the most exuberant of his colleagues. The emergency organisation worked well, amidst every kind of rumour. On the whole the police coped calmly and well with incidents which might have ended in serious bloodshed. In one district of Leicestershire, where feeling was especially inflamed, a small contingent of police disarmed the hostility of a large group of miners by giving a timely and warm rendering of 'The Red Flag'.

Baldwin exploited to the full during the General Strike his mastery of the intimate broadcast talk. Using a phrase which Neville Chamberlain was to employ in 1938, he said 'I am a man of peace' and described how he was longing, working and praying for peace. 'But I will not surrender . . . the security of the British constitution . . . Cannot you trust me to ensure a square deal for the parties, to secure even justice between man and man?'

By 8 May the situation had improved a good deal and a considerable quantity of flour was moved from London docks that morning. A battalion of the Scots Guards had marched thither on the previous day with pipes playing and had been received with cheers. They had taken possession of the dock and later, when the flour had been unloaded, each lorry was guarded by soldiers with fixed bayonets. Rather surprisingly, there was no serious protest and not a stone was thrown. That evening the Cabinet approved a bill to forbid sympathetic strikes. The intelligence services had intercepted a cable from the Soviet Government sending £26,000 to the strike committee, but the TUC had the wit to refuse the gift, saying that it would be 'wilfully misrepresented'. In other words, they showed that they had not forgotten the Zinoviev letter. It was perhaps just as well for everyone that the strike was now on the point of collapse. When eventually, late on the morning of 12 May, the deputation from the TUC waited upon Baldwin, some of them indicated that in deciding to call off the General Strike they had taken into consideration the Prime Minister's broadcast message. Perhaps fear of starvation and anarchy had also played its part.

Alas, neither the miners nor the owners would accept the proposals of the Government. For many weary months the struggle in the coalfields dragged on, leaving behind a legacy of pride, stubbornness, self-sufficiency and indifference to the opinion of others which was often not understood by those who moved in a different world and which certainly had its effect in the winter of 1973–4. That Baldwin wished to settle the strike is not in dispute; whether he or anybody else could have done so, save by the continuation of direct subsidy, is more debatable. As for the General Strike itself, it had been possible for the Government to succeed because the processes of concentration and specialisation which have become so familiar to us since the Second World War had not advanced so far in 1926, with the result that the country was less vulnerable to action by a determined handful; the Government's own precautions had been considerably improved between the summer of 1925 and the spring of 1926; and the hearts of many trade union leaders were not in the strike anyway. There were plenty who confessed afterwards that they felt they had no choice but to join

in at the outset. Nothing that has come to light in the fifty
years since the General Strike suggests that Baldwin and his
colleagues were wrong in regarding such an act as incompatible
with parliamentary government. The strike split the miners
from the TUC and convinced most trade union leaders that
political ends must be sought through parliamentary machinery,
industrial ends through negotiation.

Baldwin allowed the business of trade union legislation to
drift along for the first two months of 1927. Eventually, in
mid-March, a special meeting of the Cabinet was called. The
Prime Minister said that he was strongly impressed with the
desirability of two proposals; a declaration that a General
Strike would be illegal and an amendment of the law about
'peaceful' picketing. He was undecided about the question of
the political levy, but inclined to bring this within the scope of
the bill on grounds of political expediency. On the first two
issues the whole Cabinet agreed with the Prime Minister. On
the point of the political levy, there was a good deal of division.
The two main opponents of including this item in the bill were
Douglas Hogg and Neville Chamberlain, but the majority
were disposed to include it, although admitting that it would
produce little result. There were wide differences of opinion
about the funds of trade unions.

Chamberlain had been most anxious that the bill should contain some positive measures, and had pressed the point upon
Baldwin early in the new year. His principal suggestion,
however, was that in the case of any stoppage which would
affect a great number of people, there should be a period
in which neither strike nor lock-out would be permitted
while the facts were investigated impartially and the results
published. The purpose was to allow public opinion and information to be brought to bear, and tempers to cool. When
these suggestions were first considered by the Cabinet, most
members favoured them. At the last, however, Baldwin declared himself strongly opposed to the suggestions on the
grounds that they had not been properly discussed with representatives of industry. The proposal was therefore defeated by
11 votes to 7. Chamberlain's diary describes this as a most
unfortunate decision, which he ascribed essentially to Baldwin's
inability to lead or act. The Prime Minister came to Chamber-

lain after the Cabinet and said that he hated to disagree with him more than with anyone else and that he would not have minded at all putting the proposals into a separate bill and having them examined. 'I believe that to be true', Chamberlain wrote, 'but the maddening thing is that if he would only set his mind to the problems and grapple with them in time we need never disagree at all. But he puts off the decision and avoids discussion for fear of disagreement until the last moment with the result that others have gone too far to stop without a painful jar.'[6]

The fact is that Baldwin was already very tired. Attending a dinner, he suffered from a fainting fit and had to be taken home. His doctor said that although there was nothing organically wrong his heart was strained and he might have to take a prolonged holiday. If that could not be managed, he must cut down his engagements and cease the habit of living on cheese sandwiches for lunch. Baldwin seems to have felt low and depressed. Chamberlain noted in mid-June that since this episode Baldwin's indisposition to take a lead had been more marked than ever. After Easter the Prime Minister had affected a jaunty air which was obviously forced and soon wore off. However, he returned invigorated after the Whitsun holiday. The Trades Disputes Bill, which came to be regarded in later years as an outrageous assault upon the rights of the working-class, was sadly deficient in constructive proposals and attracted little parliamentary excitement. Labour members had much difficulty in keeping the debate going. This Act, repealed some twenty years later, was of far greater importance as a symbol than for its practical effect. Most of it was inoperative from the start. The Act outlawed certain features of a General Strike and it caused those trade unionists who wished to pay the political levy to contract in. There is no evidence that it did any serious harm to the trade unions; it caused the Labour Party loss of members and funds. The Conservative Central Office issued nine million pamphlets on this one issue alone.

During the summer of 1927 Baldwin's mind was dwelling on the future shape of the Cabinet and the Government's policy for the election. Chamberlain, with whom he discussed it all, said that he would like to see the Prime Minister personally associated with a movement for conciliation in industry. Baldwin's idea was to set up committees of ministers in the autumn to work out a policy for the election. He mentioned among other subjects agriculture and the extension of safeguarding, believing that if the Government had protected steel it might not now be faced with the problem of 150,000 unemployable miners; but he did not know how Churchill would take such a proposal. To this Neville Chamberlain remarked that he thought Churchill was coming along nicely and would go much further if Leo Amery could be kept from nagging at him. The Prime Minister believed that if the Conservative Party could hold the rural seats it would win the election; whereas if it lost any substantial number Lloyd George might well turn the balance. Baldwin himself did not wish to retire, doubting whether the party was ripe for a successor; did not think that the Conservatives would take Churchill, whose candidature would divide them deeply; and judged that they would prefer Douglas Hogg or Chamberlain, probably the latter. Chamberlain merely rejoined that he thought Baldwin's disappearance from the party would be a disaster and for himself he wanted nothing since he was very happy at the Ministry of Health.

A few months afterwards, Hogg was asked by Baldwin to take the office of Lord Chancellor; if he accepted he would be effectively debarred from becoming Prime Minister. When Hogg first told Neville Chamberlain of the offer and suggested that he might already have committed himself, Chamberlain protested vehemently and said he realised that each of them had been talked of as a possible successor to Baldwin. On his brother's authority he knew that Birkenhead and Churchill would both take office under Hogg, but was not sure whether either would do so under himself; and in any case, he still had no wish for the office. He would not shirk the post of Prime Minister if it were a duty to take it, but would not lift a finger to get it and knew that it must be fatal to his peace of mind. However, Hogg swiftly became Lord Chancellor and Chamberlain was not consulted, to his distress, by the Prime Minister:

'To my mind this is a great misfortune for I believe he would have had a very good chance and I am sure he is the best man we have for such a position . . . I would gladly serve under him as I believe he would under me but I have never regarded him as a rival, having no ambition to become P.M. myself, and I have on the other hand always looked on him as a man who might well stand between us and a Churchillian domination, which would be a very dangerous contingency.'[7]

No serious reconstruction of Baldwin's Government was attempted. When Austen Chamberlain was compelled to rest for some months in 1928, Churchill suggested to the Prime Minister that if another Foreign Secretary had to be found, Neville Chamberlain should be chosen. 'He is one of our best men and he is a strong man. You want a big man in that office.' Some time later Baldwin toyed with the notion – ironical in view of what was to happen quite shortly – of putting Churchill at the India Office. For his part, Neville Chamberlain told the Prime Minister that although he would prefer the Colonial Office to the Exchequer, he would not refuse to consider the Treasury. Baldwin said that this would be an extremely popular appointment with members of the party, because for one thing they liked to have the next man to the Prime Minister in that office and, moreover, they did not want Churchill to be there. Chamberlain encouraged a notion which Baldwin put forward tentatively, namely that with the exception of Austen Chamberlain everybody over the age of sixty in the Cabinet would retire in order to make way for younger people. However, all this petered out.

The Ministry of Health, either on its own account or in collaboration with other departments, had continued to bring forward a whole series of measures, ranging from slum clearance to grants for the improvement of sub-standard properties, smoke abatement, the development of garden cities and the inspection of nursing homes. In more substantial questions, where strong vested interests were at stake, Chamberlain had much greater difficulty. There was a vital point of timing. A government which intends major reforms, likely by their nature to arouse a good deal of opposition, is wise to put them through early in its life. Partly because of the General Strike, the long-drawn agony with the miners and all the economic disruption which they caused, and partly because the measures themselves were so complicated, several of the more important were passed only in the closing months of the Government's life. Chamberlain argued vigorously, and in the end successfully, that it would be wrong to be unduly frightened of the electoral consequences of Poor Law reform: 'We shan't win elections by doing nothing, but by establishing a record of useful work.'

The suggestion which has gained currency in recent years – that Chamberlain's reforms of the 1920s were carried through in the face of bitter hostility from the Labour Party, that he was deliberately provocative, abrasive and sneering in Parliament – is misleading. It is quite true that occasionally he would lament the inability of his opponents (of whatever political complexion) to grasp the point of a clause or an amendment. However, there are few ministers in charge of lengthy and detailed bills who do not commit that sin. It is also true that in debating style Chamberlain and Douglas Hogg were different from most of their front-bench colleagues because they made speeches directly attacking the Opposition, while Baldwin did not care to make that kind of speech and in any event was ill-fitted to make it even when it was needed. There was an occasion in 1927, which Chamberlain had the candour to record, when 'Stanley begged me to remember that I was addressing a meeting of gentlemen. I always gave him the impression, he said, when I spoke in the H. of C. that I looked on the Labour Party as dirt. The fact is that intellectually, with a few exceptions, they *are* dirt.'

All the same, the passage of the main measures was notable not for violent opposition from the Labour and Liberal parties, but for a large area of agreement. There is no evidence of special hostility between Chamberlain and the Labour Party during the 1920s; rather the contrary, in fact, for his sincerity and ability were widely recognised. His extreme reserve and somewhat remorseless efficiency meant that by contrast with Baldwin he was never likely to be a popular or well-loved figure with MPs of either party.

After many vicissitudes, not to mention rows with Churchill, the shape of major reforms was hammered out between the Ministry of Health and the Treasury. Just before Christmas 1927 matters became so serious that Chamberlain formally warned the Prime Minister that there might soon be a Cabinet crisis. This was at a time when Churchill was contemplating a very large scheme for reform of the rates, the first draft of which involved some 35 million pounds of extra taxation. The permanent head of the Treasury, Sir Warren Fisher, discussed it all with Chamberlain and spoke of Churchill as a baby, who must be handled as a child and not as a man. The Chancellor received what he described as some very 'knobbly' criticisms from others and plainly had no intention of risking another Gallipoli episode, where he found himself hopelessly committed to a course and then obliged to resign. Chamberlain reacted in a characteristic way. He prepared a paper of criticism intended to reduce the more grandiose features of Churchill's plan but also to combine a scheme for partial exemption from rates with a reform of the Poor Law. In this question, as in respect of housing and pensions, Chamberlain was very conscious of following pioneering efforts of his father. The Local Government Bill which he introduced in the autumn of 1928, a vast measure consolidating and codifying many existing provisions, embodied the substance of a number of official reports and of two Royal Commissions. Health policy was at last separated from the Poor Law, and the basis of Exchequer grants was changed. Many voluntary and public services were pulled together and this Act, probably the most important of its kind which Parliament has passed in the twentieth century, united two streams from a century before, that of 1834 (Poor Law Relief) and 1835 (Local Government by Corporations). Chamberlain's speech in moving the second reading, heard with complete attention on all sides for more than $2\frac{1}{2}$ hours, was a masterpiece of presentation and easy dominance over the material. He was much struck and touched that Liberals and Labour men should join with great heartiness in paying their acknowledgements. However, there is all the difference in the world between winning triumphs in Parliament and winning elections in the country.

The changes in the franchise had converted an electorate of less than 8 million in 1910 to one of almost 30 million by the election of 1929. A great number of women had the vote for the first time. All this meant marked changes in the organisation of the political parties. In the constituencies the Conservatives made tremendous strides in the late 1920s; at the Central Office a good deal of the machinery was overhauled and reorganised. In the choice of candidates, the local associations were in effect liberated from the Central Office. Membership of the party rose almost everywhere, large sums were subscribed and much literature distributed. As it became more democratic, it also became more middle-class in its outlook and membership; which made all the more valuable Baldwin's ability to command a very large number of working-class votes. As for the organisation of the party itself, the annual conferences grew in size and significance; Cabinet ministers began to attend them and the Prime Minister himself would occasionally go to meetings of the Executive Committee of the National Union or to the Central Council. Reliance upon the machine was indeed part of Baldwin's political strategy and the moment of really serious challenge to his leadership, in 1931, occurred when he thought he had lost the support of the rank and file. Baldwin came to recognise the importance of the 1922 Committee, widened a couple of years after its formation to include the whole Parliamentary Party, and developed the practice of sending one of the whips to the meetings to discuss business for the coming week. On the whole this committee has been a source of strength to the established leadership of the Conservative Party, not least because it has given loyal members of Parliament a platform previously available only to the rebellious.

Baldwin spent a great deal of his time in the House of Commons, either upon the bench or in the smoking room. There cannot have been a Prime Minister in the twentieth century who knew individual members better, or sensed the movements of parliamentary opinion more readily. Since no Prime Minister can carry out all the duties which he is supposed to execute, the corollary of Baldwin's wholehearted devotion to the parliamentary side of his duties was that the executive side – the framing of programmes, discussion of points of policy with colleagues, the preparation of speeches – suffered somewhat.

During the 1920s, the party's machinery for publicity improved out of recognition. In the general election of 1922 $18\frac{1}{2}$ million leaflets were sold, and 93 million in the General Election of 1929. Indeed, in this latter contest the Central Office produced more than four leaflets for each voter, quite apart from election addresses and other materials published in the constituencies. The quality of the literature was much enhanced. Books on each main area of policy were produced at low prices and Baldwin's speeches endlessly reprinted. It appears that there were close connections between some of the staff of the Central Office and the intelligence organisations. Furthermore, the Conservative Party had informants in the Labour headquarters and at the printers which normally produced that party's publications. Frequently the Conservative Central Office had copies of Labour leaflets and pamphlets before they even reached Transport House, so that the reply would sometimes be ready as soon as the original appeared. All this was well known to J. C. C. Davidson; indeed, a good deal of it was organised under his direct authority, and it is highly probable that in essence these proceedings were known to Baldwin.

It was certainly in agreement with Baldwin that Davidson set out to ruin the organisation of Maundy Gregory, most brazen of all the middle-men who had profited from the sale of honours under Lloyd George. This was achieved after some years, but not without many apprehensions about what Gregory might reveal in court. Although the Conservative Party was supposed to stand inflexibly against any trafficking in honours, there is plenty of evidence now available to indicate that in practice the position was not quite so simple. For instance, when Sir Patrick Gower was lured away from the Civil Service to the Conservative Party organisation in 1927, he asked for an honour as part of the compensation and was duly given a knighthood. It was also necessary to secure his pension rights and the rich friend of Davidson who put up the money was given a peerage in the following year. The three chief donors to the Conservative College at Ashridge all received peerages, though one at least had been a long-standing contributor to the party. It need hardly be said that Davidson, like any other chairman of the party, was approached by people who openly solicited honours for themselves; and on one occasion he went to much trouble to get a baronetcy recommended for such a suppliant through the India Office or the Colonial Office. The most that can be said, therefore, of the 1920s is that while it is probably true that no honours were sold after 1922 in the sense that bargains had been struck in advance, subscribers to party funds did continue to receive honours and a high proportion of the honours recommended did go to supporters of the party.[8]

Even Amery had accepted that the Government could not propose at the General Election either new food taxes or a general tariff. Churchill, though still against the safeguarding of iron and steel, did admit that an inquiry into the conditions could hardly be refused; which of course implied that a duty would be put on if a verdict were favourable. It seemed that at last some of the vitally necessary amalgamations and rationalisations in the cotton and steel trades were beginning to take place, despite many human and financial difficulties. If after this kind of process steel was still unable to meet foreign competition, the case for safe-guarding would be unanswerable. When the Prime Minister spoke to the Party Conference in the autumn of 1928 there was unmistakable enthusiasm over safeguarding and no doubt that the audience would have liked a stronger pronouncement, especially on iron and steel. Baldwin was proceeding very cautiously, determined not to make again the mistake of 1923.

The Government elected to fight upon its record. In foreign affairs, the chief success had been the Locarno Treaties, the improvement of feeling between France and Germany, and the lightening of the burden of reparations. However, the movement for planned disarmament had thus far failed; a conference for naval disarmament at Geneva had broken up with the loss from the Cabinet of Lord Robert Cecil, champion of the League of Nations Union; and the Government was freely accused of insufficient devotion to the ideals of the League of Nations. As for domestic affairs, it has been well said that Chamberlain at the Ministry of Health probably contributed more than any minister of the century to the conception of national policies locally administered which underlies so much of British government to this day. 800,000 houses had been built. For those who were in employment real wages were rising. But the registered unemployed, just below one million in May 1926, were nearer to a million and a quarter in 1928. The inability to make a better showing on that front presented the Opposition parties during the election campaign with an obvious target. Moreover, the reform of rating, completed only just before the election, meant that many householders and shopkeepers received their new and increased assessments just before polling day.

In the upshot, the Conservative Party, having won over 400 seats in the election of 1924, came back in 1929 with only 261, while Labour had 287 and was thus for the first time the largest party in Parliament; the Liberals had 59. Had not Lloyd George insisted on putting up candidates for five-sixths of the seats, the majority of which he could not conceivably win, the result might have been different. Conservative strength in rural areas declined. The great advance of the Labour Party lay in the industrial constituencies, which confirmed a trend which had continued since the war. Furthermore, the other parties had been in office continuously except for the brief interlude of 1924. In the short run at least, the Government record of social reform had not been sufficient and even Chamberlain admitted that the Conservative Party probably lost votes by the pension scheme and by the successes in housing:

'No-one has voted for us on account of these things who would not otherwise have done so, but thousands have voted against us because they or their relations or even someone they knew had not got a pension or house. I see no way of stopping this Labour advance except such a dose of Labour Government as will in turn disappoint and antagonise its supporters.'

This was shrewdly said, though Chamberlain would not have claimed any more than others to foresee the circumstances in which the Labour Party's aspirations would collapse. Baldwin himself was subject to a good deal of criticism for his leadership, or lack of it, during the election; the complaints against the Central Office, already substantial, became in due course so powerful that J. C. C. Davidson had to go; and for a time Chamberlain was blamed because he had antagonised traditional supporters, passed measures which many people did not understand, and mistimed the reform of rating. Whereas Austen Chamberlain appears to have surrendered office with some equanimity, his brother, who observed tersely 'my pleasure is in administration rather than in the game of politics', felt profound disappointment, for he would have liked to begin on a reforming tenure of the Colonial Office.

Chamberlain's record in the 1920s, upon which his later promotion depended, was much assisted by the Prime Minister's view of what the Conservative Party should be. Baldwin did not wish the right wing to dominate the party and thus to leave the way open perhaps to the Liberals, but more probably for Labour; on the contrary he wished to point to the Conservative Party's record in social questions, which meant that the party must have ministers capable of producing and carrying through Parliament detailed proposals. This was exactly Chamberlain's long suit, whereas Baldwin's abilities lay rather in creating a tone or mood. Balfour, no mean judge, even described Baldwin as a genius, admitting that he had at first regarded the Prime Minister as being in no way exceptional. He said that nobody could achieve what Baldwin had achieved without putting into it something of his own, and defined genius as 'the right man doing or saying the right thing at the right moment.'[9] It goes too far, perhaps, to claim that Baldwin steered Britain away from revolution. Certainly that was his conscious aim, and it does not meet the point merely to say that Ramsay MacDonald, or J. H. Thomas, or Arthur Henderson needed no conversion to parliamentary methods. The question is whether with a different kind of Conservative Party or a different kind of Conservative Government in the 1920s, the political and industrial following of Labour would have remained convinced that use of the established system would produce benefits more dependably than resort to less orthodox methods. In other words, Baldwin had to enable the moderates in the Labour Party to remain in control. His Government had a very substantial tale of achievement, though in the matter of tariffs and Protection its policy was governed by the need to compromise, and especially by the presence of Churchill. However, that was the inevitable price of Conservative reunion, and an issue which had racked the party for the best part of thirty years was soon to be resolved.

Baldwin's natural diffidence, and the presence in the Government of leading figures who had difficulty in reconciling themselves to his leadership, probably increased his reluctance to give a clear lead to the Cabinet, though this tendency diminished somewhat in the later phases of the ministry. He had shown patience and sincerity, had treated his opponents fairly and, because considerate, was ill-fitted for the vigorous attacks in which leaders of the Opposition are supposed to indulge. The

account given by Baldwin's first authorised biographer of the
Prime Minister surfacing at the end of the afternoon with arm-
fuls of private letters, or sleeping ostentatiously in the Cabinet
when foreign affairs were discussed, is of course pure caricature.
There is more force, however, in another observation; that after
periods of intense effort he was apt to relapse into moods of
lassitude. It was not in his nature to derive deep satisfaction
from the knowledge that he was dominating a great administrative machine, whereas to Chamberlain or Curzon or
Churchill that sensation meant a great deal.

Although both Baldwin and Neville Chamberlain are far
better known for their part in the affairs of the 1930s, their
position in the history of Conservatism is essentially established
by their record in the 1920s, for what happened after 1931
imposed severe constraints. Until 1934 or 1935, almost all
domestic policy was dominated by the need to restore the economy and to reduce the total of unemployed; and thereafter,
when large social reforms would in more normal circumstances
have been taken up again, the outlook was at first darkened
and then wholly overshadowed by the dangers from abroad.

CHAPTER 3

The National Government

It was not long before the deep divisions over Protection showed themselves in public. Lord Beaverbrook campaigned for 'free-trade within the Empire'. Simultaneously, Chamberlain suggested a rather different line, by which tariffs or customs duties should form part of a larger imperial trade policy. It is hard to realise how intensely the political world was pre-occupied with this issue, or at least with the tussle for political power which it represented, in 1929, 1930 and 1931. Baldwin detested Beaverbrook and Rothermere because their antics, their scant regard for truth, their vanity, all seemed to him a prostitution of what a good popular press should be, and likely to work most mischievously upon the spirit of the people. To Chamberlain, the promotion of inter-imperial trade meant more than to Baldwin. He was seriously interested in the details of the agreements which might be worked out, and Baldwin was not; he was intermittently on close terms with Beaverbrook, whom he thought probably sincere in his imperial aspirations; and he regarded the performances of the popular press as a regrettable but predictable act of commercial policy. Thus within a few months of its defeat the Conservative Party presented a spectacle of some disarray. Chamberlain remarked, and it may well be that Baldwin was of the same mind, that he did not think this mattered very much, his main anxiety being that the Government should remain in office long enough to hang itself.

The leading former ministers held almost every possible position. In particular, Churchill was resolutely hostile to food taxes or, as Chamberlain recorded, was against anything which would make more difficult a bargain with Lloyd George. 'He has absolutely no instinct in these matters and cannot see that apart from any other difficulties it is impossible to deal with Ll.G. because he couldn't deliver the goods, i.e. he could not take his party into the lobby with us against the Government.' Chamberlain wished to place the emphasis on Empire trade and development, with a strong campaign of education to explain that the intention would be to make treaties with the Dominions and Colonies, or groups of Colonies, under which each side would benefit and that until the negotiations were complete it was not possible to tell what Britain might offer. We may readily sympathise with the predicament of Baldwin, whose mind was concentrated much more upon India than upon the economic problems or imperial preference. He had determined that whatever else transpired, India should not be made the shuttlecock of British domestic politics. This stand showed courage and he recovered for a time a good deal of his parliamentary position by speeches which lifted the discussion to a plane of idealism or even of mysticism, reviewing the long collaboration between Britons and Indians, pleading for trust in their new relationship.

It would be otiose to record here each development of the tussle between Baldwin and Beaverbrook and Rothermere. It was not until 1931 that the challenge, which would not have been serious enough in itself to threaten Baldwin's position had he not self-confessedly lacked some of the qualities of a leader, was beaten off. By that time the economic crisis had become so serious, and the Labour Government's incapacity to control the problem of unemployment so patent, that greater events swept Beaverbrook and Rothermere off the stage. Thereafter the normal conditions of party politics hardly applied.

The threat lay partly in the capacity of the United Empire campaign to attract disgruntled Conservatives and partly in its announced intention to oppose every parliamentary candidate, of whatever colour, who did not adopt the policy of Empire Free Trade. Baldwin was at one moment tempted to arrange a simultaneous test of strength of the Empire Party in four

constituencies where by-elections were pending. Davidson
pressed him strongly not to do this, on the grounds that while
most of the local constituency organisations were loyal, many
of the rank and file had been attracted by the Empire Free
Trade campaign and that in order to win them back it would
be needful to mount a strong counter-offensive, which must
take time. He thought, moreover, that Beaverbrook was
diluting his policy and weakening in the intention to put
candidates into the field against Conservatives. Nothing would
weld Beaverbrook and Rothermere together so surely as to
force them to run common candidates, whereas it was plainly
in the interests of the Conservative Party to split them. For a
while it seemed that Baldwin had succeeded in doing this.

He had a talk with Beaverbrook early in March 1930,
and announced on the next day that the Conservative Party
would ask for a free hand to negotiate with the Dominions; if
the latter wanted food taxes, there would not be a second
general election to seek a mandate for such taxes – the course
previously suggested – but a simple referendum. This reconciliation, temporary as it proved, transformed the political situation.
For instance, Churchill eagerly accepted the proposal.
Chamberlain, returning from East Africa later in the month,
did likewise. However, he discovered that Beaverbrook was still
dissatisfied, and found him smarting under the criticisms and
abuse being levelled at him because he had apparently abandoned the United Empire Party founded only a few weeks
before. Beaverbrook's line was that he had proposed a referendum as the only way of saving the Conservative Party from
destruction, though he did not like it and he hoped that
presently the Conservatives would drop it. Chamberlain,
begging him to say nothing of this kind to anybody else 'as it
would scare the Party blue', agreed that if the country really
showed signs of its willingness to adopt food taxes it might
be possible to get rid of the referendum. 'But I begged him
not to take the line that food taxes were inevitable until at
any rate we had got our party safely into the fold. Those who
had been most afraid of the food tax cry would now have to
defend it under the cover of the Referendum but presently
they would defend it on merits – if they were not frightened by
too hasty a run.'[1]

Baldwin was induced to agree to weekly meetings of what was called a 'Committee of Business', a kind of inner Cabinet formed of the leading ministers of the previous government, which would concern itself with questions of general policy, and also to form a committee, to which Beaverbrook would be invited, to discuss ways and means of promoting 'Empire Free Trade'. Beaverbrook was glad to escape, temporarily at least, from the embrace of Lord Rothermere; he said as much to Davidson. He was also powerfully impressed by his talk with Neville Chamberlain and Davidson wisely proposed that the latter, in every way better qualified for the role, should take off Baldwin's shoulders most of the work of keeping Beaverbrook sweet. At first this procedure worked well. Beaverbrook became very forthcoming and Chamberlain confessed that he was growing to like him. However, there were many difficulties within the Business Committee, with the Central Office and with Beaverbrook himself. In the first batch of documents drawn up under Davidson's guidance for a campaign to stir up the party, no allusion was made to the new policy. Beaverbrook, not unnaturally, refused co-operation on these terms and soon said that he intended to revive the Crusade. Meanwhile, Churchill still favoured a coalition or an alliance with Lloyd George. He asserted that by its attitude on food taxes the Conservative Party had alienated the Liberals and driven them into the other camp, so that at the next election eight million Conservatives would be suffocated under thirteen million Liberal and Labour voters.

After a whole series of difficulties about the literature to be issued by the Conservative Central Office, Chamberlain had become convinced that Davidson must be replaced. His own name had been freely canvassed for this post in the summer of 1929, but he had then no reason to believe that Baldwin was considering a change and felt no enthusiasm for a position which would deprive him of his work in the House of Commons and of the opportunity to supplement his income. In the spring of 1930, Chamberlain wanted as Davidson's successor a banker and businessman who had lost his seat in the election of 1929 but who had taken a close interest in the reform of the Central Office. Chamberlain intimated to Davidson that he ought to resign before he was forced to go. Davidson told Baldwin that he was ready to leave. It remained therefore to arrange the timing. It is an open question whether anybody could have negotiated with Beaverbrook successfully, and Chamberlain himself confessed that he found Beaverbrook disappointing and unable to stay put. From his own point of view, Beaverbrook was playing a dangerous game, since attacks on the Conservatives could only weaken the one party capable of carrying out at least part of his programme. On the other hand, he was rendering some service by uniting the Labour and Liberal parties in defence of Free Trade, a policy which had an increasingly poor expectation of life.

Depressed by the constant complaints and grousing, Baldwin even said to Chamberlain, though perhaps he did not mean it seriously, that it would not take much to make him throw in his hand. His friend Bridgeman, who had much shrewdness, remarked that because Baldwin did not recognise the centre of discontent to lie in London and in the House, he spent too much time and energy in speeches around the country when he might have occupied himself more profitably in conciliating leading Conservatives and the rank and file of members of Parliament. Chamberlain, who commented to his sister in mid-May that the party was in a very disgruntled and disheartened condition, had begun to wonder how much longer Baldwin could go on, anticipating that if he should abandon the leadership a most unpleasant situation would arise. 'I know a great many would like to see me in his place but many others would not. I myself would hate it; it would be end of all peace and probably of any chance of the C[olonial] O[ffice] but I should not refuse it if the party wanted it. Lately, however, it has occurred to me that they might well take Horne as leader. I could work with him all right.'[2]

Eventually Chamberlain was summoned to see Baldwin, with whom he found Davidson and Eyres-Monsell, the Chief Whip. After debating procedure for an impending party meeting, they fell to a discussion of possible candidates for the chairmanship. Finally the Chief Whip said, 'Of course there is only one man who could really completely restore confidence and pull the whole thing together.' They all looked at Chamberlain, who replied, 'Well, Stanley, you know you have never asked me yet, and I should want a lot of pressing to consider what is an extremely unattractive task.' To this Baldwin remarked that he had not liked to do so because it seemed so much to ask. 'But of course if you did take it, it would be a wonderful thing for the party. If I could announce *that* on Tuesday, it would make things go.'

Chamberlain went away to consider and to seek advice. In fact, he had made up his mind that he would take the office if it were offered and had put it out of his thoughts only because Baldwin did not seem favourable. In sum, Chamberlain came to the conclusion that Davidson must leave the Central Office long before he had any expectation of succeeding to the chairmanship, a post which he plainly took with reluctance. This was not because he thought that partial withdrawal from the parliamentary limelight would spoil his chances of the leadership, for there is no reason to doubt the sincerity of his repeated statements that he would much prefer the Colonial Office. The strongest single reason seems to have been a desire to render the party a service which, if matters developed well, might make the difference at the next election and thus enable 'the great policy' to be carried into operation.

The position of chairman of the party was certain to be a difficult one in such circumstances, and not least because the internal strains had been visible for some considerable time. Relations between Davidson and the deputy chairman, Edward Stanley, had been distinctly cool, and sometimes worse. Indeed, Stanley had once voted in favour of a motion of no confidence in Davidson! The chairman was appointed by the leader of the party, but then had to give that leader supposedly independent advice. He had also to run the machinery of the party, no easy task because of the proper jealousy of their independence felt by the constituencies. One of the chief reasons for which Chamberlain's brief assumption of the chairmanship is significant is that he was acknowledged to have direct access to Baldwin, and to be able to talk on terms of near-equality with the leader, as Davidson had not been able to do. In this respect Chamberlain's tenure of office anticipated what has been common practice since the Second World War. Under his reorganisation, Topping became General Director of the Central Office, with supervision of the activities of each department, and directly responsible for organisation, in which there were comparatively few advances or changes during the 1930s.

Perhaps the lack of a serious threat from the socialists after 1931 contributed to this period of relative calm. The party agents had become a professional body of men, carefully trained; the organisation in the constituencies had developed considerably; and Central Office had become large and specialised. Baldwin's sharp remarks about the fate which would inevitably await a party looking for candidates who could provide their constituencies with £1,000 a year had produced a considerable effect. By 1933, the Official Handbook issued by the Central Office claimed that the time had now gone when money was a criterion in the selection of a candidate and it was generally appreciated that each local association should be self-supporting. There had been another development pregnant with importance for the future: a Research Department, financially independent of the Central Office and endowed by a rich supporter, had been established in November 1929. This was Davidson's doing and was intended to repair the deficiency which had been pointed out five years before.

Soon the chairmanship passed to Neville Chamberlain who, in his methodical way, laid down some clear rules and confessed that he was becoming very much interested in the work: 'it seems to me that through my new department I shall have my finger on the springs of policy'. He arranged to take his instructions from the Business Committee and to report to it; every committee set up under the Research Department should have proper terms of reference and a small membership, so as to sharpen the individual sense of responsibility; the committees were composed mainly of young men, including back benchers. The purposes of the department were to provide material for the senior members of the party, and to undertake research into major problems. Results were not to be published but to be made available to the Business Committee, the Central Office and the Conservative College at Ashridge. In its first few months, the Research Department began investigations into unemployment insurance, social and industrial problems, and agriculture. Thus the Conservative Party was provided with an organ which, outside the immediate press of business at the Central Office, could devote time and detailed study to large questions. It was possible in this way to report upon tariffs and Protection, an immensely detailed and complicated subject, before they became the official policy of the party. Much of what was done in the negotiations of 1932 depended upon investigations by a committee working under the aegis of the Research Department. The new mechanism went some way to make good the weakness which every party in Opposition experiences, lack of access to the information and expertise of the Civil Service. Nevertheless, the Research Department was never large in the 1930s and its full flowering was delayed until the period of re-thinking and re-appraisal after the Second World War.

It can hardly be denied that Baldwin benefited a good deal from the posturings of his opponents. Whereas Beaverbrook was thought by many to be no more than congenitally erratic, Rothermere was widely believed to be mad. Mad or not, he was foolish enough to write to a Conservative member a letter that was passed to Baldwin, and which Rothermere authorised him to use in public, just before the party meeting of 24 June 1930. Baldwin assured this audience that he had made up his mind and they must now make up theirs. On the lines agreed with Chamberlain, Baldwin asked what would be thought of the Conservative Party if it changed its view at the bidding of newspapers? He derided Beaverbrook's plea that personalities should be avoided. As for Rothermere, he had been against food taxes in January, in favour of them in February, against them in May and was now alleged to be supporting them. As Baldwin remarked, with a studied simplicity, 'You cannot take your politics from a man like that.'

Baldwin drew an analogy between the events of 1926 and the newspaper barons' desire to dictate policy to a great party, to choose a leader and to impose ministers on the Crown. He had accepted the one challenge then and would accept the other now. Rothermere's letter stated that under no circumstances would he support Baldwin unless he knew exactly what his policy would be and had complete guarantees that the policy would be carried out if the Conservatives took office. Furthermore, his Lordship would need to approve at least eight or ten of Baldwin's more prominent colleagues in the next ministry. Afterwards, Baldwin used to remark with some truth that the Lord had delivered Rothermere into his hand:

'Now those are the terms that your leader would have to accept, and when sent for by the King he would have to say: "Sire, these names are not necessarily my choice, but they have the support of Lord Rothermere." A more preposterous and insolent demand was never made on the leader of any political party. I repudiate it with contempt, and I will fight that attempt at domination to the end.'

For the moment, this was enough to hold the position. Nevertheless, it remained far from comfortable. A motion in favour of the existing policy was carried by a margin of about two to one.

At this point Chamberlain took over the chairmanship from Davidson, in the middle of a by-election in Norfolk. During the campaign it became evident that the Conservative Party and Beaverbrook could hardly go on as they were. Either they had to reach some compact, or declare open warfare. Chamberlain went to lunch with Beaverbrook and Rothermere. After much talk about the value of rows to newspaper proprietors keen on circulations, the root of the matter was reached. Rothermere said that he had asked Beaverbrook whether there was anyone whom he could trust in the Conservative Party and he had replied 'Yes, there is one.' It was not Horne, who was insincere, but Neville Chamberlain. 'If you make that transformation,' said Rothermere, meaning the substitution of Chamberlain for Baldwin, 'you get him and you get me 100 per cent.' After this, as Chamberlain's account records, there was nothing more to be done. The party broke up, Rothermere saying to him as they parted 'Think over what I have said. Believe me, it is the straight tip.' Chamberlain noted that while the commonest loyalty made it impossible to listen to such suggestions, he had with much reluctance come to the conclusion that if Baldwin would go the whole party would heave a sigh of relief.[3]

By the later part of September 1930 the reports reaching the Central Office were still more gloomy. Meanwhile, Chamberlain had taken advantage of the forthcoming Imperial

Conference, and of the Labour Chancellor's fanatical devotion
to Free Trade, to press for an emergency tariff, drastic economies at home, a reform of unemployment insurance, a quota
for wheat, no tax on meat, and a free hand for all the other
commodities. He suggested that talk of a referendum and a
second general election should be dropped. Baldwin accepted
the whole programme on his return from Aix-les-Bains, to
which he had repaired for his usual prolonged summer holiday.
A statement in Baldwin's name was given to the press on 8
October, seizing upon speeches made by Dominions' ministers
at the Imperial Conference, when they had declared for the
extensions of tariff preferences. The Conservative Party stated
that it accepted the principle, would formulate its own proposals and submit them to the electorate 'for their definite and
final assent.' At a stroke (as the saying is) the party had thus
sloughed off the referendum and the second election. Moreover,
it had dealt a smart blow to Beaverbrook and others, who had
just written a letter for publication implying that Baldwin
was too feeble to take this splendid opportunity.

When the Business Committee met again on 15 October, it
was clear that Churchill was looking for a point of disagreement. Because the Prime Minister of New Zealand had indicated that he would like a tariff on mutton, Chamberlain had
abandoned the idea of excluding meat from taxation. Churchill
announced that he could not accept this policy and would have
to disagree in public. Since he took the opportunity of bidding
his old associates a formal farewell, he had evidently determined upon this decision in advance. Churchill thanked his
colleagues for their consideration, expressed his regrets at
parting and declared his intention of acting as a benevolent
friend. An awkward silence ensued. Neville Chamberlain
passed a note to the Chief Whip: 'Vex not his ghost. O! Let
him pass.'

Now that Baldwin had adopted the policy of the free hand
he was in a position to challenge Beaverbrook, as he duly did,
to stand by a declaration of the previous February that he
would withdraw his opposition if Baldwin took this very step.
Meanwhile, some forty-seven Members of Parliament had
asked for another party meeting to discuss the situation.
Baldwin decided to confront those who wished to get rid of him.

Beaverbrook helped, not for the first time, by running a candidate in a by-election to be held on the very day of the meeting, at which he was received with boos and hisses and for which he had prepared nothing. By saying somewhat incautiously, 'I don't care who is the leader so long as he accepts my policy', Beaverbrook pointed up neatly the observation of Douglas Hogg that anybody who succeeded Baldwin would have to take his orders from the *Daily Express* if he were to avoid the same hostility as Baldwin had incurred. Chamberlain drafted the resolutions for the meeting, whereby a ballot – so that there should be no doubt that the rebels had polled their last man – confirmed the leadership by 462 to 116.

Baldwin absented himself from this part of the proceedings, but had earlier made a short speech on policy and moved that it be approved, which was unanimously done. It took about five further months for Baldwin's position to be firmly re-established. In January 1931 Churchill publicly severed himself from his former colleagues over the Indian question. Baldwin, however, stood out for his own line. Since the princely rulers of India had declared their acceptance in principle of a federal structure, he refused to play for any immediate advantage and emphasised the importance of preserving a common view between the parties in Parliament, without which no Prime Minister or Secretary for India would have any chance of coping with the government of that country. It need hardly be said that Beaverbrook and Rothermere took the fullest advantage of this position. Chamberlain, who became for a time the object of Beaverbrook's hostility, noted that the latter was as unstable as water, without patience, balance or self-control, incapable of waiting and consumed with a restless vanity. Indeed, he put up a candidate at a by-election at Islington and proclaimed his purpose to break up the Conservative Party if that party did not adopt the policy of Empire Free Trade. Rothermere had come to the conclusion that because of Churchill's campaign on India and Beaverbrook's on Empire Free Trade, the Conservative organisation would collapse. This was a delusion, but a plausible one, since Churchill, by predicting the likely result of Conservative policy a complete abandonment of formal ties between Britain and

India, was able to join with many who differed from him over the issue of Free Trade.

Chamberlain's position as chairman of the party became acutely embarrassing, for he was still receiving reports of dissatisfaction, confusion and loss of confidence in the party's leadership. Although it has been widely assumed that he desired to supplant Baldwin and to leave the Central Office for the purpose, his letters and diaries indicate that he was absorbed in the reorganisation of the Office and had no intention of leaving in the near future. On 23 February the Chief Agent intimated that he must give formal warning of the dangerous situation which the party was approaching. To this Chamberlain replied that he would accept a memorandum with reluctance but could not refuse to receive it. The paper referred to a gradual drifting away of support:

'a very definite feeling that the Leader is not strong enough to carry the Party to victory, and that feeling appears to have grown stronger every day.

'This is clearly apparent not only to me, but to my colleagues in the office, who have the opportunity of coming in touch with the officials of the Party throughout the country ... No day now passes without anxiety being expressed to us about the present situation.

'I have gathered recently that our officials in other parts of the country have the same experience and although the feeling of apprehension is greater in some districts than in others, from practically all quarters one hears the view that it would be in the interests of the Party that the Leader should reconsider his position.'

Topping added that there was a feeling of grave disquiet in the minds of some supporters lest a sudden development might bring about what he delicately called 'a change which would not eventually prove an advantage to the party.' This meant that many Conservative supporters took a view on the Indian issue which was much nearer to that of Churchill than to that of Baldwin, but would prefer that if a new leader were to be chosen he should be selected on broad policy rather than on a single issue. Chamberlain asked the Chief Agent to alter one or two passages which he thought too wounding to be passed on to Baldwin. He consulted six senior colleagues; all agreed that he was bound to show the document to Baldwin and all confirmed Topping's view of the rapid decline in the latter's position. Chamberlain sent the paper forward on 1 March, after reading in the press that an anti-Baldwin candidate would stand in an impending by-election at St George's, Westminster. The man favoured as the official Conservative had withdrawn on the grounds that he was not prepared to champion the leader. There was little doubt, Chamberlain noted that morning, that the anti-Baldwin candidate was standing at the instigation of Rothermere and Beaverbrook. 'We cannot possibly sit down under that or allow S.B. to resign at their bidding. Therefore just at the moment when the train was laid and the match actually lighted, Max has once more blundered in and upset the applecart.'

Chamberlain was asked to call upon Baldwin that afternoon. He recorded that he found Mr and Mrs Baldwin together and that she had remained in the room for a few minutes while her husband said their reactions to the paper, which had not come altogether as a surprise, were identical. They both felt that he should leave, since it was clear he no longer commanded the support of the party and his continued presence would be harmful to it. 'I did not seek', Chamberlain wrote, 'in any way to combat this resolution and after Mrs B. had left we continued to converse on the basis that it was settled. S.B. said he would not ask his colleagues for their opinion but would inform them of his decision.' Baldwin even discussed the domestic consequences and said that he and his wife had already decided to move into a smaller house. He expressed the hope that Chamberlain would be his successor and said that he would gladly help to that end if he could. He added that he thought it would be disastrous for Churchill to have the leadership but he did not imagine for a moment that he would get it. Chamberlain supposed Baldwin to have arrived at a settled conviction. According to his later recollection, Baldwin asked whether he thought the colleagues would agree with the course he was taking, to which he replied 'Yes'; whereas Baldwin understood Chamberlain to say that they wished him to go. This is not probable, since Chamberlain had not been authorised to say what they wanted Baldwin to do.[4] Doubtless it was a genuine misapprehension, understandable in the agitating circumstances of such an interview.

That evening Mrs Baldwin greeted Bridgeman and Davidson with the words, 'Well, we four were together at the beginning of Stanley's leadership, and now we are together for the farewell.' To this Bridgeman retorted, 'Farewell be damned'. He contended that Baldwin should himself come out as a candidate in the by-election, whereas by resigning at once he would disgust the very large body of Conservatives who had been quietly supporting his leadership. Mrs Baldwin smiled upon the idea and her husband seems momentarily to have reached the same conclusion. However, the obvious disadvantages of this course prevailed; an excellent candidate was found for St George's in the person of Duff Cooper, and the question of the leadership was at least postponed for a while. Neville Chamberlain, who believed that Baldwin would not be able to remain leader much longer, discussed the issue again with Hailsham; to whom he said, 'I do not wish to be leader and would prefer to serve under you, though if the Party wished me to take it I should not refuse.' This was exactly Hailsham's position also. Baldwin had by then made up his mind not to go unless forced out and was said to be very angry with some of his colleagues who, he believed, had been plotting against him, and sore against Chamberlain for not having supported him more stoutly. When the Business Committee met on the evening of 11 March, Sir Austen Chamberlain, without any previous communication with his brother, bluntly asked when the latter would leave the Central Office. He argued that the debating strength of the front bench had been weakened, but added something to the effect that Chamberlain's influence in the House and country must suffer by his absence from the Chamber. As Neville Chamberlain noted, it was pretty plain what he had in mind. Baldwin replied that Neville Chamberlain had not asked for a release and that he was ready to discuss it whenever he desired. On thinking this over, Neville Chamberlain concluded that his brother was probably right, though not on the grounds which he put forward. Shortly afterwards, it was agreed that Neville Chamberlain would resign.

These were the circumstances in which Baldwin reasserted
his leadership. The vigour with which he did so compels
admiration. On the day after the meeting of the Business
Committee he made a long speech in Parliament on the Indian
issue, reminding the Conservative Party that the Empire was
no dead matter, but alive and in the constant process of
evolution. It could not be supposed that in the world of
evolution India alone was static. Baldwin made skilful play with
extracts from Churchill's own speeches of years before, paid
tribute to the work of Edward Wood, Lord Irwin, as Viceroy
and showed that he understood the difficulties of conviction
and old ties within the party. In the concluding passage,
Baldwin served notice that he was willing to face a renewed
challenge to his leadership:

'If there are those in our party ... who would have to have
forced out of their reluctant hands one concession after
another, if they be a majority, in God's name let them choose
a man to lead them. If they are in a minority, then let them at
least refrain from throwing difficulties in the way of those who
have undertaken an almost superhuman task, on the successful
fulfilment of which depends the well-being, the prosperity and
the duration of the whole British Empire.'

Then Baldwin spoke in the by-election, shrewdly seizing upon
the shifts in attitude of Rothermere and Beaverbrook and
identifying the interest of the Conservatives in resisting such
tactics with the interests of the Liberals and Socialists, neither
of which parties fielded a candidate. Baldwin also used a phrase,
supposedly provided by his cousin Rudyard Kipling, which has
taken its place in the coinage of British political life. Having
said that the papers conducted by the two press lords were not
newspapers in the normal sense but engines of propaganda for
their constantly changing policies and dislikes, he described
their methods as

'direct falsehood, misrepresentation, half-truths, the alteration
of the speaker's meaning by publishing a sentence apart from
the context ... suppression, and editorial criticism of speeches
which are not reported in the paper ... What the proprietor-

ship of these papers is aiming at is power, but power without responsibility – the prerogative of the harlot throughout the ages. This contest is not a contest as to who is to lead the party, but as to who is to appoint a leader of the party. It is a challenge to the accepted, constitutional parliamentary system, and that is why Liberals and Socialists alike resent this interference with the liberty of a political party just as much as we do, because it may be their turn tomorrow to suffer for what we have to suffer today . . .'

Duff Cooper duly won in St George's. Though a meeting of the Business Committee, at which Austen Chamberlain explained with brutal candour the deficiencies of Baldwin's leadership, cleared the air somewhat, it is doubtful whether the scars inflicted by these episodes ever healed entirely. Fifteen years later, Baldwin politely but firmly declined to discuss with Neville Chamberlain's biographer the events of 1930 and 1931. For practical purposes, however, their collaboration resumed and indeed from the autumn of 1931 that collaboration became indispensable to the life of the Government; for the conditions of British politics were soon to change, and in the most dramatic way. The total of unemployed, which stood early in 1931 at more than two and a half million, made nonsense of Labour's earlier claims. The Chancellor of the Exchequer proclaimed the financial position to be very serious and called for sacrifices. MacDonald's administration continued to be kept in power by the votes of the Liberals, some of whom were becoming distinctly restive. In the concluding days of his chairmanship of the party, Chamberlain haggled with a somewhat chastened and deflated Beaverbrook to arrive at an agreed agricultural policy, which was announced at the end of March and marked the end of the Great Empire Free Trade Campaign. Two skills, possessed in most unusual measure, had enabled Baldwin to beat down the challenge: an acute sense of timing, which assisted him to make the utmost play at the meetings of June 1930 and March 1931 with particularly offensive and indefensible effusions; and an instinctive facility with words. The hostility of the press lords mattered far more then, when the sound-film was in its infancy and television had not been invented, than it has done since the

'Second World War or even since the later 1930s. The importance which was attached to the compact with Beaverbrook is indicated by a remark of Chamberlain that the support of the Beaverbrook newspapers in the next general election might make all the difference; and Chamberlain was extraordinarily fortunate in the moment of his departure from the Central Office, because Churchill's behaviour and definite separation from the Conservatives made it appear natural that he should resume normal parliamentary work.

During the spring of 1931, as the economic situation became steadily more threatening, quiet soundings went on between the Conservatives and some Liberals. The more percipient of the latter undoubtedly realised how absurd their party was beginning to look, with its frequent announcements of despair at the Government's proposals followed by the announcement of an intention to vote for them. By the middle of the summer, rumours of a coalition government and a financial catastrophe were bruited abroad. Baldwin took the line that he would support MacDonald in any measures necessary for the national interest, but plainly had no inclination to join a coalition. Nor had the other leading Conservatives. The crisis, however, developed suddenly, overturning assumptions made in July. By 13 August Baldwin and Chamberlain were being told by the Prime Minister that when the Cabinet had agreed on cuts in expenditure, Conservative support would be requested for a second budget.

Here indeed was a startling reversal of fortune. By the somewhat enlarged standards of the 1960s and 1970s, and even when allowance is made by a handsome multiplication for the decline in the value of money, the figures in question were small. This does not mean that the crisis was taken too seriously, or that it was simply a bankers' ramp, or that a superior knowledge of economics would have enabled a later government to cope without difficulty. The fact was that the ability to enforce some cuts had become a touchstone of the Government's fitness to remain in power. MacDonald's second administration had been singularly unfortunate. The unprecedented contraction of international trade was bound to strike Great Britain severely. The interlocking crisis in the American and European economies meant the eventual collapse of the reparations settlement and the whole elaborate system for payment of war debts. It has become customary to deride Chamberlain as an unduly strict and rigid Chancellor, though by comparison with Snowden he was bold and adventurous to a degree; and there was a prolonged period, during what may be termed the posthumous reign of Keynes, when it was thought sufficient to utter the words 'deficit financing' in order to answer the question 'What then should the Government have done in 1930 and 1931?' In fact, Keynes imagined at this stage of his intellectual progression that most of Britain's troubles stemmed from the artificially high parity of the pound, and he predicted that once Britain had come off the gold standard the depression would soon be over.

The immediate situation in mid-August was that a Labour Government was actually contemplating a large cut in public spending. It appears that Baldwin, recalled while travelling to his annual sojourn at Aix, had given little thought to the situation. He made no significant contribution to the discussions, was evidently anxious 'not to be drawn into something'. Baldwin said that he wanted to get a holiday and asked Chamberlain to undertake the further negotiations. He thereupon left for France, sending Chamberlain a message of gratitude for sparing him the need to return and saying that he would back his colleague to the end.

For the second round of the negotiations, Chamberlain therefore summoned Hoare, to whom he explained that the problem was one of restoring foreign confidence in British credit, which could be done only by announcing such a cut in spending as would convince foreigners that the British had enough courage to tackle the situation. Chamberlain put the figure at one hundred million pounds, an economy which could not be reached unless Unemployment Insurance benefits were substantially reduced. Not until several crucial days had passed, during which the Labour Cabinet began to break up, did Baldwin return from Aix. On the next day, 23 August, the Prime Minister told the King that he could carry neither his Cabinet nor his party. It seemed at that moment that MacDonald would simply resign and the King would send for Baldwin, who would then have to discover what the Liberals would do.

Neville Chamberlain strongly pressed on Baldwin that he should try to secure the support of MacDonald, Snowden and one or two members of the outgoing Government, even if they brought no one else with them. With this tactic Baldwin agreed. Late that night at 10 Downing Street, the Prime Minister said that he would try to help the Conservatives in passing proposals for economy through Parliament, but that it would be of no use for him to join a government; he would be a ridiculous figure, unable to command support and bringing odium upon the Conservatives as well as upon himself. It is important to emphasise that what was then contemplated, in the circumstances of immediate crisis, was a temporary administration which would carry the economy bill and dissolve Parliament. Then MacDonald changed his mind overnight and with Snowden undertook to form such a government himself. The election would be fought on party lines. Economies would be sought to the tune of about £70 million and £50 million would be raised by additional taxation. The senior Conservatives approved, and authorised Baldwin to say that any of them would be prepared to serve.

It was decided that there should be a small Cabinet of ten. This had the advantage of marking the serious nature of the crisis and helping MacDonald, since it could produce a division of offices between the parties of four, four and two. Baldwin and Chamberlain would clearly be two of the Conservatives and were agreed that they wanted Cunliffe-Lister[5] and Hoare as the other two. Samuel and Reading represented the Liberals, the potential difficulty about Lloyd George being overcome because he was still convalescent. Besides MacDonald, the representatives of Labour were Sankey (the Lord Chancellor), Snowden and Thomas. Conservative membership of the Government at large, with 21 ministers out of 46, was disproportionately low, and Liberal representation unduly high.

Baldwin incurred a good deal of criticism for his failure to stand out more vigorously on behalf of his party – which may have occurred because he thought that the arrangements would last no more than a few weeks – and for his barrenness in council. It is still not certain why Baldwin, who after all his experiences with Lloyd George had little wish to join a coalition, still less to be its chief architect, abandoned his preference for a Conservative government. Probably the urgings of the King played a part; there was obviously much to be said for making at least some Labour ministers share the responsibility; and, though this mattered less to Baldwin than to Chamberlain, there were already signs that a tariff would have to come. The Conservative Party warmly supported the action of Baldwin, who announced that once the budget had been balanced the agreement would end and the parties go their separate ways. 'When this Parliament dissolves, you will then have a straight fight on tariffs, and against the Socialist party.' Simultaneously, most of the former Labour ministers were in process of discovering that after all there had been no crisis of national credit but rather a sinister manoeuvre by bankers. Many alleged, and rumours which had circulated freely in July gave a certain verisimilitude to the charge, that MacDonald had for some time been intent upon ditching his colleagues in favour of more congenial company. The Lord Chancellor, nominally a Labour supporter though little attached to party politics, had a knack of reducing complicated issues to the bare essentials. His diary for 29 August observes: 'Politics are queer. I am supporting a policy which a large majority of my late colleagues voted for in the Cabinet, and they daren't say so for fear of the Trades Union Congress. God help England.'

An emergency budget was introduced in September amidst revelations about the earlier willingness of Labour ministers to make cuts. Taxes were increased, unemployment benefits and some salaries reduced. The purpose for which this allegedly temporary government had been formed, to arrest the flight from the pound, was not fulfilled. On the contrary, renewed credits negotiated in New York and Paris ran out with alarming rapidity and the new ministers were informed that the unfavourable trade balance would probably lie between £50 million and £100 million that year. There was a minor mutiny in the fleet, a first-class financial crisis in India and an imminent danger of the fall of the pound. It is necessary for readers of another generation, who have become accustomed to treating this latter event as a normal occurrence, to remind themselves that in 1931 it all looked very different. On 19 September Chamberlain recorded that it had been a terrible week: 'The Prime Minister is worn out and seems unable to make up his mind to decisions, S.B. is useless and everything seems to fall on me.' All members of the Cabinet except the two Liberals wanted a very early election. So far had the situation developed in a matter of weeks that Chamberlain, whom no-one ever accused of undue solicitude for the Labour and Liberal parties, or of feebleness in advancing the interests of his own, also observed:

'But if we do go to the country, how are we to go ? Our idiotic party thinks it has the game in its hand and wants us to fight on party lines. I believe the only way to secure the sort of majority which would give the world confidence is to go as a National Government, perhaps even as a National Party, carrying MacDonald and his colleagues with us together with as many Liberals as we could get. It is very interesting to find that Topping wants this too, though you could hardly find a stronger party man.'

In the next two days the reserves were depleted by £28 million. The gold standard was abandoned forthwith. The Liberals naturally said that this step made a tariff unnecessary, since it would increase the price of imports and the competitiveness of exports. On the evening of 24 September the Business Committee met under Baldwin, who said he had come to the conclusion that an election should take place as soon as possible, with an appeal on a national rather than a party programme, asking for a free hand and including tariffs, to be made by a National Government reconstructed after the resignation of any who could not accept the programme. Baldwin felt that MacDonald should be the head of that government but had not made up his mind who should be Prime Minister in a government formed after victory. There were besides Baldwin thirteen leading Conservatives present at this meeting. All favoured an appeal by a National Government under Ramsay MacDonald, provided that the programme embodied the full tariff. All agreed that the election should be held at the earliest possible moment and that if they went into the election with MacDonald as Prime Minister he must be accepted as Prime Minister in the event of victory.

This was a much more important decision, for the longer term, than the entry into the Government a month before.

Nothing could indicate so clearly the seriousness of the crisis, or at any rate the seriousness with which it was viewed, as the willingness of these senior figures to support to the full a Prime Minister who had spent his life in opposing them. Their readiness to subordinate immediate party and personal interest to the national interest stood in happy contrast with the behaviour of most members of MacDonald's Labour Government. With justice Chamberlain remarked that if Baldwin had not been leader of the Conservative Party the agreement to join forces with MacDonald and some of the Liberals could hardly have come about.

MacDonald too had concluded that an early election must be held. There followed a succession of pilgrimages by prominent Liberals to the oracle at Churt, whence Lloyd George protested vehemently against the prospect of an election and urged his Liberal colleagues to resign from the Government. After numerous further haverings, Baldwin and Chamberlain together had to tell MacDonald on 5 October that he must reach a decision that day. The Conservatives informed him that unless he could agree that the manifesto must contain a plain request for power to control imports – whether by prohibition, tariffs, the effect of the devaluation of sterling or any combination of such methods – they must part company. At last it was arranged that the Government should go to the country as a supposedly united administration, one section of which advocated tariffs whilst the other declared it had an open mind but was still convinced of the merits of Free Trade.

The campaign proved less bitter than many had expected. Large numbers of people who had formerly voted Labour now supported the National Government, which was returned with a staggering majority. The Labour Opposition was reduced to a rump of 52, led by the only former minister of any seniority who had not lost his seat, George Lansbury. Parties supporting the Government had 554 seats. Of these no less than 471 were Conservatives, which meant that Baldwin had an army with a majority of over 300 against all others. It is well to remember, nevertheless, that about 7 million votes were cast against the National Government, and rather more than 14 million in favour; and it is plain that the Conservative Party could not have done anything like as well as this without MacDonald and

Snowden. Attacks by the latter upon the programme put forward by his former colleagues, 'Bolshevism run mad', were deemed particularly effective. Of the new Cabinet's twenty members, eleven were Conservatives. The National Labour group continued to hold four places; the Samuelite Liberals had three, and another brand, the Simonite Liberals, two. Since Simon himself was given the Foreign Office and Ramsay MacDonald was the unquestioned Prime Minister, the Treasury could not be withheld from the Conservative Party. In other words, the office lay between Baldwin and Chamberlain, and the former had no desire for it. The latter, on the other hand, was an avowed Protectionist, and it was thought that since Cunliffe-Lister was more or less of the same conviction he must not be put at the Board of Trade. That office accordingly went to Runciman; and the episode illustrates the weakness of any government formed in such a way, namely that ministers of different persuasions have to be balanced against each other and that in default of strong and supple leadership, policy may be whittled away to the lowest common denominator or indeed to vanishing point.

It was of course natural that MacDonald, and especially after the election, should fear to be shown up as a mere mascot of the Conservatives, a danger to which Baldwin and his colleagues were sensitive. Although it is usual to describe the National Government of 1931–5 as nothing more than a Conservative administration masquerading under a false name, what happened in the 1930s cannot be understood until it is appreciated that the situation was more complicated than that. MacDonald played, at least until 1934, a much more active role in the affairs of the Government than many accounts have allowed. In foreign affairs, most notably in relations with the United States, he was apt to keep a good deal of business in his own hands. Although numerous and powerful Conservatives expressed their discontent with Simon's performance at the Foreign Office, he remained until June 1935, then moved to the Home Office, and after that to the Treasury. Baldwin filled the kind of role as Lord President which suited him best. There were few executive or administrative duties and his principal task was to attend to the business of Cabinet committees and of the House of Commons.

A Chancellor of the Exchequer must always occupy a powerful position if he is even moderately competent, and Neville Chamberlain was a great deal more than that. The circumstances of acute financial crisis and of unprecedented unemployment increased his power within the Government in one sense and decreased it in another. Because the Government was committed to the elimination of the budget deficit and to the restoration of confidence, it was easier than in normal times for the Chancellor to justify refusals to the spending departments; and on the other hand, it was harder for that very reason for the Chancellor to strike up working alliances with important colleagues whose programmes he would undertake to finance, somewhat as Churchill had done during Chamberlain's tenure of the Ministry of Health. Even in the last years of MacDonald and Baldwin, when Chamberlain was certainly the most resourceful and efficient of the senior ministers, there were plenty of subjects of importance upon which he could not carry his view, or could carry it only in part. The Cabinet system, whereby advice is tendered to his colleagues by a minister who then has the responsibility of executing the collective decision, does not lend itself readily to dominance by any other minister, no matter how well informed, intelligent and powerful, unless he occupies the first place. The events of this administration also indicate how difficult it is for a Prime Minister to be displaced if he desires to remain in office, and especially so when his most likely successor has no anxiety for the post.

To be Lord President fitted Baldwin's inclinations much better. He insisted on moving into the residence normally occupied by the Chancellor of the Exchequer, 11 Downing Street, where, as he cheerfully remarked, 'I could always keep my eye on the Prime Minister'. David Margesson, the Conservatives' Chief Whip for most of the 1930s, who knew Baldwin intimately, said with justice that his strength lay in the fact that he only ticked over at half speed and was capable of revving up his engines in a crisis. Chamberlain, by contrast, possessing greater physical energy than Baldwin, was accustomed to run his engines just, but only just, within their capacity. Colleagues who omit to give decisions, or neglect to answer letters, or fail to prepare for meetings, are generally incapable of realising what anguish they cause to others differently constituted. More than enough has been written already to indicate what a sore trial to the patience of Chamberlain and other leading Conservatives was caused by some of Baldwin's habits; the combination of Baldwin's failings and MacDonald's must have compounded the problem during the next few years. Like others, Neville Chamberlain recognised and acknowledged in Baldwin a capacity to judge the minds of the people, to raise political debate to a higher plane and to attract affection. It is not surprising that the same feelings were not entertained by most Conservatives towards MacDonald, who did however command a good deal of respect for his courage. On the whole, Chamberlain behaved well to both of them until he succeeded Baldwin in May 1937.

The depression had given extra weight to the protective aspects of tariffs and the first moves were made within a few weeks of Chamberlain's arrival at the Treasury. To his amusement, the ardent Free Trader Snowden proposed that the President of the Board of Trade should have power to impose a duty up to 100 per cent on excessive imports. Later in the month, a tariff was placed on certain vegetables, fruit and flowers. Though the Prime Minister showed a marked lack of enthusiasm for food taxes, Snowden and Samuel both swallowed the medicine. Chamberlain resigned himself to a prolonged effort to place the finances of the country on a sounder footing. He judged that the paramount duty of a government in such circumstances was to create confidence in the probity of its policy and the value of the currency. Without those conditions, a country so dependent upon foreign investment and trade could not thrive. Once confidence revived, however, there would be a greater willingness all round to invest, employment and trade would improve and industry might be made more efficient in the process. As he said to a friend, 'the more I think of the financial situation, the more I feel like the farmer who, when his wife had been ill for some years, exclaimed "I wish she would get better – or something."'

In a Cabinet so constituted, some difficulties were bound to arise. There was one passage of arms early in December, which seemed likely to end in the resignation of Snowden. However, this crisis was averted and Chamberlain noticed that in the

Cabinet he carried more weight than before and spoke more. 'The P.M. shows much deference to what I say and as S.B. mostly remains silent our people look to me for the lead and I see that they get it.' After it appeared that the Government must disintegrate over the issue of a general tariff, an extraordinary constitutional expedient was adopted; by 'the agreement to differ' the four dissentient members of the Cabinet (Snowden, Samuel, Maclean and Sinclair) were allowed to disclaim responsibility for the tariff proposals but to remain ministers. From the point of view of those who wanted a tariff, this was a good solution. The dissentients were likely to suffer most of the embarrassment and their proclaimed attitude removed one of the main arguments of critics in the Conservative Party, who could not say that the pass had been sold. The way was prepared for the Imperial Economic Conference, to be held at Ottawa later in the year, by the exemption of Dominion products from the tariff for the time being. This gave the British party something with which to negotiate. In the meantime, and surprisingly, there had been no significant rise in domestic prices since the departure from the gold standard and in February 1932 the cost of living index actually stood six points below its level of January 1931.

Chamberlain's speech on what he described as 'the great day of my life' is well worthy of study as an example of the lucidity, clarity and order which characterised his financial statements. The measures of February 1932, and the arrangements reached at Ottawa six months later, closed an era which had opened nearly ninety years before with the repeal of the Corn Laws. Free Trade had become for many not a question of economic prudence, to be decided according to the needs of the moment, but an issue of principle, almost of religion, entwined with conceptions of international harmony and peace. The abandonment of Free Trade, a system which by definition had left the British virtually powerless to retaliate against others who suited their own convenience by practising very different systems, and the introduction of limited forms of imperial preference, were the most distinctively Conservative measures passed by the National Government. It is an index of the deeply ingrained resistance, and of the fear of dear food, that although the bulk of active Conservatives had wanted at least some reform in these directions for many years, it took the collapse of sterling, the fall of the Labour Government, and hitherto unexampled unemployment to produce a climate in which it became possible. Before the events of 1931, it would have been thought inconceivable that some Labour and Liberal members should vote for such measures.

It was all but thirty years since Joseph Chamberlain had abandoned his seat in the Cabinet to preach Tariff Reform. His son, while conscious of the historical fitness of the occasion, had at first determined to say nothing of that aspect, fearing that he might be unable to control his voice. However, when he saw all the references in the press to the completion of Joseph Chamberlain's work, he realised that a silence would be misunderstood. It is natural that politicians should try to call in aid a sense of continuity and to wrest approval from the past. This was one of those occasions when the claim could be made with some justice, the more effective for the expressive and compact English of the Chancellor's peroration:

'There can have been few occasions in all our long political history when to the son of a man who counted for something in his day and generation has been vouchsafed the privilege of setting the seal on the work which the father began but had perforce to leave unfinished ... His work was not in vain. Time and the misfortunes of the country have brought conviction to many who did not feel that they could agree with him then. I believe he would have found consolation for the bitterness of his disappointment if he could have foreseen that these proposals, which are the direct and legitimate descendants of his own conception, would be laid before the House of Commons, which he loved, in the presence of one and by the lips of the other of the two immediate successors to his name and blood.'

Chamberlain's budget of 1932 could hardly be an agreeable one. He received a certain number of abusive letters, many of them from beer drinkers angry that the duty had been put up. On the other hand, no less a personage than the Governor of the Bank of England declared that it was almost the first honest budget since the war. It was part of Chamberlain's technique to praise, in his public speeches and in his broadcasts, the spirit of resolution and self-sacrifice with which the British people had faced the crisis of 1931. The Government had then issued a national appeal for early payment of tax by companies and individuals; and it does no harm to be reminded that they responded on so heroic a scale that the Inland Revenue Authorities were unable to send out receipts to keep pace with the inflow of tax paid early. Chamberlain regretfully declined to allow any relief from taxation, though aware that the whole country was crying out for it and acknowledging the political attractions of seeking a little popularity in this way. But confidence which had already revived might easily be shaken beyond repair if the Government made concessions and then had to withdraw them. 'Hard work, strict economy, firm courage, unfailing patience – these are the qualifications that are required of us, and with them we shall not fail.'

During the summer of 1932 the National Government, considering all its difficulties, did extraordinarily well. The conference at Lausanne was expertly handled by MacDonald, who had both taste and aptitude for foreign affairs and who had come to trust a good deal in Chamberlain's support. The two of them provided an effective combination, because Chamberlain was master of all the technical and financial side of the business, and moreover understood French easily; MacDonald had neither qualification but knew how to balance the many forces at play. The conversion of War Loan, carrying a rate of interest at five per cent, was successfully accomplished; the rate of interest was reduced to three-and-a-half per cent and by further operations later in the year the total of saving to the Government in the servicing of that loan was brought to about £40 million p.a. Elaborate preparations had meanwhile been going forward for the conference to be held at Ottawa. Some of the Dominion governments had made it discreetly plain that the Dominions Secretary, Mr J. H. Thomas, did not quite conform to their conception of the higher levels of British statesmanship. Chamberlain, declaring that he cared nothing about the leadership but a great deal about the success of the conference, quietly suggested that Baldwin should go since in that case there could be no dispute about the headship of the delegation and his presence would give the conference an exceptional prestige. Baldwin had made a prolonged and memorable tour of Canada some years earlier and, as Chamberlain put it, 'although he would not contribute very much to the practical part of the business, it would be extremely useful to have him there to make dignified speeches and do things which we might not have time for. I enlarged on this theme to S.B. and although the idea came as a surprise to him, I could see he was much tickled by it and it seems to me the solution of the difficulty.'

Thus matters were arranged. The Lausanne Conference concluded just in time for Chamberlain to join the main party of ministers, crossing to Canada in those spacious days by the *Empress of Britain*. It need scarcely be said that Chamberlain soon organised his colleagues into orderly preparations. A whole series of general proposals was drawn up, on the principle that a delegation which goes to a conference knowing what it wants is much more likely to get its way than one which does not. Chamberlain even wrote Baldwin's opening speech. The conference itself proved to be a protracted ordeal. Any notion which the ministers had entertained that it would be easier to do business with their own kinsmen than with 'foreigners' was swiftly dispelled. 'It isn't hands across the sea, it's fists across the sea' Chamberlain remarked. Baldwin explained privately that he put the main burden of the negotiations upon Chamberlain and Hailsham because if the conference failed the diehards at home would know that it was not for want of trying. He might have added that they were in any case better fitted by training and knowledge to conduct the detailed negotiations. Baldwin coped with all the public side of the business excellently while many of his ministerial colleagues worked themselves to the point of exhaustion, not least because the Prime Minister of Canada, Mr Bennett, insisted upon keeping everything in his own hands and behaved in such a way that even Baldwin said he had brainstorms. Agreements were negotiated between Britain, the individual Dominions and India, based upon the principle of reciprocal preference. 'This has been a devil of a job', wrote Baldwin while the outcome still lay in the balance; 'the bulk of the negotiations have been done by Neville, "ably assisted" (as the papers would say) by Hailsham. To Neville, of course, it is a sacred trust, but he has been A.1., and most

sensible and broad minded.'[6] Chamberlain had been anxious
to obtain an agreed set of resolutions which would go towards
laying down the principles of an imperial trade policy. However, he had to be satisfied with something much milder.
Bennett made amends to a limited degree, after Baldwin had
signed the agreements between the United Kingdom and the
other countries, by announcing the signature of the Anglo-
Canadian agreement and saying that he would call upon the
son of 'that great statesman whose vision paved the way for the
task now consummated' to sign on behalf of Great Britain.

At Ottawa and Lausanne alike, Chamberlain had shown
himself a superb negotiator in all technical matters, with the
whole of the case at his fingers' ends, and with a capacity not to
lose sight of the objective; he was assiduous to a degree, could
think quickly and draft in detail. Shocked to discover how thin
the cement of Empire had worn, he concealed nothing of his
emotions in the long account which he gave the Cabinet on the
return of the delegation towards the end of August. The Ottawa
agreements, which led to a marked up surge in inter-imperial
trade, and helped materially to mitigate the effects of the
depression in Britain and in the Dominions, owed more to
Chamberlain than to any other politician. His estimate of the
possibilities deriving from the Ottawa agreements, and from
Tariff Reform in general, was a realistic and moderate one.
Having begun his political life as a devout imperialist,
Chamberlain had shed any notion that Britain could rely in
foreign policy or trade upon the unsupported strength of the
Empire. Snowden, Samuel and Sinclair, together with a
number of junior ministers, resigned because of the Ottawa
agreements. MacDonald, after some hesitations but with firm
support from Baldwin, remained Prime Minister.

The early years of the National Government show in an acute
form the paradox of Britain's economy between the wars;
unemployment rose to the better part of three millions in the
trough of the depression and yet real consumption appears to
have been almost unaffected. The cycles of British economic
activity had shown fairly sharp fluctuations in the 1920s but
towards the end of 1932 a strong recovery set in, inaugurating
one of the longest upsurges in British history and lasting till the

autumn of 1937. After that, the increase in the spending on armaments distorted normal patterns; but it is worth noticing that even an expenditure upon rearmament unprecedented in peace time failed to reduce unemployment to the levels which have been considered normal, and readily attainable, since the Second World War. The fact is that the unemployment of the 1930s, and particularly after the worst phase had passed, was not generally spread. The areas dependent upon certain old-established industries no longer competitive suffered very severely, and there is no clear evidence that a different set of policies on the part of the National Government would have promoted a much speedier recovery. By the standards of most industrial countries, indeed, Britain recovered well from the worst of the depression, and for many millions the 1930s were not a period of unrelieved gloom and misery, but rather a period of rising prosperity and falling prices, marked by a high level of house-building.

By the spring of 1933 the outlook, in short, was a good deal more promising. Chamberlain refused to accept the advice of Keynes, with whom he discussed the issue at length, that the budget should be unbalanced on a large scale. Most of those who argued for deficit financing pressed for a large increase in public works, often in deference to the view that the decline in public works had accounted for a good deal of the rise in unemployment. This was not so; the biggest single cause was the decline of British exports. The financial year 1932–3 had produced a deficit of rather over £32 million instead of the tiny surplus for which Chamberlain had calculated. He went to some lengths to assure the House of Commons that he had not dismissed the proposal for an unbalanced budget simply because it was unorthodox. Nor was he impressed with the suggestion that acceptance of this suggestion, which was generally to be achieved by a substantial reduction of income tax, would be a proof of courage on his part; world trade was shrinking, prices were falling, and it was beyond belief that by unbalancing the budget the British were going to reverse these movements. The world over, budget deficits were piling up. They did not produce the favourable results which were claimed for the same policy in Britain, whereas the policy of tightening the belt and sound finance had enabled low interest rates to be secured, greatly to the benefit of industry. Chamberlain put his argument thus:

'Of all the countries passing through these difficult times the one that has stood the test with the greatest measure of success is the United Kingdom. Without underrating the hardships of our situation – the long tragedy of the unemployed, the grievous burden of taxation, the arduous and painful struggle of those engaged in trade and industry – at any rate we are free from that fear, which besets so many less fortunately placed, fear that things are going to get worse. We owe our freedom from that fear largely to the fact that we have balanced our budget.'

The Finance Bill was not at all strenuously opposed and Chamberlain planned his concessions with the usual care, extracting the maximum of benefit from each. From the point of view of the Conservative Party, the most serious issue of the next year or two was India. The Secretary of State, Hoare, had announced in 1932 that the Government intended to pass a single measure which would provide for autonomous constitutions in the provinces of India and for the federation of the provinces and principal states. After the publication of the White Paper in March 1933, Churchill gathered together as much support as he could and in effect adapted to the 1930s the methods practised by his father fifty years before, using the party's organisation against its hierarchy and its leadership in Parliament. Baldwin fully understood the risks; this continued to be one of the issues upon which he felt deeply and on such issues he was habitually both tough and adroit. Incidentally, anyone who reads the debates or newspapers of the 1930s will realise how much nonsense has been written about the 'deliberate exclusion' of Churchill from successive governments. The fact is that by his own choice, and for better or worse, he excluded himself time after time. His marked lack of discrimination, his unwillingness to make those compromises without which no body of intelligent men can work together and call themselves a party, the extravagance of his language, all diminished his effectiveness. Austen Chamberlain, who was disposed to agree with Churchill about Germany, recorded as early as the spring of 1933 that in respect of India he had become hysterical and could see only one side of the question and listen to only one view.

To be set against the slow reduction of unemployment and the rise in prosperity were many disquieting developments, all of them arising from circumstances beyond the Government's control. The Japanese had been attacking Chinese territory spasmodically since September 1931, and the League of Nations had done precious little about it. The more vigorous enthusiasts for the League, simplifying the difficulties to a degree which causes amazement even now, blamed the Foreign Secretary in particular and the Government in general for the failure to protect China. It was widely believed that only clumsy handling by Sir John Simon had prevented the joint imposition of telling sanctions by Britain and the United States, a notion still widely credited but quite baseless. This was held to be the first test case of the League's effectiveness, since Japan was the first great power openly to flout the covenant. No British government possessed the means at that time of threatening Japan effectively or even plausibly, for Britain had no base east of Malta capable of sustaining a fleet of capital ships. Indeed it was not until 1932, under the stress of the events in the Far East, that Britain abandoned in principle the Ten-year Rule, the instruction to the Service Departments that they should prepare their plans on the assumption that the British Empire would not be engaged in a major war for the next ten years. This rule had been made self-extending after pressure from Mr Churchill, when he was Chancellor of the Exchequer and pursuing a relentless campaign of parsimony in the Service estimates. Its effects lasted throughout the 1930s and because the shortage of orders had caused a decline in research, a dearth of skilled craftsmen and the closure of many factories capable of manufacturing arms, the first thing the National Government discovered when it embarked upon a programme of rearmament was that very big sums could not be sensibly spent in the first few years for lack of capacity. Those who had been Churchill's colleagues in the 1920s and knew some of the facts must have found it hard to hold their tongues during the debates of the 1930s.

The Disarmament Conference, dragging along since February 1932, had caused British ministers a tremendous amount of labour for scant result. There were millions who equated partial disarmament with peace, and imagined that the one would be automatically secured by the other. The British had placed themselves in the worst of positions by disarming on a large scale before the Conference began. Moreover, the accession of Hitler to power in January 1933, coupled with the obvious refusal of the Japanese to take any serious notice of the League, rendered the whole idea of an international disarmament convention more than faintly ludicrous. As for relations with the United States, the British Government had after some hesitation on Chamberlain's part made a further payment against the debt in December 1932. This was one of the rare occasions upon which Baldwin expressed a decided opinion, which weighed heavily with the Chancellor. For all practical purposes, reparations payments by Germany had been abolished at the Lausanne Conference of 1932 and the British Government would have liked to see war debts cancelled all round. Small payments were made to the United States in June and December 1933, and none thereafter. Chamberlain's worst enemies would not have accused him of lack of scruple and uprightness in financial questions; indeed, the more normal charge is that he carried orthodoxy in such questions to the point of a fault. There is therefore no need to argue the proposition that he loathed the principle of default. At the same time, he had little patience with the attitude of the United States Government, and especially after Roosevelt ruined the World Economic Conference in the summer of 1933. Of the debt payments actually made to the United States at that point, 80 per cent had come from Britain, although the British debt to the United States was only about 40 per cent of the total. Mr Baldwin, walking at Aix-les-Bains, arrived at opinions which as on other occasions indicated that his powers of diagnosis exceeded his powers of prescription:

'Walking alone among these hills I have come to the conclusion the world is stark mad. I have no idea what is the matter with it but it's all wrong and at times I am sick to death of being an asylum attendant.

'I think we are the sanest but the disease is catching.'[7]

Just after Germany had left the Disarmament Conference for

good in October 1933, there occurred one of the most celebrated by-elections in British history at East Fulham, so celebrated indeed that even now it is providing the material for a volley of articles in learned journals. The bare facts are that a National Government majority of 14,521 at the general election of 1931 was converted into a Labour majority of 4,840, representing a swing of 25·5 per cent. This was one of five by-elections held in the space of a month or so. Only at East Fulham was the National Government candidate defeated, but in the other four the average swing against the National Government was over 20 per cent. The probability is that, for the moment at least, Liberals were not voting in any great numbers for the National Government. The significance of the by-election lies less in the result itself than in the effect upon the minds of the Prime Minister, who was rendered very miserable, and still more of Baldwin, who adverted to this event in conversation until the end of his life and once said with passion 'it was a nightmare'. Baldwin became convinced that the by-election had been lost on no issue but the pacifist. This judgement is open to question, but it is perfectly true that during the campaign the successful Labour candidate had placed much emphasis upon that issue and immediately after his victory he claimed that in Fulham the Conservative candidate had 'stood for armaments. In two years the Government have dealt a deadly blow to the hopes of peace by international co-operation'. Mr Wilmot alleged that Europe was again piling up armaments for a great war, which in some countries was true enough; and he claimed to have discovered feverish activity, night and day, in the armaments factories of Britain, producing hideous modern instruments of destruction. The Chancellor of the Exchequer, whose task it would be to pay for any such activity, recorded that he did not lose a minute's sleep over the election at Fulham or accept that the result was simply due to lies about war. The Government with so gigantic a majority was bound to lose many by-elections.

The deficiencies in the defences of Britain and the Empire were so glaring, the prospects of the Disarmament Conference so unpromising, that officials and ministers undertook a full-scale review. The essential fact, without which the history of the 1930s and of appeasement cannot be understood, is that

British interests were spread across the globe. The loss of the Anglo–Japanese alliance, and the conversion of Japanese good-will into distrust and then hostility, constituted the most important single change for the worse in Britain's position. Had Japanese ill-will been compensated by the active goodwill of the United States, it would have been a different story. Britain's stake in the East, whether measured in terms of prestige, or territory, or investment, or trade, was too great to be abandoned without the loss of her position as an imperial power. So long as Europe remained quiescent, the risk might be run. But the rise of Hitler, in command of a Germany which was still potentially the strongest state in Europe, transformed the prospect not only in the Far East but in the Mediterranean and the Middle East; and it was this multiplicity of dangers which dominated the minds of the leading ministers in the last five years before the war. 'We cannot', Chamberlain observed in his diary for 6 June 1934, 'provide simultaneously for hostilities with Japan and Germany.'

Baldwin and Chamberlain had already argued successfully that Britain could not adopt the policy of standing aloof from the military threats in Europe, a notion which had some adherents among senior members of the Cabinet and many supporters outside. The Chancellor, who felt deep reluctance to finance a massive programme of rearmament, expended a good deal of time during the summer of 1934 in boiling down the estimates. That aspect mattered comparatively little in the long run, because the figures which had been suggested were rendered meaningless within a matter of months by the pace of Germany's rearmament. What is much more important is that Chamberlain, basing himself largely upon the economic argument, was able to insist that Britain simply did not have the resources to provide against all dangers. She must therefore have a clear set of priorities in her defences. Secondly, because Germany had rightly been identified as the ultimate potential enemy, and because the anxieties of the British people were concentrated on Europe rather than on the Far East, British preparations – assuming that a choice had to be made – must be directed against Germany rather than Japan. Moreover, Baldwin had already promised that Britain should not remain inferior in air strength to any power within striking distance of her shores; and the Chancellor insisted upon a large increase in the sum allocated to the Royal Air Force, to be found by reduction of the sum devoted to the Army. At first, Chamberlain proposed that the policy of maintaining a fleet of capital ships capable of meeting the Japanese in battle must be postponed. This paper produced such an uproar, partly because most ministers thought that the danger in the Far East was more immediate than that in Europe, that it had to be withdrawn. The Chancellor and the first Lord of the Admiralty were bidden to discuss the naval construction programmes in the normal way and again the practical consequences were less serious than they might have been. In respect of capital ships and of cruisers, Britain was committed until the end of 1936 by the naval treaties of 1922 and 1930; and well before that date, Chamberlain was willing to sanction a scale of expenditure which he would not have considered in his worst dreams of 1934.

Baldwin accordingly announced increases in the strength of the Royal Air Force, whereupon the Opposition moved a vote of censure. By way of public education, Baldwin tried to explain that if the RAF were not expanded 'we may find ourselves later on in terrible jeopardy . . . The greatest crime to our own people is to be afraid to tell the truth . . . the old frontiers are gone. When you think of the defence of England you no longer think of the chalk cliffs of Dover; you think of the Rhine. That is where our frontier lies.'

The decisions taken in the summer of 1934 owed more to Baldwin and to Chamberlain than to any other members of the Government. The sums which it was proposed to spend were far too small in relation to the danger as it developed; but that the chief threat would come from Germany, enhanced because combined with the risk of war with Japan, and later with Italy, was correctly apprehended, and the date by which the Services should be ready for war was set at 1939.

Like a number of his colleagues, Chamberlain had been anxious to see whether an accommodation could be reached with Japan, a policy which he pressed strongly upon the Foreign Secretary and which proved abortive. He recorded a universal feeling of fear about the future, an apprehension that whether it came in two, three, five or ten years, a challenge to

Britain's safety might materialise and that it would come from Germany. Chamberlain believed that Japan did not wish to confront Britain to the point of war and would not do so unless Britain were hopelessly embroiled in Europe. Provision against the dangers in Europe, therefore, would probably mean security for the more important of British interests in the Far East. As for the alternative:

'If we had to contemplate the division of our forces so as to protect our Far Eastern interests, while prosecuting a war in Europe, then it must be evident that not only India, Hong-Kong, and Australasia would be in dire peril, but that we ourselves would stand in far greater danger of destruction by a fully-armed and organised Germany . . . The *fons et origo* of all our European troubles and anxieties is Germany.'[8]

The reputations of Baldwin and Chamberlain have been blasted to an altogether unjust degree by the failures of Britain in foreign policy and defence in the period from 1934 to 1940. A good deal of this criticism turns upon the assumption, seldom debated, that the war could have been avoided and Hitler and the Nazi Party overthrown, or tamed, or deflected, by a more skilful exercise of British diplomacy. Even now, our view of the period is affected by the strictures passed upon both men by Mr Churchill, criticisms reinforced by others with powerful reasons for wishing to direct attention away from their own performances in the 1930s. The essential failure of Baldwin and Chamberlain, and one shared by almost everyone else, was the failure to realise in time the scale and swiftness of German rearmament. In dealing with the Japanese, the Italians or the Germans in the later 1930s, armed strength and the will to use it were essential to a power which was to have any hope of treating with them. Many prominent members of the Labour and Liberal parties, and some members of the Conservative Party, were adopting not a wrong view of this or that issue, which could to some degree be remedied by argument or the presentation of fresh facts, but a false conception of the nature of international relations and of British power. At least, this is the most generous construction to put upon the ceaseless speeches about the force of world opinion, the organisation of collective security and the folly, not to say wickedness, of British rearmament.

As prosperity revived somewhat, and the date of the next general election drew nearer, questions about the future of the Government became more acute. The very size of the majority carried its own dangers, since the weakness of the Opposition might produce a feeling of security, relaxation and aimlessness. It appears that no prominent Conservative wished to fight the election on purely party grounds. Neville Chamberlain, however, was the leader of the group which became restless about the Conservatives' lack of direction. Like many others, he saw the General Election of 1931, and the slow recovery thereafter, as a triumph of patriotism and good sense over the more incompetent and unstable elements of the Labour Party. If this position was to be upheld, the Conservative Party must show itself to be the party of prosperity and responsibility, of industrial reorganisation; and Protection would be the chief symbol of its commitment to rationalisation and planned economic development. There must be a programme, based upon careful thought and fresh ideas.

This was where Chamberlain's chairmanship of the Research Department enabled him to impinge directly upon the party's policy. Early in 1934, he set the department to work on a programme which included Empire migration, the maintenance and development of the Ottawa agreements, the relations between industry and the State, and the improvement of national physique. He took care to arrange that these issues were discussed in the first instance only by the Conservative members of the Cabinet; in other words, matters were being so prepared that the Conservative Party had its own identity. Before the first meeting of this group Chamberlain drew up a memorandum under nine headings, with numerous sub-divisions ranging from reform of the House of Lords to centralised slaughtering. He discoursed upon each item and it is not difficult to credit the claim made in his diary that the paper created 'a profound impression', since none of his colleagues had any idea that he would produce such a scheme. Baldwin appears to have expressed himself enthusiastically and a series of regular meetings began.

It is not easy to find a parallel to the speed and completeness of the change of emphasis which occurred in British politics at this time. Until 1934 or 1935, the great issues were pre-dominantly domestic; thenceforward, the fate of the League, the vulnerability of Britain to attack in the air, the policy to be pursued towards Germany, the introduction of conscription and the declaration of war itself became the critical questions. For the first time in many years, the defence estimates in 1934 had shown an increase for all three Services. The increases were of the most modest dimensions, and soon to be overtaken by further announcements. Nevertheless, the Opposition objected vehemently and Mr Attlee even asserted that the Labour Party stood for total disarmament 'because we are realists . . .' Mr Churchill delivered a speech of much interest. Far from desiring Britain to throw her weight at once into the scales in Europe, he wished to use Britain's increasing strength in arms to secure the freedom to remain outside European war. Baldwin, he said, had only to make up his mind what was to be done. He had the power not only because of the confidence placed by large numbers of the British people in the sobriety of his judge-ment and in his peaceful intentions, but because he possessed overwhelming majorities in both Houses. Once he made up his mind, Parliament would vote all the supplies: 'There need be no talk of working up public opinion. You must not go and ask the public what they think about this. Parliament and the Cabinet have to decide, and the nation has to judge whether they have acted rightly as trustees.'

In the formal sense, this is doubtless true. Had Baldwin determined on a very large increase in the Air Force, he would have been supported by the bulk of Conservatives, though he might at the same time have had to face the prospect of break-ing up the National Government. The real point is, however, rather different. The last date at which an election could come was 1936 and governments normally do not like to let a Parliament run its full term. But rearmament on this scale would be a slow business, certain to lead to increased spending for the indefinite future. Baldwin evidently feared that if he pressed ahead too fast, the tide of pacifism and easy talk about collective security would overwhelm the Government. The Permanent Under-Secretary of the Foreign Office argued that

Baldwin could afford to lose many seats and still have an ample majority. Baldwin replied that he knew much more of these things than did Sir Robert Vansittart. He feared a landslide; 'and then you will have the Socialists, who will give you no rearmament at all, instead of me who give you not enough.'[9]

It was inevitable that so great a disparity in the parliamentary forces would occasionally lead to prickliness, and but for Baldwin's tact, skill and lack of self-importance, such differences would probably have ruined the National Government. Many Conservative MPs had been urging for some time the repeal of a land tax imposed during the second Labour Government, and in the spring of 1934 Baldwin told Ramsay MacDonald that he feared it would be impossible to hold back this tide any longer; he received a reply refusing to allow repeal. Baldwin did not wish to carry the issue further. Chamberlain therefore spoke to the Chief Whip about it, whereupon Captain Margesson waited upon the Prime Minister and told him plainly that the Government would probably be defeated on an amendment unless it took the initiative. MacDonald talked of resignation and it was only at this stage, late in April, that Chamberlain learned from him of a memorandum sent to Baldwin in the previous August. In this paper MacDonald had reviewed the position and had concluded that the formation of a new party in advance of the next general election was probably unpractical, suggesting that he should resign the Premiership and take a place without portfolio shortly before the election. This was the solution which many leading Conservatives were inclined to favour. There were powerful arguments for waiting until the India Bill, an enormously complicated measure with divisive effects inside the Conservative Party, had passed through Parliament; which would not be until about the middle of 1935.

The preparation of a programme proceeded during the autumn; Chamberlain devised a plan, gratefully accepted by MacDonald and Baldwin alike, for the initiation of schemes which would stimulate economic development in the most severely depressed areas, and by-pass all the normal cumbersome business of reference to Government departments; in the early part of 1935 the total of unemployed at last fell below two million; and there was for the second year running a modest surplus. Within the Conservative Party the situation was less happy. Churchill had made no attempt to mend quarrels over India. Endless time was wasted during the summer of 1934 over his complaint, which proved to be a mare's nest, that the Secretary of State had been guilty of a breach of parliamentary privilege. This futile episode merely caused irritation. Baldwin stuck to his guns in supporting the policy of an all-India Federation. At a vast meeting of the party's Central Council, attended by something like 1,500 delegates, he pleaded once more that India should not be pitch-forked into the party warfare of England. Britain had preached democracy to India for a century and now India wanted the promise to be honoured. He used a phrase which Mr Macmillan almost borrowed, quite unwittingly, a quarter of a century later: 'There is a wind of nationalism and freedom blowing round the world, and blowing as strongly in Asia as anywhere in the world. And are we less true Conservatives because we say: "the time has now come"? Are those who say "the time may come – some day", are they the truer Conservatives?'

Baldwin carried this policy easily. The worst of the danger within the Conservative Party was over. The India Bill was brought before Parliament in February 1935 and had passed through all its stages rather less than six months later. Though the Federation established by the bill never operated, a strong case may be made for the proposition that his firm stand upon India, which enabled the partial introduction of parliamentary government in that sub-continent and a voluntary though sanguinary transfer of power in 1947, constituted the most remarkable achievement in the last phase of Baldwin's political life. Long afterwards, and with many qualifications, Churchill confessed that he had been wrong about India.

If it be true that the most serious failing of the British Government in foreign policy during this period was not an inability to identify the enemy correctly, but a failure to rearm on a large enough scale in time (whether the failure was inevitable or not), special attention is owing to the years 1934 and 1935. The fact is that MacDonald, though never as decrepit as some accounts have alleged, was by then physically unequal to the never-ceasing work of a Prime Minister and mentally and ideologically ill-attuned to the new times.

Having devoted his life to the processes of conciliation and a striving for peace, he detested the very idea of heavy expenditure on armaments. There had been an increasing impression, of which MacDonald was himself conscious, that the Government lacked drive and direction. The Prime Minister's considerable powers of oratory were failing; he had been hampered for years by eye trouble; and, as Simon put it most perceptively, 'he seldom enjoys the refreshing stimulus, so necessary for anyone bearing the burdens of Premiership, of making a rousing and effective reply to the Government's critics in the House of Commons amid the plaudits of all ranks of his followers . . .' The Liberal members of the Government had no hesitations about the prospect of serving under Baldwin. Simon recorded on 14 February that Baldwin and Chamberlain had both given the most positive assurances that they meant the National Government to go on and had no hankering after a purely Conservative administration.[10]

It is a natural tendency of diarists and letter writers to exaggerate their own role. Even when a discount is made, however, there is little doubt that Chamberlain was justified in claiming that to an increasing degree he was carrying the National Government upon his back. The situation in which neither the Prime Minister nor the Lord President could handle detailed business day by day was impossible; no government on the British pattern could function efficiently in such circumstances. However, the position became clearer in the next month or two. MacDonald made up his mind to retire and Baldwin indicated to Chamberlain at the end of April that it would be much more difficult than he had imagined not to succeed MacDonald. 'I shall have to see the King and if he wants me to go on I shall have to do so for a year or two.' Chamberlain behaved very loyally to Baldwin, and the more so because he felt as much as any minister the effects of Baldwin's hesitations and indecision. He merely responded 'You know I shall fall in with whatever I am wanted to do'. Baldwin replied, 'Well, I should like to see you have a turn before you finish up.'

It is easy to sympathise with Baldwin's position; he had known the frustrations of serving under MacDonald, it is highly probable that he already had serious apprehensions about the Prince of Wales, he evidently hoped to inaugurate better relations with Germany. All the same, it was six years since he had been Prime Minister. The dangers abroad had increased out of recognition: Hitler had just announced conscription and the building of a military air force; Mussolini made it clearer every day that he intended to attack Abyssinia, and therefore to call into question the whole standing of the League, and its usefulness as a curb upon aggressors; and Baldwin, as matters proved, was no longer fit enough for the post of Prime Minister. His return to 10 Downing Street meant that Chamberlain did not succeed to the post until he was in his sixty-ninth year.

MacDonald resigned early in June. The India Bill being in its last stages, Baldwin had considered the inclusion of Churchill in the Cabinet, to which he felt no personal objection. He acknowledged that Churchill would be a disruptive force and there was certainly much feeling in the Conservative Party about Churchill's long campaign against the Government's Indian policy. On the other hand, his warnings about German air strength appeared to have been vindicated, and even to have been vindicated by Baldwin himself; and there was, moreover, the problem of Lloyd George, whose programme to revive the British economy and reduce unemployment had been exhaustively discussed with ministers in the spring and who had left an impression of failing vitality. Chamberlain continued to say that he would not serve in the Cabinet with Lloyd George; but it also appears that no other leading minister wanted him. Churchill and Lloyd George together, Baldwin said, would be an impossible combination. Eventually he decided to take in neither. All the evidence of the later 1930s suggests that Lloyd George was by then incapable of bringing much strength to the Government. Churchill stood in a very different category. On a long view, his exclusion may well be thought a disaster. It was, however, disaster which he had to a considerable degree brought upon himself. His record as a minister in the second Baldwin Government had been rather a mixed one, and he had a reputation far and wide for interfering unnecessarily with his colleagues; he was on intermittently intimate terms with Beaverbrook; and in a whole series of issues, before and after the reconstruction of 1935, he chose to make difficulties for the Government in a way which was not likely to facilitate his return. Churchill himself, evidently anxious to stand on better terms with Baldwin now that the Indian issue was disappearing, wrote to him in July:

'You have gathered to yourself a fund of personal goodwill and public confidence which is indispensable to our safety at the present time. But there lies before us a period of strain and peril which I do not think has been equalled – no, not even in the Great War, certainly not in the years preceding it. Naturally this will never fail to govern my action.'[11]

There is force in the comment made by the Foreign Secretary, Sir Samuel Hoare, towards the end of July, that there must be an election soon because Baldwin would never be master in his own house till then. This had been the trouble when he followed Bonar Law in 1923. 'You cannot succeed to a government.' Apart from this consideration, there was of course the looming Abyssinian crisis. By then it was plain that the French would not run, if they could possibly avoid it, any serious risk of estranging Italy. The most that France under Laval was likely to do was to apply somewhat tepidly a minimum of sanctions. The British were ill-placed to urge more strenuous opposition since they could offer France no additional security to make good the loss of Italian help.

At the end of July Baldwin told the senior ministers that he did not intend to make even a provisional decision about a general election until after his return from Aix. His colleagues generally favoured an early date. The Central Office's estimate at that stage gave the National Government a majority of 105, but 57 of these seats were described as doubtful. Both Baldwin and the Central Office had been working on the assumption that the election would turn on unemployment and especially on the depressed areas. They were therefore anxious to produce attractive programmes which would include projects to bring employment to those areas and Chamberlain observed that some plans to be announced in the autumn would help. However, he was quite convinced that they would never do for an election, though serviceable enough for a debate: 'What we want is some issue that will put them in the background and if possible substitute for the hope of fresh benefits a fear in the public mind – always the strongest motive to induce people to vote.'

He therefore urged that the obvious intention of the Labour Party to fasten on the Conservatives the label of warmonger should be turned to advantage. Clearly Britain must rearm, though Chamberlain had yet no conception of the scale on which it would be necessary; and if the Government tried to keep its plans secret until after the election it would either fail or, if it succeeded, lay itself open 'to the far more damaging accusation that we had deliberately deceived the people. In view of these considerations I have suggested that we should take the bold course of actually appealing to the country on a defence programme, thus turning the Labour Party's dishonest weapon into a boomerang.'

Baldwin remarked that this would be something to think over at Aix but that he would prefer not to express an opinion. With unwonted mildness, Chamberlain noted that it would have been very helpful if Baldwin could have expressed an opinion at the beginning of the recess, since it would have enabled the party to prepare accordingly. However, this is another of those instances in which his chairmanship of the Research Department enabled him to act somewhat independently. He instructed the director to consider a plan of campaign. Chamberlain acknowledged that there might be trouble with the National Labour members of the Government over a programme of rearmament. Whereas the Liberal Nationals (Sir John Simon and his followers) could contemplate without anxiety a future which might bring them into the Conservative Party, the National Labour people were socialists and must remain so. He realised that there was no future for them with the Conservative Party; 'and I can hardly blame them if they take any convenient opportunity of separating off.'[12]

There matters rested during the late summer, save that every new display of Mussolini's determination to attack Abyssinia gave point to Chamberlain's argument. Baldwin, very tired, asked Chamberlain to take over a speaking engagement towards the end of September. Although nothing had been decided about the election, it clearly had to come soon. The speech which Chamberlain delivered at Floors Castle marked the opening phase. It contained a plain admission that Britain had been grievously handicapped by the low level of her defence forces. Unilateral British disarmament had been 'a complete, a costly and a dangerous failure'. The time had come when the realities must be faced and Britain's forces brought up to the minimum required by self-respect. Pointedly, and with Churchill in the audience at the Party Conference, Baldwin spoke of the deficiencies in arms for which 'all of us are responsible since the war ... I am not satisfied with the position as it is today ...' By then the long-awaited invasion of Abyssinia had taken place, the Labour Party had shed its venerable but pacifist leader, George Lansbury, and under the impetus of Ernest Bevin had voted for sanctions. It appears that Baldwin did not wish to make defence the prime issue at the election, preferring to state as his main reason for going to the country the probability that a long and anxious period was impending in foreign affairs, which must be faced by a stable government. Chamberlain grasped eagerly at this notion and, among his other duties, had that of writing Baldwin's election address.

It is important to set out these issues in some detail because of the persistence of the myth that serious rearmament was not a major issue at the 1935 election. Whether or not Baldwin wished it to be so, he was left with no choice. True, he said in his election broadcast that no one proposed huge forces for Britain; but he also said that the Navy and Royal Air Force must be modernised and that he would not remain responsible for the Government if he were not given power to remedy the deficiencies. He put much the same point in the House of Commons, adding with a disarming candour: 'One of the weaknesses of a democracy, a system of which I am trying to make the best, is that until it is right up against it, it will never face the truth.'

Conservative speakers naturally attacked the obvious contradiction in the policy advocated by the Labour Party, which simultaneously condemned the Government for not using or threatening force against Italy and for saying that it intended to rearm. If this signified anything in practice, it merely meant that those who went to war in such circumstances must fight their battles with antique ships and wooden aircraft. The poster used by most Conservative candidates, including Churchill, read thus:

A STRONG BRITAIN MEANS A WORLD AT PEACE VOTE NATIONAL

In the Labour Party's broadcasts during the election, the principal speakers do not seem to have been under any delusions about the place of armaments in the campaign. Mr Attlee, the new leader of that party, stated that what the National Government really wanted 'is big armaments in order to play the old game of politics. This way leads to war, but it will mean big profits for the private manufacturers of arms.' Morrison took the same line in his public speeches and even accused the Chancellor of having no money for the unemployed, the depressed areas or the social services. 'He will spend on the means of death, but not on the means of life, and that is the sort of fellow he looks like.' This was too good to miss. Chamberlain replied that he did not wish to spend long in bandying such remarks with so magnificent a specimen of humanity as Morrison. 'I was not surprised at his description of my personal appearance. We ordinary people cannot expect to have such luck in that respect as, say, Clark Gable or Mr Herbert Morrison, but when he said that I had nothing for the unemployed and social services, I thought his memory must have played him false.'[13]

Baldwin made an address to the Peace Society, closely based on a draft provided by Dr Tom Jones. His defence of the Government's rearmament programme was altogether more apologetic than it need have been, even in front of an audience containing a large number of people singularly reluctant to see the world as it was and is. Nevertheless, Baldwin has been unduly blamed for the statement 'I give you my word there will be no great armaments', language which had a particular significance to anyone who knew, as all members of that audience would have done, the most celebrated passage in Lord Grey's *Twenty Five Years*. Baldwin was saying that Britain was not going to lead an armaments race; and indeed it already lay beyond her capacity to do so because she lacked the technical and manufacturing strength to produce large numbers of sophisticated weapons in a short time. This speech, couched in

language which matched or perhaps excelled the best level
which Baldwin had attained in his second spell as Prime Minister, drew from Neville Chamberlain a letter characteristic both
in its openness and in its willingness to admit Baldwin's special
talents:

'I will frankly confess that at times I have felt some transient
impatience when it has seemed difficult to bring your thoughts
down to the earthy decision I wanted. But when I read a speech
like that, I can only think of our good fortune in having a
leader who can raise us so far above ourselves, and can express
what we should like to believe we had thought ourselves, in
such moving words.'

The Labour Party's manifesto stated that Labour would
efficiently maintain such defence forces as were necessary and
consistent with membership of the League. A Labour Government would propose to other nations the abolition of all
national air forces; the creation of international air police
forces; large reductions in armies and navies; abolition of the
private manufacture of arms. What on earth was to be done if
this policy could not be carried out, and what Hitler was likely
to say to it, the party's manifesto did not reveal. It is right to
add that the Labour Party rejected the policy of one-sided
disarmament; and that if Labour leaders meant what they
said in supporting armed forces sufficient to enable Britain to
take its share in a system of collective security, they would in
the circumstances of the late 1930s have been compelled to
meet a bill of the most startling proportions. On this whole issue,
Baldwin did himself far more harm than was ever caused by the
attacks of his opponents.

During a later debate, Churchill reminded the House of
Commons that from the summer of 1935 Baldwin began to
make very serious statements about the need for rearmament
and that he had 'fought, and largely won, the General Election
upon that issue'. Mr Churchill also pointed, not unjustly, to
the difficulties of reconciling those statements with some of the
others which Baldwin had made during the election campaign
about no great armaments. However, when Baldwin himself
replied to the debate, he said that in 1933 and 1934 there had
probably been a stronger pacifist feeling running through

Britain than at any time since the war. 'Supposing I had gone to the country and said that Germany was rearming and that we must rearm, does anybody think that this pacific democracy would have rallied to that cry at that moment? I cannot think of anything that would have made the loss of the election from my point of view more certain.' This remark has been widely taken to refer to the General Election held in November 1935. It is clear from Hansard that it does not. Baldwin went on to point out that the country had learned by the events of the winter of 1934–5 what might be its dangers and at the election of 1935 the Government had obtained from the country a mandate 'for doing a thing that no one, twelve months before, would have believed possible.'[14] The majority, though reduced, was indeed still enormous. Against 154 Labour members and 20 Opposition Liberals were ranged 432 supporters of the National Government.

Chamberlain had proved himself a practical planner, with a streak of imagination; a devotee of limited intervention by the State in the interests of greater efficiency; and the chief provider of drive. He sometimes found the role a wearisome one, and (as he acknowledged in the winter after Munich) lacked during his own time as Prime Minister a colleague who would stand towards him as he had stood to Baldwin. On the morrow of the election, receiving alarming reports about the sums which would have to be spent on arms, Chamberlain asked himself why he did not retire at once, with the laurels of four years' successful finance, instead of remaining in office to be cursed and kicked by the ungrateful British public:

'I suppose the answer is that I know no one that I would trust to hold the balance between rigid orthodoxy and a fatal disregard of sound principles and the rights of posterity. And, perhaps, when I come to think of it, I don't really care much what they say of me now so long as I am satisfied myself I am doing what is right. For it isn't as if I had ambitions which might be ruined by present unpopularity. I believe S.B. will stay on for the duration and by the next election I shall be 70 and shan't care much, I daresay, for the strenuous life of leader even if someone else has not overtaken me before then.'[15]

The Ascendancy of Chamberlain

Taking skilful, audacious and (for himself) ultimately fatal advantage of the increased room for manoeuvre and bargaining power which the rise of Hitler conferred upon him, Mussolini had committed Italy to the invasion of Abyssinia. This was clear well before the election. It is probable that he had failed to realise how deeply opposed the British would be to any such adventure, not because of the local consequences in East Africa but because an attack on a small state by a great power would put to the test the League of Nations and indeed the whole settlement of 1919. Everybody knew that if the League could not prove itself effective against Mussolini, it would not arrest Hitler's progress. Baldwin had been impressed with one central fact; namely, that although the Admiralty was confident of winning a war against Italy in the Mediterranean, it might cost several capital ships, and none could be replaced inside four years. He understood the connection between Europe and the Mediterranean and the Far East, and between economic sanctions and military sanctions. In short, there were powerful reasons, strategic and diplomatic, for not antagonising Italy unduly. There was also a strong case for outright opposition to Italy, which might bring down the dictator, uphold the League, and deter Hitler. It is perhaps hardly surprising that the Cabinet ended by taking a course which neither protected Abyssinia and vindicated the League nor kept Mussolini on friendly terms.

The French Government continued to show no intention of pressing sanctions against Italy. The Permanent Under-Secretary of the Foreign Office, Sir Robert Vansittart, never ceased to urge the importance of compromising with Italy. It was for a mixture of these reasons that the pact was initialled between Hoare and Laval on 8 December 1935. This episode perhaps damaged Baldwin more than any other in his political life. Although Hoare had gone to Paris intending to see what terms he could get from Laval, none of his colleagues had understood that he would commit the Government; and he had been unable to extract any clear instructions from Baldwin. At all events, the Foreign Secretary had to be thrown over; Baldwin cut a sorry figure in the House of Commons and indeed might have been defeated had not Attlee described the issue as involving the Prime Minister's honour and thus brought Austen Chamberlain, the most influential back bencher, to Baldwin's defence; and the Government's standing suffered a most severe blow, not least in the eyes of its own supporters. The Prime Minister was perhaps especially harmed because of the concern which he had expressed for the sanctity of electoral pledges. It was as if he had fought the General Election of 1931 on a platform of defending the pound and then had devalued it immediately after winning. In private, Baldwin said he felt sure, and the intelligence services may well have provided some evidence in this sense, that Laval had been bought by Mussolini. However, he could hardly announce this in the House of Commons!

Eden was appointed Foreign Secretary at the age of thirty-eight. No more than Hoare did he feel able to run the risks of a policy which might conceivably have saved Abyssinia. And within three months Hitler, seizing upon the disunity of the former allies, already edging Italy over towards his side, with an unerring instinct for his opponents' weaknesses and hesitations, seized the demilitarised zone in the Rhineland, the last physical security enjoyed by France and her eastern allies, centre of many German war industries and springboard of any future invasion of France and Belgium. The strategic balance in Europe had changed and France, by her refusal or inability to act at the moment when German troops moved back into the Rhineland, had demonstrated her own defensive mentality and timidity.

Between January and July 1936 the Cabinet passed through a miserable time. The sudden realisation of British weakness in arms, admissions which Baldwin had made (though discovered after the war to be largely unnecessary) to the effect that he had quite underestimated the expansion of the German air-force, the inability of the armed services to agree on a strategic doctrine, all made irresistible the arguments that defence policy and spending must be to some degree coordinated by a minister, and that such a task was beyond the powers of any Prime Minister. There was a debate in mid-February, during which Sir Austen Chamberlain quoted freely and with effect from some of the Prime Minister's earlier speeches. Having done a good deal to save Baldwin in December, Chamberlain took advantage of this non-party debate to voice opinions which were now widely held: 'I thought that the time was overdue for trying to shake him out of his self-complacency. Of course it is true that no man can do all the work which in these days the Prime Minister is supposed to do, but what angers me is that the present Prime Minister does none of it . . .'[1]

This was a somewhat unkind exaggeration, but it had a certain point. Baldwin was now nearly seventy. For all his stolid appearance he was a man of acute sensibilities and much nervousness, who went through agonies of anticipation before each speech. Although he used to advise intending politicians to avoid logic and cultivate the hide of a rhinoceros, he probably found it easier to do the former than the latter. His doctor examined Baldwin at the beginning of February 1936 and judged him sound in health but very tired. The Prime Minister, saying that he wanted to see the new King well started and that he would like to reach some agreement with Germany, mentioned casually to Neville Chamberlain that he thought of retiring in 'about two years'. It is clear that he hardly under-stood the effects of such pronouncements upon his likely successor. Later in the summer, after the Rhineland crisis and the collapse of Abyssinia, Baldwin talked despondently to Chamberlain about himself, saying that he was 'very fagged' and woke every morning at 5.30. He found MacDonald nothing but an incubus. 'I have heard', Baldwin remarked mournfully, 'of carrying on with a sack of flour fastened to your back; Ramsay is an eiderdown around my head'. On another occasion he complained of the constant badgering in the House of Commons.

A month after Abyssinia had fallen and the Emperor had fled, Neville Chamberlain said at a dinner that to continue with the economic sanctions against Italy, a course advocated by the League of Nations Union, would be the very mid-summer of madness. Clearly sanctions had failed in their purposes; they could not restore Abyssinia, and there was no point therefore in attempting to pretend that the unpalatable had not happened. This was essentially the line of Chamberlain's reasoning and, as he recorded in private, he felt that he should speak thus because the Prime Minister was not likely to give any such lead. Eden was placed in an invidious position, which he accepted with much grace. Britain did duly propose the raising of sanctions. Lloyd George thereupon delivered one of the most tremendous onslaughts which any government between the wars had to endure. Referring to Eden's announcement, he averred he had never before heard a British minister come to the House of Commons and say that Britain and her Empire were beaten. Baldwin, so exhausted that he could neither understand clearly what Lloyd George was saying nor think of any answer, was visibly unhappy and shaken. As he recognised, he could not rival Lloyd George in that kind of oration. 'To L.G. and Winston', Baldwin said to his friend Tom Jones, 'it is all part of a game; as for me, I cannot make speeches which are sheer and mere dialectic . . . If I had made the sort of speech about L.G. that I could have made, it would be a cruel attack on an old man and it would have done no good.'[2]

Baldwin told Neville Chamberlain that if he did not feel better on his return from holiday, he might not be able to continue, in which case he hoped Chamberlain would not think that he was shirking. 'He evidently does not fully realise', Chamberlain noted, 'how completely he is leaving his work to be done by others now and how little help he gives us.' By a later stage of that month, July, Baldwin's condition was worse. He suffered from a couple of hours of intense depression each morning and felt nervous even in answering ordinary parliamentary questions. The doctors insisted upon three months' rest. The Prime Minister had suffered a physical and nervous collapse. It was even thought that his heart was affected; and in conditions of great secrecy an electrocardiogram was taken at Chequers. Baldwin and Mrs Baldwin sat in the library to receive the verdict. The specialist showed him the tracing and explained how the heartbeats are recorded. Baldwin asked, almost impatiently, 'Well, come on; what do you think of it?' and the doctor replied, 'If ever I write a book on the subject for the guidance of medical students, I would insert a record like this as a frontispiece to illustrate a normal electrocardiogram belonging to a healthy subject.' Thereupon Baldwin jumped at once to his feet, beat his chest with his hand and exclaimed, 'I knew my heart was all right. I would be quite well if things settled down at home and abroad.' He seized a pipe from the pocket of his dressing-gown and was quickly wreathed in clouds of white smoke.[3]

During this period Neville Chamberlain's position as heir-apparent first became obvious, since he had to deputise frequently for the Prime Minister. Moreover all informed observers knew that in many aspects of policy the Chancellor had been supplying the motive power. Hence Mr Churchill's reference to Chamberlain as 'the pack-horse in our great affairs'. When they next met, Chamberlain accepted the description as a compliment, which indeed it was intended to be. Churchill himself spoke to Chamberlain about it, saying, 'Don't be angry; I called you a pack-horse, but read the context. It comes out of *Henry VI*, when Clifford is dying.' A little later, Chamberlain said that while he was much obliged for the generous allusion, the quotation came from *Richard III*, not *Henry VI*. 'No' said Churchill, 'I think I am right; it comes from that speech when the King compares himself to a shepherd'. The thought suddenly occurring to him, he asked, 'Have you looked it up?' Of course Chamberlain had; and he noted in his wry way that it was thoroughly characteristic of Churchill first of all to have remembered the phrase, which was not a familiar quotation; then to have given it the wrong attribution; and then not to have troubled to check it even when his attention had been drawn to the mistake.

In a work dealing with the history of the Conservative faith, there is no need to dwell on the unhappy events of the abdication. Baldwin had long known how ill-suited was the Prince of Wales to succeed his father. It was not a question of personal animus; on the contrary, Baldwin knew the King well, liked him, and toured Canada with him in 1927. But he must also have known of King George V's apprehensions and only a week or two after the old King died Baldwin, who was evidently well informed about King Edward VIII's relations with Mrs Simpson, is recorded as saying to an intimate friend, 'You know what a scrimshanker I am; I had rather hoped to escape the responsibility of having to take charge of the Prince as King. But perhaps Providence has kept me here for that purpose . . . When I was a little boy in Worcestershire reading history books I never thought I should have to interfere between a king and his mistress.'

The King and Baldwin appear to have said nothing to each other on this subject until the third week in October, when the comments and pictures in the foreign press had become too lurid for the Prime Minister to ignore. Moreover, divorce proceedings between Mrs Simpson and her second husband were about to come to court at Ipswich. By general consent, Baldwin handled this most delicate situation with consummate sympathy and firmness. He used to remark that his worst enemy would not say he did not understand the British people. He also understood the significance of the issue for the British Empire and for the social and political cohesion of the United Kingdom itself. Nothing could have been more divisive than a prolonged struggle between partisans and opponents of the King. It was one of the sadder features of the situation that Churchill, who had a strong feeling of romantic attachment to the sovereign, and no excess of affection for Baldwin, was widely suspected of taking up an attitude of protection towards the King because he wished to upset the Government.

King Edward himself, Baldwin believed, behaved very well and had the wisdom to ignore his more foolish counsellors. At all events, the Prime Minister and his small circle of confidants in the Cabinet made no serious error. They addressed the King courteously, did not attempt to hustle him and were scrupulously careful and neutral in taking the opinion of the governments in the four white Dominions. All the evidence suggests that Baldwin and his colleagues were right to judge the King and his intended wife essentially unsuitable occupants of a post demanding the utmost dedication, dignity and self-sacrifice. The King evidently had little taste for many of his duties, for which it would be wrong to blame him too severely; and he simply felt that without Mrs Simpson's presence and comfort he could not manage. He resolved to go and appears to have been determined from the start that if he could not marry Mrs Simpson and remain on the throne, he would choose marriage. The speech in which Baldwin described the events leading to the abdication, a speech of about an hour, delivered to a House of Commons more packed than at any time since August 1914, proved to be one of his apparently artless masterpieces, couched in a simple but conversational English and proceeding with a strong spinal chord of narrative. It was made from slips of paper recording the main events and supplied by Sir Horace Wilson, who had been involved with every stage of the abdication. Some of them fell on the stairs at 10 Downing Street and were only discovered at the last minute, when Baldwin was trying to shuffle the documents into some sort of order like a pack of cards and said plaintively that he knew there were some missing.

It was well for the Commonwealth, in which the Monarchy played then, and indeed still plays, a role more considerable than most outside observers realise, and well for Britain, that this crisis should have been met by a minister of ripe experience who not only knew how to handle it but, as often matters more in politics, believed in his own capacity to handle it. It was also well that Baldwin came to the issue – he touched little other business between mid-October and mid-December – refreshed by a rest of three months. All the disasters of Hoare-Laval, the Rhineland, the lifting of sanctions, were forgotten. There was a chorus of praise and admiration for Baldwin's dexterity and firmness. '*On ne baldwine pas avec l'amour*', said the French.

Tired out and counting the hours to the day of release, Baldwin determined to resign at the Coronation of King George VI. That Chamberlain would succeed him was no longer in doubt.

They discussed the crucial offices at intervals during the next few weeks. When they talked about the new Chancellor of the Exchequer, Chamberlain said that although he had formerly thought of Hoare, he was now more disposed to take Simon. This course Baldwin approved, saying that Hoare's judgement was not infallible and that Simon would be more useful. And it would be 'most valuable' to have the Liberal leader quite satisfied. On this latter point Chamberlain entirely agreed; indeed, there is every evidence that he was as anxious as Baldwin to keep the National Labour and National Liberal people contented with their place in his Government. In these last months of his political life, Baldwin delivered a whole series of speeches warning against ill-considered constitutional change, the inappropriateness of fascism or communism for British conditions and the importance of a Conservative Party committed to constructive reform. Quoting Burke about the duty of a citizen to cultivate the mind and rear to maturity every generous and honest feeling, he spoke of the inseparable connection between ordered freedom within the law, the secret of British government and the British Empire, and a view of man's nature, a value placed upon the individual and derived from the Christian religion:

'Every compromise with the infinite value of the human soul leads straight back to savagery and the jungle. Expel this truth of our religion, and what follows? The insolence of dominion, and the cruelty of despotism. Denounce religion as the opium of the people, and you swiftly proceed to denounce political liberty and civil liberty as opium. Freedom of speech goes, tolerance follows, and justice is no more.

'The fruits of the free spirit of man do not grow in the garden of tyranny. It has been well said that slavery is a weed that grows in every soil. As long as we have the wisdom to keep the sovereign authority of this country as the sanctuary of liberty, the sacred temple consecrated to our common faith, men will turn their faces towards us and draw their breath more freely.'[4]

Baldwin took a peerage, reflecting that there was perhaps a certain retributive justice in the step, since he had sent so many others to the Lords hoping that he would never see them again.

At the party meeting which elected his successor, Churchill said simply that there were no rivals or competing claims; Chamberlain stood forth alone with the goodwill of all sections of the whole party and the credentials of memorable achievement. This speech is of special interest because of its tribute to the way in which Chamberlain had restored confidence swiftly and had rebuilt British credit at home and abroad; and unless British credit had stood at the highest level, British commercial integrity and economic strength had been revived, 'we should not have been able to provide the vast sums which have been required to meet the primary needs of national and Imperial defence.' This was exactly the ground upon which Chamberlain justified his policy at the time and later. Churchill acknowledged that when at length the previous Government had been convinced of the urgent need to rearm, no one had been more active in pressing forward that policy than Chamberlain 'and in providing the immense supplies of money which had been rendered available, largely through his own foresight and prudence.' Chamberlain himself had to begin his tenure as Prime Minister by a rare act of retreat. His proposal for a national defence contribution, payable upon the increased profits which the armaments firms would make, was designed partly to prevent the scandals of the First World War and partly to make rearmament more palatable to the Labour Party and the trade unions. There was a considerable uproar from the City and from Conservative back benchers. Eventually, and with the aid of one of Churchill's best chaffing speeches, the Prime Minister had to acknowledge that the money would be found in a different way. His remarks about the decision to withdraw tell a perceptive reader a good deal about his character:

'I do not think . . . that I have ever been inclined to show a pig-headed obstinacy. Provided I could get what seemed to me the important thing, I have never boggled over particular ways of achieving it nor allowed anything in the way of *amour propre* to prevent my taking what I should call a common-sense attitude.'

Whereas Baldwin had come to the post of Prime Minister chiefly as the result of chance and accident, Neville Chamberlain's advancement had been of a different kind. His very early elevation to the Treasury in 1923 was due, no doubt, to the absence of senior figures from that Government; but his claim to a high place rested essentially upon his work at the Ministry of Health between 1924 and 1929, his expertise in domestic questions, his chairmanship of the Research Department; and upon his record as Chancellor. In short, he became Prime Minister because of a proved pedigree of administrative competence, executive capacity, skill in exposition, and knowledge of the party.

Baldwin had been so exceptionally gifted in the smoothing down of asperities and so alert to the unspoken, sometimes even unconscious, assumptions of his opponents, that almost any successor was bound to suffer by the comparison. Chamberlain, however, stood out the more obviously because he was in his mental and physical habits very unlike Baldwin, and because he believed his predecessor's habits too dangerous to be continued. He knew that he had not Baldwin's skills, though he had other aptitudes. 'I can't do all the things that S.B. did', he wrote in one of his private letters, 'as well as the things he didn't do, and I consider that at present at any rate the latter are more important.' He thought that the country, and the Conservative Party, had been rudderless for too long, and that the times were too far gone to allow a continuation of Baldwin's methods. The consensus which he was seeking would be found through forensic ability, through the orderly and careful formation of policy, through determined public defence of it. This style of politics was related to Chamberlain's career and temperament. He did not suffer fools gladly enough, he was perhaps insufficiently evasive, he lacked the minor civilities which ease the transaction of business.

In effect Chamberlain was saying that the way to secure agreement was not that pursued by Baldwin. Without immediate threats and pressure, his might be the best; but those were not Britain's circumstances. To have a clearer policy, in foreign affairs and defence, was not therefore a matter of taste but a matter of necessity. From 1933 until 1937 endless discussions had proceeded. In the closing months of Chamberlain's time at the Treasury it had been only too evident that the Services could produce no agreed strategic doctrine or division of resources. Until binding decisions could be reached, which meant a serious risk (because the decisions might be wholly or partially wrong), there would only be further debate and diversion of resources, which in Chamberlain's view would be still more damaging. The discussions about the role of the British army are a case in point. Some, like Chamberlain himself, thought that on grounds of public opinion, of strategy, and of finance, it would be wrong to plan to put into Europe a great army. Others thought differently. The debate reverberated until Chamberlain insisted in 1937 that a conclusion must be found, and by then finance decided the issue. Even Eden, still Foreign Secretary, who for a number of reasons would have liked to plan a substantial expeditionary force, was driven to tell the Cabinet that he found the financial arguments against it irresistible. He declared that the situation was quite different from that of 1914. In other words, the policy of deliberate obscurity, which used to be dignified by the description 'keeping Hitler guessing', was one which Chamberlain thought pointless; as he remarked, most of the guessing was done by Britain.

Chamberlain's style of leadership and parliamentary manner discounted the possibility of open co-operation with the Opposition parties, and given the Spanish question, it is difficult to see how any such collaboration would have been possible in foreign policy so long as the strategy of non-intervention was followed. This was particularly so in the later phases of the war when the Prime Minister was repeatedly urged to intervene on the Republican side. It is probable that Chamberlain, though he recognised the risk of war and was indeed as much responsible as anyone for spending vast sums on arms, was more hopeful of averting it than, say, Eden. He was therefore less disposed than the latter to act upon the argument that the Opposition must be handled gently because one day war might be unavoidable. Chamberlain would not follow a policy acceptable to the Liberal and Labour Opposition, since that would in practice have meant a policy which could not produce a useful result; this was especially so in relation to Italy, and the military advice laid strong stress upon the importance of avoiding a hostile Italy lying athwart the main line of communication from home waters to the Far

East. Chamberlain reasoned also that wholehearted public support for British engagement in war would be more likely when every possible effort had been made to avert it. In his mind the moral argument was no mere piece of window-dressing; quite apart from all the practical consequences of engagement, and especially premature engagement, in a great war, he believed in every fibre that the statesman had an overriding duty to engage in war only when other courses had failed. He was never a pacifist; far from it, but in the broadcast which he made on the night of 27 September 1938, when war seemed to be imminent, he did say and mean 'I am a man of peace to the depths of my soul', having first dictated 'I am a pacifist to the depths of my soul.'

It is open to doubt whether a softer handling of the issues of foreign policy would have made very much difference to the eventual outcome, or would have enabled Chamberlain to carry opinion more unitedly. The official Opposition, and a good part of the intelligentsia, were deeply wedded to notions about international affairs which had no roots in history. Once the Germans, the Italians and the Japanese set about the up-setting of the international order, blame was certain to be heaped upon anyone who had to bear the responsibility for adjustment to the new conditions. It may well be that Chamberlain would have been wiser to say much less about the League and merely to leave events to make it and collective security what they were in reality, ambitious plans which in the circumstances of the later 1930s could not be effective against challenges so determined. It is probable, nevertheless, that even then he would have been as fiercely denounced as Baldwin at the time of the Hoare-Laval pact; and difficult to resist the impression that hostility focused to an abnormal degree upon Simon, Hoare and Chamberlain because all three were thought to have betrayed the League as an act of deliberate policy: Simon by his supposed failure to enforce collective security, and thereby to make the League an effective deter-rent to others, in the Far Eastern crisis; Hoare because of the agreement with Laval; Chamberlain because of the speech about the midsummer of madness and the Munich Agreement; while Halifax, whose policy was in all essentials indistinguishable from theirs, has to this day escaped a good deal of the odium.

There is no reason to conclude, as has sometimes been suggested, that the Chamberlain Government's policy was largely conditioned by calculations of domestic politics. It would be nearer the mark to say that Germany, Italy and Japan, and most of all Germany, consistently held the initiative in foreign affairs between 1935 and 1939. Much of British policy, especially given the advice which the Cabinet received about the country's military weakness, was determined by factors well beyond British control; and it is important not to overlook the quality of the opposition. Hitler in particular displayed boldness, astonishing power of will, a satanic facility in detecting the vulnerable points of his opponents, and a genius for using Anglo-Saxon attitudes and feelings of guilt to his own advantage. In justifying the union of Austria with Germany, and in demanding the absorption of the Sudetenland, Hitler was turning against the British principles which they had proclaimed at the end of the First World War.

It was not a question of an unconscious departure by Chamberlain from Baldwin's habits, or of a style unreflectively adopted. Baldwin's practice had been to bring policies to fruition in an atmosphere of general agreement, and he used to say repeatedly that democracies would learn only by bitter experience. He justified thus, to the end of his life, the decision not to undertake a major programme of rearmament, and put it to the country, until the end of 1935. On this thesis, only events would convince a sluggish-minded, insular people. The most that politicians could aspire to do was to change the atmosphere a little. Only when facts – in the case of this example the rearmament of Germany, the nature of Hitler's régime, the Italian attack upon Abyssinia – had sunk into the public consciousness could the politician step in and act. It followed that politicians must do nothing to hinder emerging agreement and the process by which serious events percolate into the general consciousness; they must therefore be conciliatory to their colleagues and even more so to the Opposition. Being a much better debater than Baldwin, and ready to make innumerable parliamentary speeches, Chamberlain inevitably attracted the hostility of the Opposition. It ought to be pointed out, as can be verified by anyone who cares to read Hansard and the newspapers for the later 1930s, that although Chamberlain is commonly described as being harsh, abrasive and aggressive, his opponents assailed him with a vehemence and bitterness quite unequalled on his part. Nevertheless, Chamberlain was deliberately abandoning centre-party politics and he had to reconcile his determination to give a clear lead, and to produce a coherent policy, with the need for unity in certain practical matters. For instance, he understood that the re-armament programme could not go forward without the active goodwill of the trade unions. Chamberlain accordingly watched, largely with the help of Sir Horace Wilson, who had many contacts in the trade union world, the industrial realities which lay behind the rearmament programme. Partly because some aspects of that programme brought employment to districts and industries where the depression had struck severely, there was little disposition to make undue difficulty so long as too many hurdles were not taken at once. Chamberlain saw a good deal of trade union leaders in private and came to feel a high confidence in Sir Walter Citrine, General Secretary of the TUC, in whom it was his habit to confide with startling candour.

We may question whether Baldwin, for all his emollience, personal charm and sympathy, would have fared much better. The issues which history picks out as the most significant and the issues which contemporaries selected are by no means the same. The Labour Opposition had fixed its gaze with especial intentness upon Spain. It is not unfair to say that the Spanish Civil War represented, and indeed to many of that persuasion still seems to represent, not so much an issue as an obsession, resting upon the assumption that the war was an open contest between fascism and the forces of the Left, which chanced to take place in Spain. The Civil War attracted more parliamentary questions, and more parliamentary debate, than, say, German designs on Czechoslovakia or Poland. The Spanish policy pursued by Chamberlain's Government was that for which Mr Eden was essentially responsible and for which he was heavily criticised by the Labour Opposition for most of his time as Foreign Secretary. Eden himself, being excellent in the House, generally gave as good as he got; and the kind of policy which he was recommended to pursue bore so little relationship to the possible benefits, Britain's other risks, or the Labour Party's long opposition to rearmament, that on one occasion he said that Palmerston paled into insignificance beside the peevish truculence of Mr Attlee.

There is a closer concordance than has generally been conceded between the Government's moves in foreign policy and the military advice which it was receiving. Chamberlain listened carefully to the Chiefs of Staff, to the Service Ministers and to the unique Hankey, Secretary of the Cabinet since 1916 and Secretary of the Committee of Imperial Defence for an even longer period. It was he who urged in July 1937 that Britain could not feel more safe at least until the summer of 1939. He argued for an approach to Mussolini, not because he lacked confidence in Britain's capacity to defeat Italy if the two powers were left alone in the ring, but because victory could only be secured by uncovering more vital interests elsewhere; a world war would almost certainly be precipitated 'and for that we are totally unprepared'.[5] This was at the time when Chamberlain began serious efforts to secure Italian friendship or neutrality. It is clear that Chamberlain's judgement in the period from 1937 to 1939 was influenced by the Far Eastern risks. The balancing act was particularly difficult at the end of 1937 and early in 1938, because the Japanese behaviour in attacking British and American ships on the Yangtse showed an open indifference to the opinions and reactions of those powers, and at the same time Britain was trying to begin talks with Italy. Chamberlain pressed for these conversations vigorously, noting that an early start would be as well, 'for the Japs are growing more and more insolent and brutal.' And again: 'We are a very rich and a very vulnerable Empire, and there are plenty of poor adventurers not very far away who look on us with hungry eyes.' He ruled that despite all the fresh threats in the Far East the fleet should not move to Singapore because its presence in the Mediterranean was the strongest card Britain had to play in the negotiations with Mussolini. It was partly because he was more sanguine about the outcome, but partly because he was determined to try to buy off a potential enemy, that Chamberlain was prepared to sacrifice Eden by his insistence upon opening conversations with Mussolini in February.

There is no denying that the loss of Eden was a most serious one on all grounds, and not least because he had a wide following, with an appeal far outside the bounds of the Conservative Party. Identified with the high ideals of the Covenant, he stood head and shoulders above the other young members of the Cabinet. It was not a question of personal hostility, certainly not on Chamberlain's side; on the contrary, he liked Eden, was always glad to see him and encouraged him to call frequently at 10 Downing Street. Chamberlain entertained fewer hopes than Eden of useful American intervention in international affairs; the overwhelming majority of the Cabinet agreed with the Chiefs of Staff; and in the eyes of the Prime Minister (and of many others, including the Secretary of the Cabinet) Eden would not begin serious talks with Germany or Italy. That the Foreign Secretary should wish to see some clear evidence of Italian fulfilment of promises, since Mussolini had broken plenty before, was entirely reasonable, and it is hardly possible to contest that such faith as the Prime Minister had in Mussolini's goodwill was ill placed. It is fair to Chamberlain to add that he was not trusting entirely in Mussolini's goodwill; he was also hoping that the facts of Italy's position would cause Mussolini to think long before aligning himself irrevocably with Hitler.

Though the Labour opposition was not powerful between 1935 and 1939, it was much more formidable than Lansbury's tiny band of the 1931 Parliament; whereas the opposition on the National Government's side, though significant after Eden's departure from office, was never as strong in numbers as the opposition which Baldwin had faced on the issue of India. Chamberlain attached the highest importance to hearty, as distinct from merely passive, support in Parliament. He recorded after one debate in April 1938:

'It was so long since our people had heard a real fighting speech that they went delirious with joy and I don't remember ever hearing the cheering so prolonged as it was when I sat down. The Chief Whip says he has never known such enthusiasm over the lead the party is getting and of course that is not surprising when you remember that for 14 years they have had only S.B. or Ramsay.'

Chamberlain realised that the policy of taking firm decisions about foreign affairs, and of making deliberate efforts to purchase peace with Italy and Japan and stay out of the Spanish Civil War, had many domestic implications. In the spring of 1938, at the time of the Anglo–Italian agreement, he was told by the party chairman that he could not remember the Conservatives so united, 'but on the other hand he thought my outspokenness and precision had probably frightened the rather weak-kneed Liberals who felt safe with S.B. I expect that is true . . . but it was inevitable. I can't change my nature and I must hope to make up for Liberal defections by greater enthusiasm in our own Party.'6

Chamberlain did not feel his parliamentary or public position shaken by the German entry into Austria. Indeed, his statement about British foreign policy, identical for all practical purposes with those which Eden had put forward repeatedly in 1936 and 1937, but leaving open the option of fighting if Germany should move into eastern Europe, was well received. The Prime Minister paid no attention to the occasional rumours of dissent in the Cabinet, remarking that such differences as there were arose mainly from the fact that some of his colleagues always asked initially about any proposal, not 'Is this right?' but 'How will it affect the House of Commons or my constituents?'; whereas, as Chamberlain expressed it characteristically

'My method is to try and make up my own mind first as to the proper course and then try and put others through the same course of reasoning as I have followed myself. As for the House of Commons, there can be no question that I have got the confidence of our people as S.B. never had it. They show it in lots of ways; by the tremendous reception they give me whenever I speak, by letters and by stopping me in the lobbies to tell me of their wholehearted support. . . . I tell myself not to lose my head over this week's success, for there are days of ups and downs and the downs are bound to come and perhaps very soon.'7

The decision not to offer a direct guarantee to Czechoslovakia, or to France in connection with her obligations to

Czechoslovakia, was not reached lightly. The policy of the Grand Alliance, as Mr Churchill used to term it, was carefully examined and at first blush attractive to the Prime Minister. Eventually he decided not to follow it. The Chiefs of Staff had advised that no pressure that Britain and her potential allies could bring to bear would prevent Germany from overrunning Czechoslovakia; and they feared that if such a struggle began it was more than probable that Italy and Japan would seize the opportunity to further their own ends. A guarantee to Czechoslovakia, in view of this military advice, would be not a matter of local defence but an occasion for going to war with Germany. Though Chamberlain loathed the very idea of a great war, which was generally anticipated to produce horrors still more dreadful than those of the First, he did not rule it out on any grounds of principle. Rather, he said that he would not contemplate such a guarantee 'unless we had a reasonable prospect of being able to beat her [Germany] to her knees in a reasonable time, and of that I see no sign.'

When the British and French ministers discussed the whole issue at the end of April, Chamberlain put the point in similar terms, adding that he thought a time would come 'when a gamble on the issue of peace and war might be contemplated with less anxiety than at present.' In other words, the buying of time remained a strong element in British foreign policy, as it had been for several years. This was the line which Eden had recommended to the Cabinet early in 1936; to reach agreements with Germany where they could honourably be reached, to be under no illusions that Germany would keep them when they ceased to suit her, and to accelerate British rearmament, the spending upon which was moving swiftly forward in 1938 and 1939 and which far exceeded any expenditure upon arms ever undertaken by Britain in peace time. This is not to say that the sole purpose of the policy pursued in 1938 was simply to obtain a breathing space. Chamberlain had some sympathy for German grievances, and was acutely sensible of Hitler's capacity to exploit them; he felt much doubt about the outcome of a war; he could hardly bear to think of the wanton destruction; but there is not a sign that he felt any fondness for dictatorships or sneaking sympathy for fascism. On the contrary, he had a rather marked racial dislike for

Germans, whose food he thought awful, whose womenfolk
hideous, whose statesmen malevolent or thick-witted. Chamberlain was perfectly ready to put the worst complexion upon
Germany's actions. During the first Czechoslovak crisis of
1938, over the weekend of 19–22 May, allegations of troop
movements by Germany were freely made and as freely re-
butted. Chamberlain had no doubt, though we now know that
he was almost certainly wrong, that the denials were lies.
'The fact is', he wrote to his sister, 'that the Germans,
who are bullies by nature, are too conscious of their
strength and our weakness, and until we are as strong as
they are, we shall always be trapped in this state of chronic
anxiety.'[8]

The policy of trying to maintain the peace by concession, to
Germany and to Japan, and later to Italy, was not personal to
Chamberlain or suddenly inaugurated when he became Prime
Minister in the spring of 1937. It was not a policy pursued in
defiance of the considered advice of a united Foreign Office
and body of ambassadors. On the contrary, appeasement in
the broad sense was supported, no doubt for an assortment of
reasons, by the British ambassadors in every major capital; the
decision not to go to war over Czechoslovakia in 1938 was
warmly approved by the Permanent Under-Secretary at the
Foreign Office, by the Foreign Secretary, and by each of the
Chiefs of Staff, as well as by the Secretary of the Committee
of Imperial Defence. All this is shown up fully in the official
papers, as is the detailed advice given to ministers about the
terrible consequences which would follow the outbreak of a
war characterised by indiscriminate bombing. We now know
what they could not know, namely that the predictions were
exaggerated. Ministers were being invited to plan for the kind
of effect we should expect from limited nuclear warfare. That
they should shrink from such a prospect on moral grounds, and
desire to postpone it until they were better able to defend the
country, if they could not avert the crisis altogether, was
entirely natural. Chamberlain realised full well, as he remarked to his sister on 11 September 1938, that if eventually
aggression took place there would be many, including
Churchill, who would lay the responsibility on Britain and
assert that if only the British Government had had the courage

to warn Hitler at this early stage against the use of force, on pain of war, he would have been stopped:

'By that time it will be impossible to prove the contrary, but I am satisfied that we should be wrong to allow the most vital decision that any country could take, the decision as to peace or war, to pass out of our own hands into those of the ruler of another country and a lunatic at that.'

In other words, Chamberlain had concluded that the issue and the occasion were not great enough for a European, or world-wide, war. But that did not mean that Germany could behave as she pleased indefinitely. On the afternoon of 26 September, after it was agreed by all parties that the Sudetenland should be ceded, Chamberlain telegraphed to Germany: 'French have definitely stated their intention of supporting Czechoslovakia by offensive measures if latter is attacked. This would bring us in. And it should be made plain to Chancellor [i.e. Hitler] that this is inevitable alternative to peaceful solution.'

The unfortunate Sir Horace Wilson had the task of conveying this news to Hitler, who certainly understood what it meant. He raged, implied that he was indifferent to a holocaust, said that he had spent $4\frac{1}{2}$ billion marks on fortifications in the west. All the same, he did change front somewhat during 27 September, and although the Munich terms proved in practice to be little different from those of Godesberg, the probability is that nothing short of willingness to go to war on the side of Britain and France would have altered the outcome. The only minister who resigned, Mr Duff Cooper, was also the only figure of any importance who faced the real question and said outright that he would sooner have fought.

Between Munich and the German entry into Prague, Chamberlain's mood fluctuated a good deal. As he once expressed it to the Foreign Secretary, 'Edward, we must hope for the best while preparing for the worst.' Further enormous sums were released for rearmament. The British were intercepting and deciphering some of the German telegrams, in which the Prime Minister found unpleasing references to himself. Patient diplomacy was followed, nevertheless; Chamberlain tried to demonstrate his willingness to make an agreement on reasonable terms, but indicated plainly enough that there would be no more concessions without a substantial German contribution. He told Mussolini that the armaments of Germany went beyond any purely defensive purpose and that the attitude sometimes expressed in the German press, of contempt for the fighting qualities of the democracies and disbelief that they would face the test of war, was wholly misplaced.

The line which Chamberlain was taking was of its nature perilous. By the summer of 1939 British production of tanks and aircraft equalled that of Germany; but on many fronts there was much leeway to make up and whereas Britain was preparing for a long war in depth, relying on the moat defensive in the last resort, upon financial power and upon an optimistic view of the strangulative effects of blockade, Germany was preparing for a quick war in width. Moreover, Germany was essentially a central European power, and Britain a world-wide power, with far greater dangers spread over a wider area and requiring a variety of forces. Chamberlain did not wish to lay too much emphasis in public upon the progress of British arms, since the probable effect would be to give extra impetus to Germany's propaganda about encirclement and perhaps to a desire to strike before the democracies were stronger; in private, however, he expressed the belief that the period of acute danger – the risk of being knocked out at the beginning of the struggle – was passing. He seized with eagerness upon every sign that Germany might after all be satisfied with the large gains which she had already made.

Towards the end of January the British Government had undertaken in private that Holland should be guaranteed. On 6 February it was announced that Britain and France would support each other in all eventualities. Later in that month it was at last agreed – though no one knew how the later stages were to be financed – that a large army should be equipped for service on the continent of Europe. The guarantees given to Poland at the end of March, and shortly afterwards to Roumania, Greece and Turkey, did not constitute a promise of local defence for those countries, any more than a guarantee to Czechoslovakia would have done. Rather they were meant as an intimation to Germany and Italy that another aggression would mean a general war. The change of policy was nimbly managed and first announced to the world on 17 March in a speech at Birmingham, just after the triumphal entry of the German dictator into Prague.

Chamberlain considered very carefully whether to invite his most experienced and eloquent critic into the Cabinet. Churchill himself had asked the Chief Whip to dine and told him explicitly that he wished to be made a minister. Acknowledging that Churchill's authority and debating power would strengthen materially the Government front bench, Chamberlain asked himself whether that strengthening would be purchased at too high a price. That Churchill would have to come in at once if war occurred was not in dispute. Chamberlain had no doubt that his inclusion would be taken by the dictators as a sign that Britain intended war at an early date. If there was any chance of avoiding it, and clearly he did not feel convinced that it was impossible, then he did not wish to take the risk. Moreover, Chamberlain did not judge his position in the country or in Parliament to be so weak that he must take in Churchill or anyone else. On the contrary, the polls of public opinion remained remarkably consistent and the amount of public support received by Chamberlain as Prime Minister, from such indices as are available to us, remained much the same in the midsummer of 1939 as it had been in the month of Munich. He continued to be welcomed everywhere, even in political strongholds of Liberal and Labour parties, with the utmost enthusiasm.

During that summer, while the war of nerves was screwed up in Europe, Japan took advantage of British preoccupations. So serious did the situation become that ministers considered the despatch of a large fleet to Singapore. In private, Chamberlain lamented the attitude of the United States, which remained passive, and correctly predicted that no firm support would be forthcoming from that quarter. He continued to balance the Far Eastern risks against the European, and to conclude, correctly, that since the heart of the British Empire might be pierced by Germany, but not by Japan, it was right to endure almost any provocation in the Far East. 'It is maddening to have to hold our hands in face of such humiliations, but we cannot ignore the terrible risks of putting such temptations in Hitler's way.'

In those same months Chamberlain determined that no doubt must be left in Germany's mind about the consequences if she resorted to war. However, it is a powerful criticism of the events of 1938 that after a capitulation of that kind it was hard to make Hitler believe in British and French resolution. It would have been harder still had the British given a guarantee in 1938 as a piece of bluff. By a variety of methods the Prime Minister, the Foreign Secretary and other members of the Government tried to indicate that while they remained anxious for a settlement with Germany on reasonable terms, they were not prepared to see Poland overrun. Neither Chamberlain nor Halifax had ever been among those who said that a guarantee must be given in Eastern Europe only with Russia's support; those who followed that line should logically have been opposed to a declaration of war in September and some, notably Lloyd George, soon approached that position. When the news came of the impending signature of a treaty between Germany and Russia, Chamberlain's mind was dwelling on the events of July 1914 and upon the charge that if only Sir Edward Grey had been able to make the British position clear, the First World War might never have started:

'Whether or not there is any force in that allegation', Chamberlain immediately wrote to Hitler, 'His Majesty's government are resolved that on this occasion there shall be no such tragic misunderstanding. If the case should arise, they are resolved and prepared to employ without delay all the forces at their command, and it is impossible to foresee the end of hostilities once they are engaged. It would be a dangerous illusion', he added, evidently anticipating a swift German victory in Poland, 'to think that, if war once starts, it will come to an early end even if a success on one of the several fronts on which it will be engaged should have been secured.'[9]

At the outset of the war, Chamberlain invited Liberal and Labour members to join the Government, which they refused to do. He seems to have concluded that until the circumstances of the war changed there would be no hope of bringing the

Opposition parties in, though it is clear from his reaction in May 1940 that the full importance of their active goodwill to the war effort was prominent in Chamberlain's mind. There was scant evidence from the record of the late 1930s that many members of the Labour front bench would make especially distinguished ministers, a point which was forcefully put by Herbert Morrison to an official of the Foreign Office at the end of November 1939. He argued that an Opposition was necessary to the English Constitution and should not be dispensed with unless those who composed it could bring exceptional and valuable gifts to a coalition. This was not the case with the Labour Party and he doubted whether it had half a dozen members who could add anything in strength or decision to the Chamberlain Government. Moreover, most of the Labour front bench were – at least in Mr Morrison's view – frightened of power and few were capable of drive unless they had a strong committee behind them. He took the line that if the war continued as it had begun, Chamberlain would probably see it through as Prime Minister and he doubted if there was a better man.

This latter judgement may seem surprising, but will be the less surprising to those familiar with the newspapers of the period. They contain numerous tributes, some of them rather grudgingly given by political opponents, to the effectiveness of Chamberlain's speeches and to the freedom of gesture, voice and mannerism which he increasingly allowed himself, to the excellent reactions abroad and to the contrast between his own firm but unswaggering declarations of British purpose and the ravings of Hitler and Goebbels. The same impression of vigour and decision is conveyed by film and sound records, as well as by accounts of eye-witnesses.

During the war twilight, as he called it, Chamberlain was anxious to build up the strength of the allies as far as possible and to convince the Germans that they could not win. He continued to hope against hope that the result might be achieved without bloodshed on the grand scale. This course posed obvious difficulties, not least those of sustaining morale at home, unity with the Dominions, good relations with the United States and the neutrals. Moreover, it might at any moment be upset by a major offensive in the West. The

Government announced very early that it was planning for a war of at least three years. It was decided that Britain should build up an army of no less than fifty-five divisions and should aim at a production of over 5,000 aircraft per month. After the Cabinet discussion on this question, Chamberlain received the following note from Churchill:

'My dear Neville,
　'I hope you will not think it inappropriate from one serving under you, if I say that in twenty years of Cabinets I have never heard a more commanding summing-up upon a great question.'

Indeed, on most broad aspects of strategy Chamberlain and Churchill agreed. For instance, they were at one in the view that it would not be to the advantage of the allies to initiate the bombing of Germany. Even on the question of Scandinavia, the disagreements were less clear cut, and Churchill's own line less consistent, than the casual reader of *The Gathering Storm* might apprehend. Chamberlain took much trouble to manage Churchill tactfully and to appeal to his generous instincts. He also understood perfectly well that Churchill had no intention of leaving office. As for relations with the Opposition parties, Attlee and Sinclair were provided in secret with a great deal of confidential information. In theory a party truce prevailed; in practice, it frequently did not. Not unnaturally, there were many members of the Labour Party and Liberal Party who could not resist the temptation to make capital out of the difficulties inseparable from wartime. Moreover, it was – to put it no higher – very convenient, for people who had only a few months before opposed the even sharing of the military burden of conscription, to appear as the apostles of zeal and efficiency in the prosecution of war. Chamberlain, less resilient than he had been and oppressed with the uselessness and misery of war, expressed himself tartly in private about the behaviour of some of the Labour members. After the enforced resignation of Hore-Belisha in January 1940, Attlee made a careful speech and, according to a Labour member who told Chamberlain's parliamentary private secretary, many of the party were angry with him for missing such a unique opportunity of embarrassing the Prime Minister. 'A fine patriotic spirit in wartime!' Chamberlain remarked. During his own speech he had been interrupted constantly with shouts and derisive laughter and more than once the hubbub became so great that he had to pause in order to make himself heard.

'I don't show any signs of disturbance, so people naturally think that I am not disturbed; but it makes me sick to see such personal prejudice and such partisanship when I am doing my best to avoid any party provocation in the national interest. I need hardly say that Ll.G. was conspicuous in encouraging and approving the behaviour of the opposition riff-raff.'[10]

It is too simple to represent Chamberlain as being solely responsible for his own political downfall. Having alienated a substantial section of his own party, the argument runs, and the whole of the official Opposition, he was bound to fall once the policy with which he had too openly identified himself failed in its avowed object of averting war. In reality, Chamberlain had abandoned appeasement with decisiveness and adroit timing after Prague, though he never abandoned a desire to go to great lengths to prevent a war. His two most weighty critics on the Conservative side, Churchill and Eden, had at once been taken into important posts at its outbreak. That the Liberal and Labour parties would refuse to enter a coalition was predictable enough. It is possible, but not certain, that they would have been willing to enter a coalition under someone else. The extraordinary circumstances of the first eight or nine months of the war, with all the inconveniences to which Britain was not accustomed, including the blackout, the progressive introduction of rationing, the closing down of places of entertainment, compulsory evacuation from the cities, all leading to every kind of grievance and all recklessly exploited by the press, unredeemed by many triumphs of arms; the unexpected stalemate on the western front; the failure of Germany to launch the confidently-expected and devastating attack from the air; on the personal level, the hostility which seems to have concentrated even more upon Simon and Hoare than upon Chamberlain; a general conviction, which probably no government could have avoided, that more decisive methods would bring success against Germany; a sense of shock when the Royal Navy, hitherto thought to be practically invincible, proved to be rather less than that in conditions of modern warfare; the gap between performance in Norway and the expectations fostered by the press; all these were factors in the demise of the Chamberlain Government after the debate of 7 and 8 May, 1940.

Mr Morrison had picked out Chamberlain, Simon and Hoare for special criticism in their conduct of foreign policy between 1931 and 1939 and as lacking in war the qualities they had always lacked – courage, initiative, imagination, liveliness, psychological understanding and self-respect. 'I regard them as being perhaps more than any other three men responsible for the fact that we are involved in a war which the wise collective organisation of peace could have prevented.' The Opposition felt that the House must divide at the end of the debate and he asked members in all parts of the House to realise the full significance of the vote, which would indicate whether or not they were satisfied with the conduct of affairs. As soon as Morrison sat down, Chamberlain (whose speech on the first day had been unconvincing) intervened to say that this challenge to the Government in general and the attack upon the Prime Minister in particular made the occasion graver still. As head of the Government he accepted the main responsibility for its actions, and his colleagues would not be slow to accept their share of responsibility:

'It is grave, not because of any personal consideration – because none of us would desire to hold on to office for a moment longer than we retained the confidence of this House – but because . . . this is a time of national danger, and we are facing a relentless enemy who must be fought by the united action of this country. It may well be that it is a duty to criticise the Government. I do not seek to evade criticism, but I say this to my friends in the House – and I have friends in the House. No government can prosecute a war efficiently unless it has public and parliamentary support. I accept the challenge. I welcome it indeed. At least we shall see who is with us and who is against us, and I call on my friends to support us in the lobby tonight.'

No doubt the language, used without preparation or reflection, was unwisely chosen; but in referring to his 'friends' Chamberlain did not go beyond the normal parliamentary parlance and it is clear from the context of his remark that whatever else the Prime Minister meant, he was not appealing to his personal and political friends to keep him in office. Lloyd George, at the climax of their mutual dislike, put this interpretation upon Chamberlain's words; but he had not been present in the House when they were uttered. In accepting the challenge Chamberlain was preferring an open vote to the kind of intrigue through which Lloyd George himself ousted Asquith from the Premiership in 1916.

It was an irony that Chamberlain's Government should fall after a debate on the conduct of the campaign in Norway, many of the failings in which had been Churchill's direct responsibility. Without Chamberlain's loyal support, Churchill could not have formed or sustained a government. He acknowledged the fact in generous terms on the evening of his appointment, 10 May 1940:

'My first act on coming back from the Palace is to write and tell you how grateful I am to you for promising to stand by me and to aid the country at this extremely grievous and formidable moment . . . The example which you have set of self-forgetting dignity and public spirit will govern the action of many, and be an inspiration to all.

'In these eight months we have worked together, I am proud to have won your friendship and your confidence in an increasing measure. To a very large extent I am in your hands – and I feel no fear of that.'

Chamberlain retained the leadership of the Conservative Party, helped Churchill with much domestic business and soon established good relations with his new colleagues, Attlee, Morrison, Sinclair and others with whom he had so recently been embattled. The Prime Minister, having warned presciently against Germany, had every right to discourage heresy-hunting, and Labour members of the Cabinet knew well where the parliamentary battalions were ranged. As Mr R. A. Butler expressed it in his inimitable way, 'If intrigue or attacks on the Government grow to any great extent, all we have to do is pull the string of the toy dog of the 1922 Committee and make it bark. After a few staccato utterances it becomes clear that the Government depends upon the Tory squires for its majority.'[11]

Chamberlain was by this time mortally ill, though he did not yet realise it. Churchill behaved towards him with the utmost consideration, sending papers and messages by despatch rider almost every day. After watching the progress of a great air battle at Fighter Command Headquarters in mid-August, Churchill returned to 10 Downing Street and immediately instructed his private secretary to telephone the good news to Chamberlain: 'Your attitude to me', Chamberlain wrote to the Prime Minister at that time, 'is as loyal as mine to you, and I can't say more.' When Chamberlain insisted upon returning to work, Churchill told him, much as Baldwin had once done, that they were complementary; 'he was up and down, I was more steady. Therefore it was helpful to feel that his decisions were approved by my judgement.' Soon it became plain that Chamberlain could not continue amidst the air raids in London. At the Prime Minister's instance, the King offered a knighthood of the Garter, which he declined gratefully, saying that he wished to die plain 'Mr Chamberlain', as his father had done.

Churchill, who had come to admire many of Chamberlain's gifts, delivered a valediction after which one well-qualified observer said that while there might be room for several opinions of Mr Churchill as a politician there could be only one opinion of him as a poet:

'It is not given to human beings . . . to foresee or to predict to any large extent the unfolding course of events. In one phase men seem to have been right, in another they seem to have been wrong. Then again, a few years later, when the perspective of time has lengthened, all stands in a different setting . . .

'History with its flickering lamp stumbles along the trail of the past, trying to reconstruct its scenes, to revive its echoes and kindle with pale gleams the passion of former days.'

By this very process of lengthening perspective and fresh

balancing of the evidence, Baldwin, Chamberlain and the Conservative Party of the inter-war years may be seen to deserve more kindly judgement than has usually been accorded to them. Even now, it is probably true that *The Gathering Storm* has coloured the perception of more people about the 1930s than any other work; and in a sense justly so, because there is a stamp, a sweep and a vigour about Mr Churchill's judgements which others cannot match, and under his guidance the reader feels himself swept inexorably along towards a tragedy which wiser men with keener foresight would have avoided. Indeed, Mr Churchill himself used to say with a mischievous twinkle that he thought it would be found best to leave these contentious matters to the judgement of history, 'especially as I propose to write that history myself.' It need hardly be added that the concentration of responsibility upon Baldwin and Chamberlain, or Simon and Hoare, or MacDonald and the bankers, though convenient and consoling, embodies a fundamental historical fallacy. There is a constitutional and a real, but limited, sense in which a modern Prime Minister is 'responsible' for the successes or failures of British policies. Very often the outcome is determined by factors which he may be able to influence but is unable to control. No British government of the later 1930s, for instance, was in a position to determine the policy of Germany and Italy. Simply to record, as does the index to *The Gathering Storm*, 'Baldwin, S. . . . confesses to putting Party before country' obfuscates and burkes the issue; the fact is that in immensely complicated matters of policy, the responsibility of a Prime Minister is limited because shared with leading colleagues, with civil servants, with the thousands or hundreds of thousands of people involved in executing the policy and, in another sense, with all those who help to create the mood of the times. Even Sir Winston, musing upon Baldwin's record, felt moved to say, 'You must remember that the climate of opinion on people is overwhelming'. It is not sufficient simply to state that the government of the day is responsible for the nation's defences; the government of the day has to work a parliamentary system, it has to think of the next election, and it must therefore pay attention to the susceptibilities of the parliamentary Opposition, to the undertow of opinion in the country at large.

These are the limiting factors; and the man who cares to reflect upon the differences in public opinion between, say, 1908 and 1934 will learn a good deal. In the former instance, there was a strong body of opinion which determined that the Royal Navy must remain superior to its enemies. One of the more powerful governments of the twentieth century, including Mr Churchill, with a comfortable majority, felt obliged to change its policy and to lay down additional battleships under stress of the cry, 'we want eight and we won't wait'. When we cast a glance forward to the middle 1930s, we find a very different situation. Successive British governments of Conservative and Labour complexion alike had thought fit to reduce the Royal Air Force, the largest and most efficient in the world at the close of the First World War, to such a level that it ranked sixth by 1934 and was equipped solely with obsolescent wooden biplanes. There was a widespread and exaggerated fear of the power of the new arm. Yet such was the change in psychology, so marked the shock caused to this insular people by prolonged exposure to a continental warfare from which Britain had previously been detached, so swift the loss of nerve, that the rising threat in the air produced no pressure of opinion comparable with that which the Liberal Government felt before the First World War.

Baldwin and Chamberlain shared a mistrust of sectional control, a belief in historic institutions adapted to changing needs, and in the importance of service, at national and local levels. Both believed in the practices of parliamentary government, but neither wished to extend the economic or political power of the state unduly, on grounds of practicality – because the affairs of the State in such circumstances would become impossible to manage with economy and efficiency – and because the freedom of individuals would be too much compromised. Their essential legacies to the Conservative Party were, in Baldwin's case, a marked diminution of party hatreds and strife between the classes; in Chamberlain's, a record of sympathetic and practical social reform, bringing local authorities, the voluntary agencies and the central government into partnership, but avoiding the crippling burden of providing for all benefits needed only by some. Both, and especially Baldwin, made notable contributions to the development of the Commonwealth; both, contrary to fashionable opinion, understood that diplomacy without force is like an orchestra without instruments; and their governments set in train, belatedly, the processes which enabled Britain to survive by far the most determined assault made in modern times upon her interests. These were no mean achievements, as anyone who reviews the history of the 1960s and 1970s may see for himself. No human habit is more natural, or in the historian more reprehensible, than the exercise of hindsight; and to acknowledge at once that Churchill was a greater man than Chamberlain or Baldwin, fortunate because his qualities coincided with the demands of the hour, does not in the least oblige us to disparage his predecessors.

BIBLIOGRAPHICAL NOTE

These chapters draw heavily upon material held in the Public Record Office and in many collections of private papers, especially those of Sir Austen Chamberlain and Neville Chamberlain. I am indebted to the Librarian of Birmingham University, and to Mrs Stephen Lloyd, for permission to quote extracts from these papers. Dr John Ramsden, Mr John Barnes and Mr Alan Beattie have generously allowed me to use material from their unpublished writings and have provided many helpful references. I should like to record my gratitude to Lord Butler and to the Vice-Chancellor of my own university, Lord Boyle, for patient guidance and correction.

The inter-war period has already given rise to an enormous literature. The best book about Baldwin is by R. K. Middlemas and A. J. L. Barnes, *Baldwin, A Biography* (1969). The first authorised biography, *Stanley Baldwin* (1952), by G. M. Young, was an unsatisfactory work, not worthy of its author's talents; for a fairer view see A. W. Baldwin, *My Father: The True Story* (1955). D. C. Somervell, *Stanley Baldwin* (1953); D. H. Barber, *Stanley Baldwin* (privately printed, 1959); H. Montgomery Hyde, *Baldwin, The Unexpected Prime Minister* (1973); and earlier works by Wickham Steed, Arthur Bryant and A. Gowans Whyte all contain, in varying degrees, material of interest. Baldwin's volumes of speeches [*On England* (1926); *Our Inheritance* (1928); *This Torch of Freedom* (1935); *Service of Our Lives* (1937); *An Interpreter of England* (1939)] are indispensable for the understanding of his assumptions and interests, and are full of reminiscences of his early life.

There are important articles on Baldwin by R. Blake in J. Raymond (ed.), *The Baldwin Age* (1960); A. J. L. Barnes in *Crossbow* (May, 1973); R. K. Middlemas in H. van Thal (ed.), *The Prime Ministers*, vol. 2 (1975); C. L. Mowat in *The Journal of Modern History*, vol. XXVII, 1955; Rt Hon. Lord

Butler in Sir J. W. Wheeler-Bennett and the Earl of Longford (eds.), *The History-Makers* (1973). Some references to other, more detailed, articles are given in the notes.

The most perceptive biography of Neville Chamberlain remains that published by Sir Keith Feiling, *The Life of Neville Chamberlain* (1946). The study by the Rt Hon. Iain MacLeod (1961) is somewhat slight. As in the case of Baldwin, earlier biographies have a good deal of useful material culled from contemporary sources easily overlooked by later generations; see, for instance, D. Keith-Shaw, *Prime Minister Neville Chamberlain* (1939) and D. Walker-Smith, *Neville Chamberlain* (1940). Many of Chamberlain's speeches as Prime Minister were published under the title *In Search of Peace* (1938) and, in an extended version, as *The Struggle for Peace* (1939). The pamphlet by A. J. Beattie, D. N. Dilks and N. Pronay, published by the InterUniversity History Film Consortium to accompany the film about Chamberlain, contains material about his use of the newsreels and films. There are helpful articles on Chamberlain by C. Cook in H. van Thal (ed.), *The Prime Ministers*, vol. 2; Sir E. Boyle in *The Birmingham Post*, 18 March 1969; and W. N. Medlicott in *History Today*, May 1952.

Works which deal with the background to the events of 1923–39, or with the nature of Conservatism, and which I have consulted freely, include Lord Eustace Percy, *Some Memories* (1958); D. Southgate (ed.), *The Conservative Leadership, 1832–1932* (1974); T. Jones, *A Diary With Letters* (1954); R. R. James (ed.), *Memoirs of a Conservative* (1969); M. Cowling, *The Impact of Hitler* (1975); R. Blake, *The Conservative Party from Peel to Churchill* (1970); N. H. Gibbs, *Grand Strategy*, vol. 1 (1976); Sir Graham Vincent, *Stanley Baldwin and Rearmament* (unpublished typescript in the Library of Leeds University); R. K. Middlemas (ed.), *Thomas Jones: Whitehall Diary* (3 vols, 1969–71); W. S. Churchill, *The Gathering Storm* (1948); W. N. Medlicott, *British Foreign Policy since Versailles* (1968) and *Contemporary England, 1914–1964* (1967); B. E. V. Sabine, *British Budgets in Peace and War, 1932–1945* (1970); I. M. Drummond, *Imperial Economic Policy, 1917–1939* (1974); James Stuart (Viscount Stuart of Findhorn), *Within the Fringe* (1967); Rt Hon. Lord Templewood, *Nine Troubled Years* (1954); Rt Hon. Earl of Avon, *Facing the Dictators* (1962) and *The Reckoning* (1965); R. J. White (ed.), *The Conservative Tradition* (1950); J. H. Grainger, *Character and Style in English Politics* (1969); H. Glickman, 'The Toryness of English Conservatism' in *The Journal of British Studies*, vol. I, no. 1, 1961.

NOTES TO PART THREE

Chapter 1

1 A. W. Baldwin, *My Father, the True Story*, p. 327.
2 Neville Chamberlain's diary, 31 December 1921.
3 Lloyd George to Austen Chamberlain and reply, 16 March 1922.
4 A. W. Baldwin, *My Father, the True Story*, p. 327.
5 C. Hazlehurst, 'The Baldwinite Conspiracy' in *Historical Studies*, vol. 16.
6 Neville Chamberlain to Ida Chamberlain, 26 May 1923.
7 Austen Chamberlain to Mrs Chamberlain, 27 May 1923.
8 Neville Chamberlain to his sisters, 20 and 26 August 1923.

9 Neville Chamberlain to Hilda Chamberlain, 24 January and 9 February 1924.
10 Austen Chamberlain to Ida Chamberlain, 9 February 1924.
11 Austen Chamberlain to Baldwin and reply, 20 May 1924.
12 Baldwin to Austen Chamberlain, 26 October 1924.
13 Neville Chamberlain to Ida Chamberlain, 26 October 1924.
14 ibid., 1 November 1924.

Chapter 2

1 S. Baldwin, *On England*, pp. 6–7.
2 Bridgeman's diary, 22 July 1925.
3 Sir Eyre Crowe to Austen Chamberlain, 15 March 1925; see also D. Johnson, 'Austen Chamberlain and the Locarno Agreements' in *University of Birmingham Historical Journal*, vol. VIII.
4 Neville Chamberlain's diary, 26 November 1924.
5 G. M. Young, *Stanley Baldwin*, pp. 102–3.
6 Neville Chamberlain's diary, 16 and 25 March 1927, and letter to Ida Chamberlain, 26 March 1927.
7 Neville Chamberlain to Hilda Chamberlain, 31 March 1928.
8 I am deeply indebted to Dr John Ramsden for information upon these and many other aspects of the Conservative Party's organisation.
9 Note by the Secretary of the Cabinet, 30 May 1929; Hankey papers 1/8.

Chapter 3

1 Neville Chamberlain's diary, 12 March 1930.
2 Neville Chamberlain to Ida Chamberlain, 19 May 1930.
3 Neville Chamberlain's diary, 28 July 1930, and letter to Ida Chamberlain, 26 July 1930.
4 Neville Chamberlain's diary, 1, 3, 8 and 25 March 1931, and letters of 1, 7 and 28 March 1931 to his sisters. Bridgeman's diary, 1 and 28 March 1931.
5 Previously Sir Philip Lloyd-Greame; later Lord Swinton.
6 T. Jones, *A Diary With Letters*, p. 49.
7 T. Jones, *A Diary With Letters*, p. 115.
8 K. Feiling, *The Life of Neville Chamberlain*, pp. 253–54.
9 Lord Vansittart, *The Mist Procession*, p. 444.
10 Lord Simon, *Retrospect*, p. 205.
11 Churchill to Baldwin, 9 July 1935 (Baldwin papers, vol. 85).
12 Neville Chamberlain's diary, 22 July and 2 August 1935.
13 The *Daily Telegraph*, 8 November 1935.
14 Hansard, Vol. 317, cols. 1103–4, 1144–5; R. Bassett, 'Telling the Truth to the People: The Myth of the Baldwin "Confession"' in *The Cambridge Journal*, vol. II.
15 Neville Chamberlain to Ida Chamberlain, 8 December 1935.

Chapter 4

1 Austen to Hilda Chamberlain, 15 February 1936.
2 T. Jones, *A Diary With Letters*, pp. 206, 227.

3 W. Evans, *Journey to Harley Street*, pp. 216–17.
4 S. Baldwin, *Service of Our Lives*, pp. 156–67.
5 Memorandum by Hankey to Chamberlain, Premier I/276; Public Record Office.
6 Neville Chamberlain to Hilda Chamberlain, 9 April 1938.
7 ibid., 27 March 1938.
8 ibid., 22 May 1938.
9 *Documents on British Foreign Policy*, series III, vol. VII, p. 127.
10 Neville Chamberlain to Ida Chamberlain, 20 January 1940.
11 R. A. Butler to Lord Templewood, 20 July 1940 (Templewood papers 13: XVII).

Part Four

From Churchill to Heath

by
John Ramsden
Lecturer in Modern History at Queen Mary College, London

CHAPTER 1

Winston Churchill and the Conservative Party

Although he was leader of the Conservative Party for almost fifteen years, Winston Churchill's leadership was a time full of paradox. He reached a pinnacle of popularity with the party rank and file such as few other leaders have ever done, and his personality overshadowed all of the party's many activities in his time. In that he provided such a personal focus for loyalty and leadership – nationally as well as in the party – the party can be appropriately described as Churchill's party during the fifteen years from 1940. Yet, in the longer term, his lasting influence was small, in some fields almost non-existent. This strange relationship makes sense only in the context of Churchill's career as a whole, for his fifteen years as party leader were less than a quarter of his long and distinguished political career. And even in those fifteen years, his role as party leader was far from being the centre of his world or of his importance to the nation.

Elected first as an Imperialist Unionist in 1900, fresh from his triumph in the Boer War, he soon deserted the Unionists over the issue of tariffs and, crossing the floor of the House, joined the Liberals. Other party leaders have changed sides – Derby would be one example – but few have castigated the party that they left so immediately and with such devastating candour. He described the party and its tariff policy as: 'a party of great vested interests, banded together in a formidable confederation, corruption at home, aggression to cover it up abroad, the trickery of tariff juggles, the tyranny of the party machine.'[1]

No wonder that Churchill was such a catch for the Liberals, included immediately in the Liberal Government of 1905 and promoted to the Cabinet at the age of only thirty-four in 1908. No wonder also that he was regarded as a particular *bête noire* by Conservatives, treated with the hostility reserved for prominent renegades whose desertion is thought to have harmed the party's interests. In 1908, when Conservatives rejoiced to hear of his by-election defeat in Manchester, the *Daily Telegraph* celebrated with the news that 'Winston Churchill is out – out – OUT!' Such attitudes remained for the next decade; Churchill's removal from the Admiralty was one price of the Conservative decision to join Asquith's Government in 1915, and his appointment to the Ministry of Munitions in 1917 was described by the Council of the National Union as 'an insult to the Army and Navy and an injury to the Country.'[2] This hostility goes far towards explaining why the party regarded Churchill's return to Conservatism in the 1920s with rather less than enthusiasm, but this was more than simply a refusal to forget the past.

In the attitude of Churchill quoted above, and in much that he had said and done since then, Churchill had expressed his contempt and dissatisfaction not only for the Conservative Party, but for the party system itself. In 1910 he had been the most enthusiastic supporter of Lloyd George's schemes for a national coalition; during and after the war he was a keen coalitionist; right up to 1924 he was supporting attempts to form a new centre party – an idea that was anathema to all good party men. Like Lloyd George and Joseph Chamberlain, he was regarded – and regarded himself – as a sort of dynamic force that would not fit into the constraints of the party system. In his own view, he was always capable of achieving more than the party system would allow him even to attempt; in the view of many Conservatives, he was prepared to risk all that they held dear to follow the whims of a moment. Moreover, the idea had become firmly fixed in the common political memory that Churchill was irresponsible – a political gadfly whose intellect was remarkable but whose judgement was fatally flawed. The list of examples built up, Sidney Street, the Ulster 'Pogrom' of 1914, Antwerp, Gallipoli, intervention in Russia, Tonypandy. All of these charges were unfair and some can be entirely dismissed with the benefit of hindsight and inside documentation, but they added up to a formidable list for those who were prepared to believe the worst.[3]

Churchill's role in the party from his return in 1924 to the outbreak of the Second World War did much to confirm these suspicions. His appointment as Chancellor of the Exchequer by Baldwin in 1924, when he had not even been elected as a Conservative MP, was greeted with amazement by many in the party and was scarcely believed by Churchill himself. He was unlucky to be the Chancellor responsible for the return of the gold standard in 1925, unlucky because any Chancellor would probably have taken the same decision and because Churchill himself had severe doubts about it. He was less unlucky though in the reputation that he earned himself during the 'Cruiser Crisis' of 1925 and the General Strike of the following year; his actions in the former went far to confirm his reputation as an intriguer who was prepared to divide the party, and his belligerence in 1926 demonstrated his intemperate hostility to Labour and his apparent readiness to resort to extreme measures. He threw himself as always into the work of his department and at the Treasury in the 1920s this involved holding down or cutting expenditure, largely at the cost of spending on defence. He reduced the level of annual spending on the army and navy and was the originator of the 'ten-year rule' whereby it was assumed that no preparations need be made for a war within ten years.[4] In the 1920s all of this made sense – he left the Treasury in 1929 more than ten years before war broke out – but it was hurled back at him when defence once more became the priority in the 1930s. His resignation from the Shadow Cabinet in 1930 was over an issue on which he had much support within the party, the future of India, but he damaged his position again by associating with the equally-unpopular Lord Beaverbrook in attempts to split the party. Throughout the 1930s he was treading on very thin ice, always out of harmony with the Government and the overwhelming majority of the party, always treated by the party as a rogue elephant who might be motivated as much by ambition as by policy. In Lord Birkenhead's much-quoted verdict, 'Winston is often right, but when he is wrong, My God!'

In the 1930s though, Churchill was often playing a tune that harmonised well with traditional Conservative attitudes – even if it clashed discordantly with the policy of the party at the time. In the long debates over the future of India, he was able to mobilise the imperialist wing of the party behind his policy of no further concessions to the Nationalists; over the abdication crisis, he spoke out for many who felt that Edward VIII was being treated unfairly; in his campaign against 'appeasement,' he appealed to the old-fashioned virtues of national strength and self-reliance that had been a distinctly Conservative stance before 1914. And yet, in all of these fields, his policy and attitudes were decisively rejected, not only by the leaders of the time but by the party as a whole. Baldwin felt that the trouble that Churchill had caused since he had personally resurrected Churchill's career in 1924 justified him in now keeping him as far away from power as possible, and Chamberlain felt that Churchill was too dangerous and irresponsible to be involved in crises as sensitive as those of the 1930s; Churchill more than repaid Baldwin and Chamberlain for such attitudes in the account of their policies that he painted in his war memoirs. The leaders of the party certainly felt that Churchill had shot his bolt, but his policies were rejected equally decisively by the rank and file. It was after all in the parliamentary party and the National Union that the debates took place that endorsed the Government of India Act; it was the reaction of Conservative MPs to the views of their supporters in the country that brought about Churchill's humiliation in the House of Commons over the abdication; and the party was solidly behind the National Government's policy towards Nazi Germany. Right through 1938 and 1939, the Executive of the National Union was deluged with constituency resolutions supporting Chamberlain's efforts to preserve peace. The critics were under severe pressure from their own constituents, and Churchill himself came close to being disowned by the local party at Epping in the winter of 1938–9. Even Conservatives

who shared his critical attitude over defence and foreign policy
were most reluctant to associate with him; whatever Churchill's
success in public opinion, he was less significant in Parliament
than the group that gathered behind Eden after his resignation
in 1938.[5]

The war of course changed most of this, but by no means all
of it. For those who felt that war was his proper element and
that his year at the Admiralty showed that he was the man of the
hour, there were others who remained as critical as ever, adding
Norway to the list of his irresponsible failures. His public
standing grew rapidly in the winter of 1939–40, spurred on by
his shrewd use of public relations, but this did not break down
forty years of mutual antipathy. In the political crisis of May–
June 1940 he was suddenly propelled into the premiership and
it is popularly believed that he was placed there by the nation
as a whole, finding the right leader in the moment of crisis. The
reality is different; Chamberlain was displaced only because he
handled the crisis very badly, because he lost the support of
some of those who had previously been reliable supporters, and
because in the end he threw in his hand when he might well have
been able to fight off the challenge. Churchill succeeded to the
vacancy because only a Conservative could be supported by an
overwhelmingly Conservative House of Commons and because
the Labour Party would not serve under Chamberlain or
Halifax.[6] There is little doubt that Halifax was much preferred
as Prime Minister by most Conservative MPs. In the end,
Churchill pressed his claims most strongly and secured the job.
It all added up to a most unlikely and implausible end to his
long career. A forty-year apprenticeship of mutual hostility
between Churchill and the Conservative Party was followed
by fifteen years of harmony that culminated almost in hero-
worship. But the change should not be exaggerated. For several
months, Neville Chamberlain remained the leader of the
party while acting as one of the most powerful and influential
members of Churchill's Government. Chamberlain's erstwhile
supporters remained in positions of power for the rest of the
war and some, like Sir Kingsley Wood, were even promoted
by Churchill from positions held under Chamberlain. There
was no clean sweep of the old guard, but there was a gradual
infiltration into Whitehall of politicians who had been close to

Churchill for many years and who were to remain powerful influences on him for the rest of his career, men such as Beaverbrook, Brendan Bracken, and Lord Cherwell. Even during the war, when Churchill's stock stood at its highest with the nation (and no doubt also with the party rank and file) there were murmurs of discontent. Some of the party felt that he was not partisan enough in his attitudes; two wartime party chairmen did not even think it apt that he should be described as a Conservative at all. In view of past feelings, this is not especially surprising, but it explains much about his leadership after 1945.[7]

Churchill during the war revelled in the opportunities that a global war presented for exciting forays into Grand Strategy and for important public pronouncements at a high emotional level; for all of this he was well suited and both he and the country knew it. He also enjoyed working a government of all parties, untrammelled by the need to consider short-term tactics of electioneering and parliamentary business. What he was not so good at was presiding over the rethinking of policy and attitudes for the post-war years that had been necessitated by the war. He was not interested in such things and had little enough time to spare for them anyway. For the director of the war effort, the actual achievement of victory always had to take priority over the distribution of its fruits and that was always the policy that he enforced on the Government as a whole.[8] At the same time though, the trend of public opinion, the activities of reformers within Whitehall, and the activities of the Labour ministers on the home front had generated a demand for change which had to be planned for execution once the war was over. Preparation for this took place on the Conservative side, but never with Churchill's active support and often in the teeth of his opposition. Thus, R. A. Butler piloted through Parliament the Education Act of 1944, the only large reforming measure for which the party could claim credit; Churchill was at first hostile and always indifferent, partly from a general doubt about the wisdom of such reforms, partly from fears that it would distract attention and resources from the war.[9] Even when the war was drawing to a close in 1944–5, he gave little support to post-war planning, focusing instead on the need to go on and defeat Japan and on the increasing danger of war with Stalin's Russia over the corpse of Hitler's Germany. The public and the majority of politicians, however, remained as blind to such fears in 1944 as they had been blind to the danger of Hitler in the 1930s. As VE-day came and went, Churchill tried desperately to hold the National Government together into the post-war world, an attempt that was destroyed by Labour's insistence on independent action after the war.

On the Conservative side, too, there were many looking forward to a resumption of party politics, hoping to use Churchill's name to win a mandate for a post-war Conservative Parliament. Few politicians on either side believed that the electorate would reject the national hero, but with retrospect it can be seen that Churchill's popularity as war leader was always coupled with the proviso that he would not be suitable after it was all over.[10] He conducted the actual election campaign of 1945 very rashly, largely on the advice of Bracken and Beaverbrook and taking little account of either the party chairman or the Chief Whip.[11] Although most commentators have stressed the importance of long-term factors in producing the Conservative defeat of 1945, contemporaries placed at least some of the blame on Churchill himself. Thus, *The Times*:

'When all allowance has been made for the emergence of a new generation of voters and for the "swing of the pendulum" among the old, it will still be necessary to seek the explanation of the Conservative defeat largely in the circumstances and conduct of the election itself. Mr. Churchill himself introduced and insisted on emphasising the narrower animosities of the party fight. As a result the great national programme was allowed to slip into the background.'

Most of the press had been emphasising how much common ground there was between the policies of all of the parties and so there may be some truth in the claim of *The Times* that the way in which Churchill fought the election had a disproportionate effect on its outcome. The *Economist* noted more bluntly that, for all of Churchill's stature as a war leader and as an international statesman, he could still take lessons in party management from Baldwin.[12]

The election defeat of 1945 brought to a head all of the fears and frustrations in the party of the past few years. Churchill was, not unnaturally, bitterly disappointed by his rejection at the hands of a nation that he had served so well; as he characteristically put it, he was 'deeply distressed at the prospect of sinking from a national to a party leader' – hardly the most hopeful attitude with which to start a period as Opposition leader.[13] His reaction was to resist the transformation to the utmost, to draw back as far as he decently could from the routine work of party leadership, and to reserve himself for statements of an international significance. Not for him the long and arduous task of redefining the minutiae of policy and organisation, not for him the slow grind of legislation in the House of Commons; rather, he persisted in thinking of defence and diplomatic problems, delivering his conclusions in the weighty accents of an international statesman rather than the partisan tones of a domestic party leader. This fortunately left the field open in the party for the very considerable achievements of Butler, Macmillan and Woolton.

Churchill had been much hurt by the events of 1945, not only the result of the election, but also by the tone with which it had been fought – although he had injected more fury into it than any other combatant. The result of this was that he made a distinguished and distinctive contribution to the political argument of the Opposition years, but only in his chosen and limited field, and in such a way that his contributions affected the thinking of all the nation, all the parties, rather than shaping directly the thoughts of his own. His speeches at Strasbourg and Fulton are rightly seen as significant pronouncements on the future of Europe and Britain's role in the world, but it is more difficult to cite a speech on a domestic question that made as much impact – either at the time or since. It was not that he did not speak on domestic issues, or that his speeches were not good, well-researched (by Reginald Maudling in the main) and polished, but that they were simply not given on *his* subject, not delivered with the same conviction and not as original. In foreign affairs, he was leading the nation, in most other areas he was leading his party from a position firmly in the middle. His lack of leadership as such has perhaps been exaggerated and there were some consequences of his semi-retirement that did the party positive good: he was allowed a much-needed rest after the exertions of six years, he could in any case be relied on to come into the deliberations of the party and deliver the results of policy reformulation with appropriate emphasis, and in the meantime he preserved his reputation as a leader above and beyond British politics.

Churchill's own brand of Conservatism therefore made no great contribution to the re-thinking of party policy and philosophy that took place, and his influence was negative rather than positive. As a Conservative, he described himself as a 'Liberal Tory', following the distant steps of his father, and his idea of Conservatism was of a paternalist but magnanimous State, that would not be afraid on the one hand to act to preserve its strength and integrity, nor on the other to intervene to protect the weak in its midst. In many ways this helped the re-thinking of policy that had to take place; the leader was sympathetic to State action as some Conservatives were not (but as traditional Toryism always had been), and he was relatively open-minded as to the means that should be used to secure desired ends. It was useful in combating charges that the re-thinkers of philosophy were leading the party to 'pink socialism' to have at the helm a leader so unshakeably committed to the preservation of the institutions of Church and State, and personifying a traditionally robust patriotism in his very self.[14] All of this helped to open the way for changes without damaging the unity of the party.

Churchill had a more direct influence on the way in which the party functioned as an Opposition; he kept the party on a loose rein and called for only a limited commitment from his senior colleagues, partly no doubt because he was giving a limited commitment himself, partly through conviction. Thus, Shadow Cabinet meetings were gatherings that were as social as they were political, speakers for the week's business were chosen on an *ad hoc* basis with no Shadow ministers allowed or expected to specialise in one field to prepare for power, and the emphasis of re-thinking was always on re-establishing principles rather than on laying down detailed policies. All of this helped to restore the unity and identity of the new team of party leaders, gave them experience in a wide range of fields, and gave an impression of the wholesale reconsideration of

policy without committing the party to very much in advance
of actually getting into power. It should be stressed that this
system, as fully operational after 1948, could only work when
plenty of time was available and in the relatively leisured
political communications world that still existed in the 1940s.
Pragmatic opposition was the order of the day; Shadow
ministers developed no special field that would lead them to
expect a particular job in power, policy-makers stopped short
of dictating the terms of policy for the next government. While remaining more or less aloof from the
battle, Churchill kept the party's future securely in his own
hands.[15]

    The election defeat upset more people than Churchill. The
election seemed to have marked a decisive shift in electoral
history, the end of a long period of Tory predominance; there
had been only one non-Conservative majority Government
elected in the whole of the previous sixty years, but the future
looked considerably less rosy. When Sir Hartley Shawcross
proclaimed that Labour were 'the masters at the moment, and
for a very long time to come' there were few disposed to argue.
For a party so suddenly thrown down from the expectation of
power, it is (as Enoch Powell subsequently wrote) 'a grave
operation to recover belief in the unity, the consistency and the
rightness of its principles and policies.'[16] In the aftermath of
1945 then, the relations of the Conservatives with the British
people were characterised by 'doubt, hesitation and pain'; nor
was this ever followed by a 'glad confident morning' on which
the doubt and hesitation were finally lifted. The failure to win
the South Hammersmith by-election in 1949 brought another
bout of self-doubt in the party, the election of 1950 was a severe
disappointment, the victory of 1951 was seen as a fortuitous
consequence of the electoral system and of Liberal withdrawals
since 1950. Not until the victory at South Sunderland in 1953
did the sun really begin to break through, and not until ten
years after was the gloomy ghost of 1945 finally laid. In the
meantime, everything that the party did, said, or stood for was
subjected to searching scrutiny. *The Times*, in a friendly spirit,
even suggested that no good would be done unless the party
changed its name. None of this is especially surprising when it is
remembered that the party was coming to terms with a political

world that was markedly less favourable than the one that had existed before the war.

What emerged was strikingly unoriginal in terms of pure policy but very successful as party strategy; in Butler's view, what was attempted was a major piece of cosmetic surgery, as large a modernisation of method and approach as the party would accept without the danger of a split.[17] As strategy, the principle was to withdraw from the positions that the Socialist Government were preparing to attack, leaving only a parliamentary force of skirmishers to occupy their attention, and to re-form the party in prepared positions to resist the next wave of socialism.

Much of the change was seen by its chief advocates as the updating of traditional and eternal principles of Conservatism, re-writing Burke and Disraeli for the post-war world. So Quintin Hogg called for a new 'Tamworth Manifesto', a reformulation of party philosophy to meet an acknowledged social revolution like that of 1832, and the Industrial Policy Committee considered Peel's text of 1834 as one of their starting-points.[18] There was indeed a great effort to present what was being done as both original and yet at the same time firmly within the Tory tradition. Butler certainly believed that he was by Conservative standards unorthodox, but that he could legitimately claim to share that unorthodoxy with Bolingbroke, Burke and Peel. The reformers could thus have it both ways, combining tradition with change, rewriting policy while proclaiming eternal principles; in this at least they were well within the mainstream of Tory history, for Peel, Disraeli and Baldwin had all carried out the same cosmetic job for their party in their time. It was, however, more than a trifle disingenuous; in 1955, the Conservative Political Centre published an anthology of the results of policy reviews since 1945 and proudly called it 'The New Conservatism'; in 1962, Iain Macleod, who was thought by many to be almost the embodiment of the changes that had taken place, told the party conference that 'there is then no new Conservatism, only a restatement of old beliefs in modern terms.'[19] Such contortions follow naturally from sincere attempts to modernise policy while remaining faithful to the past.

In a more direct way the party had been able to re-establish its contact with the past. Central Office and the CPC published new editions of Disraeli's speeches, restatements of the Tory faith in traditional terms, and the by-then traditional lists of legislation on social problems carried by Conservative governments since the 1830s.[20] These seemed to give a clear indication of the continuing commitment of the party to an advanced social policy. More specifically, attention was given to the refutation of Labour's claims that Britain before 1939 had been a social desert and that Labour alone was responsible for the advances that had been made from that pre-Keynesian and pre-Beveridge state of nature. With the exception of Harold Macmillan, who had been a rebel against the party's economic and social policy in the 1930s,[21] Conservative leaders spent a great deal of time defending their party's pre-war policy and claiming equal credit for the advances that had been made since.

Churchill pungently refuted the entire Labour argument by pointing out that most of the new policies had derived from a National Government of which he had been the head. Thus, on employment policy, he told the Party Conference of 1947: 'To this document, which Lord Woolton drafted and I approved as Prime Minister, and of which Mr Bevin boasts so loudly, the Socialists have not yet added one single coherent idea.' Churchill was an expert at such historical games, re-establishing the past in the present, as when he remembered that the Webbs had spoken highly of Disraeli's policy towards the trade unions, or when he introduced *The Right Road for Britain* in 1949 with a long and entirely appropriate quotation from a speech of his father's, seventy years earlier.[22]

Only in one area did the party completely ignore the past, and that was the question of pre-war foreign policy. Only Quintin Hogg in *The Left was Never Right* sought to refute Labour's criticisms of the policy of 'appeasement', and that book had been written before the 1945 election anyway. It was left to Baldwin's family to defend him from the attacks on his reputation made in G. M. Young's official biography, and the name of Neville Chamberlain was hardly mentioned by party spokesmen, even when they were praising the social reforms that he had carried out at the Exchequer and the Ministry of Health. It is hardly surprising that old wounds were not re-opened after they had been so successfully bound up in and after 1940, but the result was that the party missed the opportunity to challenge myths about the 1930s before they were firmly established. It was an unnecessary exercise anyway, since Labour could make little political capital out of denunciations of appeasement when they were faced by a party led by Churchill and Eden.[23] In domestic, economic and social policy, though, the party missed no opportunity to re-establish its past and to stress the elements of continuity in what it sought to do in the present and the future.

The immediate reaction to defeat had been to blame the sadly deficient party organisation, run down after years of war. So constituency parties had almost folded up, money had not been raised, agents and candidates had been diverted to war service or other national work. It will not do to explain this away simply as a hysterical refusal to accept defeat, nor to show that Labour was equally badly organised in 1945; what is at issue is the relative organisational strengths of the parties and whether the position in 1945 differed from the usual position.[24] The Conservatives have drawn an electoral bonus from the superiority of their organisation at every modern election *except* 1945, a bonus based on different methods as well as different levels of efficiency. The party has based its appeal to the voters on an intensively-organised, professional structure that co-ordinates a large network of activists who are otherwise ineffective. Labour and the Liberals on the other hand have made less use of professional organisers, less use of an active mass-membership, and more use of the enthusiasm that can be generated on the left under the urgent pressure of an election. In 1945 the Tory machine was in ruins, both centrally and locally, and the party's campaign was a shambles; on the left, enthusiasm was perhaps greater than ever in the aftermath of war, nothing had been lost in professional organisation because little had existed anyway, and the campaign ran much as always. Labour may not have been more efficient than the Conservatives in 1945 – it is impossible to make exact comparisons – but the very fact that Labour was not obviously *less* efficient reflected a change from each election before or since. Part of the emphasis given to organisation in the Conservative Party after 1945 comes from that simple fact; disorganisation was by no means the only explanation for defeat, but it was certainly a contributory cause. It was a cause that stared every party activist in the face, and it was a cause that could be remedied by the party's own efforts. If it put its own house in order, it would make at least some recovery at the next election.

But changes in the party organisation had a wider aim than the winning of the next election. The organisation embraced all those from MPs to the humblest party workers who gave the party its collective style and its public face; an elector could be influenced as much by what he saw of the party as by what he heard of its policies. In 1945 the party's defeat had been a rejection of men as well as measures and it was necessary at least to give the impression that both were changing. Thus the Maxwell-Fyfe Committee changed the rules regarding candidates' subscriptions to constituency parties, so that finance could no longer be the over-riding criterion in the selection of candidates.[25] Henceforth, it could be said that the career of a Conservative MP is open to all the talents – an important step towards harmony with the post-war world. In fact, the situation before the rules changed had not been as bad as its critics alleged, and the consequence of the new rules in changing the social character of the parliamentary party was both limited and gradual. Most important, though, something had been seen to be done, and in time the results were considerable. The expansion of the local parties into mass organisations with large numbers of activists and expanding subscription lists also helped to express the policy of the party towards individualism and participation. Finally, the developments in organisation keyed in with the changes in the party policy through the expansion of the party's drive for political education and the foundation of the Conservative Political Centre. The newly-enlarged membership in the constituencies could be kept in touch through the two-way movement of ideas; policies could be reported down through the party machinery and reactions from the constituencies could be fed back. This mechanism helped to hold the party firm in a time of much stress and helped the policy-makers to advance at a rate that was acceptable to the party as a whole. The relative lack of dissent when the major policy statements came up for endorsement at the party's

Central Council or Conference says a great deal for the improved intra-party communications run through the CPC.[26]

The recasting of policy had not begun only after defeat in 1945, for the reformers had been active in the preparation of schemes and plans for the post-war world at least from 1941. The Post-War Problems Committee had been sitting since 1941 under the leadership of Butler and Maxwell-Fyfe, and was transformed into the Advisory Committee on Policy and Political Education in 1945. Yet little had been done by 1945, partly because Conservative ministers were inevitably restrained by the demands of their own departments, partly because their work overlapped with the Government's Reconstruction Committee under Lord Woolton, and partly because the climate of opinion for policy-making was so frigid in Churchill's wartime Government.

Most important perhaps was the Tory Reform Group, led by Quintin Hogg and Lord Hinchingbrooke, more effective in the main because its members were free of the restraints of office and free also of an official status in the party. The TRG did have some success in pressing the acceptance of the Beveridge Report upon the Conservative members of the Government and went on to exert similar pressure on other questions, notably on catering wages. The reformers before 1945 had then at least begun the work of clearing the ground, questioning the party's assumptions and challenging its beliefs. It needed only the impetus of defeat and the restoration of the party's research and secretarial apparatus to open up the flood-gates of change.[27]

The Research Department went on in fact to play a more important role in the party than it had ever done before 1939. Under Butler's chairmanship, the department provided the professional backing to all of the policy reviews that were undertaken, supported the party's leaders with material for speeches, and wrote much of the party's literature. It also provided an apprenticeship in politics for a whole new generation of leaders, men like Iain Macleod, Enoch Powell, Reginald Maudling.

Defeat made all Conservatives except the extreme right more ready to look again at the party's policy, and the end of the war brought a useful ally to the reformers with the return to England of Harold Macmillan, always the spokesman for the

militant left in the party before 1939 but exiled to a ministerial
post in Africa since 1942. The jibe that the new party policy
amalgamated the Tory Party with the YMCA was near the
truth in one respect; Macmillan's group of left-wing social-
conscience Conservative MPs in the 1920s had been known as
the YMCA and his return to influence party domestic policy
from the inside was in itself a move towards the views that he
had always held. 'The Middle Way' had been Macmillan's
contribution to political philosophy in the 1930s, and it was as
accurate a description as any of the stance that the party took
up after 1945. Many men were important in the re-thinking
of policy. Oliver Lyttelton and David Maxwell-Fyfe are obvious
examples, but the powerful intellectual and political influences
behind it all were Macmillan and Butler, with Eden always
available to support whenever necessary – especially when
Churchill needed to be convinced.

Lord Fraser of Kilmorack, at that time a member of the Conservative Research Department and later its chairman, has noted
that without Butler, 'the recovery would not have happened
in any lasting way . . . He was the only person at the top level
who really put drive and coherence into the policy exercise,
recreated the Research Department and got the show on the
road. Macmillan was the next greatest influence but at that time
relatively limited, since he had not got an army and Butler
had.'

So the Industrial Policy Committee duly produced its
Industrial Charter, deliberately written in unprovocatively
obscure and unexciting terms, and was somewhat surprised by
the relative ease with which it was accepted as party policy by
Churchill and the Conference.[28] From this flowed the many
other statements of policies, little charters, and minor investigations that were codified into *The Right Road for Britain* in 1949.

In policy-making, there was little attempt to cash in on the
difficulties that the Labour Government was experiencing in
managing the economy. Most of the new policies were deliberately framed very widely – a framework of philosophy and
guidelines for administration rather than an immediate programme for the next Parliament, summed up in Butler's description of the exercise as 'impressionism'. The long series of
policy statements enabled Conservatives to resist the Labour

demand that the Opposition should provide alternatives to the policies that they were criticising. After 1949 it certainly could not be said that the Conservative Party did not have any policies – a charge frequently levelled in 1945. Nor could Labour attack the new policies at what was their weak point – the fact that they provided little that was distinctive from what Labour themselves were actually doing. This was clearly the case, but it was hardly possible for Labour to say so; in fact the Labour leaders did not seem to grasp how real was the Conservative conversion to the welfare state, the mixed economy, full employment and Keynesian economic management. Labour was determined to claim the sole ownership of such attitudes, arguing that the Tories threatened them all, and so they missed a chance to point out that the Conservatives had little to offer that was different.

Much of this was in any case fortuitous; Conservative and Labour policy-makers had often reached the same conclusions by different routes, sometimes for different reasons, usually at different times; both were reacting to the changes that the war had brought about in Britain's economy and society, so it is hardly surprising that they came up with some of the same answers. In some of the answers though, the Conservatives clearly believed with more certainty than their Labour counterparts, as in the case of the dismantling of controls; it might be the policy of both parties, but it was clearly more to the liking of the Conservatives. Labour had already reduced the level of income tax since the end of the war, but it fitted more logically with Conservative thinking to reduce it further. Labour would certainly have continued the anti-Communist policy necessitated by the Cold War, but it fitted more reasonably into the Conservative view of the world. In these as in other areas, the refurbished Conservative policies were brought up to date alongside those of the Labour Party, but into areas where Churchill's team was more at home than Attlee's.

The Conservatives had been discredited in 1945 not because their policies differed greatly from those of Labour, but because the electorate clearly believed more strongly in Labour's intention to carry them out; in 1950 and 1951 this happened in reverse with Labour now appearing the less credible of the two parties to carry out the agreed policies. Nor is this clear only

with the wisdom of hindsight, for the point was made at the
time by commentators on the 1945 Election and on the Conservative declarations of policy as they appeared thereafter. In
1945, *The Times* had suggested during the campaign that 'the
electors are fortunate in having in effect before them a minimum programme to which all parties are pledged.' After the
results were declared, the paper remained faithful to that view,
with the City Editor consoling his readers with the reflection
that 'the area of agreement between the parties is considerable.'
He went on with great perception to note where the parties
disagreed on longer term policies:[29] 'The first and much the
more important is that of nationalisation of key industries. The
second is the question whether the detailed location of industries
and the direction of the flow of capital to industries should be
primarily the decision of private enterprise or primarily the
decision of government.'

An observer in 1945 could thus see not only how far the
parties already agreed but also where disagreement left room
for different policies in the longer term. When the Industrial
Charter was published, highlighting exactly the same areas of
general agreement but specific differences, the only grounds for
complaint were from those who shared Labour's doubts as to
whether the Conservatives would do as they said. So the *Daily
Telegraph* and *The Times* both stressed how much of the new
policy was shared with the Labour Government, while the
Economist doubted whether the bulk of the party was really
behind interventionist policies to secure full employment. The
Telegraph noted that:[30] 'There is nothing partisan or reactionary
about these proposals. For the most part they consist of securing
in more effective ways what the present government is trying
to secure. The difference is largely one of method.' *The Times*
though went a stage further and linked its verdict with a view
of the nature of democratic government that went close to the
heart of the matter. It noted that the two parties would put very
different emphases on different parts of what was fundamentally
the same programme, and went on:

'This is as it should be. In the British Parliamentary system the
programme is dictated by the wishes of the people and the
requirements of the nation, not by the parties. The question to

be decided at each election is which of the parties will carry out the programme most effectively and most fairly. In 1945 the choice fell on the Labour Party. It is a question of confidence, and the task of the Opposition today, as always, is to persuade a majority of the electors before the next election that they would serve the national interest more competently and more justly than the government.'

In one of his best speeches, fifteen years later, Iain Macleod explicitly accepted the same explanation of what the policy review after 1945 had really been about:[31] 'It would have been impossible for the Conservative Party, after its defeat in 1945, to reform and reorganise itself if it had contemptuously said that the electors had chosen wrongly. Instead we started from the assumption that it was we, the Conservative Party, who were at fault and not the people of this country.'

The comparison with Labour's reaction to defeat in the 1950s was a good one; the humility with which the Conservatives had reacted to defeat in 1945 was testament again to the realism and flexibility that had characterised the party throughout its history.

But, as we have seen, the changes were not as difficult to make in the 1940s as they have sometimes appeared to be in retrospect: working from different premises and arguing in different ways, *The Times* in 1945, the Industrial Policy Committee in 1947, and Quintin Hogg in *The Case for Conservatism* all reached strikingly similar conclusions about the main lines of party policy. Much of the same course of argument had indeed been followed, again independently, by Harold Macmillan's *The Middle Way* in 1938. The facts of the economy and of British society, interpreted by Keynes and by Beveridge and his precursors, were too strong to be denied.

Only in one area did the party succumb to the demands of electioneering before the return to power in 1951, over the question of housing. Before this, there were indeed regular complaints that the party leaders, MPs and policy-makers were not being partisan enough, not hitting Labour hard enough, and not making enough electoral capital from the Government's mistakes. The debates over steel nationalisation and the inter-mittent campaign to harry the ailing Labour Government to death in 1950–1 helped to silence such critics, but the new policy on housing was the first overtly electioneering concession to the party rank and file. Housing had been the Labour Government's most obvious failure, mainly because it had given such specific pledges on the subject in 1945, and the clear temptation was to exploit this fact with an equally specific Conservative pledge. The demand became irresistible at the Blackpool Party Conference of 1950 and Lord Woolton acceded to the demands with a pledge to build 300,000 houses a year, despite warnings of the probable economic cost from others on the platform – notably Butler.[32] It was an isolated example, if an effective one in helping to win back power for the party, but it gave as good an indication of what would happen in government as did the six years of remarkable restraint that it crowned.

The other late shift of emphasis was the increasing weight placed in the party's election manifestos on the elements of policy that stressed freedom. This had been an important part of the argument of the *Industrial Charter* and *The Right Road for Britain*, but it became the dominant note of the 1951 Manifesto, *Britain Strong and Free*, when the election campaign was centred around the slogan 'Set the People Free'. This increasing emphasis was a consequence both of public demand and of an increasing conviction that the Labour Government was not in fact dismantling controls as quickly as was possible. The first few years of Conservative government after 1951 demonstrated the truth of both points.

The Government formed by Winston Churchill after the Conservative Party won the General Election of 1951 conformed closely to what might have been expected by an informed observer of the past few years of his career. The new Government reflected Churchill's personal attitude to government itself, it reflected the demands of the parliamentary situation, and it reflected the changes wrought by the war and by post-war reconstruction. It was clearly Churchill's Government in that it maintained something of the flavour of the war-time and 1945 caretaker governments. It was run by a small Cabinet – perhaps as small as Churchill could get away with in peacetime – and included several non-party and semi-party figures who lent to the Government a flavour that was less than usually partisan. Churchill had indeed tried to avoid forming a party government at all. In the introduction that he contributed to *The Right Road for Britain* in 1949, he claimed that[33] 'We are not only reviving the Tory Democracy of Lord Beaconsfield and after him of Lord Randolph Churchill, but are giving expression to the spirit of liberalism with its sense of progress, tolerance and humanity.'

The National Liberals had come finally within the Conservative alliance with the Woolton–Teviot agreement of 1947, but Churchill was claiming rather more than this and was aiming for a wider measure of Liberal support. After the victory of 1951, when there was a clear but small Conservative majority in the House of Commons, he offered places in the new Government to the Liberal Party. It was only because Clement Davies turned down the offer and thereby kept the Liberals independent that Churchill was forced to form a party government at all in 1951.[34] Apart from the Prime Minister, whose partisanship was thus again seen to be ambivalent, the Cabinet included Lord Woolton as Lord President (a prominent Conservative since 1946 but not even a Conservative until 1945); Lord Simonds as Lord Chancellor (one of the few to occupy that post without an apprenticeship in the other political law officerships); Lord Ismay at the Commonwealth Relations Office and Lord Cherwell as Paymaster-General (both relics of Churchill's war staff). The Government did not include either Lord Beaverbrook or Brendan Bracken, but both visited Downing Street regularly as Churchill's courtiers and probably wielded more influence as informal advisers than they could ever have done as departmental ministers. To these must be added Lord Salter, a non-political economic specialist, and Earl Alexander of Tunis, who became Minister of Defence in 1952. All of these no doubt helped Churchill to feel continuity with the great successes of the war years and strengthened his claim to be more than just a party leader. There has rarely been a government that contained so many members who held office merely by the will of the Prime Minister and who had no conventional political backing to support them in office. Perhaps there was never a one-party government that seemed to owe so little to the party that put it in office and kept it there.

For this reason, the appointment of R. A. Butler as Chancellor

of the Exchequer was a vital one; this signified clearly enough
that Churchill was aware how far the party had actually moved
since 1945 and constituted almost a guarantee to the country
that the new Government would not put the clock back. The
appointments of Harold Macmillan to the Ministry of Housing
and of Peter Thorneycroft to the Board of Trade were also
significant pointers of the way in which the party had moved,
but it was a significance that few noticed at the time. Harold
Macmillan, to become a pivotal Cabinet figure within a year
or two and Prime Minister in less than six years, was not even
among the first eight men appointed by Churchill to his
Cabinet and was sent to the Housing Ministry only after Woolton's request to go there had been turned down.[35] Such apparently limited concessions to the new mood in the party are now
quite explicable, but at the time they lent credence to Labour's
belief that the old enemy had changed little and was bent on a
course of reaction. Little more could have been done largely
because of the lack of experienced talent available to Churchill
in 1951: it was twenty years since the party in the House of
Commons had received an infusion of new blood, and the new
recruits of 1950 and 1951 were scarcely yet experienced enough
to leap straight into the Cabinet. The junior appointments of
1951 therefore told a better story than the Cabinet; men such
as Iain Macleod, Anthony Head, Derick Heathcoat Amory,
Selwyn Lloyd, Alan Lennox-Boyd, and Reginald Maudling
were given their first posts. Time would bring the changes of
the 1940s to the top ranks of the party in Parliament and in the
meantime the party's appearance would belie its real character.

The functioning of the Government, as well as its composition,
reflected the nature of its head. Lord Woolton reflected that
'the Cabinet under Mr Churchill was often reminiscent of
bygone times' and he was not the only one who was concerned
by the unbusinesslike way in which the Prime Minister dealt
with the agenda. Often the whole time allocated for the meeting
was taken up with general discussion of political problems, none
of which were on the agenda or prepared for by the Secretariat
and the ministers present. Other ministers were kept waiting
for long periods outside the Cabinet Room while those inside
were not even dealing with the agenda. Woolton added that
Churchill's lengthy lectures on the sum of his political experi-

ence were often useful and always interesting but that they became intensely frustrating to a team of busy men.[36] This was no doubt a particular source of grievance to those who had had to forgo valuable business careers in order to give time to their ministerial careers in 1951.

The scheme of 'overlords' was also a Churchill innovation that caused more disruption than the resulting gain in co-ordination could justify. To co-ordinate policy and reduce the number of men in the Cabinet, Churchill appointed some ministers to oversee the work of others who would not be in the Cabinet. This sensible scheme, much imitated in later years with the growth of monster ministries and the amalgamation of ministries, was vitiated in 1951 simply by the fact that the 'overlords' were in the House of Lords themselves, whilst most of their subordinates were in the Commons. Problems of accountability arose at once and were never satisfactorily resolved until the system was abandoned.[37]

Despite all of this, the Government's record of achievements justifies the claim that it carried out most of its election programme of 1951 and this in turn says much for the realism of its approach in the 1951 Election itself. Butler was a great success as Chancellor of the Exchequer and earned tributes both in the Treasury itself and in the financial press. At first he was hedged about with considerable limitations on his power, a semi-independent economic adviser appointed by Churchill, and a reluctance of the Cabinet as a whole to accept his advice on matters of economic strategy; gradually his freedom of action increased. By 1954 he was earning tributes not only for his success in turning the national economy around the corner from deficit to substantial surplus, but also for the modesty with which he attributed much of the success to economic forces beyond his control. Macmillan at the Ministry of Housing was equally successful, gathering around him an expert team of advisers, modelling his methods on those of the wartime production departments, and easily reaching the 300,000 figure that had been set. The costs of such a massive diversion of resources to consumption were perhaps more serious than was seen at the time, but the success of the policy itself cannot be denied.[38]

Walter Monckton at the Ministry of Labour had a similar success with similarly-dubious long-term effects. It was the intention of Churchill and Monckton to keep the temperature of industrial relations as low as possible and so refute the Labour claim of 1951 that the return of a Conservative government would turn industrial relations back to the battlefield that they had been in the 1920s. The upshot was that by keeping unemployment down – it fell every year from 1952 to 1956 – by avoiding anything that could be considered provocative, and by giving way where necessary in wage disputes to avoid political confrontation, the Government managed to achieve its ends. The number of men involved in industrial disputes was – with the single exception of 1953 – no higher than it had been under Labour. The cost of this in inflationary wage settlements was considered justifiable. Once again the cost was really felt later.[39]

In the general field of economic policy, the most commented-upon feature of Conservative policy was again its lack of provocation. Iron and steel and road haulage were removed from the public sector as had been promised, but no further denationalisation plans were brought forward. The other areas in which the new Government changed the plans of Labour in the organisation of industry were in regard to broadcasting and the provision of public houses for 'new towns'. In both of these, private enterprise was given an opportunity to compete in what was felt to be its proper field of activities, but not without severe restrictions being imposed in the case of the new Independent Television Authority.[40] Controls, rations and Government intervention were scaled down or removed altogether; the Ministry of Materials was wound up and its stockpiles sold off, thereby removing not only the intervention itself but the agency that spoke for such government intervention from the inside.

With the exception of the two measures of denationalisation, little of this was controversial, and these were rallying points for the party faithful intended to establish points of principle, rather than starting points for the wholesale destruction of the public sector. Commentators tended to complain indeed that the policy of the new Government was indistinguishable from that of Labour – a view summed up in the idea of 'Butskellism', a compound of Hugh Gaitskell and R. A. Butler. Such a view is borne out more by an examination of the means and methods used in economic policy than the ends for which they might be designed. Butler was as convinced that Keynesian policy towards the economy was a secure foundation for competition, individualism, and the survival of capitalism, as Gaitskell had been convinced that the same means could secure the purposes of socialist collectivism. Each used monetary and financial policy to carry out his aims – each had learnt the lessons of the war and of Keynes – but the ends remained distinct. Even the means might have diverged sharply if Butler had been allowed by the Cabinet to let the pound float in 1952 – a policy that was attacked bitterly by Gaitskell as dangerous and irresponsible. Supported only by Oliver Lyttelton and hesitantly by Churchill (perhaps remembering the consequence of the fixed parities of 1925?) Butler gave way to the rest of the Cabinet. Insofar as there ever was a Butskellism of economic methods, it was imposed on Butler by the rest of the Cabinet.[41] All in all, the policy was not to challenge the broad consensus of popular agreement on economic policy that had arisen in the 1940s, but to impart a distinctively Conservative emphasis within that area of agreement. It can hardly be doubted that Labour Chancellors in the 1950s would have reduced controls, but nor can it be doubted that they would have done so with less enthusiasm and less conviction. 'Setting the Nation Free' was a policy that fitted both the broad consensus and the Conservative emphasis within it. One final area in which public opinion and party aims could come together was in taxation policy; reductions in taxation were the consequence of both an improving economic position and of the careful economic management of the first two years. When taxes could be lowered in 1953 and 1954, these decisions were naturally popular and the party equally naturally derived a great satisfaction from saying so.

Hardly surprisingly in a Government led by Churchill and with Eden as its second in command, Commonwealth and foreign affairs occupied a large part of the Government's time. Eden was unchallenged in his control of these fields, even by Churchill himself, and the Cabinet as a whole played little part in the formulation of policy. Over the Korean War and relations with Russia and America, this probably mattered little: opportunities for independent action by Britain were limited, American policy made few concessions to British interests, and Russia certainly regarded Britain as little more than an adjunct of the United States in Europe. Desperate attempts by Eden and by Churchill to halt the deteriorating relations between the two super powers therefore achieved little. Churchill in particular was profoundly upset by the way in which events progressed and stayed on after 1954 largely because of his conviction that he could make a personal contribution on the world stage by his own considerable reputation. The chances of this were perhaps more limited than he was ever ready to admit. In relation to Europe though, the lack of Cabinet policy control was more serious; Eden had little sympathy for the emerging institutions of Europe, developing through the European Coal and Steel Community into the EEC, and the opportunity for British involvement was therefore missed. There were certainly Cabinet ministers more sympathetic than Eden – Macmillan and Maxwell-Fyfe for example – but foreign policy remained Eden's personal sphere of influence.[42] Perhaps no chance really existed, for British opinion in the 1950s was very hostile to involvement in avowedly supra-national institutions and opinion on the Conservative back benches was far more interested in the Commonwealth than in Europe. Agitation over foreign affairs was more confined to the consequences of withdrawing from the Suez Canal Zone in 1954 than to a possible missed opportunity in Europe.

Determination to deal personally with the new Russian leaders provided Churchill with an excuse in 1954 – as in 1945 – for staying on in office when the party might have reasonably expected him to retire. Most senior ministers had suggested retirement to him after his stroke in 1953 and his age was becoming an increasing problem to the functioning of the Government, an increasing frustration to the party as a whole. There was a great sense of relief in both Cabinet and party when he finally announced his resignation in March 1955. But Churchill's role in the re-establishment of the post-war party should not be understated, especially in the years of Government. He was in those years a partisan figure who considered himself, and was widely considered by others, to be something of a national leader. He therefore refused to use Central Office press officers when in Downing Street, involved the leaders of the Opposition parties as much as possible in the formal business of Government and insisted on a restrained and national policy towards the trade unions. All in all, he did much to bring the party back into the dominating position of natural government that it had lost – apparently for ever – in 1945. His was a vital role, for his stature provided an umbrella beneath which the party could regroup, rediscover itself and its sense of purpose, and readjust for the new situation. Perhaps most important was his sense of history – a sense that led him to describe Butler's budget of 1952 as a continuation of the 'Tory Democracy' of his father in the 1880s. This sense of history, and the continuity that he helped to establish within it, enabled the party to make a vital and difficult transition into the post-war world.

In terms of strategy, much was gained from Labour's bad tactics, deriving largely from their failure to recognise the way in which the Conservatives had changed. In 1951, as Harold Macmillan then noted, they had fought the election on the question of fear, in the sure belief that a Conservative Government would destroy all that had been gained.[43] By 1955 Churchill's Government had done enough to destroy such fears for a generation – and had in the process discredited those who had spoken the language of fear in 1951. Lord Woolton had never been allowed by the Labour Party to forget his demands that the people should have a little more 'red meat'; by 1955, meat rationing, like so much else, was a thing of the past. The achievement of the Churchill Government was to set out to achieve things that were realistic, to carry them out, and to reap the benefits that then deservedly accrued.

CHAPTER 2

Despair and Recovery
1955-59

The new Prime Minister, who was the near universal choice of the party, was greeted with at least modified rapture by all sections of the party and press, and won a considerable personal triumph in the general election that was held immediately after he succeeded Churchill. That this should even need to be said of Sir Anthony Eden is comment enough on the speed with which his career and prospects were eclipsed by a few short months of the highest office. It had been agreed for several years among senior ministers that Eden was to succeed Churchill; it was re-emphasised when Churchill considered retiring in 1954 and taken for granted in 1955. Eden had indeed been the Crown Prince to Churchill ever since 1940, and he had Cabinet experience that went back to 1935 in one of the great offices of state. It was certainly known that he was predominantly interested in foreign affairs, but this need not be exaggerated. As Churchill's deputy, he had had to involve himself in the whole range of party policies and to speak on them in the country and in the Commons. He certainly regarded foreign affairs as his field, but he was by no means a one-sided politician. He had received Churchill's stamp of approval in particular as a foreign specialist when Churchill restored him to the Foreign Office in 1940; this had been more than confirmed in 1948, when the first volume of Churchill's war memoirs was published. If there is a hero in *The Gathering*

Storm then it is not Churchill but Eden, and one of the most memorable passages of the book describes Churchill's profound gloom in 1938, induced by the news of Eden's resignation. From all of this, Eden was to be measured by Churchillian standards as a statesman of the world rather than as a British politician.[1]

In the first place though, Eden's advent was greeted not because it marked continuity but because it seemed to herald change. The party, in the Cabinet as well as in the country, had felt that Churchill had outstayed his welcome and, though they would never have forced his retirement, they now accepted it with relief. Eden seemed to stand for the new post-war world as surely as Churchill had stood for all that was continuous and unchanging. Thus, press reactions to Eden's elevation pointed to his youth and looked forward to a different future now that youth was at the helm. All of this evidently irritated Eden himself, who had to be reminded by Lord Woolton that the public were not measuring his age forwards from zero, but backwards from Churchill's age.[2] In reality, he was more a prisoner of the pre-war situation than Churchill had ever been, but this was far from apparent in the spring of 1955. His welcome from the press was remarkably unrestrained. In view of later events, it may be as well to quote the *Daily Telegraph*, whose editor noted that: 'Training, knowledge and courage are in high degree the unquestionable assets of our new Prime Minister. He incarnates as well as any man the new Conservatism.'

In those first few weeks, the press credited him with all sorts of outstanding abilities, a personal skill for the maintenance of Anglo–American relations, a particular understanding of his party, and a special qualification to head the Cabinet itself because of his knowledge and understanding of Cabinet methods and procedure.[3] The General Election that was declared within a week of his elevation seemed to confirm all of this; wherever he went, he was welcomed warmly and in many places he received a better reception than even Churchill had had. Thus, in Glasgow he 'not only filled the enormous St Andrew's Hall but two overflow halls for his relay. On the next night, Attlee could not get the St Andrew's Hall more than half full.' Indeed, faced with such a popular opponent and with a Government riding on the crest of successful policies, the Labour Opposition and its press supporters hardly tried at all in the 1955 General Election. Eden was warned by Lord Woolton that his electioneering should not look too much like a triumphal progress, but this is effectively what it became; the upshot was a considerably increased Conservative majority in the House of Commons and a personal triumph for Eden in the result at Warwick and Leamington.[4] He was after all a more glamorous public figure than his predecessor or his opponent, a man who perhaps more than any other this century has actually *looked* the part of Conservative Prime Minister. His speeches, if not as one unfriendly commentator has called them 'banal', were solid, down-to-earth stuff that went down well enough with the Conservative audiences that he had to address. And he had done enough to present himself, as the *Daily Telegraph* suggested, as the incarnation of the new Conservatism.

In speech after speech during the war and since, he had sought to propound the new approach to society that he believed that the war had made necessary. Such speeches, few in number when compared to the huge list of his official statements on foreign affairs, had nevertheless done much to help in formulating the new approach. While Churchill had usually talked about the eternal verities of power politics and British history, and while Butler had concentrated on expounding the details of the new policies and on justifying them through their own logic and desirability, Eden had tried to link the new approach to domestic policy with Britain's position in the world and with the foreign situations that he knew so well. So, in October 1946 at Plymouth, he asserted that:[5]

'The essential problem facing the modern world is to reconcile freedom and order. It is no new problem. It has been with mankind ever since civilisation began. To each succeeding age it presents itself in a different form, and each generation must find its own solution. Wherever you look you will see how in essence this problem, the reconciliation of freedom and order, underlies the struggles and the difficulties of statesmen and governments.'

A few weeks earlier, at the Party Conference at Blackpool, he had given his answer and the party's answer to this recurrent problem in re-introducing and popularising the concept of a 'property-owning democracy' – a neat idea that at once accepted the changes wrought by the war and at the same time called for a halt to such changes. Emphasis was placed not on division but on how much was agreed by the parties, and the onus was placed on the Labour Party for breaking that consensus with its more advanced schemes. It was through this idea that the party rediscovered and re-popularised the idea of freedom within capitalism, central to all of the new policies of the 1940s and culminating in the 'Set the People Free' slogan of 1951. Much of this was common to the bulk of the parliamentary party and the Shadow Cabinet, but it fell to Eden to articulate it and to link it with the defence of freedom in Europe. But he also set firm limits to freedom and accepted this as a determinant on policy. Thus, speaking on industry at Walthamstow in August 1946:[6]

'We accept that there is a field for State action in relation to our national economy and to our industrial life. But that certainly does not mean State Ownership, for ownership is only one, and usually the worst form of State intervention in the affairs of industry . . . State action in the economic sphere is normally thought of as wholly negative and restrictive . . . but I believe that should be only part of the story. There is no doubt that close and genuine co-operation between Government and private industry in these post-war years can bring valuable financial and economic benefits to this country.'

These few examples, all from a few weeks in 1946 could be amplified endlessly from the speeches of the next ten years and explain the high hopes that followed Eden's elevation to the Prime Ministership in 1955. Here was an ideal Prime Minister, well qualified in the vital field of foreign affairs, marked out with Churchill's personal seal of approval, and yet with a clear and moderate attitude to domestic problems too.

What is surprising is not so much the high hopes as the speed with which they were abandoned, and the reasons for this sudden reversal were as much reasons of personality as of policy. Once in office, Eden turned out to be far less good at the actual job of Prime Ministership than colleagues or party had expected; the Cabinet was run on more businesslike lines than under Churchill, but there soon emerged an indecisiveness that had not been there before. Thus, on the vexed question of capital punishment, the Home Secretary was left in a highly exposed position in the House of Commons, defending a line of policy that the Government would neither formally espouse nor resolutely reject and both he and the Government as a whole were considerably damaged. Lord Woolton has described the difficulty that he had in actually leaving office in 1955, although he had made it clear from the start that he wanted to resign and so leave room for the promotion of younger men into the Cabinet. Eden was most reluctant to tamper with the team that Churchill had bequeathed to him; the re-shuffle that did take place in December 1955 was widely regarded as both too long delayed and insufficiently thorough; when men *were* replaced in 1956, as were both the First Lord of the Admiralty and the Minister of Defence in the weeks before the Suez invasion, it was unexpected and ill-judged. As Prime Minister, Eden behaved strangely, irritating his colleagues by his alternate high-handedness and irresolution, and especially by his frequent loss of temper. It was all as though the job was too much for him, that Churchill's enormous mantle was smothering him.[7] All of this was doubtless exacerbated by the troubles in matters of policy that beset the Government immediately after the elections were over.

If ever a government was 'blown off course' from the start by the unfavourable winds of policy, then surely this one was. In the summer of 1955, the warning signals of economic overheating and accelerating inflation became too loud to be ignored. Butler was forced to introduce an autumn budget that took away much of the reductions in taxation that he had been able to distribute in April. This provoked a howl of rage from the Opposition, convinced as they were that they had been the victims of an electioneering economic policy that had now served its turn. Such a verdict was without doubt unfair; Eden had supported Butler's decision to restrict the give-away side of the April budget to a minimum, and Treasury advisers had been wholehearted in their support for the Chancellor's policy.[8] The state into which the economy would fall by the autumn had been foreseen by almost no one in the spring. Nor were the problems as severe as may have appeared at the time; the deficit on the Balance of Payments could be dealt with by short-term restrictions and the rate of inflation could be brought down without too much pain or industrial strife by a sensible and moderate financial policy; in both fields the decisions of 1955 and 1956 had substantially dealt with the problems by 1957, but in the meantime the Eden Government went through a rough time.

At the end of 1955 the by-election at Torquay marked the first sign of a Liberal resurgence at the expense of Conservative candidates in suburban and middle-class strongholds. Early in 1956 the party almost lost Hereford, Gainsborough and Taunton; in June there was a remarkably close contest at Tonbridge. Throughout Eden's time as Prime Minister only one by-election failed to show a swing against the Government and there was a continuous Conservative deficit in the opinion polls; the proportion of the electorate approving of Eden as Prime Minister fell spectacularly from 70 per cent in autumn 1955 to 40 per cent in the spring of 1956.[9] All of this seems to have rattled Eden and to have added considerably to the discontent already felt by his colleagues and party supporters. Press criticism became widespread and was to be read as frequently in the *Daily Mail* and *Daily Telegraph* as in more hostile journals. Speculation mounted at Westminster and in Fleet Street that Eden would have to resign and the flames of speculation were certainly fed by Eden's ill-judged decision to issue a public denial of any such plans, and by the ill-concealed frustration of some of his colleagues. Donald MacLachlan's article in the *Daily Telegraph* in December 1955, in which he called for the 'smack of firm government' and added insult to injury by framing his attack in terms of Eden's speaking style, was especially hurtful but was no more outspoken than others had been.[10] Eden himself reacted in a way uncharacteristic to both himself and his office, being more hurt than most professional politicians would be by such attacks, but, far worse, by allowing himself to be seen to be hurt. As 1956 wore on, the continuation of press attacks and the backstairs criticism of colleagues told more and more heavily on his nerves, nerves

that were already frayed by the burden of office and by bouts
of illness. And all of this before any of the events occurred that
were actually to bring about his downfall.

It should be emphasised though, particularly tragic as it is,
that it was in his own field of foreign affairs that the greatest
failures came about and that Eden's prestige was correspond-
ingly lowered. In the handling of the Russian protests over
Commander Crabb's espionage activities in Portsmouth Harbour and in the reaction to the dismissal of General Glubb by
King Hussein of Jordan, Eden's standing as a diplomat was
lowered. When the Government was reshuffled in December
1955, Macmillan was removed from the Foreign Office, partly
at least because Eden found it hard to get on with a strong
personality in an area where he meant to be personally involved, and so chose Selwyn Lloyd as his successor, confident
that this would give the Prime Minister more freedom of action.
For any diplomatic problems of 1956 then, the Prime Minister
would be directly responsible and would be seen to be; in this
field, he meant to keep direct control, even to the extent of
leaving the Embassy at Washington without an Ambassador for
the crucial month before the Suez invasion.

It was in the context of a relative failure at home, both
personally and in policy, that Eden set about restoring his
fortunes and those of his Government with a bold stroke in
foreign affairs. All seemed set fair, for in Colonel Nasser he
appeared to have an adversary that he could recognise (as a
sort of substitute Hitler) and a situation that he could be
expected to master – in his own words, a repetition of the
Rhineland Crisis of 1936. The melancholy sequence of events
that followed need not be described, but a few comments must
be made. First, it must be emphasised that Eden's original
analysis of the situation and of the analogy of the problem with
that of the 1930s was widely shared in Britain, in both parties,
and perhaps more stridently in the Labour Party than among
Conservatives. What he failed to see was that immediate reactions in July were far from a readiness to contemplate an
actual war in November; nor was he alone in following policies
designed to prevent the outbreak of the *last* war, for that was
exactly what the appeasers had been doing in the 1930s. In the
1950s as in the 1930s, it was the factors that had changed that

should have been emphasised, not those that appeared to be the same. But Eden was surely right in one point, his assurance that popular opinion was with him and that the British people as a whole would accept military action if necessary in defence of national interests. In that belief he drew still on the experience of his pre-war career, for his opposition to appeasement, his resignation from Chamberlain's Government, and his later justification of his actions, would only make sense if the British people would support a more adventurous policy; whether they would have done in the 1930s cannot be proved, but they surely *would* have done in 1956. Eden himself continued to assert this even after the policy had collapsed and so gave the basis of a policy to his successor. Speaking at a Young Conservative rally on 17 November 1956, he received a quiet hearing until he asserted that,[11] 'We make no apology and shall make no apology for the action that we and our French Allies took together,' a statement that received a torrent of applause, almost a standing ovation. Thus was born the strategy of no apologies that Harold Macmillan was to carry to such a successful conclusion in the next three years.

In two areas, however, Eden's handling of the Suez affair was more lasting in the damage that it did to the party. The new factor that he had so consistently excluded from his calculations was the question of American support – perhaps characteristically, for it was not a significant factor in the European diplomacy of the 1930s. Without American support, or at least the benevolent neutrality of the State Department and the US Treasury, the Suez invasion was in truth doomed from the start. Pressing independent action by Britain to its very limits and beyond them merely exposed for all to see, at home and abroad, how dependent Britain had now become. Britain might not apologise, but she could hardly fail to note what Suez had demonstrated, and neither could others in the world. Finally, Eden himself and to a lesser extent the entire Cabinet, was damaged by the way in which the invasion was justified as a neutral intervention to prevent the Israelis and Egyptians from destroying the Canal. This was a convenient device that fooled very few – not least because the military plans had been begun in July long before a Middle East War seemed likely – and moreover it seriously weakened Britain's position because it took away all justification for intervention once the Egyptians accepted a cease-fire. Eden has specifically denied that the Government had forewarning of Israel's plans or that there was collusion between Israel, Britain and France. But there was clear collusion between Israel and France, and it was quickly asked at the time what sort of alliance did Britain have with France if such information was not passed on; and why did not British intelligence find out about it anyway. The entire affair, not just in its origins, but in its detailed handling, shattered Eden's great reputation for diplomacy and for some at least compromised Britain's position in the world as a moral force.[12]

Ironically though, the greatest effect of the Suez Affair on British politics was on the Prime Ministership rather than on matters of policy or prestige. Since Suez had confirmed existing doubts about Eden's fitness for the job, and since he himself was now even more unsure of himself than before, it is likely that it would have brought about his resignation. After such a colossal defeat for his personal policy in his central area of interest, it is hard to see how the party could have allowed him to stay on; at the Christmas-time of 1956 Eden himself was considering resignation. But Suez had not just damaged his reputation but had also shattered his health. After the worst part of the crisis he was ordered to Jamaica for a complete rest – leaving Butler as acting Prime Minister, with the unenviable task of withdrawing the troops from Suez and stabilising the financial position. After his return, a few weeks went by, during which he was treated coldly by the party in Parliament and with intense hostility by the Opposition. Early in January his problem of decision was taken from him and on the instructions of his doctors he resigned from office.

The enforced retirement of Eden really marked the ending of a chapter of Conservative Party history, the passing of a generation. The change was marked by the new leader and by the men that he chose to have around him, then and in the entire period of his leadership. Macmillan's preparation for the supreme office had been almost as stormy and unconventional as Churchill's had been. Regarded from the start of his career as a rebel on the left of the party, he had resigned the

Whip in 1936 to register his personal disapproval of Government inaction on the question of unemployment, and he had gone on to be even more critical of the National Government's foreign policy. The advent of Churchill to power had been the making of Macmillan's career, in 1940 when he was brought into Government for the first time, in 1942 when he was given his first position of real power – as Minister Resident with Eisenhower's HQ in Africa, in 1945 when he was promoted to the Cabinet, and in 1951 when Churchill gave him a chance to show his abilities as Housing Minister. Moreover, the Macmillan that emerged from this training was a very different politician from the rebellious member from Stockton in the 1930s; no longer an affected and mannered speaker but a self-confident and effective debator, no longer an impractical if worthy idealist, but a proven man of action, no longer a soft-hearted MP of the 'YMCA' variety but a resilient man of the world more at home in power politics than before. He had not troubled to hide his ambition to get to the top in politics, even when this exposed him to ridicule, perhaps because he could never feel satisfied in any subordinate position. Thus in the 1930s he was well-known to be displeased by the promotion of such near-contemporaries as Butler and Eden while he himself remained on the back benches. In 1955, he agreed to move from the Foreign Office to the Treasury only if it were accepted that this was a move towards rather than away from the Prime Ministership, an insistence that provoked amused comment among colleagues.[13]

Eden's eclipse suddenly opened up the situation for Macmillan. Butler had antagonised many in the party by his barely-concealed frustration with Eden as Prime Minister, by his open discontent with the Suez expedition, and by his general readiness to evangelise for the left of the party at the expense of popularity on the right. There were many who resented the fact that a Conservative Chancellor could be popularly linked with the Labour leader in the word 'Butskellism' as denoting no great difference of policy between them. Ironically, Macmillan had been outspoken in his demands for military intervention in Egypt, outspoken outside Parliament as well as within, just as Butler had not hidden his doubts about it all. The failure of the policy though strengthened Macmillan

rather than Butler, for it placed the Government and the party
under such strain that the one thing that could *not* be admitted
was that it had been wrong. Many Conservative MPs effectively
took out their frustration with Nasser and Dulles on Butler, and
expressed their admiration for Eden's gallant failure through
their support for Macmillan. Even if it had all been foredoomed
to failure, it had at least been tried, and Macmillan had at
least given his full support to the attempt. He had, as Harold
Wilson jibed, been 'first in and first out' over Suez, the hardest
of hard-liners in his demand for intervention and the first to
see the consequences for sterling – as his position at the
Treasury made inevitable. He therefore emerged from Suez
with his reputation enhanced in two ways, with a new streak
of apparent toughness and with a renewed basis for respect in
his undeniable realism. Suez had shown that he would risk a
great deal on 'one turn of pitch and toss', but also that having
lost he was prepared to 'start again at your beginnings, and
never breathe a word about your loss.' In opening the way for
Harold Macmillan, the party never made a wiser choice. For
him the opportunity had come at last, as Anthony Sampson
commented:[14]

'With Eden out of the way and Butler in retreat, Macmillan
at last had a clear field. We should not be deceived by the
histrionics, the casual air, the reading of Trollope, the determined unflappability. Here was a man at the height of his
powers of extreme ambition who had waited thirty years for
this opportunity.'

Although Macmillan's elevation to the Premiership was a
surprise to many commentators, it should be stressed that it
was far less controversial in 1957 than it was to become in
retrospect. The 'usual processes' evoked less criticism when
handled quietly and quickly in 1957 than when conducted in
the full glare of publicity in 1963. The serious criticisms, such
as those by Emrys Hughes and Gerald Sparrow came out in
1962 and 1965 respectively.[15] In 1957 itself, Macmillan was
certainly the overwhelming choice of the Eden Cabinet and
of the elder statesmen consulted by the Queen; no accurate
account of the views of MPs has been published, but it is clear

that Macmillan at least had no substantial body of entrenched opponents in the parliamentary party, as Butler certainly had at that time. There can rarely have been a time when a Conservative Party leader so certainly 'emerged' as Macmillan did in 1957, the man of the hour and the unifying choice of the party. He provided the lead that the party was looking for in 1957 and the party responded with a loyalty in adversity that astonished friends and enemies alike.

Macmillan signalised the change that had been made by the sweeping changes that he instituted in the Government, far more widespread than Eden had made, but in the same general direction of promoting talented younger men. So far was this carried that by the middle of 1957, the Cabinet included only five men who had sat in Churchill's Cabinet in 1951. The transitional regime of Churchill was now over, and the post-war generation of recruits was entering into their inheritance. Ironically, the change was presided over by a man who was actually three years older than Eden and ten years older than the average age of his first Cabinet. It may truly be that, as Sampson said, Macmillan's chance had come 'ten years too late.'[16] This was perhaps underlined by the difficulties of the situation that he inherited from Eden, a party on the point of mutiny, the economy in a weak condition, the country in diplomatic isolation, and all looking to the new Prime Minister for the wherewithal to remedy the situation. Little wonder then that the characteristic of the first three years of Macmillan's Premiership was rebuilding structures and re-establishing confidence rather than radical re-thinking of policies and attitudes. The keynote was summed up in Lord Hailsham's word 'unflappable' that soon caught on sufficiently to be almost universally applied to the Prime Minister.

Selwyn Lloyd was kept on at the Foreign Office, much to his own and everyone else's surprise, for Macmillan felt that 'one head on a charger was enough'; in any case, Macmillan intended to make much of the running of foreign affairs himself, drawing on his personal standing with Eisenhower to re-build the 'special relationship' with the United States, and such intervention would be much easier with Lloyd at the Foreign Office than with Butler there.[17] Butler had wanted to go to the Foreign Office but it suited Macmillan to keep Butler in a position where he would not become the focus of rivalry to himself, for the party needed some years of undisputed and indisputable leadership in order to get over 1956. Butler accepted all of this with good grace; both have written in their memoirs that they were aware how deeply the future of the party depended on their ability to get on with each other and work together closely in the Cabinet and outside.[18] The party can rarely have had the good fortune of two such able contenders for the leadership as when it had to decide between Macmillan and Butler, each at the height of his powers in 1957. They represented between them the two ongoing themes of Tory history, Macmillan the inspirational and romantic, even sometimes flashily vulgar tradition of Disraelianism, Butler the more sober, administrative assiduity of Peelism. The combination of the two at the head of the party for the six years from 1957 was indeed a formidable combination. At the next level the same was true; the party had rarely fielded a team of such all-round ability as the one that Macmillan was able to assemble in his Cabinet.

Macmillan had therefore provided himself with a Cabinet that was mainly less experienced than himself, with a Foreign Secretary who could be kept more or less under his personal control, and with a deputy who had loyally knuckled under to him for the good of the party. He was never challenged in the leadership during his six years as Prime Minister and even at the end of that time, with his policies far from successful, there was little disposition to challenge him. There was little doubt of this from the start, but any doubt that did exist was swiftly dispelled by the resignation of Lord Salisbury from the Cabinet a mere two months after it was formed. Romantic Tories who still thought of the Cecils as carrying an effective moral influence far beyond their actual power were soon to change their views; Salisbury resigned rather than accept the Government's policy in Cyprus, but also because of his lack of sympathy with the Prime Minister on colonial issues and on the aftermath of Suez. It was Salisbury who was defeated and the policy of the Government did not change in the slightest.[19] Less than a year later, Macmillan reacted to the resignation of the entire Treasury team of ministers with an airy description of the crisis as 'little local difficulties' and set off at once for a long-planned Commonwealth Tour. Whenever he needed to do so, he asserted his personal control in such ways, refusing to give the appearance of concern or indecision.

In the Cabinet itself, his control was equally masterful: several colleagues have commented favourably on his efficient and direct way of running Cabinet meetings from the chair, dominating proceedings by intellectual mastery rather than by personality. He also refused to operate with an 'inner Cabinet', and although this made him rather remote from many of his colleagues, it helped greatly in getting them to work as a team of equals. As we can now tell from his memoirs, and as the best-informed commentators were saying at the time, the appearance of decision and confidence was a mask that was assumed painfully and nervously to hide much inner tension. He had long realised the value to his own career of giving a greater appearance of self-assurance than he actually felt and he now transferred that attribute from himself to his Government and party. The keynotes would be confidence and inspiration; thus in his first major speech, he ridiculed the idea that Suez had exposed Britain to the world's gaze as a third-rate power and asserted his confidence in Britain's present and future strength. None of this had much implication for actual policy, for it was clearly the only viable stance for Eden's successor to adopt Eden's position of 'no apologies' – the restoration of national confidence was more important than any actual decision of policy. As Harold Wilson observed, 'The man's a genius. He's holding up the banner of Suez for the party to follow, and he's leading the party away from Suez.'[20]

Macmillan had himself made a considerable contribution to the thought of modern British Conservatism through his writings and speeches before the war. This gave him a head start as a Prime Minister, not because what he now said was very new or original, but because what he had always said had suddenly become fashionable and popular. He defined his view of Conservatism in this way in an address to the Conservative Political Centre in March 1958, linking present policy directly to the ideas that he had expounded in *The Middle Way* twenty years earlier.[21] He asserted the distinction between matters of absolute belief, the irreducible minimum of freedom and independence, and the rest of the area of political debate which was more susceptible to pragmatic and undogmatic resolution. In the latter category, he placed the whole area of economic policy, and especially so because the resignation of Peter Thorneycroft and his colleagues from the Treasury a few months earlier had been on this exact point; Macmillan had demanded a pragmatic approach to economic management and his Treasury ministers had refused to budge from a more dogmatic attitude to public expenditure. To Macmillan, the business of Conservatives in this central area of politics was to resist the ruling panacea of the day, whether it be from the left or the right, whether it be individualistic Liberalism in the nineteenth century, whether it be doctrinaire Socialism in the 1940s, or monetarist economic policy in the 1950s. For this reason, the Conservative Party could only pursue the middle way, the way between extremes, and use its judgement in matters of short-term policy as it thought best at the time. Such was the secret of the party's success in the past, and such would be the basis of its survival into the future. This idea echoed strongly *The Case for Conservatism* put forward by Lord Hailsham in 1947 and the views of others in the party who were inherently distrustful of any dogmatic views at all. Few Prime Ministers had ever expressed their pragmatism so baldly, but in Macmillan's case this was accompanied by a strong sense of party history and by firm convictions about policy in the present that prevented pragmatism from ever being an excuse for inaction, a negative defence for an arid policy or for no policy at all. So he told the Party Conferences of 1958 and 1960 that the Tory responsibility to counter the current dogmatism of the left now gave them a duty to 'proclaim the right of the individual against the State and other large-scale concentrations of power.' On economic affairs he was even more specific as to the clear responsibilities of government, as he told the Conservative Political Centre audience in 1958:[22]

'The older ones have not forgotten. I was a Member of Parliament in those years on Tees-Side. As long as I live I can never forget the impoverishment and demoralisation which all this brought with it. I am determined, as far as it lies within human power, never to allow this shadow to fall again upon our country. Even the social injustices suffered by a minority in the post-war period – and they are very real – are more tolerable than this major injustice.'

To Macmillan then, as to Eden, the Thirties could never be forgotten, but their lesson was a lesson as to ends, not as to means; the end was greater prosperity, and it was to be achieved by any means that lay to hand and seemed to be appropriate. He had stressed this frequently, and it came almost to be his catchphrase in the party, as was emphasised by Sir Richard Proby in introducing Macmillan to speak at the Party Conference in 1958:[23]

'In the course of the last eighteen months Mr Macmillan has impressed his personality first on the Party, then on the House of Commons, then on the Nation, and month by month he is impressing his personality on the world. How has he done it? Well of course, we all know that he is a pastmaster at television, and television is not an art which any twentieth century Prime Minister can afford to neglect. But of course, there is something deeper than that, and I think that at an informal occasion when I happened to be present he let us into the secret. This was what he said on that occasion: "In the conduct of affairs what is needed is constancy of purpose with flexibility of execution." I want to suggest that that is the technique which Mr Macmillan has wonderfully mastered.'

Macmillan asserted that such had been his aim on several occasions, and it was said about him over and again by colleagues and admirers alike.

This was carried a stage further in public meetings when he urged the country not to forget what had been achieved since the 1930s or how fragile were those achievements. Thus, at Bedford he asserted in a characteristically off-hand phrase that 'some of our people have never had it so good', a phrase taken up by the Opposition as a base piece of materialistic electioneering and constantly flung back at him. Like so many successful slogans, it was not designed to be one, was popularised by its critics, and vindicated by its truth.[24] (The same process occurred when the cartoonist Vicky sardonically characterised Macmillan as 'Supermac' and drew him a cartoon hero, only for the parody to boomerang when the rest of the press took up the name and used it about Macmillan for several years.) However 'Never had it so Good' was devised, it became a convenient electioneering shorthand for Conservative policies of growth and prosperity, policies that had by 1959 paid full dividends in both the economy and the electorate. When he reviewed the election victory of 1959 at the Party Conference of 1960, though, Macmillan commented merely that the party had given the people both what they wanted and what they needed, stressing rather the theme that 'materialism is not enough'.[25] However, the sense of achievement in the long term remained with him, as he pointed out in his resignation letter, read to the Party Conference of 1963 by his successor:[26]

'Since 1945 I have lived to see the party of our dreams come into being ... I have seen our policies develop into that pragmatic and sensible compromise between the extremes of collectivism and individualism for which the party has always stood in its great periods. I have seen it bring to the people of our own country a degree of comfort and well-being ... such as I and my comrades could not have dreamed of when we slogged through the mud of Flanders nearly 50 years ago. Thus, the silent, the Conservative revolution has come about.'

There were expressed at once Macmillan's acute sense of history, his feel for the vital importance of pragmatic compromise and his ambivalent materialism. Against all of this must be set Macmillan's well-known preference for inflation over unemployment; in the view of some, the years of Macmillan's leadership were the time when the relatively insignificant inflationary wage settlements of the early 1950s went on at a higher rate to become potentially dangerous. To some extent, Macmillan may come to be remembered as the Prime Minister who taught the British people to live with inflation and even to expect things that could only be paid for with inflation. In his defence can be cited his obvious good intentions and the ever-present memory of Stockton in the 1930s. But, as his favourite author Trollope might have reminded him, 'a man can't govern well, simply because he is genuinely anxious that men should be well-governed.'

Although Macmillan's leadership had steadied the party almost from the first, it took longer for both the leader and his policies to get across to the nation. In the short term, 1957 seemed almost as bad a year as 1956 had been, with a succession of defeats in by-elections culminating at Rochdale where the Conservative came third in what had been a Conservative seat. Local elections and opinion polls confirmed the same view, but in the winter of 1958–9 the signs began to improve. The lengthy aftermath of Suez was at last finished and the entire subject could be legitimately treated as one that was now over and done with; Labour indeed seems to have antagonised a good many voters by insisting on raking the coals over and over again; this certainly helped to keep Conservatives loyal and to strengthen partisanship on the right. The economy too was improving in 1958 and was on the point of breaking into a full-scale economic boom by the spring of 1959. Foreign problems had eased very little, but Macmillan's constant attempts to bring East and West together had gained him a good deal of support and the appearance of being an international statesman as Churchill and Eden had been.

Most of all Macmillan had revived the party's morale, through his efforts and through the considerable achievements of Lord Hailsham as his party chairman. Macmillan outlined the problem in a leaflet intended for a recruiting campaign in 1958:[27]

'When a political party has been in power for several years – as ours has been – and is setting out on a campaign to recruit new members, it must base its appeal on a double claim. It must show by its achievements that it deserves a renewal of confidence by the people. It must also show that it has confidence in itself and its power to go on to still further achievements.'

In 1957 and 1958, the problems of policy were slowly coming round, but the problem of party morale and confidence was less easy to resolve. Debates at the Party Conference on the failure of the leaders to explain their policies adequately showed the low state of morale; like Plantagenet kings, Conservative leaders are never attacked directly by their subjects, but only through their bad advisers and their failure to explain themselves. But in 1958 this tide too turned; no Party Conference debated the failure of publicity or public relations again until 1962. Much was done in this area by adding to the Liaison Committee between party and Government, set up by Churchill in 1951, a small and secret steering committee, charged with the task of overseeing the tactical side of politics and preparing the ground for the election. This consisted of Macmillan (in the chair) with Butler, Hailsham, Macleod, Heath, and Michael Fraser as Secretary. It enabled ministers to meet regularly outside the constraints of the Cabinet and wearing their party rather than their public hats.

The rising morale of the party showed itself in a greater enthusiasm for the General Election in 1959 than had seemed likely a year earlier. It was also shown in the success that met Central Office opposition to Conservative–Liberal pacts in the constituencies. Only in Bolton and Huddersfield, where pacts were well-known and well-established, were pacts approved and despite some disagreements Central Office and the party chairman were able to get what they wanted. The contrast with ten years earlier shows clearly the gain in morale; in 1949–50, the party had tried hard to establish itself as the heir of Liberalism as well as of the Tory tradition, while in 1959 it stood aside from the Liberals and challenged them to do their worst.

CHAPTER 3

The Zenith and After, 1959-65

Economic and diplomatic recovery from the trough of 1956–7 led on to a political recovery of equal proportions, a recovery that was certainly assisted by the current state of the Opposition. Gaitskell's feud with Bevan had been healed by the time that Macmillan called a General Election in 1959, but Gaitskell remained unconvincing as a leader and unsure of his colleagues. The General Election of October 1959 seems in retrospect to have been a foregone conclusion, but only in retrospect. At the time many commentators were unable to believe that the Macmillan Government would really be able to live down its unpopularity of 1956 and opinion polls published during the campaign seemed to confirm that the result would be close. If there was any real chance of Conservative defeat – an unlikely proposition in itself – then it was easily dealt with by the masterly way in which Macmillan conducted the campaign, using his considerable skills and that of his team to project the picture of a forward-looking party in strong contrast to an outmoded and old-fashioned Labour Party. Labour's discomfiture was underlined by the disastrous way in which Gaitskell fought the campaign. Macmillan's use of the visit of President Eisenhower to London during the election, and Gaitskell's tactical blunder in promising not to increase taxes, may stand for their respective campaigns.[1]

In reality the Conservative victory was based on firmer

foundations than this; at the most the campaign may have increased the size of the Conservative majority. The Government was returned with a majority of 100, the first occasion when any party had improved its position at four successive elections, and went on to improve its position still further in 1960. At Harrow, there was a swing towards the Government, and the Government actually won the seat at Brighouse and Spenborough from Labour, a very rare Government gain from the Opposition in a by-election; in the local elections of 1960, Conservative candidates wiped out the losses of 1957 and took more council seats than at any election since 1951.[2] 1960 was the zenith not only of Macmillan's premiership but also of Conservatism in the post-war years. So widely was this seen that politicians and commentators of all the parties and of none began to ask themselves whether any other party but the Conservatives would ever win an election again. Professor Beer examined the prospects of a 'democratic one-party government' for Britain, and Anthony Crosland asked 'Can Labour Win?' echoing Mark Abrams' question, 'Must Labour Lose?'[3] Gaitskell showed how seriously he took the consequences of his party's third successive defeat by plunging Labour into a bitterly-fought attempt to change the party's constitution and image.

All of this was eloquent testimony to the scale of Macmillan's success, not just in winning an election but also in destroying the morale of his opponents; in the years after 1959 several of Labour's front benchers so lost confidence in the future of their party that they left politics altogether – men like Robens, De Freitas, Marquand and Johnstone. With Bevan dead, Gaitskell discredited by the election and its aftermath in the Labour Party, and with Wilson scheming for the leadership, the Labour Opposition became so weak as to offer no serious challenge to the Government. When Macmillan's team began to run into serious troubles in 1961, they were challenged not by Labour but by the Liberals and by critics outside Parliament. One long-term effect on British politics of a *fourth* Tory win in 1964, had it occurred, would surely have been profound – perhaps a realignment of the other parties.

The reasons for this considerable triumph must be analysed. Some of it was certainly the result of favourable economic circumstances that the Conservatives had been able to exploit to party advantage; whatever government had been in power through the 1950s, such factors as a favourable shift in the terms of trade would have helped them to give a great measure of prosperity to the electorate. But it is not as easy as that. Many in Parliament and the press were openly hostile to the arrival of mass affluence in the later-1950s, as the outcry that greeted 'Never had it so good' shows; this feeling was popular most of all on the left and it seems likely that a Labour Government in the 1950s would not therefore have taken the opportunity to raise living standards as eagerly as Macmillan had done, first at the Ministry of Housing and later as Prime Minister. It was after all the consistent policy of Conservatism, at least since Disraeli, to improve the 'condition of the people' in the sure knowledge that this policy would be both wise and popular. Disraeli had pointed out that a 'policy of sewage' was more popular with the people and more in their interests than 'all the pains and pleasures of the Ballot Act'; Macmillan in the 1950s was reasserting the same tradition of Conservatism when he portrayed his own party as the believers in material well-being and the other parties as believers in moral changes and structural reforms. Nationalisation was in 1959 much what the Ballot Act had been in 1872, an irrelevance to the everyday lives of at least a large section of the population. It has been a Conservative belief, re-emphasised by Macmillan, that politics is not the whole of life but that economics is much more nearly so.

Labour implicitly accepted this view of Macmillan's success when in their inquests on defeat they asked themselves questions about the relationship between affluence and voting behaviour. The most popular explanation of Conservative success was that affluence had weaned Labour voters away from their older loyalties of class; more specifically it was asserted that home-ownership, together with the possession of cars, washing-machines and televisions, had 'embourgeoised' working-class electors into middle-class attitudes – and hence into voting Conservative. Assiduous research failed to find hard evidence for this theory – these mysterious 'affluent workers' failed to show up in surveys or research programmes. But the theory must be accounted at least half proved; at the very least, the years of

Conservative affluence had the effect of confirming and strengthening Conservative opinions among working-class Tories and bringing them out to vote in force, while having an equally discouraging effect on Labour voters. It needs only an assumption of differential turnout, a very likely explanation in itself, to reconcile the theory and the evidence.[4]

Macmillan had contributed more directly to the party's success in his personal leadership and in his contributions to the international scene. It was a personal triumph for the Prime Minister that relations with the United States were repaired so quickly and so completely after the rupture of 1956 and so it was in a way fitting that Macmillan's televised conversation with Eisenhower should help him to win the election. It was also undeniably to the Prime Minister's credit that he had striven so hard to bring America and Russia to the conference table; his much-quoted preference for 'jaw-jaw rather than war-war' may have played the same part in foreign affairs as 'Never had it so good' did domestically, summing up as it did the trend of years of policy and aspiration in a single and memorable catch-phrase. Ironically, neither phrase was Macmillan's own, although both were associated with him. But Macmillan's success went deeper than catch-phrases, in a sense deeper than policy itself. In a way that is difficult to express, Macmillan himself seemed to stand for the hopes and fears of the British people at the end of the 1950s, caught at the end of their days as an imperial power but not yet reconciled to the post-imperial era. With such a self-confident and self-assured Prime Minister cutting such an impressive figure on the world stage, it was hardly possible to believe (much less to assert) that Britain had 'not found a role'. Macmillan was highly amused by the determination of the press to label him as 'Edwardian', but this both expresses an important truth and hides one. As a figure apparently from Britain's imperial past – a controlled and confident ruler such as David Niven had played in a generation of Empire films – Macmillan himself did much to reassure the nation in a time when morale might have suffered badly. At the least, he managed to postpone the national crisis of confidence for a decade, so that the nation could reassess itself more slowly than had seemed likely in 1956.[5]

While seeming to be a figure from the past, Macmillan was

also very characteristically a man of the time, perhaps even too much so. His assurance was external rather than internal, and the praised unflappability was the product of years of inner tension; in his ambiguity and his ambivalence, Macmillan stood for the nation in the 1950s as surely as he stood for the things that it had achieved in the past and hoped to achieve in the future. Like Baldwin, his very complicated nature expressed the *Zeitgeist* of Britain – he was the Hegelian 'man of the hour'.[6]

Perhaps it was Macmillan's very timeliness, his aptness for the situation, that ensured the decline of his popularity when the public mood changed. Certainly the luck and good fortune of the Government changed with dramatic suddenness in the winter of 1960–1. The first set-back came with the failure of the Summit Conference at Paris in May 1960; Macmillan had staked a great deal on success when Eisenhower and Krushchev came face to face, but his manifest good intentions as an honest broker between the two at least ensured that Britain's prestige and his own did not suffer from the breakdown. If the failure at Paris affected Macmillan at all, it was to persuade him that greater power would be needed to play a more active role in the world, and if it damaged his reputation at home it was by raising the suggestion that for all his good intentions, he might not be quite as skilful or as effective as had been believed. In the following year though, far worse things went wrong. As Lord Kilmuir noted, the Government had not put a single foot wrong for the whole period since early 1958 – now all went wrong for them at once.[7]

Opinion in the party had been surprised when Macmillan kept on Selwyn Lloyd at the Foreign Office in 1957, but the same people were astonished when Lloyd was moved to the Treasury in 1960, replaced himself by the Earl of Home. Lloyd was not regarded as a politician of independent mind or of outstanding judgement but, while this had not mattered much in an office so closely under the Prime Minister's supervision, it was vital at the Treasury. In 1960 and 1961 the concentration of the Prime Minister and the Cabinet was mainly on foreign problems, the Summit Conference, relations with South Africa and the rest of the Commonwealth, EFTA and the decision to apply for membership of the EEC. In all of these

Home won good opinions and demonstrated that he was a Foreign Minister with views of his own. But meanwhile the domestic situation was deteriorating badly; in his first budget, Selwyn Lloyd made little change, but was able to give tax concessions to a number of surtax payers. A few months later, with the economy becoming dangerously overheated, the Chancellor had to introduce special measures that included a recommended wages standstill, credit restrictions and cuts in spending programmes. On the domestic front, the Macmillan Government never really recovered the initiative from this unlooked-for set-back.

The economic problems were difficult enough in themselves, dictating as they did unpopular measures for about two years, but they also brought the Government into a series of damaging industrial confrontations and revived the Labour Party by giving them a target to attack. In order to encourage private employers to support what was virtually an incomes policy without statutory backing, Lloyd had to adopt a policy of no concessions whatever in the public sector where he had got powers; this led to highly-publicised battles with the nurses and the teachers, and in both disputes the Government got the worst of the publicity. Labour revived because they now could argue that the 1959 election had been fought on a bogus prospectus, that Gaitskell's claim in 1959 that the economic boom was not soundly based was now validated, and because they could castigate the Conservatives' entire policy since 1951 in one brilliant over-simplification – 'stop-go'. In the public mind, the party that had won by 'Never had it so good' was hoist by the reappearance of 'stop-go'. Whatever their real responsibility for the economic situation – and it was only partial responsibility for failure in 1961, just as it was only partial responsibility for success in 1959 – the Government could not now expect a revival of their popularity until the economy revived and controls could be relaxed.

Meanwhile, almost everything beyond the Government's control also went wrong – as with the disastrously cold and prolonged winter of 1962–3, which greatly increased the level of unemployment. On the positive side, Selwyn Lloyd set up a new and lasting institution, the National Economic Development Council, in the attempt to involve employers and trade unions as well as Government in the framing of long-term economic strategy; Macmillan's sympathy for economic intervention and for such methods of indirect planning went back into the 1930s and so he doubtless approved of this aspect of Lloyd's policy. Lloyd also set up the National Incomes Commission – the forerunner of many such bodies, but the first of its kind – but this was far less successful. The trade unions were moving into a more radical phase than at any time since the 1920s and were in any case highly critical of the Government's pay policy; instead of the industrial relations harmony that had characterised most of the Conservative governments since 1951, 1962 was a black year for disputes, with more men on strike than in any other year since 1926.

A more direct effect on Government popularity was perhaps caused by the high level of bank-rate and the consequences of this for Conservative supporters who had taken out cheap mortgages in the boom years of the 1950s; Conservative voters began to rebel in large numbers, with the Liberals the main beneficiary in the first place. This reached its height in the spring of 1962 with the loss of Orpington to the Liberals in an electoral tidal wave. After the summer of 1962, the Liberal tide receded steadily but was replaced by a Labour threat that was more serious for the Government in a future general election. For Macmillan, the effect of such deep unpopularity was profoundly shocking and the 'unflappable' suddenly seemed to panic. When Labour held the marginal seat of North-East Leicester in July 1962 with the Liberal a strong second and the Conservative a very poor third, Macmillan's nerve seems to have given way. He had been considering a Government re-shuffle with the intention of bringing forward younger men and brightening up the Government's image. In the aftermath of North-East Leicester, seven Cabinet ministers including Lloyd were suddenly sacked, some of them receiving only a few hours' notice. This event, dubbed by the press as 'the night of the long knives' destroyed Macmillan's reputation as the cool, controlled politician. For some time the Government had been receiving the rough end of the new satire boom, and Macmillan was certainly conscious of the need to fight back in some way, but this action had exactly the wrong effect. Most of all it seemed to emphasise the Government's lack of control, lack of unity, and lack of direction.[8]

It should be stressed that the Government's loss of direction and unpopularity were actually past their worst point by the time of the Profumo Scandal that was to complete its political discomfiture. In one vital area, Macmillan's political strategy had been utterly destroyed before Profumo was a word that the average citizen had ever heard of. Following the Summit failure of 1960 and the unsatisfactory Commonwealth Conference of 1961, and following also the disappointing position of British trade, Macmillan came round gradually to the idea of applying for admission to the EEC. He had always been more sympathetic to the ideas of European unity than most of the party, but had accepted the logic of Eden's more cautious policy. After the Treaty of Rome was signed and after the relative lack of success of the EFTA alternative, he tried to use the European Free Trade Area as a bridge to a wider economic union between the Six and the Seven. It is difficult to know what finally tipped the balance of the argument in favour of applying in the winter of 1960–1, but it was probably matters of strategy and general policy rather than the state of the economy. He was keenly aware of the need to provide both for the Government and for the nation a focus of policy and aspiration that was different from the Empire of the past but greater than Britain and her domestic problems. Europe therefore became for Macmillan the hope that would inspire future generations as the Empire had inspired the past; on the way, participation in Europe would also give Britain a much more real say in the affairs of the world than could be expected from outside.[9] The great snag with this conversion to Europe was that it could not be made as publicly as would give it an assurance of success. The public – and the Conservative Party – would not stand for such a sudden abandonment of the past as would be entailed in a wholehearted conversion to supra-national Europeanism. Britain therefore applied for admission to the EEC, while protesting that she was still the centre of the Commonwealth and part of a special relationship with the United States. Such protestations no doubt did much to reduce public opposition to the move and to keep party opposition within manageable proportions, but they also did much to convince Europeans that Britain had not really changed her attitude at all. At Brussels, the British delegation under Edward Heath pressed on with all speed, but Macmillan still maintained his ambivalent attitude in public. In the end it may well have been Britain's ambivalence that ensured the failure of the application and with it the failure of Macmillan's entire political strategy. For when President De Gaulle delivered his veto in 1963, the whole strategy went down in ruins, as a Central Office official told David Butler:[10] 'Europe was to be our *deus ex machina*; it was to create a new contemporary political argument with insular socialism . . . It was Macmillan's ace, and De Gaulle trumped it. The Conservatives never recovered.'

In retrospect, it can be seen that the Profumo affair in the summer of 1963 gave the *coup de grâce* to the Conservative Government. This was mainly because it seemed to chime in so well with ways in which the Government was already being attacked – especially by the satirists of *Private Eye*, the BBC's 'That Was The Week That Was' and the 'Establishment' night-club. Profumo seemed to demonstrate to a fault Macmillan's decline in the popular estimation – from the self-confident world statesman of 1959 to a shy old man who did not want to pry into distasteful matters in 1963. It gave credence to the Labour assertion that the Conservative Party under Macmillan was in the hands of 'an effete aristocracy' that was far too closely involved with such sordid underworld entrepreneurs as Stephen Ward and Peter Rachman. Profumo also inflicted a problem of leadership on the party before any question of health might have brought it about naturally. Although Macmillan survived the actual debates over Profumo in May 1963 and had resolved by the autumn that he would lead the party into the next election, this was now possible only by ignoring an embattled minority that was inflexibly opposed to him. Nigel Birch was the bitterest of these opponents; he had been opposed to Macmillan since his own resignation with Peter Thorneycroft and Enoch Powell in 1958 and he had led the Prime Minister's critics in the debates of May. Such opponents were a small minority, but they constituted a continuous threat to Macmillan's position such as he had not had to meet before, and they did not seek to hide their views. From May 1963 then, the question of the party leadership was a matter of public debate.

Macmillan had no sooner resolved to soldier on – partly because he could genuinely envisage no successor who would give the party a better electoral chance than himself and partly no doubt because, like Churchill, he found it almost impossible to render himself dispensable – than ill-health ended the question by compelling his retirement anyway. The result of this was that the party went into a public leadership contest after alternative candidates had already been canvassed for six months. The timing of Macmillan's collapse was particularly unfortunate in two senses. It turned the Party Conference at Blackpool into a sort of American convention and, although there was no attempt to take the real decisions until the following week, the hot-house conditions of a party conference did a great deal to raise the temperature and to fix loyalties that were an embarrassment when the action shifted to London the following week.[11] In the view of one experienced observer, the party might have won under Home, Butler, Hailsham *or* Maudling, but was unlikely to have won under any of them after a public row.

Lord Home's emergence as party leader was the result of a wider and more systematic canvassing of party opinion than had ever been taken before, but the impression given was nevertheless one of manoeuvrings behind closed doors. This was emphasised when the Prime Minister had to switch candidates in mid-stream, a second result of the events at Blackpool. When Lord Hailsham was adjudged to have discredited himself by his lack of restraint, Macmillan casually switched his support to Home, but this drew out the 'customary processes' for longer than was usual and left some in the Cabinet with a sense of betrayal. This was all compounded by the fact that no detailed results of party soundings were ever published; it was claimed afterwards that each of the areas in which soundings had been taken had yielded an independent majority for Home and that these had added up to a case that was cumulatively over-whelming. All depended on what questions were asked, what alternatives were posed, and when the questions were put. Without publishing the actual figures, it was impossible to refute the charge – levelled specifically by Iain Macleod a few months later – that Macmillan and the whips had set out to make a majority for Home as a candidate with no enemies. Whatever the truth of such charges, they remained in existence throughout Sir Alec's time as Conservative leader – reinforced by Randolph Churchill's book and by Iain Macleod's unforgiving review in February 1964 – and soured his position.[12] Sir Alec himself always felt that his position had been made more difficult by the fact that democracy had not appeared to be done and hence he resolved that no successor should ever have to suffer such a bad start to his career.

It is of little value to speculate whether Butler, Hailsham or Maudling would have been a better bet for the party in 1963; Butler would have carried more assurance on the crucial domestic front and would have given the appearance of leading the party from the centre ground; Hailsham would have done more to inspire the party activists and to brighten up the party's appearance; Maudling would have done more to meet the demands of a new generation and to meet Harold Wilson on his own ground. But perhaps the unpalatable truth is that the party had already as good as lost the next election by the autumn of 1963 and that it did well to come so close to winning a year later; whatever Sir Alec's successes or failings as leader, there is no clear case to suggest that an alternative candidate would have done better.

It was not only Sir Alec's method of emergence as leader that ensured that he would have a difficult start as leader, for he started off with disadvantages enough of his own. As a peer, he had to go through the distasteful business of disclaiming his ancient title and fighting a much-publicised by-election before he could be a real leader at all. After that he had to return to the Commons and make his first speech there for twelve years as a new Prime Minister, with the Opposition baying for his blood. He then had to take on an unaccustomed role in the party's appeal to the country, undertaking an almost continuous sequence of major speeches in provincial centres and marginal constituencies, and making for the first time a regular series of appearances on television.[13] He seemed to be a Daniel flung unexpectedly into a den of political lions; if like Daniel he could expect to gain some credit for his sincerity and his unaffected honesty, he could nevertheless expect also that he would be eaten in the end. In the short term, the party's fears for its new leader were at least partly set at rest by his early performance; on television he made a good impression with his first broadcast as Prime Minister, promising 'plain speaking', and in Parliament he proved to be much more capable of looking after himself than had been forecast. But such good impressions were made because the party had set its expectations so low; had it made a realistic comparison with either Harold Macmillan or Harold Wilson, it could only have been less impressed. Sir Alec was better at the political crafts of modern party leadership than had been feared, but less good than either his predecessor or his opponent. This was vital in the circumstance when a general election had to be held in a minimum of one year. Sir Alec told the MPs who elected him as leader in October 1963 that the party's eyes must now be fixed unalterably on the coming election; but this focused more attention on his apparent failings as an electioneering leader and less on his far greater qualities as a leader in other senses.[14]

As a chairman of Cabinet, Sir Alec conducted business in a straightforward way; he was more available to his ministers than Macmillan or Churchill had been, less interfering and ever-present than Eden. As party leader, he was more disposed to think of the problems of party politics in the widest context of public morality and popular attitudes than most leaders have been, but such qualities were hardly required of him in a year that became one uninterrupted election campaign. The 'testament' that he wrote in December 1963 to familiarise his advisers and staff with his political attitudes is a remarkably far-sighted and well-thought-out analysis of the state of the nation; such a face was all too rarely exhibited though in twelve months as Prime Minister.[15] As he reflected in retrospect, he had such a vast amount to learn of the craft of leadership and of the unfamiliar domestic situation, that he relied too heavily on speeches written by others and on ideas and concepts that were demonstrably not his own.[16] His volume of 1964 speeches, *Peaceful Change*, makes impressive reading, but it does not add up to a really coherent political position or to a personal statement of political attitudes. As the 'testament' shows, his chief concern was with the problems that would occur for Britain with the running down of Christian morality as a basis for personal action and with the breaking down of imperial connections that had served as a focus for patriotism and common action. An awareness of Britain's fundamental problem in the 1960s was all too obviously there, but this was in private; all too little of his personal convictions was allowed to show through in his electioneering.

In other ways, Sir Alec inherited a strategic position that placed him on the defensive for his whole time as Prime Minister. At the beginning of the Parliament, Macmillan had shrewdly initiated a series of policy reviews so that a government at the end of twelve or thirteen years would be able to come up with new or re-furbished policies without the charge of obvious inconsistency; thus, for example, the Robbins Royal Commission on Higher Education reported in 1963 and provided a basis for the prominence given to education in the Government's programme in 1964. But the central points of Macmillan's political strategy had been successful negotiations to enter the EEC, successful timing of the handling of the economy, and his own survival at the head of a Government of younger ministers. All of this had gone dramatically wrong before Sir Alec took over as leader; the failure to join the EEC left the Government without a clear aim in its foreign policy, the slow recovery from Selwyn Lloyd's credit squeeze inhibited Government policy and took away freedom of manoeuvre, and Macmillan's enforced retirement had of itself upset the balance of the Government. Sir Alec made few changes in the Cabinet but important factors were beyond his control; Macmillan's aim had been to preserve the balance of experience and youth through the changes made in 1962, with a small group of older ministers of his own generation and the rest of the Cabinet promoted from the generation of the MPs of the 1950s. But this balance was destroyed by Macmillan's retirement – since he was the only man who could easily bridge the gap of the generations – by Butler's increasing withdrawal from the domestic front, and by the refusal of Macleod and Powell to serve under the new Prime Minister. Macmillan's unique blend of tradition and change, so successful in 1959–60, might well have been equally successful in its new form in 1963–4, but its ambivalence was torn apart by the change of leadership and its consequences.

Sir Alec was by no means the right-wing figure that he was

sometimes portrayed as by the Labour Party and the press, but he was undeniably a representative of social Conservatism in contrast to the bulk of his Cabinet. Harold Wilson's jibes had been cut short by Sir Alec's description of him as a 'fourteenth Mr Wilson' but he soon returned to the attack. Wilson promised to 'play the ball and not the man', but he could hardly be expected to miss the opportunities that Sir Alec gave him as Conservative leader. Nor could the Conservatives complain when, already under attack for their 'grouse-moor image', they chose as their leader a man who owned 50,000 acres of Scotland. That had been the reason for the well-known attempts to form a 'stop-Home' cabal at the last moment, and it was Macleod's reason for refusing to join Home's Cabinet.[17] The new professional class in the party felt slighted by Home's selection as leader; Macleod and Powell on the back benches seemed to be a perpetual confirmation of the fact. Macmillan's leadership had been based on his own ambivalence; he had been at once a progressive, modern-minded Conservative in his policy but also a social Conservative from a traditional Conservative background in his style and appearance. Sir Alec's leadership seemed to be victory for one side of Macmillan over the other. Sir Alec gave great freedom to Maudling at the Treasury and to Heath at the new Department of Industry, Trade and Regional Development, but neither of them could remedy the defects in the party's strategic position. Maudling at the Treasury had no room for manoeuvre between a deteriorating economic position and an imminent election; Heath, in his urgent desire to win a domestic triumph for the Government, alienated many Conservatives by the way in which the Resale Price Maintenance Bill was forced through Parliament.

In one field Sir Alec was of course able to shine, that of Foreign Affairs. In this area he regularly demonstrated his superiority over opponents and it naturally figured prominently in his thinking and in his electioneering. He believed passionately in the necessity for Britain keeping up an independent deterrent as a ticket to any conferences that might decide Britain's long-term future, and he believed equally that this was threatened by Labour's plans. He could also draw much political benefit from his regular involvement in international events, his visit to the United States with its modest success over

Malaysia, and his successes over East Africa and Cyprus. He drew much credit retrospectively from having signed as Foreign Secretary the Nuclear Test Ban Treaty of 1963.[18] In this field too, he had the full support of his party; he had from R. A. Butler as Foreign Secretary the same loyal backing that Butler had given to Macmillan.

As well as foreign affairs, Sir Alec drew benefit from the improvements in the British economy, recovering from slump and not yet over the height of boom in the spring of 1964. After six months, the dust of the leadership controversy seemed at last to be settling, Sir Alec was warming to his task as leader, the Tories' 'secret weapon' of loyalty was operating at full stretch, and it seemed conceivable that he might just be able to pull it off. Central Office advice carried the day against a plan to hold an election in May or June 1964, but this in itself carried the seeds of ultimate defeat. The greatest advocate of an early election had been Maudling, whose concern about the economic future was mounting; but Central Office almost guaranteed defeat in June. By the time that a long, hot summer and several months more of economic boom had done their work, the Conservatives seemed likely winners of an autumn election. This all fell away again at the last moment, apparently during the campaign itself, and almost certainly because the state of the economy was now giving rise to the justified alarm that Maudling had expected. In this sense, perhaps the only time when the Conservatives could have won was in August or September 1964 – but more likely there was no such opportunity, for the campaign would have stirred up economic fears whenever it had come. The surprising thing about 1964 is not that Sir Alec lost the election but that he came so close to winning it (within 0.7%) and that anyone at all expected him to win. After the economic misfortunes of 1961 and 1962 and after the political agonies of 1963, the recovery had been remarkable. In this, Sir Alec's patent sincerity and honesty – exploited to the full when set against Harold Wilson – had played a great part.[19]

Within less than a year of the party's narrow defeat in the General Election of 1964, it had acquired a new leader, a new image, a newly-thought-out set of policies, and a new generation of politicians at its head. All of this had to be done so quickly because of the narrowness of defeat in 1964; Labour could not govern for long on its small parliamentary majority and so Conservatives had to prepare for an election which might come at any time and at short notice, but which was certain to come within a year or two. Sir Michael Fraser's description 'redeployment in the face of the enemy' was necessary. In these circumstances, some of the changes that were made naturally reflected the demands, tactical and strategic, of the short-term situation. But what is most striking overall is how naturally this series of changes blended into developments that had been taking place in the party in the last few years. In some ways then, the developments of those first nine months of Opposition marked a decisive change from the past, a change that was dictated by the party's current position, but in other ways the developments followed paths that had been clearly marked out since 1962.

The first essential was the re-establishment of the unity of the party; although the bulk of the party had rallied to Sir Alec in 1964, the wounds created by his selection as leader had never quite healed. The return of Iain Macleod and Enoch Powell to the Shadow Cabinet immediately after the election was a public sign that bygones were now to be treated as such. A signal for the future was the decision to purge memories of October 1963 by adopting a new system of electing the party leader. Sir Alec himself had keenly felt the perceived inadequacies of the system that had made him leader and the arguments over its workings had rumbled on through his year as Prime Minister. He was determined that one of his legacies to the party should be to leave it with a more open and straightforward method of choosing its leader so that none of his successors could be criticised unfairly, as he felt that he had been. The difficulty was to reconcile an open system of election with the two great strengths of the old system, whereby it could be ensured that votes were counted *against* a candidate as well as *for* him, and by which appropriate weight would be given to all sections of the party inside and outside Parliament. The system adopted was therefore a complicated one that aimed to select the leader openly but without generating open contests that would create lasting bitterness.[20] After being used twice, in 1965 and 1975, the system cannot be said to have been successful in the latter aim, but it has certainly removed charges of unfairness such as were made about 1963 and 1957. Democracy is now being seen to be done.

The second priority was the re-examination of the party's policy. This job was given specifically to Edward Heath, who became Chairman of the Advisory Committee on Policy immediately after the election defeat. Under his aegis, a number of small policy groups were set up, each with a specific remit and each charged to report back in a short time. These policy-groups were composed partly of MPs and partly of outside specialists, businessmen and civil servants. The groups were usually chaired by the appropriate Shadow minister and all were serviced by the Research Department, in touch with party opinion through the CPC. Co-ordination of all of these activities was assisted by the integration of the CPC into Central Office early in 1965 and by the reform of the party's structure to bring Central Office and the Research Department into closer touch. Sir Michael Fraser, Director of Research Department from 1951, became deputy chairman of the party and acted as the Secretary of the Shadow Cabinet while remaining a member of the Advisory Committee on Policy. The urgency with which the policy review had to be conducted made it impossible to consult party opinion as widely as would have been desirable to allay fears of what was going on behind the scenes. And this problem was exacerbated by the public protests of some MPs when they discovered that the names of the non-politicians in the policy groups were not to be released. This decision was taken so that expert advice could be drawn from people who would not wish it to be known that they were sitting on a party committee, but again secrecy and urgency led to a certain amount of antagonism.[21]

The parallel most widely drawn was with the re-thinking of policy in and after 1945, but in vital ways this parallel was misleading. The historical case that fitted most exactly with the policy review of 1964–5 was that of 1924; in 1924 similar groups of MPs and outsiders had worked in similar conditions of secrecy and urgency and the whole process had been managed by Neville Chamberlain – in 1924 a likely successor to Baldwin as Heath was to Home in 1965.[22] The differences from 1945 are clear enough, but they must be emphasised since they contri-

buted largely to the form of the review when it was completed.
In the 1940s there was no shortage of time, and so it was possible to canvass party opinion more widely than in 1965; in the
1940s there was positive virtue in not completing the process
in less than three or four years. Most different of all was the
philosophy that underlay the entire enterprise: R. A. Butler and
his colleagues had begun their review from the first principles of
Conservatism and had taken great pains to emphasise that what
was proposed was consistent with what had been done in the
past. In 1965, by contrast, Edward Heath decided not to use
the limited time at his disposal with an examination of the
party's philosophy but to concentrate instead on the rapid
production of detailed statements of policy that could be written
into an election manifesto at short notice.[23] So the review was
complete by July 1965 and was published as 'Putting Britain
Right Ahead' in time to be approved by the Party Conference
in October. Again the difference from the 1940s was clear, and
again it was largely missed: the Industrial Charter had described itself as a statement of policy but had actually been a
statement of general principles, while 'Putting Britain Right
Ahead' was described as a statement of Conservative aims but
was actually a statement of policy.

The reaction to 'Putting Britain Right Ahead' was a mixed
one, largely because press and political commentators concentrated on trying to divine from its text whether the Conservatives had moved to the right or to the left since losing power.
The *Economist* described the document as moving the party
'very slightly towards the radical left'; the *Daily Telegraph*
regretted that there had not been a clearer statement of
Conservative principles, and the *Spectator* noted that,[24]

'It is possible to argue that the document (trades union –
immigration) represents a shift to the right. Equally possible to
argue (Europe – Social Services) that it is a shift to the left.
These terms have little meaning inside the Tory Party. Basically, the document is an expression of the thinking of the
Party's new leader.'

Comment also centred, as in the 1940s, on how similar were the
policies put forward by the two parties and on how far the

Conservatives were reacting to the political style of Harold Wilson. Alan Watkins in the *Spectator* noted the similarity of language between the new Conservative statement of policy and many speeches by Harold Wilson, and the *Economist* agreed that 'Mr Heath has gone a long way towards pinching the management efficiency consultant's coat that was Mr Wilson's most attractive dress before the last election.' Heath had indeed gone out of his way to invite such comments in his introduction to the new document, when he had explained his intentions:[25] 'As I go around the country, I find that people are asking for an entirely fresh approach to the country's problems. They are looking for constructive policies – *how* we do things rather than what needs to be done.'

The area of central agreement between the parties, detected by *The Times* in 1945 and described by the *Economist* as Butskellism in the 1950s, was now proclaimed as a fact of political life by the Conservative Party leader. It is perhaps little wonder that the Liberal Party campaigned a few years later with a poster that showed the faces of Edward Heath and Harold Wilson and the slogan 'Which Twin is the Tory?'

In reality though, the policy review had made major advances from previous Tory policy and the link between the new policies was not only the personal style of Heath but also the party commitment to the EEC – as in 1963 it remained the vital core of Conservative strategy. Tax reforms and reforms in agricultural finance were cast in such a way as to make harmonisation with the EEC an easier process when it should come; the decision to undertake the reforms of trade unions was taken partly at least in an effort to enable Britain to survive the economic shock of transition to EEC membership; the changes in the social services and in other policies were also conceived with the EEC in mind. Most of all, the European Community was to provide the focus of attention and loyalty that Britons were thought to need in the 1960s – it was to provide the role for Britain now that she had lost her Empire.

The review was also conceived as part of a political programme to win back ground lost in 1964 when, as Iain Macleod remarked 'for the first time in five elections, our grip on the Centre has weakened. We must offer something better because we believe in something better.'[26] The loss that had most worried forward-looking Conservatives like Macleod in 1964 was the party's failure to win the support of a new generation of young professional people. This point was made strongly by William Rees-Mogg, one of the keenest advocates of the new policy review:[27]

'The last years of the Macmillan and Douglas-Home administrations did not seem to many of the young managers and technicians to be relevant to their problems. In the first year of Opposition, the Conservative Party has been trying, partly instinctively and partly consciously, to realign itself with these social forces.'

In this sense then, 'Putting Britain Right Ahead' was not a move to the right or to the left, but a move to a new generation, across a social rather than a political frontier. It was perhaps appropriate that the cover of the document itself bore the imprint of a familiar road sign that forbids turns to left and right alike. The emphasis was more on putting Britain ahead than on putting Britain right.

The review of 1965 was to be the foundation of the Conservative manifesto of 1966 and from there it fed into the policy statements of the later 1960s, the manifesto of 1970, and the policies pursued by Edward Heath's Government. But by then it was somewhat out of date, far less original than when it had been conceived in 1965. Thus, for example, the commitment to the EEC, central to the whole plan, could not play the inspiring role in the 1970s that it had been intended to do. Moreover, it was difficult to keep the programme up to date once proposals had been published in as much detail as in 1965; little account was therefore taken of the failure of the Labour Party's attempts to reform the trade unions in 1969, with evident consequences for the Conservative policy on industrial relations. Moreover, when the policies were implemented in and after 1970, the lack of an agreed philosophical base that was generally accepted in the party became a severe disadvantage. Instead of a philosophical base, the policies were founded on an interpretation of social trends, an interpretation with which Edward Heath felt especially close. Some of this though had been seen in 1965; Colin Welch had indeed put his finger on it in the *Daily Telegraph* review of 'Putting Britain Right Ahead':[28]

'"What men and women want, quite rightly, is not theories but results in terms of more dependable service and better performance." Thus Mr Heath in the new statement of Conservative aims . . . This sounds blunt, businesslike British stuff. Yet even in this fog-enveloped island there must be grey pedants who suspect that theories and results are closely connected, that wrong theories will produce wrong results and right, right.'

The failure to base the 1965 review on firm foundations of theory and belief was thus to have major implications later. It was perhaps the greatest consequence of the urgency with which the party was forced to react to the narrow defeat of 1964.

But all of that was far in the future. In 1965 the crowning touch to the new regime came with Heath's election as leader in July 1965, just before the results of the review of policy were announced. Sir Alec had not exactly been pushed out of the leadership, but it had become increasingly clear that his leadership was dividing the party. In such circumstances he resigned with a suddenness that surprised everyone and Heath was elected as his successor with only one ballot. The feature of the leadership contest that showed clearly how far the party had come since 1940, and even since 1957 and 1963, was the lack of any real choice. It proved difficult to identify any ground of policy on which Heath and Maudling clearly disagreed and in background they were again very similar. But in voting for Heath, MPs were consciously voting for a particular style of party and a particular line of leadership. They were voting for an abrasive and aggressive leader who might seek to divide the country rather than unite it – voting for a Neville Chamberlain rather than for a Baldwin. They were voting in fact for much that they complained of when it actually came to pass in the 1970s; but that too was far in the future. They were voting most of all for a leader who could face the future with confidence and who would accept the need for change, would indeed embrace it with open arms.

The speed of the advance needs emphasising; as late as October 1963, Macmillan had, in his valedictory message to the party, given weight to both tradition and change:[29]

'We must accept – indeed we must welcome change. But not change for its own sake. Not change that means discarding moral and religious values which long experience has taught the British people to respect. The Conservative Party has always had the faith to honour the things that history has taught us to cherish and revere. But it has also had the courage to grasp what is new and fresh, so that a constant process of renewal and re-invigoration takes place in our national life.'

In 'Putting Britain Right Ahead' no attempt was made to stress elements of continuity and no attempt was made to stress what should be preserved. The emphasis was entirely on 'modern Conservatism' and on the 'supreme importance of economic reform'. The election of Edward Heath also marked an unusual chapter of party history in that the party came, had already come, to derive so much of its vitality from one man who was clearly on one side of the Tory tradition; in its finest moments Conservatism has always represented the dualism of the tradition, Peel and Disraeli, Salisbury and Joseph Chamberlain, Baldwin and Neville Chamberlain, Macmillan and Butler. In the triumph of Edward Heath, Peelism triumphed absolutely over the spirit of Disraeli, as William Rees-Mogg noticed in welcoming 'Putting Britain Right Ahead':[30]

'The document itself . . . fits in well with the pragmatism which is one part of the Tory soul. It lacks on the other hand the romantic idealism which has also recurred in Tory history. "Putting Britain Right Ahead" might have been drafted by Peel, but would never have been drafted in these terms by Disraeli. There may again be a time for Disraelianism later. At the moment the real national and international situation of Britain is one which needs attention by men of detail rather than by men of dreams.'

Such was the supreme confidence with which the party cast off its past and looked to its future in 1965.

The post-war generation of Conservatives, who had entered the party at its nadir after 1945, who had entered Parliament and chafed under Churchill and Eden in the 1950s, who had been promoted by Macmillan and dissatisfied under Home, had now come into their own under a leader of their own. A new turn was being taken, a turn not only of measures but also of men. The death of Sir Winston Churchill after his final retirement from the Commons in 1964 had severed the last link with the Conservative Party before 1914; the retirement from politics of R. A. Butler in 1965 ended the last link with the Conservatism of Baldwin. In 1965 the process started by Churchill and Butler in dragging the party back from the abyss of 1945 had at last come to an end and a new phase had begun.

NOTES TO PART FOUR

I would like to thank the many people who gave up their time to talk to me about their part in the events that I am describing, especially Lord Hailsham, Lord Home, Lord Butler, and Lord Fraser of Kilmorack. I would also like to thank Lord Fraser for his valuable comments on the text and for permission to quote from them.

Chapter 1

1 Randolph S. Churchill, *Winston S. Churchill* (1967), vol. II, p. 99.
2 National Union Central Council Minutes, Meeting of 8 June 1917.
3 For this part of Churchill's career, see Robert Rhodes James, *Churchill: a Study in Failure* (1970), and Randolph S. Churchill and Martin Gilbert, *Winston S. Churchill* (1966–76), vols. II–V.
4 Michael Howard, *The Continental Commitment* (Penguin ed., 1974), pp. 89–90.
5 Neville Thompson, *The Anti-Appeasers* (1971), pp. 197–8.
6 Paul Addison, *The Road to 1945* (1975), pp. 75–102.
7 ibid., p. 231, and passim.
8 ibid., p. 173 and p. 223.
9 Lord Butler, *The Art of the Possible* (1971), p. 94.
10 Addison, op. cit., p. 251.
11 ibid., p. 260.
12 *The Times* (leading article), 27 July 1945; *Economist*, 28 July 1945.
13 J. D. Hoffman, *The Conservative Party in Opposition* (1964), p. 23.
14 Butler, op. cit., pp. 132–4.
15 ibid., p. 135; Hoffman, op. cit., pp. 110, 135–6; Earl of Kilmuir, *Political Adventure* (1964), pp. 148–9.
16 Andrew Roth, *Enoch Powell, Tory Tribune* (1970), p. 48.

17 Butler, op. cit., pp. 145–6.

18 ibid., p. 133.

19 *The New Conservatism*, CPC pamphlet no. 150 (1955); Conference Minutes (1962), p. 127.

20 *Conservative Social and Industrial Reform*, published by the CPC for the centenary of the Ten-Hours Bill in December 1947 is the best example, but there are many others. Even the Industrial Charter had an appendix tracing its precursors in Tory history.

21 Macmillan, when introducing Churchill to address the party conference in 1947, went so far as to describe the 1930s as a dead period for Conservative policy in all fields. He thus linked and legitimated his own opposition to the party's domestic policy in the 1930s with Churchill's opposition to its foreign policy.

22 Conference Minutes (1947), pp. 116–18; *The Right Road*, Central Office pamphlet no. 3984 (1949).

23 G. M. Young, *Stanley Baldwin* (1952); A. W. Baldwin, *My Father, the True Story* (1955). Churchill himself contributed effectively to the making of the myths in *The Gathering Storm* (1948). For this see Donald Watt, 'The Historiography of Appeasement' in C. Cook and A. Sked (eds.), *Crisis and Controversy* (1976), pp. 110–29.

24 Addison (op. cit., p. 258) is one of many who does not make this important distinction and so dismisses the entire argument about the part played by organisation in the 1945 result.

25 Hoffman, op. cit., pp. 94–6; Kilmuir, op. cit., 157–8.

26 Butler, op. cit., p. 137.

27 T. F. Lindsay and M. Harrington, *The Conservative Party 1918–1970* (1974), pp. 147–8.

28 Butler, op. cit., p. 148.

29 *The Times* (leading articles), 5 and 27 July 1945.

30 *Daily Telegraph*, 12 May 1947; *Economist*, 17 May 1947; *The Times*, 12 May 1947.

31 Conference Minutes (1962), p. 124.

32 Butler, op. cit., p. 155.

33 *The Right Road for Britain*, Central Office pamphlet no. 3969 (1949).

34 Roy Douglas, *The History of the Liberal Party 1895–1970* (1971), p. 265.

35 Earl of Woolton, *Memoirs* (1959), pp. 364–5.

36 ibid., pp. 375–8.

37 H. Daalder, *Cabinet Reform in Britain 1914–1963* (1964), pp. 109–22.

38 Michael Pinto-Duschinsky, 'Bread and Circuses' in V. Bogdanor and R. Skidelsky (eds.), *The Age of Affluence* (1970), pp. 55–63.

39 Woolton, op. cit., p. 380; Butler, op. cit., p. 164.

40 Kilmuir, op. cit., pp. 225–6.

41 Butler, op. cit., p. 160.

42 Kilmuir, op. cit., p. 177.

43 Quoted from Macmillan's memoirs in Lindsay and Harrington, op. cit., p. 173.

Chapter 2

1 W. S. Churchill, *The Gathering Storm* (Penguin ed. 1960), p. 232.
2 Woolton, op. cit., p. 417.
3 Randolph S. Churchill, *The Rise and Fall of Sir Anthony Eden* (1959), p. 197.
4 ibid., p. 200; Kilmuir, op. cit., p. 246.
5 Anthony Eden, *Freedom and Order* (1947), p. 426.
6 ibid., p. 409.
7 Woolton, op. cit., p. 419; Kilmuir, op. cit., p. 243; Butler, op. cit.,
   pp. 256–7.
8 Samuel Brittan, *The Treasury under the Tories* (1964), p. 177.
9 C. Cook and J. Ramsden (eds.), *By-Elections in British Politics* (1973),
   pp. 194–5; Lindsay and Harrington, op. cit., p. 186.
10 R. S. Churchill, *Eden*, p. 207.
11 *British Prime Ministers*, BBC Gramophone Record REB 39M (1969).
12 Hugh Thomas, *The Suez Affair* (Penguin ed. 1970); P. Calvocoressi
   (ed.), *Suez Ten Years After* (1967); Anthony Nutting, *No End of a Lesson*
   (1967).
13 Anthony Sampson, *Macmillan, A Study in Ambiguity* (Penguin ed. 1968),
   p. 112.
14 ibid., p. 140.
15 Emrys Hughes, *Macmillan* (1962), pp. 126–36; Gerald Sparrow, *R.A.B.*,
   Study of a Statesman (1965), p. 147.
16 Sampson, op. cit., p. 140.
17 Harold Macmillan, *Riding the Storm* (1971), p. 186.
18 ibid.; Butler, op. cit., p. 196.
19 Macmillan, op. cit., pp. 228–30.
20 Paul Foot, *The Politics of Harold Wilson* (1968), p. 127.
21 This address was published by the CPC in 1958 and was reprinted as a
   preface to the new edition of *The Middle Way* in 1966, pp. xiii–xxix.
22 ibid., p. xxiv.
23 Conference Minutes (1958), p. 160.
24 Macmillan, op. cit., pp. 350–2; Lindsay and Harrington, op. cit.,
   pp. 202–3.
25 Conference Minutes (1960), p. 146.
26 ibid. (1963), p. 140.
27 *This is what we have done*, Central Office pamphlet no. 4442 (1958).

Chapter 3

1 D. E. Butler and R. Rose, *The British General Election of 1959* (1960),
   pp. 45–67.
2 Kilmuir, op. cit., pp. 311–14.
3 M. Abrams and R. Rose, *Must Labour Lose?* (1960); C. A. R. Crosland,
   Can Labour Win?, Fabian pamphlet (1960); S. H. Beer, 'Democratic
   One-Party Government for Britain' in the *Political Quarterly* (1961).
4 J. H. Goldthorpe et. al., *The Affluent Worker: Political Attitudes* (1968).
5 L. Siedentop, 'Mr. Macmillan and the Edwardian Style' in Bogdanor
   and Skidelsky, op. cit., pp. 17–54.

6 Keith Middlemas, 'Stanley Baldwin' in H. Van Thal (ed.), *The Prime Ministers*, vol. II (1975), pp. 268–9.

7 Kilmuir, op. cit., p. 314.

8 ibid., pp. 323–4; Butler, op. cit., pp. 232–4; Lindsay and Harrington, op. cit., pp. 212–13.

9 Sampson, op. cit., p. 207.

10 D. E. Butler and A. King, *The British General Election of 1964* (1965), p. 79.

11 R. S. Churchill, *The Fight for the Tory Leadership* (1964), pp. 108–24.

12 *Spectator*, 17 January 1964.

13 Kenneth Young, *Sir Alec Douglas-Home* (1970), pp. 174 and 210–11.

14 ibid., p. 175.

15 ibid., pp. 188–94.

16 ibid., pp. 184–5.

17 Alan Thompson, *The Day before Yesterday* (1971), pp. 218–19.

18 Young, op. cit., pp. 195–205.

19 ibid., pp. 206–19.

20 ibid., p. 224.

21 D. E. Butler and A. King, *The British General Election of 1966* (1966), pp. 53–6.

22 K. Middlemas and J. Barnes, *Baldwin, a Biography* (1969), pp. 264–8.

23 Lindsay and Harrington, op. cit., pp. 242–3.

24 *Economist*, 9 October 1965; *Daily Telegraph*, 7 October 1965; *Spectator*, 8 October 1965.

25 *Putting Britain Right Ahead*, Central Office pamphlet no. 4778 (1965).

26 Quoted by James Margach, *Sunday Times*, 10 October 1965.

27 Leading Article, *Sunday Times*, 10 October 1965.

28 *Daily Telegraph*, 13 October 1965.

29 Conference Minutes (1963), p. 140.

30 *Sunday Times*, 10 October 1965.

EPILOGUE

by The Rt Hon. Lord Butler, KG, PC, CH

This book has not attempted to deal with the more recent political events since these cannot yet be dispassionately described as part of history. It has, however, carried the story on over the never-to-be-repeated leadership scramble of 1963 in order to include an account of the policy-making of 1965, a date which really opened a new era for the party, not only in policy matters but in respect of personalities with experience who retired, making the way for younger men. Dr Ramsden makes clear that the new programme was produced in a hurry; thus the review was not based on the firm fundamentals of theory and belief but rather on immediate policy needs, and this was to have major implications later. Dr Ramsden also shows that the document did not stress elements of continuity or what should be preserved, as had been done in 1945. After the experience of what followed the 1965 policy-making, a new attempt now is being made to face the party's future, and I only hope that the attempt this time will bear in mind the values which made the party great in the past and will ensure its greatness in the future.

The Conservative faith is so akin to the features and characteristics of human nature that it will always reappear and prevail, especially in periods of national danger or difficulty. It has suffered terrible reverses, especially at the time of the Stuart decline and the holocaust of 1906. But there has always been a restoration. It is unlikely, in modern times, that Conservatism will be restored to power through a coalition as was virtually the case at the end of the 1914–18 war or in 1931, for coalitions between major parties are not today practical politics and the immediate problems of the future, as affecting politics, are the Scottish and Welsh devolution questions.

Much depends on how the devolution question is settled. My hope will be that the Conservatives finally get an absolute majority; but although the future is all surmise, what is certain is that the Conservatives who look back on history will have many precedents and precepts to guide them and they will find that 'the Tory tradition is the Tory hope'.

INDEX